OUTWARD BOUND
U.S.A.

OUTWARD BOUND U.S.A.

Learning Through Experience in Adventure-Based Education

Joshua L. Miner
and
Joe Boldt

WILLIAM MORROW AND COMPANY, INC.

New York   *1981*

Library of Congress Cataloging in Publication Data

Miner, Joshua L
    Outward Bound U.S.A.

    "Morrow quill paperbacks."

    Includes index.
    1. Outward Bound, inc.—History.   2. Outward bound schools—United States.   I. Boldt, Joseph R., joint author. II. Title.
[GV200.53.M56   1981b]   613.6'9   80-28007
ISBN 0-688-00413-X
ISBN 0-688-00414-8 (pbk.)

Printed in the United States of America

First Morrow Quill Paperback Edition

1 2 3 4 5 6 7 8 9 10

BOOK DESIGN BY MICHAEL MAUCERI

TO THE MEMORY OF KURT HAHN

Contents

Introduction

At long last, a book that takes us back to the basics of learning and healthy growth. Of course, learning the three "r's" is basic; no one questions that. But too exclusive an emphasis on only reading, writing, and arithmetic that ignores a youth's sense of self, values, and interpersonal skills too often distorts healthy growth and ultimately blocks mastering even the three "r's" themselves.

Formal schooling is not a youth's "natural" mode of learning. A youth is built not just to think but also to feel and act. But within the past several hundred years, especially the past several decades, society has encroached upon more and more of its young people's feeling and acting space. No person who cares for young people should ever forget that by the time they graduate from high school, they will have had more than 29,000 hours of conditioning to sit immobilely, passively, apathetically, drugged by 17,000 hours of TV, 12,000 hours of schooling in which teachers have talked about 85 percent of the time, and 2000 hours of yellow school bus rides. Nor should we forget that youth nowadays attend large impersonal schools in which they no longer have as much opportunity to participate in extracurricular activities, to hold positions of leadership, to see their friends, to come into close sustained contact with adults who know them well, to grasp hold of responsibility for their own growth. A survey of Minnesota high school students reported that they felt school was a "waste of time, boring, endless, dumb, repetitious, tedious and childish." Nor should we forget that today's youth grow up isolated not just from nature—its unpredictability, its wilderness, its solitude, but also from others—young brothers or sisters or grandparents for whom to care, intact families to which to belong, neighbors to trust and with whom to work and cooperate.

Have these dramatic changes in the living and growing space of young people furthered their sense of wholeness? Those who have worked closely with them over the years say, "No." More, though certainly not all, young people seem to be excessively dependent upon novelty, rapid changes in pace as well as on direction. Cease-less noise, like stereos, is needed to block out silence; drugs are needed to release inhibition and imagination; sex and violence are needed to make one feel "alive." Relationships with others, while seemingly more carefree, mask for many deeper fears of rejection; putdowns and sarcastic bantering block the development of em-pathy; and fears of tenderness stifle compassion. And what of youth's hope and dreams for a better society, out of which passion for and devotion to service can spring? Surveys show that youth are more pessimistic about the future and more self-absorbed than at any time in the past several decades. Fears of war, eco-nomic collapse and nuclear catastrophe constantly lurk around the fringes of adolescent consciousness.

What way can adults offer today's youth for growing more wholely, or, in the perceptive words of Kurt Hahn, whose phi-losophy inspired this book, for having "health-giving experiences" in which they can learn how to "harvest the lessons of . . . life . . . in aloneness," "defeat . . . defeatism," and become compas-sionate to those "in danger and in need"? How can we empower youth to be able to say, "I never thought I could do that" or "I learned . . . I could trust and cooperate with other people in ways I had never experienced before"?

Joshua Miner and Joe Boldt show us one powerful way by which to speak to the needs of today's youth. Outward Bound, inspired by Hahn, doggedly and creatively shaped by Josh Miner and a host of passionately caring and dedicated persons, provides just that shaking-up, intense experience many youth (and adults too) need. It provides the types of experiences we now know are essential if healthy growth is to occur: high expectations of a youth's potential; challenges that stretch capabilities; intense physical, social, and intellectual experiences that test core values and ideas about one's self; sustained involvement with small groups of peers and adults that one cannot escape; a silence with one's self that cannot be avoided or narcoticized.

I began this book and could not put it down: not just because it is humanly and movingly written; nor just because I cherish warm memories of so many the book describes; nor just because the attitudes that undergird this book resonate so fully with all that I have learned professionally about healthy growth; and not just because the book beautifully illustrates how basic are a youth's capacity to feel and act in the face of challenge to his subsequent sense of competence, even academic. No, the book is absorbing because it reflects in every chapter how a vision takes shape and grows through the inspiration and devotion of adults who care for youth. *Outward Bound U.S.A.* is a case study of hope!

—DOUGLAS H. HEATH
Haverford College

Scottish Journey

My heart's in the Highlands, wherever I go . . .
The birthplace of valor, the country of worth,
Wherever I wander, wherever I rove,
The hills of the Highlands forever I love.
                                        —ROBERT BURNS

From Glasgow north to the Moray Firth is 120 miles "as the craw flees." By rail it's a fair piece more. I had been warned that the train stopped in every field to see if the hay was ripe. In June 1950 the journey consumed seven hours.

The train swung around northwestward into the valley of the Tay, following the river upstream. The country grew wilder, the station names more wonderfully Scottish. Dunkeld. Pitlochry. Through the Pass of Killiecrankie, to where the headwaters of the Garry and the Spey nearly touched, the one stream flowing southward, the other north.

Some thirty hours earlier, I had taken off from New York's Idlewild Airport. Fourteen hours later—3 A.M. in Princeton, New Jersey—the prop-driven Constellation had put down at Prestwick. The courteous, burred questioning at customs, and a one-and-one-half-hour bus ride to Glasgow. The telephone call to Gordonstoun, with Mr. Hahn's puzzling instruction not to buy a ticket through to Forres, the stop closest to my destination. Instead I was to get off a full hour sooner, at Aviemore.

In league now with the Spey as it flowed to the North Sea, the train called more on brakes than power. The wild moors merging with the mountains, the ancient rugged Cairngorms.

13

Thirty hours out of Idlewild with little sleep, I dozed off and on. Though I no longer directly remember the reverie of that journey, I can recall its sense. Uncertain of what lay ahead, I reflected on whence I came. The day's stream of consciousness comes back, thirty years later, as a kind of internal slide show—image succeeding image on an interior screen.

We can skip lightly over the early scenes. A youngster growing toward adolescence in an American suburb amid the certainties of the 1920's. The snug family suddenly buffeted by the Great Depression, improvising its defenses, wondering where the certainties had gone. In my high school junior year I won a scholarship to a school named Exeter. I was an enthusiastic, curious kid, fooling around with radio in a time when kits did not yet exist, when I could not get the printed information I needed, when I could not get questions answered. At my new school I was told I would find people who knew an awful lot, and it was difficult to wait to have them answer my questions.

But at Exeter nobody had time for those questions. Too busy teaching me what they thought I ought to know, they paid scant attention to my own innate curiosity. My preparatory-school record was not distinguished.

As a college student, I was still out of synch with the educational establishment. At Princeton I flunked out, twice. Technically, I did not flunk out that second time, at the end of my junior year, because I did not give them the chance. It was six months after Pearl Harbor, and when I was supposed to be sitting in the big examination halls, scribbling in a blue-covered book, I was on Staten Island, standing naked in line for hours, enlisting in the United States Army. At Fort Dix I heard someone say you must have an IQ of 120 to qualify for officer candidate school. IQ! Maybe that had been my trouble all along. A panic-stricken youngster in a phone booth, calling a girl he had dated at Princeton who worked in the dean's office: "Get my folder out and see what my IQ is and call me right back."

The 696th Armored Field Artillery Battalion of Patton's Third Army, in which I served as forward observer, landed on Utah Beach on D-plus-26. From there it was a long trek. The breakthrough at St. Lô, Coutances, and Avranches. The Battle of the Bulge, the relief of Bastogne. Holland. Across the Rhine, across the Elbe. VE day found us forty-five miles from Berlin, swapping stories with the Russians. In February 1946 I was honorably discharged.

The same classrooms, the same lecture halls, the same courses—and a whole new world. In Princeton's McCosh 10 the day's lecture ended, the huge class rose and flooded out the exits. I was elbowing my way down the center aisle against the stream to get at that silly fool on the platform gathering up his notes. I pounded on the floor at his feet: "What in the name of the Lord were you trying to tell us? If you can't do better than that, I've got to get out of this course. I'm twenty-six years old, I can't be wasting my time here!" One or two other veterans joined me. Together we nailed the poor devil to the wall, and that ten o'clock lecture was not over until midafternoon.

We were a subgeneration that had come back full of questions, hungry for meaningful answers. I was taking courses and on paths of inquiry I had never before dared. At Exeter a failure in American history had cost me my diploma, but now I found I could do history as readily as my "good" courses like math and physics. In my economics major I dug into the history of economic thought, the lives of the economists themselves. I was enjoying courses in philosophy and art and music composition. I was suddenly aware of how ignorant I was, alive with curiosity, doing academic work at a level I would not have thought possible a few years before. I did not know it yet, but I was learning the basic educational fact of life: the answers are meaningless until the questions are asked.

To eke out my GI scholarship income, I took on a job at the Hun School, a small boarding school for boys located in the town of Princeton. At first I was a sort of preserver of law and order and tutor. Mike Morgan, on the university staff, had said I could have the job on one condition: "Promise me you'll never go into education." I told him, "Couldn't be further from my mind." The Hun students were mostly combat veterans, as anxious to get their high school diplomas as I was to get mine from the university. We were a tight group. We spoke the same language, had the same reference, had been through it together. Every night they sprawled on the floor of my room, struggling with math or physics or chemistry. These were things I could help them with. Sometimes they had no money to pay the school a bill, and I said, "Hell, you can work it off," and they paid by doing some painting or plastering or glazing that the school needed.

I had been having such fun with these guys, and working so hard at my own courses, that I had not done much thinking about a career after graduation. Bob McAllen, who had taken over as headmaster, said, "Why don't you stay on here and teach?" I said, "Great—I'd love it." I was to teach algebra and physics, do some coaching, and help with administration. In June 1947 I graduated from Princeton *cum laude* in my major, and I married Phebe Stevens.

In that time the Hun School was a great place for a young educator to learn about education, and about operating a school. Within three years the school had four headmasters, and I was helping to break in each in turn. I was doing everything from teaching to coaching to balancing the books, hiring teachers, firing kids, dealing with trustees, dealing with accreditation authorities. We had needed a history teacher, and over at Princeton I found a graduate student named Tom Hartmann. Tom and I became partners. We swapped every job in the school. You be dean, I'll be director of studies. You be treasurer, and I'll be in charge of grounds and buildings. You be director of admissions, and I'll be director of athletics. You be varsity baseball coach, and I'll be development officer. We bought the supplies and the food. We emptied our savings accounts to pay bills to keep the merchants off our backs. And all the time we were counseling with parents who had problems with their kids, and with kids who had problems with their parents.

The school plant was a former private estate. There was not enough money for upkeep of the grounds and buildings and equipment. From the precedent of letting the veterans work off a bill came the idea of giving the kids varsity letters for doing work—cutting the lawns, painting, floor waxing, plumbing, and so on. You could not tell a football player's letter from the one a truck-engine specialist was wearing. The football players looked down their noses a little, but how envious they were of the kid driving the three-gang power mower!

One day in the spring of 1950 my father-in-law came to see me. Jack Stevens was a businessman with a lively interest in hopeful things that were happening in the world, and quite often he got involved in fund raising for one or another cause.

He told me: "Josh, some friends of mine have asked me to help raise money for the work being done by a German headmaster of a school in Scotland. One of these friends is Peggy Douglas, whose husband, Lewis Douglas, is our ambassador to Great Britain, and another is her sister Ellen McCloy, whose husband, John McCloy, is American Allied High Commissioner of Germany. They think that this man can have a helpful influence on post-war Germany. His name is Kurt Hahn. Just what he is up to I can't tell you. He seems to be involved in several different projects—his Gordonstoun School in Scotland, some other schools on the continent, and some kind of an outdoor and rescue training school. My friends say the things he's doing are extremely worthwhile. I asked them if they've ever had an American schoolteacher look at his work, and they asked me if I knew one, and I said I might just. How would you like to go over and take a look at this, and write a report on it?"

"I'd like it," I said.

The train rolled on, following the Spey down through the mountains. Studying my map, I wondered again why Mr. Hahn had instructed me to get off at Aviemore, fifty miles short of the northern coast where the Gordonstoun School was located. The "ticket inspector" leaned into the compartment. "Aviemore!" I gathered my baggage. In another minute the train puffed to a stop, and I stepped down to the platform. I was thirty years old. I had no notion that I was keeping a rendezvous with the rest of my life.

Gordonstoun

Plus Est en Vous.
(You've got more in you than you think.)
     —The Gordonstoun school motto,
          found on the wall of a Belgian church

Whoever was to meet me apparently had not arrived, for the only vehicle in sight was, singularly, a London taxicab. My musing that this vehicle made no sense in the middle of the Scottish Highlands was interrupted by a man who came up and introduced himself. He was Hunter, Mr. Hahn's driver. The London taxi was Mr. Hahn's car. It was a standard black Austin model, with glass separating the driver and passenger compartments. I sat in front with Hunter, who explained that Mr. Hahn had arranged for me to proceed from Aviemore by automobile the better to see the countryside that lay between us and the coast. In particular, Mr. Hahn wanted me to experience "the evening light." Hunter was to get me out of the car at various points, the better to enjoy the vistas in the evening light.

It was a glory ride for all time. Knee-high purple heather, riots of yellow broom. As we left the Cairngorms behind, the moors stretched endlessly, the sky grew bigger, the clouds more enormous. Pushing northward through Forres, we swung a bit to the east.

> How far is't called to Forres? What are these
> So wither'd, and wild in their attire,
> That look not like the inhabitants of the earth,
> And yet are on't?

18

These moors were Macbeth's blasted heath—and had Hunter called on my credulity, I could readily have believed that somewhere in this wild terrain the three witches still laid their choppy fingers upon their skinny lips.

The long twilight had only just set in when we arrived at Gordonstoun at 9:30. I had a sense of old buildings and long-tended landscaping, then the incongruity of several quonset huts. Hunter deposited me at the door of the main building where a student was awaiting my arrival. Shorts, knee-length socks, an open-necked shirt, and a wool sweater, all the same powder-blue color. I had never seen a school uniform before.

Hunter and the London taxi bore my luggage off to the guest house. My spirits drooped as I realized I was to have no chance to change. I was travel-weary, hungry, dirty, unshaved, my eyes bloodshot, my clothes rumpled. I had scarcely slept in thirty-six hours. On the forays from the car to view the evening light, my feet had got wet. I was cold, the chill of the north Scottish night cutting through the thin fabric of my summer suit.

I was led inside and up a wide, highly polished central staircase. The student informed me that this was Gordonstoun House, which had once been a castle, and that it was more than three centuries old. Creaking stairs, antiquity, and the pungent smell of floor wax. On the second floor the student knocked on a door. As it opened and I entered, Kurt Hahn shook my hand. I would learn not to be disconcerted by that trait of a silent greeting that let the smile express it all—recognition, welcome, kindliness. But in the moment of meeting I found my host a bit daunting. A big man of perhaps sixty years. Great shoulders somewhat stooped, big hand giving a firm grip. Partial baldness calling attention to the massive skull that suggested an equally massive brain. Large features and ears, the complexion startlingly soft and pink. The deep-set eyes with their full, live gaze. The mouth, smiling now, that through some infinitesimal reflex could go instantly from stern to amused and back. An extraordinary face, experience, wisdom, goodwill in the expression.

His first words were, "But my good man, you must be tired. You must sit down immediately."

I was quickly made aware of his omnivorous curiosity about people. Abetted by the three elderly ladies who were dining with him, he simultaneously plied me with questions and bade me eat. By the end of the meal he knew a great deal about me and my family. I remember well that I was cold—particularly that my feet were cold and damp—because of an incident during the meal. The student who had greeted me entered and spoke to Hahn. This was Humphrey Taylor, he told me, and if I would step out in the hall, Humphrey had something for me. What young Humphrey had was a pair of my dry wool socks. I had no idea how the boy had received the word to fetch those socks. Nor did I realize that the fetching had required a four-mile round trip by bicycle to go to the guest house and extract the socks from my luggage. Humphrey informed me that he was the Helper of Guests. That was his post in the student hierarchy.

That evening and my whole first week at Gordonstoun tend to blur in memory, parts coming in and out of focus. Arriving on Monday, I was kept so busy that I had no chance to write home until late Thursday night. Phebe still has that letter, and passages in it help my recall.

> Breakfast at Burnside—a delightful and picturesque Scotch farm which is the guest house—9 A.M. chat with Hahn. Morning with Mr. Sime, old boy and currently farm manager and chemistry teacher. Lunch with Hahn. Afternoon spent with 15-year-old Humphrey Taylor—delightful boy— guided tour of school . . .

Why did Hahn pick Ian Sime, that first morning, to introduce me to the academic side of the school? In part, for sure, because he was a Gordonstoun old boy. Was it also because he was a very direct, outspoken young fellow, with sharp opinions of how Hahn was not running things efficiently, of colleagues who were not pulling their oar, of the shortcomings of Americans? Sime showed me his chemistry laboratories, located in one of the "naffies"— what I called a quonset hut. Gordonstoun had been taken over by the army during the war, and the school was still utilizing naffies the military had left behind. The labs were primitive, but sound.

After lunch Humphrey Taylor gave me a good look at the school through a student's eyes. Humphrey told me about the Training Plan, which was the foundation of an elaborate system of student responsibility. It was a checkoff list of each student's daily routine, starting with the morning run, cold shower, and room chores, and so on through doing of assignments, promptness for class, writing home, bedtime teeth brushing. Once a student was judged ready to be responsible for himself, he made his own daily checkoff and carried out his own penalties for such infractions as being late for class. The prescribed penalty for lateness and other infractions was to get up early for an extra long run. I asked Humphrey why, since nobody checked on him, he didn't just skip doing his lates, as he called them. "Come on, Humphrey," I said, "I would."

Humphrey smiled. "I used to," he said. "But I got tired of lying to myself." That sold me. I didn't know if the Training Plan would work in an American school, but it was working here.

> . . . Supper with Hahn + 8 foreign students—Belgian, French, Dane, Norwegian, + 4 Germans from Salem. I read *Ivanhoe* out loud after supper. Followed by private talk with Hahn.

One of Kurt Hahn's ideals for Gordonstoun was that the student body should have a strong international mix. Among his overriding concerns as an educator, and philosophically as a world citizen, was that people, retaining love of country, should rise above the constraints of nationalism. When did American schools stop reading Scott? *Ivanhoe* was new to me. Hahn, I am sure, knew it as a boy in German.

> Breakfast at 7 with Hahn—then off to the Moray Sea School— a new short course school located at Burghead (see map— due west). They were taking the final expeditionary endurance test of the course. What an experience! Home at midnight. Dead to the world!

The Moray Sea School was my first exposure to Outward Bound. No one called it that, however; I had not yet heard the name. Hahn and others simply referred to it as the short-term school. They explained to me that boys fourteen-and-a-half to eighteen came here for a twenty-eight-day course that was physically rugged and challenging, and in a general way I gathered that the purpose of the school was character building. Most of the boys were apprentices sent by industry, some were police cadets. A few were from correctional institutions or had been referred by social agencies.

That day, the next-to-last of the course, the boys were doing a final cross-country endurance test—roughly comparable to the final-day marathon in the U. S. Outward Bound schools today. Divided by age into groups of six, they had to travel cross-country, with the aid of map and compass, through a series of checkpoints in the moor wilderness. This was a difficult test in land navigation, for it is easy to get lost in the moors. The terrain has no landmarks, and the boys had to travel around boggy areas. The distance was twenty-eight miles for the oldest group and ranged down to twenty-two for the youngest, and they were to travel as rapidly as they could without breaking up the group.

These were youngsters from more or less disadvantaged backgrounds who had been born in the Depression years, had grown while undergoing the privations of World War II. Their postwar, still-rationed diets had not enabled them to recover from a poor start. They were scrawny, undersize—and wiry. It was a real eye-opener that they could cover twenty-eight miles in a day, under pressure. I had never seen anything like it with boys in the States. Sure, I had done a fourteen-mile hike, but that was tame compared to this.

> Breakfast at Burnside at 8:30 and talk with Hahn at 9:15—10:00 off to Sea School with Guggenheim to witness the final test in seamanship. Spent 3 hours in sailing cutter—delightful.

O. A. Guggenheim and his wife were fellow visitors staying at the guest house. They had a son in the school. Of Swiss extraction, the father was a textile manufacturer who had spent most of his life in India. His son, he told me, was no great shakes as a scholar, but Hahn was discovering the boy's attributes. He had been made head of the Cliff Watchers Rescue Service. Impressed by Hahn's educational ideas, Guggenheim was becoming his close friend and ally. He informed me he was a director of the new mountain rescue school. I had no idea what that was.

The students at the Moray Sea School were formed in groups of twelve, called watches. Each watch manned a two-masted sailing cutter about thirty-four feet in length. We looked on as the crews were put through a rigorous sequence of seamanship exercises. Four weeks earlier most of these lads had never been in a sailboat. Now I marveled at their deft teamwork in handling their craft.

> Spent afternoon with Hahn and the Guggenheims witnessing the Gordonstoun sea rescue group work with a breeches buoy.

A mile or so from Gordonstoun is the Firth of Moray. Running along the coast are precipitous cliffs, two hundred to four hundred feet high. The prevailing winds are northerly—this is a lee shore, strewn with rocky shoals—and at their base the cliffs have been scooped out by the sea. Above, you can lie with your head projecting over the edge and look straight down at the pounding surf. It is a gut-qualming sight.

Here, before and during the early days of World War II, the Gordonstoun Cliff Watchers, functioning as an auxiliary of His Majesty's Coastguard, stood watch for ships in distress and enemy submarine activity. After the school returned from its wartime quarters in Wales, the Watchers were reactivated. In fog and foul weather students maintained a vigilant watch around the clock, "lest," in the phrase Hahn had happily appropriated from the Coastguard manual, "a ship burn an inefficient flare."

The Cliff Watchers were organized into two rescue groups, a breeches-buoy team, and a cliff-ladder evacuation team. On the day of my visit the breeches-buoy team drove their lorry, laden with standard Coastguard equipment, to the cliff and carried out a rescue exercise. We looked on as they set up a rocket launcher and fired a line out to a small, rocky offshore island. With this line a group on the island hauled out a strong rope and secured it to a masonry ruin, perhaps the remains of an ancient lighthouse, that simulated a shipwreck. At the cliff top the rope was run over a tripod and anchored in the ground. When all was secured, the breeches buoy was suspended from a pulley that ran back and forth on the rope. The buoy consisted of a cork ring with canvas breeches attached, designed so that the person being rescued could sit in the ring with legs through the breeches. Lines attached to the buoy were used to pull it in either direction. I watched, fascinated. I had never seen anything like this either. The boys knew exactly what they were doing, and did it with dispatch. One had no doubt that were a wreck in fact out there, they would be competently saving lives.

As we hiked back through the gorse and broom, Hahn told me how the Watchers got started. He had learned about St. Gernadius, an eighth-century Irish monk who lived in a cave in the area and on stormy nights walked the rocky shoreline, waving a lantern to warn fishermen of rocks and shoals. Hoping to enthuse the students for coast watching, he recited the monk's story. "I had a bad reception," he said. "I saw in their eyes the look of mistrust that meant, 'The old man wants to save our souls.' " He looked at me, a smile touching the corners of his mouth. "The young, you know, are allergic to the manifest improvers."

Then the Coastguard, who had heard of Hahn's interest, sent two officers with an offer: if the school would build and man a lookout hut, the Coastguard would equip it and give the volunteers auxiliary status. Summoning the school, Hahn had the officers make their request directly to the students, who gave enthusiastic assent.

Hahn gave me another of those looks and drew the moral. "There are three ways of trying to win the young. You can preach at them, that is a hook without a worm. You can say, 'You must volunteer,' that is of the devil. And you can tell them, 'You are needed.' That appeal hardly ever fails."

> . . . dinner with Mr. and Mrs. Chew, who is activities director and housemaster of Duffus House. Very attractive and competent.

As director of activities, Bobby Chew was one of the school's most important people. Hahn had a unique idea of what a school's staff structure should be. Under the headmaster were two men of equal rank—a director of studies and a director of activities. The one was responsible for the curricular program, the other for everything that did not take place in the classroom, which at Gordonstoun was a broad gamut. Hahn made the two posts equal because he felt the school should pay equal attention to the academic and nonacademic sides of a youngster's development. When one program encroached on the other, the other was expected to fight back; Hahn relished that seesaw tension between his two lieutenants. Chew had taught at Salem, Hahn's school in Germany in the 1920's. In World War II he had been a colonel in the British commandos. His lovely Norwegian wife, Eva, was the widow of a Norwegian fellow commando and friend who had been killed in the line of duty.

Chew's opposite number as director of studies was Henry Brereton, a fine scholar and innovative educator, who had held the post virtually from Gordonstoun's beginning. Since he and Chew had great respect for each other, and both were intensely loyal to Hahn, the school's top administrative structure was solid.

> Hahn is extremely unique. What a personality. What drive! What energy! What vision! At 64 he is an excellent cricketer, tennis player, and beats all up and down stairs and hills alike. He has that amazing faculty for broad vision and the most minute detail! Astounding memory. Quite terrifying *except* that he always inspires anyone to his very best, at the same time somehow preventing you from saying and doing the wrong thing and in general putting your foot in your mouth. He is extremely busy. I am grateful for every 2 minutes with him and try to make the most of them. He's on the go every minute—can't sit still a second. Makes at least 4 telephone calls during any meal and the boys say he can run 3 dinner parties at a time, hopping from room to room. He is loved, admired, respected, and feared by boys and faculty alike. They never know what he will do next. He's always doing something and keeps them in same state.

How avid I was for each few minutes of Hahn's time! I was so full of questions, and each day they piled higher. The morning encounters that started my day were frustratingly short—little more than time enough for him to brief me on my always-full schedule for the day. But at night, toward bedtime, he would say, "We must go see the wonderful light of the evening." He would summon the ever-ready Hunter, and off we would go in the London taxi, perhaps along the coast, or to someplace like Cawdor Castle. Then we would get out and walk, two or three miles. On these occasions I had my best chance to get him to talk about himself and his ideas.

Even that time had to be shared with his consuming desire to know about me. I was the subject of relentless questioning—and not just about myself. I was beginning to find out that Hahn learned about people by learning about their family. He would want to know where your mother was born. How she happened to meet your father, where they lived, and what did your father do? Even more important, what did your mother do? "And tell me about your grandmothers—I am the world's greatest collector of grandmothers." When he was through with that generation, he would switch to one's mother-in-law: "I am president of the Benevolent Association for the Protection of Mothers-in-law." Then your brothers and sisters. I was to learn that every acquaintance Hahn made was subjected to this line of inquiry. It was the way he came to know every student. And he retained it all. Through the years, when he wrote, when he telephoned, he would ask about my mother, my wife's mother, my brothers, my sisters-in-law, our children, our dog. His power of recall was astounding.

Strangely, despite the relentless questioning one never felt under pressure. He had a way of putting you at ease so that your answers flowed. You found yourself being more articulate than at any time in your life. I would always feel he brought out the best in me.

So Hahn knew all about me long before I learned his story. But then, I had a great deal more to learn.

Hahn

Eccentric perhaps, innovator certainly,
great beyond doubt.
                    —HRH THE DUKE OF EDINBURGH

Kurt Hahn, who often appears so Victorian in manners
and language, belongs in a deep sense to the new age
of hope. Like the great artists and scientists, like the
astronauts, he is a citizen of global mankind.
                    —HENRY BRERETON

Rowing bareheaded on a blazing hot day in his nineteenth
year, Kurt Hahn suffered a severe sunstroke. The injury, centering at the cerebellum, where the spine joins the base of the
brain, threatened to cripple him. To ease his suffering he spent
a year in a darkened room. Periodically thereafter—"despair stalk-
ing him like a sinister shadow," as Henry Brereton has written—
the affliction returned in full force, casting him back into the
dark. Even after a great London neurosurgeon performed a series
of brain-decompressing operations that helped him greatly, light
and heat remained his lifelong torment.

In those lonely ordeals of his young manhood he was working
out a life principle that years later a remarkable physical educator would articulate and Hahn would make his *leitmotiv*:
"Your disability is your opportunity." To make his confinement
productive, he devised regimens of physical activity and disciplined thought. He practiced the standing high jump—scarcely to
the delight of the Oxford students living beneath him—and the

legend is that he broke records in that event. With the study of Plato's *Republic* fresh in his mind he conceived a new kind of school, where the worlds of thought and action would no longer be divided into hostile camps. Later he wrote out the concept and put it away for future reference.

Hahn was born into a cultured Jewish family in Berlin in 1886. His father was a successful industrialist. His mother was a beautiful woman of artistic temperament and powerful faith in the innate goodness of man. One of her forebears was Jecheskiel Landau, Chief Rabbi of Prague in the eighteenth century, whose writings on the Talmud are still taught at academies of Jewish studies. His grandmother on his mother's side was his adored "Anschulka," whose wise and droll sayings he noted down in a book. ("Anschulka, which of your eight children is the best?" "A mother is like a shopkeeper—she has various kinds of goods.") The home in which he grew up, radiating human warmth, was a gathering place for the city's intelligentsia and artists.

His father, enamored of England, built the family summer residence Wannsee in English country-house style. Kurt, the eldest of three sons, was a born teacher. In the summers at Wannsee he would gather the young people in the pavilion and read them tales of heroic adventure. Often he led them on long hikes over rough terrain. At Göttingen, one of several German universities he attended, his Greek professor told him "If you are interested in the old in order to help the new, it is not the German universities that can help you, but Oxford." He studied at Oxford from 1910 to 1914. On August 1, 1914, he took leave of his English friends to return home. Two days later Great Britain declared war on Germany.

In the war Hahn held a succession of minor Foreign Office posts from which he nevertheless emerged as a person of influence. He worked with the moderates—against unrestricted submarine warfare, for a negotiated peace—and became one of their spokesmen. Although his counsel did not prevail, the quality of his work won the attention of persons in high places. He was made adviser to Colonel von Haeften, who was in turn political adviser to General von Ludendorff.

At the war's end Hahn was assistant to Prince Max of Baden, Germany's last imperial chancellor. The prince was a scholarly, humane man who in a speech in 1917 dared to say, "To love your enemy is the sign of those who remain loyal to the Lord even in time of war." The two men shared an enthusiasm for Plato's educational ideas, and in 1920 Prince Max founded a coeducational boarding school with Hahn as headmaster. This was the Salem (*shalom, salaam,* peace) Schule; it was the school Hahn had conceived seven years before.

The times were, quite literally, fearful. Defeated Germany was on the edge of anarchy. The school thwarted two plots, one by Communists to kidnap Prince Max, another by nationalists to murder Hahn. (Typically, Hahn was more concerned over his would-be assassins' despair for the nation's plight than he was to see them punished.) Guerrilla bands were setting fire to farms. Salem boys joined the night patrols guarding the lonely countryside. It was in that time that William Butler Yeats wrote the lines, so prophetic of the coming European tragedy, that Hahn would come to quote often, a statement of his lifelong concern:

> The best lack all conviction, while the worst
> Are full of passionate intensity.

Yeats was defining the very condition that Prince Max and Hahn had set out to deal with. Through Salem, and by spreading the Salem gospel to other educators, they sought to nurture a German youth with convictions rooted in personal responsibility, kindness, and justice. The intent, in Hahn's words, was to equip young people "to effect what they have recognized to be right, despite hardships, despite dangers, despite inner skepticism, despite boredom, despite mockery from the world, despite emotion of the moment." The school's report to parents, developed at Salem and later used at Gordonstoun, evaluated the degree to which the students displayed these traits.

Hahn was at once a champion and hard taskmaster of youth in its conflicts with the elder generation. If young people were to play an influential role in society, he insisted, they must earn the right. Even as he welcomed the German youth movement of that time, he took sharp issue with indulgent adult attitudes. Long after I first knew him, in the time of the youth revolt in the England and United States of the 1960's, it was uncanny to discover that in the Germany of 1928 he had said: "With phrases such as 'Youth Culture' these people besmear the souls of the young with the ointment of flattery—as though the young no longer had to become anything, but were everything already. They rob them of their joy of development and do violence to the natural process of spiritual growth."

Inevitably, the ideals of Salem clashed with the spirit of Nazism. Apprehensive of the growing strength of Hitler's movement, Hahn stepped up his efforts to win the German educational community over to Salem principles. But the Nazi tide continued to rise. In 1932 five storm troopers trampled a young Communist to death in front of his mother. They were arrested, tried, and condemned to death. In his notorious "Beuthen telegram," Hitler hailed them as comrades and demanded their release. "Your freedom," he said, "is our honor." For Hahn this was in fact the hour when men of honor must declare themselves. He sent a letter to all Salem alumni: "Hitler's telegram has brought on a crisis that goes beyond politics. Germany is at stake, her Christian civilization, her good name, her soldiers' honor. Salem cannot remain neutral. I ask the members of the Salem Union who are active in a S.A. or S.S. to break with Salem or with Hitler." It was, said a Briton who was teaching at Salem at the time, "the bravest deed in cold blood that I have witnessed."

Sir Roger Birley, who was Hahn's contemporary as headmaster of Eton, has given us a record of his courage in the German crisis. Discussing the education provided under Hahn at Salem, Birley wrote:

> But there was a second element quite as important. It was impressively expressed in an address Kurt Hahn gave in Hamburg on 16 February 1933. (The significance of the date, seventeen days after the Nazis gained power, will be obvious.) It began with a study of the Fascist state and educational ideals, and an account of Fascism which seems to make inevitable the uncomfortable statement which is to be found in the address, that, if one looked at the educational principles of the Italian youth organizations, "you find that you might be quoting the whole Salem Certificate of Maturity with its capacity to endure hardships, to face dangers, a talent for organization, prudence, a fighting spirit, presence of mind, success in dealing with unexpected difficulties"—and then come the words, "Only one item is and must be missing: The power of carrying out what is recognized to

be just." And a little later, "*Sacro egoismo*, sacred egoism. There is also sacred lying, sacred killing, sacred perjury, sacred breaking of promises." To speak in this way of Fascist principles at that moment was indeed courageous, but Kurt Hahn went on to turn to his own country, and it was with continual references to the state of things in Germany that he gave his reasons why Salem rejected Fascist education. Among these was to be found this one: "We need to be able to feel that as a people we are just and kindly. On this consciousness depends our inner strength."

Hahn became a marked man. In the mass arrests following the Reichstag fire in February 1933, he was jailed. The shock waves swiftly reached Britain, where his friends—some from the Oxford days, others gained as Salem's fame had spread—took up his cause. When Prime Minister Ramsay MacDonald made official representations, Hahn was let go. In July he left for England.

In those first months of exile he was profoundly depressed. At forty-seven he had lost his homeland, his school, the battle for German youth. A man of means, overnight he had become a nearly penniless refugee. Worse, his spiritual resources were depleted. When he was asked to found a new school along Salem lines, he lacked the will. When he was offered an established school to work with, he said, "I do not have time to overcome the inertia of tradition." Then he returned to Moray, the north of Scotland country where he had spent the convalescent summers of his Oxford years. He met old friends among the fishermen and crofters of the district. On the wharf in Hopeman Harbor, he listened to Captain Danny Main tell tales of men of simple courage against the forces of the sea. With another friend, Lord Malcolm Douglas-Hamilton, he inspected the empty castle at Gordonstoun, badly in need of repair, as a possible site for a school. Its vistas seized his spirit, and he knew again the truth that he would summon so often in guiding others: "Your disability is your opportunity."

Gordonstoun opened as a school for boys in April 1934; by September there were twenty-one students (among them a Greek prince of Danish blood named Philip, who one day would marry the future queen of England). The board of governors included the Archbishop of York, later of Canterbury, the headmaster of

Eton, the master of Trinity College at Cambridge, a distinguished British historian, and the future governor-general of Canada. The school's enrollment grew steadily.

In 1938 Hahn became a naturalized British subject. It was in character that even as he struggled to cope with the acute money problems of an expanding, unendowed school, he poured part of his energies into national concerns—alerting the British people to the dimensions of the Hitlerian threat, calling on them to hear the muffled cries from the concentration camps, campaigning at the War Office for a system of training that in months, he declared, could make British infantrymen the equal in stamina, hardihood, and self-confidence of German soldiers whose training had started years before in the Hitler Youth.

War broke out. The British Army commandeered Gordonstoun, and the school had to trek to wartime quarters in Wales. The move was a major disability. In it Hahn found a new opportunity—and brought forth Outward Bound.

Opportunity's name was Lawrence Holt. Hahn had been trying to launch a "County Badge Scheme," an ambitious national plan for fostering physical fitness, enterprise, tenacity, and compassion among British youth. But in the wartime climate his prestigious County Badge Experimental Committee—scientist Julian Huxley, historian George Trevelyan, and others—had made small headway. At that same time Holt, a Gordonstoun father and Hahn admirer who was partner in Alfred Holt & Company, a large merchant-shipping enterprise, was gravely concerned about the human toll in the Battle of the Atlantic. He was convinced that due to faulty training, many seamen on torpedoed merchant ships were dying unnecessarily. Unlike sail-trained old-timers, he maintained, the younger men and youths had not acquired a sense of wind and weather, a reliance on their own resources, and a selfless bond with their fellows. "I would rather," he told Hahn, "entrust the lowering of a lifeboat in mid-Atlantic to a sail-trained octogenarian than to a young sea technician who is competently trained in the modern way but has never been sprayed by salt water."

Hahn proposed they join forces to start a new kind of school offering young people one-month courses that would use Hahn's county badge scheme to implement Holt's quest for training to turn attitudes around. Holt agreed, his company providing funds and the maritime staff members. The school, called Outward Bound at Holt's insistence, opened at Aberdovey, Wales, in 1941. It was not, as the mythologized version has it, a school for young merchant seamen. While many of the students were youngsters sponsored by Holt's Blue Funnel Line and other shipping companies and from the government training ship H.M.S. *Conway*, others were apprentices sent by industry, or police, fire, and other cadets, or boys on leave from their regular schools or about to go into the armed services. It was Holt himself who articulated a Hahnian concept in words Hahn never forgot. "The training at Aberdovey," Holt said, "must be less a training *for* the sea than *through* the sea, and so benefit all walks of life." The month-long course was, in fact, a mix of small-boat training, athletic endeavor to reach standards of competence, cross-country route-finding by map and compass, rescue training, an expedition at sea, a land expedition across three mountain ranges, and service to the local people. The school was fortunate from the outset in two key staff members. Jim Hogan, a resourceful young schoolmaster whom Hahn had recruited from the national educational system to be secretary of his County Badge Experimental Committee, was warden. His assistant in charge of athletic activity was Captain B. Zimmerman, who had been a great innovative physical educator in Germany until he fled his country to avoid Nazi imprisonment. Hahn had brought him from Switzerland to Gordonstoun. It was "Zim" who first exhorted his charges that their liability was their opportunity, who—seizing on Holt's phrase—talked of "training through the body, not of the body," and worked on each student until he could proclaim, "The bug has bit!"

Although beset by a prodigious series of start-up difficulties, Outward Bound worked from the first. The youths who came were the products of Britain's dozen years of depression and dole. Invariably, when they were told what they were expected to achieve in thirty days, murmurs of incredulity and derision ran through the group. But they were soon caught up by "the magic of the puzzle," Hahn's odd phrase for the phenomenon he knew so well—that when a young person "defeats his defeatism" to meet a challenge, it primes him to try for still more difficult achievement. There was a half-concealed pride of accomplishment in the assertion of the Cockney boy, exhausted and footsore after his first cross-country effort: "Cor blimey, if this had been Larndon, they'd shift them bleedin' hills." A moving human story underlay the statement of the half-caste lad from Liverpool, warmed by his watch-mates' acclaim for his self-improvement: "This is the first time in my life I have seemed to matter." Wise old Alec Fraser, the former missionary who served as the school chaplain, saw what was happening: "They come for the wrong reasons, and they leave sorry for the right ones that it's over."

Holt's prepositional distinction—training through rather than for—was always to be the essence of the Outward Bound dynamic. Life-enhancing experience is obtained through the sea, the mountains, the wild lake country, the desert. Outward Bound has evolved since those early Aberdovey days. But it has not departed from Hahn and Holt's essential concept of an intense experience surmounting challenges in a natural setting, through which the individual builds his sense of self-worth, the group comes to a heightened awareness of human interdependence, and all grow in concern for those in danger and in need.

Outward Bound and Salem

Give children the chance to discover themselves.

See to it that children experience both success and defeat.

See to it that there are periods of silence.

Train the imagination, the ability to anticipate and to plan.

Take sports and games seriously, but only as a part of the whole.

Free the children of rich and influential parents from the paralyzing influence of wealth and privilege.

> —Kurt Hahn's prescription
> for German education, circa 1930.

After a week at Gordonstoun, Hahn sent me traveling, first to visit a new Outward Bound school.

Monday. Am at the moment bumping my way to the short term 'Outward Bound Mountain School' at Eskdale, near Whitehaven, near Carlisle, on a very jouncy train. Had breakfast at 6:30 this A.M. with Hahn. On top of a 15-mile bird walk yesterday ending at 8 P.M., followed by supper with Hahn and a rehearsal of Macbeth with bed finally at 12:30. The day finds me somewhat physically bushed, but as always (in this atmosphere) ready for more. The guy certainly has something. More ideas working, and more to be worked than you can imagine . . .

The school at Eskdale brought my first awareness of the name "Outward Bound." Hahn, who had not cared for the name when Lawrence Holt insisted on it at Aberdovey, still referred to "short-term schools." (In later years he would enjoy telling audiences how right Holt, how wrong he, had been.) What I did not then realize was how significant a development Eskdale and the manner of its founding was for what would become a worldwide Outward Bound movement. A few years before, a group of prominent British men and women, strong believers in the concept that had proved itself at Aberdovey, had formed the Outward Bound Trust. The intent was to free the Aberdovey School of the insecurity of depending on the goodwill and magnanimity of a commercial firm, and to foster growth of Outward Bound on a national basis. Alfred Holt & Company (its head, now Sir Lawrence Holt) generously deeded the school to the Trust. By 1949 there were funds in hand to enable the purchase at auction of "Gatehouse," the ancestral home of Lord Rea at Eskdale, as a base for a new school.

England's Lake District, in which Eskdale is located, is in the northwest corner of the country. Its lakes are produced by the runoff of water from the Cumbrian Mountains, which rise to Scaffel Pike, the country's highest peak. Gatehouse was a large baronial structure in a splendid setting that looked out across a tarn, as the Scots call a small lake, to the higher fells of the Scafell group. On arrival I was immediately swept into the school's activity. The warden, Adam Arnold-Brown—a Gordonstoun old boy and one of its first Guardians—was about my age. The students were doing the five-mile walk, a stressful heel-and-toe exercise that consumed, it seemed to me, more energy than would jogging over the same rugged terrain. "Come along, old chap," Arnold-Brown called out, fitting our pace to that of the student pack. Accepting an invitation I could not refuse, I was soon reduced to a state of heaving lungs, aching legs, and thorough lather.

That evening, as Arnold-Brown explained the recruiting procedure for the school, I learned about the English educational scheme. At that time all British eleven-year-olds took an examination, the "Eleven Plus," that separated those who would go on to try for the universities from those who would join a vocational stream and whose formal education would end at fourteen. Most of the latter went into industry as apprentices. It was from this apprentice group that Eskdale and the other Outward Bound schools (the Gordonstoun-affiliated Moray Sea School was soon to be taken under the Outward Bound Trust's wing) drew most of their student body. Their employers paid their way—selecting them either because they showed leadership potential or problem potential, sometimes both. Other students came as cadets in such services as the police and coastguard, or as ordinary schoolboys, and a few were boys in trouble with the law referred by juvenile authorities.

> Two voices are there; one is of the Sea,
> One the Mountains: each a mighty voice.

The Eskdale course, like that at Moray, had been designed on the Aberdovey model, except that at Eskdale mountaineering and rock climbing replaced seamanship, and training for mountain rescue replaced that for rescue at sea. But again the training was *through* rather than *for*. On a rocky promontory overlooking fields green with young crops I watched the students practice first aid and lowering a litter-borne injured person down a cliff. A highlight of the first course, Arnold-Brown told me, had been an emergency "call-out" on a dark, blustery night, the boys joining in the search for a lost mountaineering party. This was Eskdale's second course, and Arnold-Brown and his attractive wife were profoundly excited by the daily revelations of the school's potential. There had been enough in the way of dramatic incident and human interplay to convince them they were committed to an enterprise capable of producing dramatic change in young people.

Back at Gordonstoun four days later, Hahn informed me at breakfast that the leader of the visiting group from the Carnegie Foundation was "a codfish-eyed Englishman of a type I cannot handle." I got the assignment. The next day I was given another, this one putting me through a Saturday's misery of preparing a talk to the Cliff Watchers at their final Sunday chapel service.

Sunday night I was off again, this time to visit the Outward Bound Sea School at Aberdovey. On the station platform at

Crewe at 4 A.M., Guggenheim was waiting with his Bentley. The sleek car's long shafts of light swept the blackness, picking out the new curve that seemed always to lie ahead. Gugg had scant respect for curves. Before Wales, another stop. I had said to Hahn: "I would like to meet a prominent British educator who disagrees strongly with your ideas." Those remarkable eyes had flashed, a note almost of glee in his voice: "Capital! You will meet the enemy!"

The enemy was the headmaster of the Shrewsbury School. "A very stiff and proper Englishman," I wrote home. He greeted us cordially, clearly relishing this chance to disabuse the young American of any faulty notions of British education he might have picked up. His school was an academic powerhouse—all stress on preparation for the university examinations. A great rowing school. Character was developed in the rowing shell and on the cricket pitch. No reference to service, no concern with matters of social conscience, with deriving education from experience as well as in the classroom. Of its kind, Shrewsbury was one of England's best. Its very quality qualified its headmaster as "the enemy."

Over morning tea and biscuit the headmaster expatiated on what was wrong with the Hahn philosophy. I perceived he did not even know—did not want to know—what Hahn was doing. He said things like, "You know, at Gordonstoun they have boys who can't read or write." This was a half-truth. He had no comprehension of Hahn's stern principle that a boy must not be penalized for something he could not help—his IQ, for example, or a childhood bombing trauma that had blighted his early schooling.

I did not have to defend Hahn in order to disagree with my host. He stood for the very emphases in education that more and more I had been coming to doubt. We got into a pretty heavy argument. Gugg kept silent. Back on the highway, he shifted the Bentley into high. "I say, old boy, I've never heard anyone speak to a headmaster as you did." I said, "How about the parents who are paying the bill? Haven't they the right to object?" "Of course not. They'd be terrified. They'd lose their child's place in the school immediately." It had helped that I had not known better. Later, on hearing my report, Hahn would laugh. Then frown. "But you see what our problem is. He speaks well for his position. This is the inertia of tradition."

The Bentley purred on, across the Welsh border, toward Aberdovey, where we were welcomed by Captain J. F. "Freddy" Fuller, the warden of the Aberdovey School. From fifteen years of age, the sea had been the only life Freddy Fuller knew until, in 1943, the experience of surviving the successive torpedoing of two ships and commanding a lifeboat in the open sea for thirty-five days had brought him a landlubber assignment. "Perhaps it was as well," he has written, "that I came to Aberdovey with no preconceived ideas of the School and the work it was intended that I should serve with my seaman's craft and skill, but I knew that I came with an added self-confidence and new-found humility, born of the trial and experience of long days in an open boat, scantily equipped for the battle with the elements, with hunger and thirst, with self!"

I was impressed by the versatility of the Aberdovey School's terrain, which included both the sea and the hills. In contrast to the pioneer ambiance at Eskdale, one sensed immediately the established quality that eight years of operation had given Aberdovey. The routine was smooth, professional, knowing. The staff, thoroughly imbued with an understanding of the Outward Bound undertaking, was in control of the process. I was struck by the active allegiance to Hahnian ideas; the evolving school remained strongly conscious of its founder and his philosophy. The rescue ethic was pervasive, and the school had built a strong tradition of service to the area.

From Aberdovey I went to London to fly to Zurich. I was going to the fount—the Salem Schule. The ferry crossed Lake Constance, the Alps at our backs. An hour's drive brought us to the extraordinary sight of Schloss Salem, the Margrave of Baden's great castle, a portion of which housed the school. At the entrance a servant led me inside. Broad, seemingly endless corridors, the walls crowded with paintings and prints—or again, with thousands of antlers, tokens of centuries of hunting in ancient forests. Finally the doorway to my room, where an attractive young woman welcomed me. What with the language difficulties and the culture shock, I was slow in realizing that this was Princess Sophia, my hostess, wife of Prince George of Hanover, headmaster of Salem. Writing home as I awaited the call to dinner, I set down:

It's all too unbelievable. This main building is 4 floors high
and forms a complete courtyard, with entrance through an
archway. Each floor must have at least an 18-foot ceiling and
the court must measure 130 by 75 feet anyway. So you get
an idea of the size of this centuries old castle. My room
opens on the court, in which there are two large Douglas fir
trees that tower out of the court, taking up all the space.
They must be 6 feet in diameter.

At Salem I was indeed at the source. I saw it all happening
in the German environment as I had already seen it in the Scottish, except that this school was coeducational. The early morning running, the midmorning Break in the sedentary hours. The
student government hierarchy—Guardian, Color Bearers, and
Helpers. The Fire Service answering a call. The practical work,
the crafts, and the individual projects. The great student orchestra and chorus rehearsing Handel's "Alexander's Feast." The
school was a scant five years out of Nazism. Apparently Prince
George was succeeding in his vigorous effort to win back its pre-
war eminence, for the school was getting more applicants than
it could accommodate.

One day I lunched with three of the Helpers—those in charge
of practical work, dormitory proctors, and athletics. In the afternoon a boy whose title was "assistant supervisor of practical
work" gave me a tour. The work the students were doing reflected the postwar poverty. Groups were gathering huge quantities of wood for the winter fires. Others were working in the
field; in this time of severe shortages, the school produced most
of its own food. Still others were grooming the athletic fields,
working in the carpentry and blacksmith shops, as electricians,
in the laundry, wherever work was needed to keep the school
going. I wrote home: "The student government is the most
amazing system and operating under the most adverse conditions
both here and at Gordonstoun (but especially here)—no money,
no equipment . . . and until recently inadequate food, so much
so, in fact, that athletics had to be suspended as too tiring."
Twenty-four hours of continuous travel brought me back to a
5 A.M. rendezvous at Inverness with Hunter and the London taxi,
and a long breakfast with Hahn to report on my trip. That afternoon was the *Macbeth* production, which Hahn had directed. It

was performed outdoors on an extremely simple stage built up against the old Gordonstoun castle, in a foggy "fair is foul, and foul still fouler" kind of weather. The casting was extraordinarily good, the authentic Scots accents wonderful. It was the most enjoyable Shakespeare I had ever seen.

My pilgrimage—it had become that—was almost at an end. On my last day I had long talks with Henry Brereton and Bobby Chew. These were salutary meetings, for those two were among the most understanding and staunchly loyal of Hahn's staff. They did not make light of the difficulties that attached to their loyalty. Hahn's very certitude that all things in his philosophy were doable could create extremely trying conditions for those charged with devising and executing the practical details. But concerning the merits and values of the headmaster's philosophy, neither had doubts.

On the flight home I studied and reflected on the Gordonstoun School Final Report to Parents. This was virtually a duplicate of the form Hahn had long ago developed at Salem. Better than any other document, it encapsulated his educational concerns. The student was rated on his public spirit, sense of justice, and ability to follow out what he believed to be the right course in the face of various physical and psychological obstacles; on ability to state facts precisely, and to plan; on ability to organize— both as shown in the doing of his work and his direction of younger boys; on ability to deal with the unexpected; and on his conscientiousness—both in everyday affairs and in tasks with which he was especially entrusted. His imagination and manners were evaluated, as were his manual dexterity, the quality of his handicraft and other practical work, and the quality of his work in music, drawing, and other artistic endeavors. Then came the report on his academic performance and, if he were a member of the Cliff Watchers, the Fire Service, or the Army or Sea Cadets, a service report by his command officer.

It was like no report card I had ever seen. For three decades, I reflected, this man had been doing things in education that I had merely dreamed of in a theoretical way, and had carried them far beyond the blurred limits of my wishful speculations. More than any other educator of whom I was aware, Hahn practiced the philosophy that education had a twin objective: to enable the student to make intelligent judgments and to develop the inherent strengths of his selfhood (to build character, in the old-fashioned phrase too likely to touch off the allergy of the young to "manifest improvers"). The report to parents was the frame of reference that defined the goal Hahn had stated so stirringly years before: "To produce young people able to effect what they see to be right, despite hardships, despite dangers, despite inner skepticism, despite boredom, despite mockery from the world, despite emotion of the moment."

Report and Decision

≡×≡×≡×≡×≡×≡×≡×≡×≡×≡×≡×≡×≡×≡×≡

Report me and my cause aright.
— Hamlet

Back at Hun I tried to tell people where I had been, what I
had learned. Few were more than politely interested. In that day
nobody saw a need to question what we were doing in education.
Actually, "nobody" was a goodly number, scattered across the
land, but we did not know each other. We were little islands. I
had no one who wanted to listen to me except Tom Hartmann.
Tom caught on fast. We talked a lot about how Gordonstoun
concepts might be adapted to American schools.

I learned something about the group of Americans who had
banded together to support Hahn's work abroad. When the war
ended, Hahn had been the first former German national in private life permitted to enter defeated Germany. Soon he was at
odds with the Allied Military Government policy for "reeduca-
tion" of the German people. "Restoration," he held, was the
proper term. In 1948 he visited the United States to win support
for his ideas. That visit led to six prominent Americans forming
the American–British Foundation for European Education as a
vehicle for helping him. The six made a formidable roster:
Thomas McKittrick, a senior vice-president of the Chase National Bank, who was chairman of the group; Allen Dulles,
ex-president of Johns Hopkins University and soon to become
director of the Central Intelligence Agency; Abraham Flexner,
director emeritus of the Institute of Advanced Study at Princeton; Congressman Christian Herter, soon to be elected governor

of Massachusetts, and a future U.S. Secretary of State; Henry Pitney Van Dusen, president of Union Theological Seminary; and Eric Warburg, international financier and senior partner in Kuhn, Loeb and Company, whose sister Lola was married to Rudolf Hahn, Kurt's brother. Despite their bond of public distinction, they were a disparate group. But somewhere, sometime, each had come under Hahn's spell. Each had come to believe in Hahn's ideas for creating "islands of healing" in a war-torn world, especially for restoring health to democratic forces in his corrupted, defeated, demoralized native land.

A three-year program was adopted for which the foundation undertook to raise funds. It called for scholarships to four German schools—Salem, Lietz, the Odenwaldschule, and Luisenlund, a new school being founded on Hahnian principles—and the creation in Germany of three short-term schools (*kurzschulen*) modeled on Britain's Outward Bound. A "German Seminary" was to be established at Gordonstoun to train the *kurzschulen* instructors. A "German Department" was also to be created there, to enable thirty outstanding German boys to spend a year at Gordonstoun on a basis that would not handicap them in the fiercely competitive examinations to German universities. In addition, some help was to be given to equipping the Gordonstoun Cliff Watchers and the Moray Sea School.

In support of the plan for Outward Bound Schools in Germany, Thomas McKittrick arranged for Hahn to meet the newly appointed American High Commissioner in Germany, John McCloy, who was immediately sympathetic. (So was his wife, Ellen, who later would join and then become chairman of the board of the American–British Foundation for European Education. So was her sister, Peggy Douglas, wife of Lewis Douglas, our ambassador to Great Britain.) McCloy provided friends to help finance a *kurzschule*, but all kinds of practical and people difficulties continued to hold back the project. A major inhibiting element was the German educational establishment, an old *bête noire* of Hahn's, which was opposed to spending energy and funds on this kind of school when normal instruction had not yet been adequately implemented. Hahn dealt with this opposition by boring from within, winning adherents among leading professional educators. He was also conducting the standard skirmishes with governmental bureaucrats. He even tangled with the Quakers, whose work in the defeated country he greatly admired. To their sensitive, but in this instance not discriminating, ears the Outward Bound concept of adventure education was too programmatically reminiscent of the regimen of the Nazi youth whose moral ravages they were working to repair. Hahn, ired by a response that he found automatic rather than empathetic, replied, "You care more about pacifism than you do about peace!"

I made my report to the foundation. Reading it years later brings vividly to mind how my exposure to Hahn, Gordonstoun, Salem, and Outward Bound had influenced me. I was sold on the short-term school concept, impressed by the British Ministry of Education's endorsement of it, and by the depth of satisfaction with the results that was motivating British companies to continue to invest in the experience for their employees. I was completely taken with Hahn's own schools, describing the Gordonstoun program in considerable detail. "The headmaster is certainly a genius and a most inspiring person," I reported. "I have never seen his equal at handling people, especially young people. His ideas of education are, however, so fundamental and so essentially sound that personnel trained by him or by his system are perfectly capable of carrying on."

I had been impressed by the Gordonstoun boys. "Naive socially perhaps, according to American standards, they are a collection of individuals, manly, confident, healthy, and enthusiastic. Above all, they are honest. I was surprised at the lack of off-color humor, obscene language, and petty vulgarities that one expects in a boys' school. This factor, however, does not place them above healthy mischief, practical jokes, and a normal amount of boy troubles."

Toward the end of the document I wrote: "A boy who respects the rights and privileges of an individual will never become a part of an organization or state that disregards those rights and privileges. There is no question in my mind that Hahn's boys are proof against these powers."

My firsthand report must have given added assurance to the directors of the American–British Foundation, none of whom had had my exposure. Their interests, however, were entirely oriented to what was happening overseas. They had no thought of trying to bring any aspect of Hahn's work to this country.

Talking with Hartmann, I realized how ill-prepared I would be to implement any American version of the Hahn philosophy. At Gordonstoun and Salem, Aberdovey and Eskdale, the visitor who ran could read, and I had indeed been running. A mere passing observer of the product of three decades of educational thought, experimentation, and energy, I had served no apprenticeship.

In October 1950 I wrote Hahn that I would like to return to Gordonstoun as a staff member the following year. Characteristically he replied by cable: "Your suggestion thrills me. I know of no man whose help would be more fruitful at this juncture. I only hope it can start soon. You can easily bring the daughters. Warmest greetings to you both. Writing."

On February 15, 1951, the entire family—Phebe, our two infant daughters, and I—sailed on the *Parthia* for Liverpool.

Return to Gordonstoun

The schools absorb so much nervous strength through mere bookwork that there is not much spirit left in the young to fashion for themselves soul-restoring activities. I do not wish to be misunderstood; I do not advocate the lowering of the intellectual standards. On the contrary, I would like to see the mind trained by a sterner exercise of the thinking faculty. I do, however, advocate less memory work. May the young, to quote Wordsworth, "not purchase knowledge at the price of power." —KURT HAHN

What avail is it to win prescribed amounts of information about geography and history, to win the ability to read and write, if in the process the individual loses his own soul; loses his appreciation of things worthwhile, of the values to which these are related; if he loses the desire to apply what he learned, and above all, loses the ability to extract meaning from his future experiences as they occur? —JOHN DEWEY

My first teaching assignments at Gordonstoun included general science, current events, and what we would call a "remedial class" in arithmetic. The latter group was my first hands-on exposure to Hahn's working principle that a boy was not to be penalized for a deficiency over which he had no control. Two factors that should not prevail in denying admission to the school were a family's inability to pay and a boy's low IQ. The impor-

tant question was: What is the boy doing with his endowment?
Many Gordonstoun students did splendidly in the university examinations. We also had some interesting youngsters who were
far from what would be considered academically qualified at
most British or American schools. Those boys in my special class
were just about mathematically illiterate. Many of these lads had
endured the bombing in the Battle of Britain, and undoubtedly
some had suffered traumas. Emotional disturbances, manifested
in such aberrations as bed-wetting, were then common among
young Britishers. But in that arithmetic class was a socially
powerful youngster who would win a place of leadership among
the students. Another would become a master farmer, the greatest grower of tomatoes under glass in Great Britain; academia
did not come easily for him, but he had fine common sense. A
third was an artist, a genius in stained-glass design.

There were sons of bricklayers in the school who had aspirations different from their fathers', and there were others who
intended also to be bricklayers. Both were equally honored.
Hahn hoped the latter would go back into their world better
bricklayers because they were better citizens. There were boys
who were going to sea; their careers in the merchant service had
already been chosen for them. They were honored at the same
level as somebody destined for a university to become a doctor.
It was a part of Hahn's greatness as a headmaster that he gave
youngsters a sense of being members of a community in which
all had the same opportunity to earn the same kind of respect
from their peers. At the same time he was on the alert for any
kind of lateral shift an individual might develop. Here comes,
say, a youngster who has a genius for working in stained glass
but whose academic tickets are subpar. He is exposed to poetry
and drama and music, and perhaps he will be enthused by one of
these. Also he is exposed to competing with others from other
streams in a political sense, in the school governing structure.
That could hardly happen to him if as a consequence of the
Eleven Plus he had been diverted into a vocational stream.

The core of Hahn's educational purpose was to conserve and
strengthen the attributes of childhood into manhood. "What
happens in adolescence," he asked, "to your children who in the
nursery are so self-confident and happy?" Too often youngsters

who were joyous, zestful, and enterprisingly curious, with the gift of wonder and an inborn compassion, grew "dimmed and diluted." Adolescence became "the loutish years," a shallow prematuring while strengths remained undiscovered and untrained. Hahn pledged himself "to unseat the dogma that puberty need deform." To this end he sought to create an educational environment where "healthy passions"—craving for adventure, joy of exploration, zest for building, devotion to a skill demanding patience and care, love of music, painting, or writing—would flourish as "guardian angels of adolescence."

Another of my early responsibilities was The Break. It was essential, in Hahn's thinking, that a healthy youngster "have his powers of resilience, coordination, acceleration, and endurance purposefully developed." The Break was his unique contribution to physical education. He had invented it in the early Salem days, and from the beginning had made it an imperative part of the Gordonstoun scheme. Four mornings a week, during a fifty-minute break in what Hahn called "the sedentary hours," each boy took part in two of a half-dozen events—sprinting or distance running, long or high jumping, discus or javelin throwing. He competed only against himself, trying to better his previous best performance. The frail youngster who broke ten feet in the long jump for the first time in his life got as big a cheer as the track team star beating his previous mark at close to twenty. Every boy had to do every event. That same star jumper might be a dud at throwing the discus. It was as important to overcome a weakness as to develop a strength.

When I was put in charge of The Break, I became a fascinated witness to its remarkable results. It was not just that the average performance would have put the average American schoolboy to shame. The great satisfaction lay in seeing the physical duffer discover that through trying from day to day he could do much better than he would have dared to dream. He had learned, in Hahn's phrase, to "defeat his defeatism." You could see him shed —Hahn again—"the misery of his unimportance." His new-found confidence would carry over into his peer relationships, his classroom performance, the quality of work on his project. It was not unusual for a timid or sensitive boy with an undeveloped physique to emerge from the chrysalis of his underconfidence a competent athlete, surprised to find himself confirming what the headmaster had so often told the school: "Your disability is your opportunity."

Sometimes Hahn stood with me, the big hat with the wide, turned-down brim angled over his ears, a pleased observer of the Break activity all around us. Perhaps at the high jump a boy would start his run toward the bar, then shy off, and Hahn would smile. "The high jumpers," he told me, "love to dwell in the valley of indecision." And then, "But they must commit themselves!" The high jump, he claimed, had cured stammerers. Distance running had cured asthmatics. There was a whole Hahnian folklore based on The Break. At least, I tended then to regard it as folklore. I have since become a believer. Medical people now tell us about stammerers being cured by a wilderness experience—why doubt high-jump therapy? And every Outward Bound school can cite cases of asthmatic students whose two-mile early morning run, perhaps undertaken in the face of a physician's concern that the boy should attempt it at all, did much to ease their affliction.

When we first arrived at Gordonstoun, there were no quarters for us at the school; we lived in Elgin, five miles away. In August we moved into Windmill Lodge, a residence on the school grounds. Nearby, some former kennels had just been converted to a dormitory, and I was master of this new "house." At that time Bobby Chew went as headmaster to Altyre, a new Gordonstoun satellite school, and I was given his post as director of activities. I taught physics and still had my class of "mathematical illiterates." My responsibilities as director of activities included all those considerable parts of the school program that took place outside the classroom.

As housemaster I learned firsthand about the Training Plan and the whole Gordonstoun scheme of student self-government. When Jones was a new boy at the school, an older student came to him each night and checked off his Training Plan. This was a list of questions that covered the gamut of Jones's daily duties, from taking his morning shower and doing his before-breakfast household chores, through completing his lessons and getting to classes on time, to brushing his teeth at night. To each query Jones would answer yes or no, and for any shortcomings the older boy would mete out the prescribed penalties. In time, perhaps after three or four months, the older boy would decide that Jones had reached a stage of responsibility where he could be entrusted with his own Training Plan and his own punishments. He would so report to McDonald, who as Helper of the House was Windmill Lodge's number one boy. McDonald would come to me and say, "I think it's time for Jones to take on his own Training Plan."

I would say, "What's the evidence? What makes you think Jones is ready?" and McDonald would say something like, "Well, sir, I'm satisfied that he is answering Williams honestly every night. And the other day something happened, and when I asked how it happened, he immediately popped up with all the facts, even though it involved him in some of the blame." So I would call Jones down and talk with him. If I was convinced, I would take the recommendation to the headmaster, who would give me a thorough grilling. I would have to have my facts and make a really good case for Jones.

Then, a month or so after he had been given his own Training Plan, I would say to Jones, "Get your Training Plan, I want to see it." Perhaps a look of horror would come over his face. He would jog over to the house and come back with his plan, on which he had made no entries for the past ten days. So he would have to go back down the line, and Williams would take over again. Then after a while McDonald would come once more and say it was time for Jones, and I would say, "Now look, don't get me in trouble again. Are you sure?" I would go to the headmaster and he would say, "Are you sure?" I would be on trial, not Jones. So Jones would get his Training Plan back, and this time when I checked up on him, it would be in good order, and Jones was well on his way to being a self-responsible member of the school community.

Eventually he might show enough leadership talent that I would say, "It's time for Jones to become a Color Bearer candidate." All the Helpers, the students in charge of the school, were Color Bearers. The Color Bearer candidates were the ones you went to when something needed doing, and you needed someone to see that it got done. They were the ones who checked the newcomers' Training Plans, ran the study halls, did the inspections, supervised all the dirty work. They were the Helpers' noncommissioned officers. During their candidacy they were paragons of exemplary behavior. Hahn maintained that once in a youngster's life he should go through a period of being a paragon, but he should not be expected to keep it up too long. The Color Bearer competition lasted three months. At the end of that time one of three things happened. A candidate was elected by the Color Bearers to their society. He was rejected and went back to his status as a Training Plan holder. Or in rare cases, he was given three more months as a candidate.

When a boy was elected a Color Bearer, he was given a highly responsible job—as the Helper of the House, or the Helper of Guests, or the Helper in charge of The Break, or of the practical work program or athletic program, or of one of the samaritan services or whatever. The whole school was turned over to the Color Bearers. Their leader, the Guardian, was head boy of the school. But the cement of the entire structure was the Training Plan, whereby every individual in the school was given responsibility for himself.

Hahn was then sixty-five. He was running the school, making frequent trips to London to raise money for it and advance other projects, and shuttling across the Channel in his campaigns to influence the postwar education of German youth. "I am," he told me, "an old man in a hurry." I wondered how many obstacles he had hurdled with that trumpet cry of his determination. The hurry part was literally true. He climbed stairs two at a time, took an entire downflight in a single *r-r-r-p-p!* His day marched. Frequently it began with three separate breakfast meetings. In theory they were staggered, but usually he wound up circulating from one to the other. On a not-untypical morning, staff members, school governors, and the sheriff of Elgin might be breakfasting at a table in his study as they made plans for the forthcoming visit of Princess Elizabeth and Prince Philip. In an adjoining room the warden of the Moray Outward Bound School might be meeting with a high official of the Schleswig–Holstein Ministry of Education and an emissary of Count von Platen Haller-Mund, principal sponsor of a proposed new German *kurzschule*. In the school dining hall perhaps some of the *Hamlet* cast, the director of studies, and the headmaster, who was also directing the play, would be inquiring into Shakespeare's intentions in Act IV. The telephoning would have started, Hahn's refrain of "We will call him [or her] immediately" running through the day. Employing the telephone as a means of persuasion, he seemed more to *play* it than simply to use it. He would speak straight to the point—he had no small talk, ever—and somehow there would be no way for the person at the other end to say no.

However tight the day's schedule, he found time to reconnoiter about the school. "A headmaster's job," he said, "is to walk around." His antennae were always out, fine-tuned and waving, probing for each lad's potential strengths that they might be developed, for his innate weaknesses that they might be overcome. Repeatedly he homed in on some shielded aspect of a boy's ego that others had missed and that cast a sudden light on deviant behavior. He was his own psychologist, drawing on a vast bank of observations.

The day's end was signaled at that hour of the evening when Hunter brought the London taxicab around to Gordonstoun House. Hunter would drive him across the moors to the sea cliffs. Then Hahn would get out and jog along the line of the cliffs, his way illuminated by the headlights of the cab following behind.

But the days did not always end so routinely. Periodically, roused from slumber by his call, four or five of us—housemaster, teachers, activity leader—would make our way through the night to his study. The call would have but one meaning—some boy was in trouble. Perhaps a student had been caught stealing. Hahn would have spent a long evening getting the report, talking with the boy and with the student leaders who knew him best. Conscious of the contrast between our disheveled aspects and his neat daytime attire, we would wait for him to stop pacing the floor and tell us why we were there. Finally, when he had given us the facts, came the inevitable dreaded question, the blue eyes boring in: "Josh! When did you first notice this boy was in difficulty, and what did you do about it?"—dreaded because one had sensed and done nothing. When a boy was in danger of expulsion at Gordonstoun, it was not he but the adult community who was on trial. A boy steals because he has some deeper trouble. If one is sensitive enough, if one cares enough, one can detect symptoms of the trouble early, when there may still be time for remedy.

On the morrow Hahn would decide the penalty, posting the facts on the bulletin board to prevent the rumor-mongering he detested: "Put it on my tombstone, 'Here lies Kurt Hahn. He scotched a rumor every day.' "

He ran the school in tensile fashion. It began with his hiring strong people who would stand up to him. Offering Henry Brereton the post of director of studies in 1935, he said, "You must defend your department. If I want to send a boy into the hills for his health just before examinations, you must resist me." He staffed the school's nautical department with a Royal Navy officer and a Merchant Navy officer, in the belief that the inevitable conflict of two traditions would be a creative force—as it proved to be. When I became director of activities, I found that Brereton and I were duty bound to maintain a rival stance, lest either poach on the other's share of school time. If Hahn thought we were not being wary enough, he took some subtle action, created some threat of encroachment, to put us on guard.

The same tensilizing principle infused his way with the young. His core tenet, stated a thousand times as though it were cut in bronze, was: *"It is the sin of the soul to force young people into opinions—indoctrination is of the devil—but it is culpable neglect not to impel them into health-giving experiences."* * The indoor type was to be chased outdoors, the introvert turned inside out, the extrovert outside in. The tough were to be gentled, the timid emboldened. Above all, the complacent were to be disturbed. "It is my mission in life to molest the contentedly unfit."

He had powerful ideas about which experiences were "health-giving." We did not play soccer (football, they called it) at Gordonstoun even though it was the Scottish national game, because Hahn felt the professional players, with their tactics of going for the man instead of the ball, had brutalized the sport. It was, in fact, another of his declared missions in life to "dethrone games," i.e., team sports. Games were good when they taught a lesson of "the good ally" and teamwork, modesty in winning, resolution in defeat. They did harm when they glorified individual performance, or brute power, and when they stifled other interests. And they did nothing for the physical development of the boys who did not take part.

Once when I was coaching the track team, we had gotten off

* Years later, when Bill Coffin and I were working on the Outward Bound program for the Peace Corps, we came up with a variation of this precept, better suited to our then needs, in which "value-forming" was substituted for "health-giving." Hahn endorsed the change. It is the later version that has become familiar in the United States.

to a good start and built a lead in a meet at Gordonstoun with another school. At first I had been troubled that the other team was competing barefoot and that our boys, all wearing proper footgear, had an unfair advantage. However, the competent showing the visitors made in the opening events had diluted my concern. After all, I reasoned, the meet was taking place on grass, not the cinder runways I was used to, and those unshod youngsters seemed at home on the thick turf. Suddenly Hahn was on the scene, talking with the visitors. He came over to me and said, "Those boys can't afford track shoes. Have our lads take off theirs and start the meet over." "But—" The decision in his eyes stopped me. We started again, the meet now more closely contested. It took a long time for me to absorb fully the meaning of that incident. The lesson of fairness was clear enough. Still, no one would have thought it unfair if the headmaster had decided the only expedient was for our team to go barefoot in the remaining events. But in matters of fairness it was not Hahn's habit to consider expedience. In time I came to realize that the heart of the incident was his instant, uncompromising doing of what he knew to be right.

Not so many years before, Hahn himself had played on the Gordonstoun cricket and field hockey teams. "Mad as a boy to win," Henry Brereton said, recalling with a chuckle Hahn's running downfield, hockey stick at the ready, exhorting his teammates: "Always say to yourself, when you are up against a more formidable opponent than yourself, Homer's memorable words, 'You have suffered worse than this and triumphed at last!' " Perhaps there was an element of self-discipline in his game-dethroning policy. It was a policy of moderation. We played competitive cricket, field hockey, and rugby, and competed in track, but the school teams practiced only two afternoons a week. The headmaster's dethroning technique was to create competition for games, finding other ways to feed the "healthy passions." The Break, offering each an opportunity to build a base for his self-esteem, was a strong antidote to the campus sports-hero syndrome. So were the samaritan services—the Cliff Watchers, the Fire Service, and a little later, the Mountain Rescue team —and the school's mountain and sea expeditions. So were the Saturday mornings devoted to crafts; likewise the project. Every student had a long-term project. It might involve a craft, but it could be in nature, science, the arts, or some other area of student interest. The chief requirement was that it demand a sustained effort.

Hahn's zeal for the educational value of the crafts is especially memorable. He was himself "mechanically illiterate," as he put it; he would have been incapable of the simplest task in a wood or metal-working shop. While his own sense of deficiency was probably a factor in prompting him to encourage others to gain some kind of creative manual competence, his chief motivation was a deep respect for craftsmanship as a social force. The decline in skill and care, a major count in his indictment of the times, was "due to the weakened tradition of craftsmanship."

Perhaps the finest of his education stratagems was his use of the sea as a classroom. In nearby Hopeman Harbor all Gordonstoun boys mastered small-boat seamanship and qualified to crew the *Prince Louis*, the school's seagoing sailing vessel. Again this was training not *for* but *through* the sea. Hahn said, "My best schoolmaster is the Moray Firth." It was Henry Brereton, scholar, historian, striver for academic excellence, who perceived that in that challenging body of water, with its strong tides, frequent high winds, and rocky shore, the elements were strict teachers of the values of discipline, order, skill—and of mathematics, learned as a tool of navigation. At the end of one holiday time the *Prince Louis* came back from a harrowing sea voyage around the Orkney and Shetland Islands having weathered three gales. Hahn asked a boy, "How did you enjoy yourself?" The boy said, "Magnificently, sir—except at the time." That became one of the headmaster's favorite stories, for it so beautifully supported his thesis that young people should be impelled into experience.

"Hahn's educational actions," noted an admiring German educator, "seems always to stem from two poles—justice and love. Should these ever be in conflict, then love conquers." He could, however, be very stern. The finer the boy being judged, the sterner the judgment.* He was most demanding of the school's leaders; a leader had not only to earn his way to leadership but also his right to stay there. We had a youngster at

---

* From Hahn's (at the time) confidential report to the Royal Navy on Prince Philip's student career at Gordonstoun: "Prince Philip is a born leader, but he will need the exacting demands of a great service to do justice to himself. His best is outstanding, his second best is not good enough."

Gordonstoun whose antisocial behavior—due apparently to a severe childhood trauma suffered during the war—became so bad that the school could not keep him. After much effort, Hahn found another school willing to take this boy. In a fury of spite on the day he was to leave, the boy made a shambles of his dormitory. When his housemates discovered the havoc, a group grabbed him arm and leg and started for the pond at the far end of the south lawn. The pond underlay the school's ropes course, and there was a rule that if you fell into its stagnant water, you had to be dosed with castor oil to purge tadpoles and other organisms you might have swallowed.

The Guardian, the school's student leader, was at some distance talking with companions when he saw what was happening. He watched as he continued talking. When, in a burst of decision, he raced to break up the kangaroo court, he was too late. By the time he reached the group, the boy had got his dunking and was suffering, if not a fit, a severe reaction. Under the Gordonstoun code, if a punishable offense took place in the Guardian's presence, only he was punished. I was astonished at the severity of Hahn's penalty. He not only relieved the Guardian of his post of leadership, he took away his Training Plan. What was most arresting was the reason for the penalty. The boy was not punished for his failure to prevent the dunking. His offense, said the bulletin board notice, was that he had hesitated before acting.

I used to tell that story but had to stop because I found it angered people. There would be murmurings: "Why, of course he hesitated. Any normal person would." Not in Hahn's book. In any moral crisis, he believed, a leader could hardly fail more grievously than not to know immediately what he should do, and promptly do it.

He had least patience with overprotective and overpermissive parents. "I know parents," he said, "who negotiate with their children as though they were a foreign power." Once when I was in his office with a student's mother, I saw his tune-out mask drop into place as she pleaded with him on behalf of a son in trouble for chronic tardiness. The boy's difficulty, she argued, was congenital—he had a faulty interior clock. "You just don't understand him, Headmaster," she said. "Madame," said Hahn, "how many vacation trains has he missed?"

It may have been another mother, the one who packed her

son off to school with pills for when he was homesick, that caused him to explode to me on the subject of pill-popping adults. The growing dependence on quiet-downers and pep-uppers, he maintained was bound to produce a youth blighted by narcotics addiction. This was years before the drug problem emerged. It was one more time when I did not know what he was talking about—not the first or last time that someone mistook as gross exaggeration his accurate sense of what was happening beneath the societal surface.

He was an intrepid traveler; a journey with him was exhilarating. To see him cope with the usual frustrations of getting from one place to the next was to observe in microcosm ways in which he advanced his grand designs. Policemen, taxi drivers, ticket agents were his instant confidants. No matter how negative an agent's initial response, the ensuing friendship almost surely produced the needed overnight train accommodation or pair of plane tickets. Henry Brereton, who accompanied him on trips to Germany in the difficult travel years right after the war, has provided a lovely reminiscence: "Timetables seem to adjust to his whim, engine-drivers are in league with him and hold up the start of the express whilst he conducts an excited invalid infinitely slowly to her reserved compartment, saying with irritating assurance as guards blow whistles and porters shout and safely seated travelers stare from the windows, 'We have plenty of time, my dear. Don't hurry. There's plenty of time.'"

Brereton's vignette catches Hahn in a moment that, in its small but touching way, reflects the very heart of his personal philosophy. This was his profound commitment to the samaritan ethic. He had one hero above all: the compassionate traveler on the road to Jericho. Again and again he called for the Parable of the Good Samaritan to be read to the school. In the years to come I was to witness the growing power of his ultimate conviction—that through help to those "in danger and in need" youth can strike the deepest chords of the human spirit. It would become a creed: "He who drills and labors, accepts hardship, boredom, and dangers, all for the sake of helping his brother in peril and distress, discovers God's purpose in his inner life."

The summer of 1952 approached, when our time at Gordonstoun would be up. The matter of what I would do on our return to the States was of growing concern. In May came a letter from John Kemper, headmaster of Phillips Academy in Andover, Massachusetts, offering a teaching post there. I had good memories of an apprenticeship summer that I had spent at Andover just before I joined the Hun faculty, and I had great respect for Kemper as an educator and a person. Andover would be a big change from Gordonstoun, but in his letter Kemper indicated that he would expect me to contribute to my new school from my Gordonstoun experience. It was an honor to be offered a place on the Andover faculty, and I decided to accept.

The day came for leave-taking. Hahn stood by the car with his gentle smile, bidding our family good-bye. "Look back over your left shoulder, but only once," he said. "Then you will surely return." When down the road we took that last look, the man who had changed my life forever was still standing with his hand raised in farewell. Turning back to the view of the road ahead, I made a promise to myself. I was resolved to help bring some aspect of his work to the United States.

Andover and The Break

≡✕≡✕≡✕≡✕≡✕≡✕≡✕≡✕≡✕≡✕≡

Let us build up physical fitness for the sake of the soul.
—PLATO

John Kemper had written that he wanted me to bring to Andover aspects of the Hahn philosophy and method that were applicable to the Andover scene, so long as they changed none of the existing structure. I was just young enough to pay scant heed to the inherent contradiction. At Phillips Academy—best known simply as Andover—I found myself part of an institution where the faculty and administrators were secure and comfortable with the school's 175-year-old traditions, its high academic standards, its splendid record in getting graduates into leading colleges, its prestige in the educational community, its eminence on the athletic field, its Andover way of doing things. They were not in search of innovation. Most of them had never heard of Kurt Hahn, or Gordonstoun, or Salem, or Outward Bound. Had they, it would not have occurred to them that Hahn or his institutions had anything to offer them or the school.

At the same time, I was intent on maintaining a low profile. I realized that were it to get bruited about that I had an innovating mission, I would have two strikes on me at the outset. Those good low-profile intentions were abruptly shattered within a month by the arrival, on short notice, of Kurt Hahn and Prince George to visit the school. Suddenly I was consorting with these distinguished guests, one of them (now Hahn's fame raced out over the campus grapevine) an educator of international renown, the other not only a headmaster but royalty. Put

60

in charge of their visit, I did not even know the names of my fellow faculty members, let alone the students.

Hahn stayed at our home. He had no more than arrived when he managed to lock himself into the bathroom. We had to call on the combined competence of the town police and fire departments to free him. Touring the school, he and the prince were a colorful pair. John Kemper was much taken with them both. In those first meetings he was somewhat disconcerted by Hahn's readiness to give him fatherly (age sixty-six to forty) instruction in the arts of headmastership, but he would grow to relish that. The two were to become great friends.

I could not wait to hear Hahn's reactions to Andover. That he was instantly impressed by the physical plant was hardly surprising. He found the Cage—a big, glass-covered, dirt-floored building that housed a full athletic program indoors—a thing of wonder. He thought the library and music and art programs superb, and he quickly perceived the high academic quality in the Andover ambiance. But when, walking home after the third day of his visit, I asked him what he thought of the school, he said, "Phillips Academy is like a ship on a first-class voyage through education, but without a member of the crew in sight."

He meant that the students, always in his thinking the most visible part of the crew, were only passengers on this cruise. He missed the sight and sense of what was the essence of his own school's environment—the total involvement of the students in its operation. That every student did not have some responsibility whereby he was contributing to the functioning and well-being of the community—or some responsibility that he was being deprived of as a penalty—was for Hahn a denial of part of the education the school owed him. He was appalled to learn that the scholarship students had to work several hours each week while the full-paying students did not. (This is no longer true at Andover.) That made a shambles of his principle that a boy should not be penalized for a factor—especially his family's income—over which he had no control. At the same time there was that nice Hahnian switch: The "underprivileged sons of the wealthy" were being deprived of a value-forming experience the scholarship students were getting.

He was impressed by the high level of performance achieved by Andover athletes. The school records in track and field, for example, were consistently superior to those at Gordonstoun. But he embarrassed us by asking for the average for the entire student body. We did not know our averages, never having measured them—but the facts would have been even more embarrassing. I was aware that whereas the average high jump for a Gordonstoun sixth former (senior) approached five feet, it would be near four for his Andover peer.

Hahn's departure left me with a depressed sense of how difficult it was going to be to weave any part of the Gordonstoun scheme into the Andover fabric. Kemper was urging me to come up with a proposal, but he made it clear I could expect no help in the form of administrative fiat. Whatever I might propose or undertake, it would be up to me to persuade the school community of its worth.

I decided that the one thing I might be able to accomplish at that juncture was the very thing that, it seemed to me, most needed doing: to set up some version of Gordonstoun's physical-education method. Andover was in the anomalous posture of having one of the finest athletic programs of any secondary school in the country, and virtually no physical education. Every student was required to put in ninety minutes four afternoons a week in some part of an extraordinary gamut of team sports. There were five levels of interschool and intramural leagues, approximating five levels of skill, that enabled every boy to take part in a competitive sport. Altogether some five thousand youngsters from other schools were engaging Andover in one or another contest each year. These contests and the practice for them made for a fine program with many virtues, but this was athletics, not physical education.

How well I now understood Hahn's, "It is my mission in life to dethrone games." Competitive sports provide exercise, recreation, physical development, the social experience of team effort, the personal and social values of acquired skills, competitive experience. Inevitably, however, the stress on competition denies to the athletically inferior youngster the chance to know authentic competitive pressure. When the contest is close, coaches are reluctant to use substitutes. Even a Class E league has its bench-sitters. Embarrassed by their poor performance, turned off by a reenforced sense of inferiority, the inept withdraw from athletic endeavor as soon as they can; yet they may well be the ones who most need to be impelled into the physical and competitive experience.

Not only was the physically subpar 'boy not overcoming his deficiencies and "the misery of unimportance" that they bred; neither, for the most part, was the competent athlete correcting his areas of weakness. And even if the desire to win was not permitted to dilute sportsmanship, there were other hazards for the physically gifted youngster. He could loaf—could become, in Hahn's phrase, "the prima donna athlete who is no friend of wind and weather, who takes a rest cure between rare maximum efforts." He could satisfy himself with a mediocre effort. He could gloss over his shortcomings by basking in the stardom of his specialty. He could get a distorted sense of his relative importance in the student mix.

John Kemper was aware of all this, especially of the potential of physical education for increasing the confidence of adolescent boys. Two years before he had brought in a young teacher named Reagh Wetmore, a fine athlete with first-rate physical-education competency, and charged him to set up a program. But Reagh too had his problems. The faculty, defending their territorial imperatives, refused to surrender any morning time. A strict rule forbade students to set foot in the gymnasium during study hours. The only concession the faculty had made to Reagh was to let him work with those students who were so low on the physical motor scale as to be clearly in need of special attention. But now the gymnasium was being rebuilt, and he had virtually no program at all. I told Reagh about The Break at Gordonstoun. He was not impressed. He was fresh from earning his master's degree at Springfield College in Massachusetts, the fount of conventional wisdom on physical education, and the Hahnian principles were not the ones he had been taught. He let me go to work with his collection of twenty or so physical misfits but took a dim view of what I was doing.

I dubbed them "the lame and the halt." What a great bunch of kids they were! Fat kids, frail kids whose muscles were virtually unused, kids who had never done anything physical, some of them terrified, one youngster who had been crippled by infantile paralysis. Most of them eventually gave it a good try, and these surprised themselves by what they could do. This confirmed my Gordonstoun experience. But the results obtained with a handful of boys who were physically very subpar were not going to sell the program to the faculty. They could perceive that this was useful therapy, but what did it have to do with the welfare of the student body at large? At the same time, I was aware that while my lads had certainly acquired an improved opinion of themselves, they still suffered the stigma of having been singled out as the poorest physical specimens in the school.

At this point Jack Hawes, an English teacher, came to my rescue. Jack had listened with interest to my Gordonstoun and Outward Bound stories, and now he was impressed by the improved physical prowess and heightened self-concept of the "lame and halt" kids. He was housemaster of Williams, one of the two dormitories that housed the "juniors," as Andover ninth-graders are called. Jack said, "Why don't you take my dormitory next year? Put them through the program, measure their progress, keep track of their classroom records, and compare them with the boys in Rockwell." Rockwell was the other ninth-grade dormitory. This looked like a way to gain credibility for The Break. We managed to persuade the faculty to approve the experiment of excusing the fifty boys in Williams from a one-hour study period two mornings a week. It was a reluctant approval. No one was really for the scheme except Kemper, Hawes, and myself. With Wetmore's counsel—he maintained his dim view—we settled on six events: the broad jump, high jump, shot put, discus, seventy-five-yard dash, and the half-mile run. We set "Standard" and "Silver" levels of achievement for each event according to age. As always in The Break, the competition was only with oneself. I posted an improvement chart for each boy in the Cage, where I conducted the course, much as I had set it up at Gordonstoun.

Beautiful! Once again the combination of release from "the sedentary hours" and self-challenge worked its magic. In the classroom, it was easy to spot the ones who had just come in from The Break. They were more alive and alert. That kid sitting back there bright-eyed and bushy-tailed, you knew what had happened to him. He had made a quantifiable gain that day. One he could measure and send home, saying, It is I who is gaining. That is important to a fourteen-year-old boy. I recall three youngsters in particular, each representative of a kind of experience common to The Break.

Frank was a short, chubby thirteen-year-old who at the start had complete disdain for the program. Fearful of revealing how subpar he actually was, he refused to extend himself and made a comical act of his poor performance. He seemed to enjoy the jeers he induced. Then, in spite of himself, he began to improve. Gradually his attitude changed. One day he ran the dash two seconds better than his previous best time, faster than a lot of the others were doing. He forgot his act. The day he first put the shot twenty feet—nine feet better than his starting effort—the onlookers gave an acclaiming shout. You could see the new self-respect in his face. He went on to earn Silvers in both these events and a Standard in the discus. His late start cost him his Standards in the other three, but he had won a great discovery—that through trying, one can do what he thought he could not do.

Art was a slightly built, high-strung boy, sincere, studious. Physically he was poorly coordinated to the point of clumsiness, with little experience in sports. A sensitive lad, he took kindly neither to helpful nor deriding comments. But essentially there was nothing wrong with his physique except development. His improvement was startling. He bettered himself by nearly four and a half feet in the broad jump, thirteen inches in the high jump, more than twelve feet in the shot put, thirty feet in the discus, one and a half seconds in the seventy-five-yard dash, thirty-five seconds in the half-mile run. His time for the half-mile beat the school's junior indoor record. By the end of the winter term this boy who had gone into The Break labeled a nonathlete by himself and his peers was on the school's junior relay team.

Tim was one of two boys who failed to win a single Standard. He was a pudgy, physically immature little boy who was all but helpless in physical activity. He lacked both coordination and the strength to carry his excess load of baby fat, and his performance measurements at the start were abysmal. He showed total disinterest. After about six weeks, something happened. He began to improve. By the end of the second term he had bettered the improvement average for the class in four of the six events. His classmates were regarding him with new respect, and so was he. One day he brought his mother to my office. He wanted me to tell her what The Break was all about and to explain what he had achieved. I guess the memory of that boy and his mother as they went out together, both with new pride in their eyes, is my favorite among the many rewards The Break brought to me. This boy who had failed to achieve a single Standard was one of my great successes.

I made a report at a faculty meeting in April 1954. After briefly reviewing the philosophy of the concept and the program structure, I gave the impressive statistics of the overall improvement in physical competence. Near the end I quietly dropped a bombshell—the comparative academic records for Williams Hall, the ninth-graders who had been in the Break program, and Rockwell Hall, those who had not. The data told a persuasive story. The average IQs of the two groups were virtually identical. In both terms the Break group had a higher average grade and higher average rank. They won honors in many more courses than the control group, failed in far fewer, and showed greater improvement from one term to next.

I said only, "It is apparent that the program was not detrimental to the academic interests of the boys involved," and sat down. There was a long, silent moment. Then Harper Follansbee, Rockwell's housemaster, stood up and said, "Next year I want my boys to have that program." That did it.

I won quite a few faculty adherents that afternoon, but Reagh Wetmore was my great convert. Convinced, he grabbed the ball, and thereafter we ran with it together. "Let's have something more than track events," Reagh said. That made sense to me; I bought his idea for a kind of indoor obstacle course in the gym, tests that would put a premium on agility and overcoming fear. Then Reagh said, "O.K., we've got something on the ground, something in the air, we ought to have something for the third element, the water." He was Andover's swim coach. But he was not thinking of just a pool counterpart to the track events. He wanted a water activity that would be different and valuable to the average youngster. He told me of a magazine article he had read about Fred Lanoue, the Georgia Tech swimming coach, who had developed a technique he called "drownproofing." According to Lanoue, anybody could be taught to survive in the water indefinitely.

As good luck would have it, we caught up with Lanoue shortly after that at a physical-education conference in New York, where the three of us huddled for a whole afternoon.

Drownproofing; Visit to Hahn

═══×═══×═══×═══×═══×═══×═══×═══×═══×═══×═══

We try to teach youngsters that a technique in the head is worth a million helping hands that may be out of reach.

— FRED LANOUE

Fred Lanoue was one of the most colorful, most profane, and most Christian persons I have ever known. Of French Canadian parentage, he grew up in Worcester, Massachusetts. He earned his way through Springfield College as a daredevil high diver. The Lanoue stories at Springfield were in the folk hero genre. They liked to tell you that he had earned a term's tuition by diving from a two hundred-foot tower into a damp wash cloth with Roman candles sticking out of each ear and his rear end. He walked with a kind of foot-slapping limp, the consequence of an injury incurred while experimenting on a wild new dive.

Fred was a natural athlete, but as a boy swimming had been his poorest sport. Thin and bony, he was that relatively rare creature, a natural sinker. The strain of keeping his head above water sapped his energy. He discovered that he did much better swimming underwater, coming up only to breathe. It was not fast, but it got him where he wanted to go without tiring him out. That discovery provided the germ of his drownproofing theory.

He maintained there are only four good reasons for drowning. One, you are knocked unconscious. Two, the water is too cold, and you die from loss of body heat. Three, there is froth on the water, and you cannot get your head above it to breathe. Four, you starve to death. If you drown for any other reason, he said, you should get a demerit. He had developed a method for staying afloat indefinitely, even with cramps. Eschewing what he called the "cosmetic crawl," he employed a "travel stroke" for negotiating long distances with minimum energy. It was sheer absurdity, Fred argued, that a mere fifty-yard swim was considered an adequate beginner's test. If you find yourself in the water one hundred and fifty yards off shore, he pointed out, being able to swim fifty yards is unlikely to help you much. His beginner's test was the ability to stay afloat one hour and swim one mile. He halved that for four-year-olds but not for seven-year-olds.

Listening to my story of Gordonstoun and Outward Bound, Lanoue was greatly taken by the ideas of Kurt Hahn. He caught on just like that. He said, "I'm doing that with drownproofing. It's self-control under circumstances that approach panic and demand self-respect. And it leads to a respect for other people that you can express in a profound way—by saving their lives. This is what I believe in. Nobody graduates from Georgia Tech, nobody, until he passes drownproofing. I even put the president through."

That fall Wetmore and I launched our new three-part version of The Break for the entire ninth grade. For an indoor obstacle course we had rigged a circuit that involved vertical rope ladders, horizontal ladders twenty feet in the air, a trampoline leap to a horizontal overhead rope that then had to be traversed for twenty feet, followed by a flying swing to a cargo net, and so on. Its effectiveness as a test exceeded our fondest expectations. It was a great leveler. A football player would traverse that horizontal rope trip in an agony of effort, apprehension, and acrophobia. Right behind him a skinny little monkey of a kid would scramble through the whole exercise as though it were just a lark. The 200-pound tackle on the freshman team who was a big shot because he had the bulk and strength to push smaller kids around learned something about humility. Up to then he had been getting his ego-building input on the football field, which was just a congenital accident. Now he was learning the difference between the self-respect that your genes give you and the self-respect that you have earned.

Lanoue came up to help us get the drownproofing started. Fred taught me a lot not only about water survival skills but about how to approach that kind of problem analytically. Most drownings, he pointed out, are due to some combination of panic and exhaustion. When even a reasonably good swimmer encounters a sudden crisis in the water—a fall into the water far from shore, a cramp, a strong current pulling him away from safety—his instinctive reaction is too often a fatal one. He may try to buck a current wearing heavy water-logged clothes. Or he may shuck clothes that he needs for warmth. He may use a stroke he is unable to maintain. He may exhaust himself trying to keep his head out of water—the equivalent of supporting a ten-pound brick as he swims. He may gasp for air at the instant a swell fills his mouth with water. A cramp may frighten him to greater exertion and quicker exhaustion. Or he may turn over on his back to rest—which consumes more energy than is commonly thought—and choke as a wave washes over his face.

Lanoue's drownproof technique is based on the natural buoyancy of most human bodies when the lungs are filled with air. The victim takes a full breath and allows himself to sink to his natural float position. The body is angled forward at the waist, face in the water, the back of the neck at the surface, arms and legs hanging loosely downward. The air does the work of keeping him afloat near the surface. Every six to ten seconds, he folds his arms in front of his head, raises his head far enough out of the water to inhale, supporting this act with a scissors kick, then resumes the float position. He expends so little energy that terrifying complications like cramps, heavy clothes, a disabling injury, rough water, or long immersion do not threaten his survival. An adaptation of this basic subsurface float enables him, using the "travel stroke," to swim through the water at about one mile per hour without tiring. A few who lack natural buoyance—only about one percent of white males (although a considerable percentage of black males) and the rare female are sinkers—must use the travel stroke to stay afloat.

To pass drownproofing, each student involved in The Break had to stay afloat for one hour, swim a mile wearing pants and shirt, and perform a sequence of maneuvers that simulated cramp conditions—first with hands tied behind back, then with legs tied Buddha-fashion. He also had to swim underwater for 150 feet, demonstrate using a pair of pants as a floating aid, and do a one hundred-yard chest-carry of another person. Over the years Reagh Wetmore refined and added to the tests.

In the 1959 spring vacation Wetmore and I made a flying trip to visit Hahn and his institutions. He was then living in an apartment in the castle that housed Hermannsburg, Salem's junior school. We spent a day with him, visited the Hermannsburg and Salem schools, the two new German Outward Bound schools at Weissenhaus and Baad, and went on to England for visits to Aberdovey and Gordonstoun and a final rendezvous with Hahn in London.

Hahn had retired from Gordonstoun in 1953 at the age of sixty-six, charging his co-successors, Henry Brereton and Robert Chew: "You will not permit Gordonstoun to descend to the level of a first-class traditional school!" The next year the University of Edinburgh conferred on him an honorary Doctor of Law. The university's chancellor, Prince Philip, Duke of Edinburgh, made the presentation. "It cannot be given to many," said Gordonstoun's most distinguished old boy, "to have the opportunity and the desire to heap honors upon their former headmaster." Presumably the university conceived its accolade as capping the brilliant career of a man entering retirement. But Hahn still had promises to keep, and some he had not yet even made. He carried on, more than ever "an old man in a hurry," dividing his time largely between Hermannsburg and London, where in a suite at Brown's Hotel he maintained a kind of personal global headquarters.

We found him in great form. His work was bearing fruit literally around the world. In addition to new Outward Bound schools in England, and the two in Germany for which he was personally responsible, others had been started in Nigeria, Kenya, Malaysia, and Australia. In the preceding year his eighteen-year campaign for his County Badge plan had won the smashing success of royal sponsorship, when Prince Philip launched it as the Duke of Edinburgh's Award Scheme. In later years Philip, reflecting on how well the scheme had taken hold throughout the British Commonwealth, would remember: "It would never have started but for Hahn, certainly not. He suggested I ought to do it, and I fought against it for quite a long time. Because you know what the British are like in relation to that sort of thing. And I said, well, I'm not going to stick my neck out and do anything as stupid as that, and everybody saying, 'Ah, silly ass,' you know?" Hahn's faith proved sounder than the Duke's apprehension. Nobody said, "Ah, silly ass." By 1970 the Award Scheme was established in twenty-eight countries. In 1980 it was established as the Congressional Award and I was asked to be one of the sixteen founding trustees.

Now Hahn was deeply involved in inventing a new institution. In 1955 Air Marshal Sir Lawrence Darvall, Commandant of the NATO Defense College in Paris, had said to him: "The conservative, nationalistic military officers attending our school are achieving a remarkable degree of international understanding in a mere six-month course. Think how much more could be accomplished by a nonmilitarist school for young people with an international student body!" Fired by Darvall's concept, Hahn had joined forces with him. The two men were recruiting committees in many countries to support their proposal for an Atlantic College—a two-year, precollege school enrolling students from all over the world. In such a school, they envisioned, Briton and Indian, Israeli and Arab, Greek and Turk, students of all colors and political persuasions would study and adventure together in a self-governing international environment.

That trip completed Wetmore's conversion to the Hahnian philosophy. He peppered Hahn with questions. How did he know this, know that? Hahn's answers were mostly grounded in homely observation. On what basis did he claim children had an innate sense of order? Ask a four-year-old to fetch you a pail of sand, Hahn said, and see how he pats and smooths the top before he hands it to you. "All the treasures of childhood come alive in the four-year-old," he told us.

Kemper had been critical of our reports on students in The Break, as being too statistical, not interpretive enough of individual development. We told Hahn about this, explaining that we were chary of trespassing into areas that were more properly the province of the housemasters and teachers. "Trespass continually," Hahn replied. He counseled us to extend the range of our reports. We should make a diagnosis like a doctor; this would help the boy's housemaster and his parents.

There was an incident on that trip that neither Wetmore nor

I have forgotten. Discoursing on one of his favorite themes—
"your liability is your opportunity"—Hahn had remarked that
people who have surmounted a serious handicap have a "glint"
in their eye. At the Hamburg Airport, intending to fly to London, we found no record of our reservations. It was close to
flight time; informed that there were no places for us, we were
dismayed at the prospect of losing a day of our already brief
time in Britain. The clerk took our situation to a colleague, who
was immediately all concern. When his initial resort to the
telephone was of no avail, he literally sprinted off. Several minutes later he came running back, his expression telling us that
all was well, swiftly wrote out our tickets, and gave us a hurried
escort to our departure gate. As we settled breathlessly into our
plane seats, deeply grateful to our rescuer, Wetmore said to me,
"Did you see the glint in his eye?" The man had an artificial hand.

We returned to Andover revitalized. Following Hahn's suggestion, we made our Break evaluating format more subjective.
Each boy's housemaster received a rather elaborate developmental
report. As Hahn had predicted, the housemasters found these
reports invaluable in their day-to-day and counseling contacts,
as well as a help when they talked with parents. The reports
stayed in the boys' files, and in time they were useful to the
upper housemasters too.

It was interesting to observe Hahn's influence on Wetmore.
He continued to improve and refine The Break. He completely
changed his method of teaching chemistry, cutting down the
theoretical, beefing up the experiential. In his first year as swimming coach, twelve boys had come out for the team. After the
visit to Hahn, Reagh recruited vigorously. The swim squad
enrollment built to more than two hundred. He had seven teams
—varsity, junior varsity, four "club" teams, and juniors (freshmen)—swimming competitively outside the school. Broadening
the base produced more champions; the school had one national
champion after another.

The Break became an Andover institution. Reagh did a lot
of speaking and writing, creating considerable interest in the
physical-education community. But it has never taken hold in
other schools. To sell it, to win institutional status for it, requires
too much educating of the educators. I still consider it the finest
physical-education program I have known.

* * *

In January 1958, in cognizance of Hahn's new centering of effort on the Atlantic College undertaking, the American–British Foundation for European Education changed its name to the Atlantic Foundation for the Education of the Free. At that time John Kemper and I were elected to the board, along with Sir Lawrence Darvall and Professor H. Wentworth Eldredge of Dartmouth College, an early Atlantic College enthusiast. A year later I was made secretary. Ellen McCloy and Eric Warburg, who had become respectively president and executive vice president in 1954, continued in those posts. By 1960 it was definite that the first Atlantic College would be established in Llantwit Major, Wales, and Hahn was urging us to launch a campaign for a second college in this country. We scouted for possible sites. But the timing was not right for the task of raising the needed millions of dollars. John Kemper and Jack Stevens (who had been a director since 1953), the foundation's two best money-raising talents, were both deeply involved in a six-million-dollar campaign for Phillips Academy.

I was strongly conscious of not yet having redeemed my self-promise to play a part in bringing Kurt Hahn's work to the United States. While an American Atlantic College was then the project closest to Hahn's heart, I continued to hope we could also find the means of establishing Outward Bound in this country. As the new decade began, I was unaware of how close to feasibility that hope lay. I did not know about a schoolmaster in Colorado seeking a way "to give students a sense of purpose and involvement in something larger than themselves." Nor about a Princeton classmate turning from a life-negating cloak-and-dagger career to a search for affirmation. The separate aspirations of the three of us were destined to come together in the founding of U.S. Outward Bound.

The Birth of U.S. Outward Bound

Whatever you can do, or dream you can, begin it;
Boldness has genius, power, and magic in it.

—GOETHE

In March 1959, F. Charles Froelicher, headmaster of Colorado Academy, a Denver independent day school, was a guest of the British consul on a Denver radio station. A second guest was Ted Hopkins, a cadet at the Air Force Academy, who had lived in England and told about having been a student at the Eskdale Outward Bound School. The young man's description of his challenging experience fascinated Froelicher, who was unable to point to anything comparable in the States. Not long afterward British educator Sir John Wolfenden, visiting in Denver, told him more about Outward Bound. His interest further whetted, Froelicher wrote to the Outward Bound Trust in London. He sought information about the course syllabus, in the thought that he might be able to use his school plant in the summer time for an adventure program on the British model. "The more I got into it," he says, "the more I realized that that wouldn't work—that Outward Bound was a much more significant educational undertaking than I had any notion of when I started exploring it. So the matter lay fallow for a while."

Gilbert Burnett came to Princeton the same year as I. He was from Kentucky, where he had grown up in an open country environment of horses and freedom. A war-accelerated graduate in the summer of 1943, Gil enlisted in the army and was tapped by the Office of Strategic Services. He completed his O.S.S. training, including proficiency in the employment of a palm-size stiletto, in Indochina, where he became part of a joint British-American operation. For Burnett it was a "good war." When it ended and O.S.S. was dissolved, he continued in intelligence for the Army General Staff, then transferred to the newly formed Central Intelligence Agency.

His C.I.A. "targets" took him to various parts of the world. As the postwar decade went by, the dirty-tricks existence palled, then soured. Gil remembers, "There came a point when I realized that as a human being I was becoming more and more kamikaze, without any roots, without any heart, without anything—a kind of smiling ego without any insides." Some time during that period of progressive disillusionment he chatted in a Washington bistro with a British acquaintance who was a correspondent for the London *Times*. The conversation took a philosophical turn that led the Britisher to tell him about the work of a schoolmaster in England named Kurt Hahn. "The *Times* man brought up Hahn in connection with William James's concept of 'a moral equivalent of war.' He talked about the idiom of compassion, something I had entirely lost touch with. There were, I gathered, elements of adventure and derring-do in Hahn's program. I was fascinated. The conversation and this man Hahn stuck in my mind. I thought of him as a romantic, but as one who was trying to do something about the appalling negativism after the war, the arms race, the Cold War, the whole filthy business I was involved in personally."

Deciding he had to make a move, wondering what he was cut out for, Burnett thought perhaps it was teaching. Through Princeton connections he found a post at the Pounahou School in Honolulu. Arriving there, he immediately noticed that the area was wonderfully suited for involving youngsters with the sea. But the school was doing nothing of that sort. Recalling the vague information he had picked up about Hahn's work, he wrote to London for information and received some pamphlets Hahn had written. "Then I did my homework. I began to read James, and look up the words 'character' and 'compassion' and this kind of thing." He came back to the States to teach at St. George's School in Newport, Rhode Island, where he set up an adventure-based program for the students. One day early in 1960 he drove up to Andover to talk with John Kemper about an opening on the Andover faculty. He arrived just as I was saying good-bye to the Guggenheims, who had been visiting us. After introductions, as they drove off, Gil asked, "Who's that?" I told him about meeting the Guggenheims at Gordonstoun and Gugg's supportive role in Hahn's work. Gil took fire. It blew his mind to discover that I had been at Gordonstoun and knew Hahn, had been exposed to Outward Bound and Atlantic College. He drilled me with questions.

Kemper perceived that here was an ally for the Hahnian cause. He gave Gil an appointment to teach biology the following year, with the understanding that Burnett would go to England that summer to learn all he could about Outward Bound. In London the Outward Bound Trust gave him VIP treatment. Eddie Dawson, England's great ex-cricketer who was then executive secretary of the Trust, opened up the files to him, and set up visits to several schools.

Guggenheim arranged for him to meet Hahn in London. Gil recalls the large, dim figure in the darkened sitting room in Brown's Hotel, the immediate sense of being in an Old World presence, the initial impact of Hahn's gentleness, of being put immediately at ease by a pleasantry about Americans. "The philosophy that he gave me at that particular time in my own life was what I was looking for. He understood about the work I had been doing and the question that I was facing, of how to shift from being a destructive representative of the postwar period. How, instead of blowing bridges, do you build a bridge in order to effect a rescue? That was an idea that had never before occurred to me."

Gil came back to Andover gung-ho to get something started. While in London he had compiled a list of Americans, including Chuck Froelicher, who had written to the Outward Bound Trust. Some time in the fall he called Froelicher and asked him if he was interested in the possibility of starting an Outward Bound school in Colorado. Froelicher said he was. Kemper gave us permission to fly to Denver to meet with him at the January 1961 end of term. Reagh Wetmore and Ed Williams, another Andover teacher, who were doing graduate study at the University of Colorado at Boulder, joined us for a lunch meeting at Froelicher's school.

Chuck Froelicher had grown up in Baltimore, where his grandfather had been president of Goucher College, his grandmother had taught Romance languages at Goucher for forty years, and his father had been headmaster of the Park School. After naval service in World War II and graduation from Johns Hopkins, Chuck became a teacher. In 1955 he took on the headmastership of the Colorado Military Academy, a Denver school for boys that had a declining enrollment of fifty-six and was in financial straits. He dropped the military component, persuaded a group of community leaders to become trustees, and set about the task of regenerating the school. When he would leave it twenty years later to become executive director of the Gates Foundation, it would be one of the West's prestigious country day schools, with more than five hundred boy and girl students.

Through the meal, with mounting enthusiasm, we kicked around the idea of a Colorado Outward Bound School. Finally Froelicher said, "Let's just decide we're going to start a school, and line out what we have to do to get it started." He still bore the scars and growing pains of Colorado Academy's rebirth, and that experience helped as we drew up a battle plan: Interest a group of influential Colorado sponsors. Find some possible sites. Bring someone over from England to advise on the site and the organizing of a school. And so on, through a long list. Money, of course. We dreamed up a rough budget and agreed in principle on the idea of half to be raised in Colorado, half by the Atlantic Foundation.

Two weeks later Froelicher came east for the foundation's annual meeting, and the undertaking was made official. By then we had a schedule. Acquire and develop the site and organize the school in the current year, offer the first two courses in the summer of 1962. The foundation voted to raise $60,000 to help get the school started. Jack Stevens made an immediate contribution of $10,000. We voted to ask Captain Freddy Fuller to journey from Aberdovey to Colorado in the following month, to advise on site and organization and to make presentations of the Outward Bound concept in support of fund raising in Colorado. We were off and running.

Froelicher stayed on for an appointment Eric Warburg had made for him and me to meet the next day with Stephen Currier, the executive director at the Taconic Foundation. Currier listened to our story and said, "Go see Harris Wofford in Washington. He's one of our directors and if he agrees, we might consider giving you some money." Kemper joined us on the trip to Washington to talk with Wofford. Congress had recently passed the Peace Corps legislation, and President Kennedy had appointed Sargent Shriver, his brother-in-law, to create it. Wofford was helping him. When he had heard us out, he said, "You simply must talk with Shriver about this, because the Peace Corps has a problem." He took us to Shriver's office, and we told our story again. Shriver's response flabbergasted us. He said, "I want you to start eight Outward Bound schools for the Peace Corps. We'll pump our volunteers through them before they go overseas." We said that was out of the question. That we were struggling with the possibility of starting one school in Colorado. We could not possibly get involved in training the Peace Corps.

Shriver grew very earnest as he explained that the Peace Corps had a serious problem. They were getting a lot of flak from people who did not think it would work. These people just did not believe the government could take young people fresh from college classrooms, still wet behind the ears, and send them out in ambassadorial roles. The Corps' problem was that it just might not get a chance to prove its case. The opposition was so strong that if the Corps should have the same rate of attrition that federal agencies traditionally experienced overseas—losing one out of two—the program would die in its first year. Shriver and his colleagues needed some assurance that if they took a youngster from an air-conditioned college classroom and sent him to Tanganyika, he would stay there long enough to find he could make a go of it. What would happen when the first bug dropped out of the thatch into his soup, or the rains came, or the mails did not come, or people would not work, or he got homesick? "I believe Outward Bound as you describe it could be the answer to our problem," Shriver said. "If you can't start eight schools for us, start one."

We realized it was going to be difficult to turn down the White House. Shriver made it clear that in the matter of the Peace Corps he spoke for the President. Also, this was an exciting challenge. It offered a dramatic way to launch the Outward Bound concept into the national consciousness. We told him we would report back with an answer.

Three weeks later, in March, Freddy Fuller arrived, and Burnett and I flew to Colorado with him. Freddy made a presentation at Colorado Academy to a group whose support Chuck Froelicher hoped to win, and we drove out to the western part of the state to look for a site in the Rockies. Our first stop was the Rocky Mountain School in Carbondale. John Holden, the school's headmaster, and Jack Snobble, his assistant, listened to Fuller's presentation and were enthusiastic. Snobble told us about a "mountain man" friend of his who he thought would be just the man to take hold of the project. "His name is Tap Tapley. He's part Indian, an extraordinary guy. There is just nothing he doesn't know about these mountains, and how to function in them." The next day we went up into the mountains where Tapley was dynamiting avalanches and stringing fence for a mining camp, and told him about Outward Bound and why we were there. He told us of a mining claim above the mountain town of Marble that belonged to friends of his named Howard and Blu Stroud. He thought it might meet the site specifications, and we decided to look at it.

The next morning we drove down to Redstone, where I transferred into an International Harvester vehicle with Tapley and his wife Lee. Soon we were on a dirt-and-rock mountain road and climbing. Tap drove with competence and said little. We would be driving, three in front, and Lee would say to me, "He means for us to get in back," and she and I would scramble over into the back seat to put more weight on the rear wheels. We would get past that tough spot and climb back in front. Pretty soon Lee would say, "He means for us to get in back." How she got the messages I never knew because Tap had not spoken.

Howard Stroud was waiting for us at Marble, a ghost mining town with a scattering of residents. We all piled into Stroud's snowcat. The snow was deep deep now, and the climb even steeper. We were smack in the middle of the Rockies, twenty miles southwest of Aspen, at 9000 feet, on a "road" where part of the track seemed to be over nothing. It was an awesome ride.

The climb leveled out. We were at the Stroud property. Under six or seven feet of snow, it formed a level bench about one thousand by two hundred feet before the mountain started to rise again. A beautiful grove of aspen roughly delineated its boundaries. In the distance, the summit of Treasury Mountain was ma-

jestic in its white mantle. We could see that the level area offered
a splendid setting for a base camp.

Later we looked at another site, which had a large old residence on it. Freddy Fuller preferred this one; it was much closer
to the British model. All the British Outward Bound schools
have a fine residence to which, most nights, the students return,
to eat and sleep in comfortable quarters. It is Hahn's "dunk 'em
and dry 'em" philosophy, and there is a lot of soundness in the
theory. But here we were getting our first variation between
British and U.S. Outward Bound.

When we got back to Denver, there was a message to call
Shriver. I reached Wofford and told him, "We'll start an Outward Bound School in Colorado for the Peace Corps." Shriver
called back. Colorado would not do. "Congress will never buy
it," he said. "We're going to be sending people to tropical cli-
mates. It doesn't make sense to prepare them in the arctic alti-
tudes of Colorado." It was the classic misunderstanding of the
Outward Bound method—the failure to comprehend that we
would be training through the mountains, not for them. But I
could understand Shriver's reluctance to battle that one out with
Congress—especially the politically unfriendly congressmen and
the ones who were doubtful about the whole Peace Corps idea.
He said, "How about starting an Outward Bound School in
Puerto Rico? As long as Captain Fuller is here, why doesn't he
come see us on the way home?"

Fuller went to Washington, and from there down to Puerto
Rico to look for a site, and Burnett and I went back to Andover.
I felt overwhelmed by the pace and mounting complications. I
was working in the admissions office, teaching, and coaching, and
now suddenly there were these two giant undertakings in Colorado and Puerto Rico for which I was responsible to the Atlantic
Foundation. The trustees were excited that something was happening at long last and they gave their enthusiastic backing to
both ventures. Fortunately, the school year would be over in
two months.

Washington, Arecibo, and Marble

What we have to learn to do, we learn by doing.
—ARISTOTLE

Early in the spring of 1961 we presented the formal Outward Bound proposal to the Peace Corps and received an official go-ahead. I began to shuttle between Andover and Washington. One day Shriver called me in and said, "I'm delighted with the reports we're getting on your progress. You're going to be the director in Puerto Rico."

I said, "I'm glad you're getting good reports, but let's get it straight that I'm not the director."

"Why not?"

"First, I feel much more responsible for Outward Bound as a private operation than I do for Outward Bound in the Peace Corps. I can't do for both. Second, for the Peace Corps you need a very charismatic kind of guy. You need somebody who can handle the press, handle Congress, handle top brass, handle ambassadors, handle the Puerto Rican government."

"Who's that guy?" Shriver asked. I said, "I know only one—Bill Coffin, William Sloane Coffin."

"You mean Reverend Coffin, the Yale chaplain? I went to Yale, I bet I can get him." Shriver flipped his intercom. "Get me Reverend William Coffin, the chaplain at Yale University." Soon the phone rang. "Bill. This is Sarge. Sargent Shriver. No, we haven't met—I'm director of the Peace Corps. I have a friend of yours here who says you're the only guy in the world to run this doggone Outward Bound program for us. I'd like to talk with you about it. What do you mean, it's out of the question? At least you can come down and talk about it. We'll pay your way. You're coming to Washington anyway? Friday? Where're you staying? The YMCA! Nobody stays at the YMCA! We'll put you up at the Sheraton. Meet you there for breakfast Saturday morning at seven-thirty." He finally persuaded Coffin to take the job long enough to get the Puerto Rican operation under way.

As soon as school was out I went to Washington. The Puerto Rico camp was due to open in three months, and Coffin and I had a prodigious amount of work to do designing and staffing a program. Freddy Fuller had reported that Puerto Rico had fine terrain for a school, but the site had yet to be selected. I went down to make a survey and was flown all over the island in a plastic bubble helicopter belonging to the Puerto Rico Water Resources Department. The environment, though mountainous, could hardly have been more different from the Rockies. In the helicopter I was following the map, but the pilot had to show me where we were; there were no landmarks that I could see. The pilot would point and shout, "We're going down!" and I would look down at a solid mass of rain forest. We would drop almost like a leaf and land in a clearing I had not seen at all. Before the blades stopped spinning we would be surrounded by fifty kids. Puerto Rico is one of the most densely populated areas in the world.

Later I returned with Coffin. The site search had just about narrowed down to an abandoned lumber camp in the rain forest twenty miles from Arecibo, a town on the north-central coast, and we were making a final check. The area had a small stream, some usable small buildings, good trees for a ropes course. Driving around, we found a beautiful reservoir. Coffin took off his clothes and plunged in. I was about to follow when someone told us that the water had microscopic worms that infected the liver. That was a blow; we had been told the water in the area was free of parasites. The reservoir spill ran in a lovely river to the sea that we had planned to use for white-water kayaking. In the end the reservoir's only usefulness was for rappelling on the steep face of the dam.

Coffin and I were invited to the governor's palace. Governor Muñoz quickly grasped the idea of Outward Bound. He was sympathetic and gave us wonderful cooperation. He hoped the

Peace Corps would not just use the camp for its volunteers, but also would make it available to the young people of his country. He saw the same problems with his youth that he saw with young people elsewhere in the world.

I was distressed by the urbanization—much of it the "Americanization"—of Puerto Rico. But as soon as you were off the main arteries and into the indigenous culture, everything changed. The traffic changed, the pace changed, the people changed. They were lovely, laughing, hospitable, delightful. The country was lovely; the people could manage cleanliness in their small *barrios*. Above all, the family ties were warm and strong. You saw poverty everywhere, but only of the pocket, not of the soul. Malnutrition was not a problem. People raised their own food, even on the handkerchief-sized plot each family lived on with its goat and chickens. You enjoyed the lighthearted ambiance, and it broke your heart to realize what a blight our urban ghettos, so far from the lovely island wildness, had worked on that blitheness of spirit.

In Washington we immersed in the charisma of the Kennedy administration. It was an extraordinary experience for me to go from a New England classroom to a sector of the national power center. We had a great gang headed by William Haddad, a creative, dynamic, hard-bitten entrepreneur sort to whom Coffin and I reported, who became a kind of inspector general of the Peace Corps. We worked furiously, often till midnight. I worked several weeks and got no paycheck. A friend in personnel investigated. "There's some difficulty about your security clearance." Ridiculous, I told him. A couple of days later he came to see me. "What's this Atlantic Foundation for the Education of the Free you're involved in?" So this was security! I dropped the names of a few of my colleagues in the foundation—Ellen McCloy, Christian Herter, Allen Dulles, Eric Warburg.

Working and living with Bill Coffin was an experience in itself. At that time William Sloane Coffin had not yet become a controversial figure at the national level. But he had been controversial enough even at Phillips Academy when he came, fresh out of Yale Divinity School, to be acting chaplain for a year. His impact on the Andover community was the same as it was going to be everywhere else—people felt strongly for him or against him, there was nobody in the middle.

Suddenly now the chapel service before Christmas vacation floods my memory. It is snowing outside, the students are packed and dressed for the trip home, and they will take off as soon as chapel is over. They have sung the hymns and said the prayers, and Coffin steps into the pulpit to say good-bye. "I hope you all have a wonderful vacation." There is a stirring and reaching for hats. "Now, wait a minute, w-a-a-i-t a minute! You're not getting off that easy! What do I mean by 'wonderful'? Wonderful means full of wonder. I want you to go home this Christmas full of wonder. I want you to wonder about your mother. What kind of a person is she? What does life mean to her? I want you to wonder about what you mean to her life. I want you to wonder about your father. Wonder about what he is worried about. What are his concerns? What's the toll of responsibility on him? Wonder about that jerk roommate of yours. He's human too, you know. Why does he have troubles? Spend some time wondering about him. And when you're dancing around with that sweet young thing in your arms, wonder about her. Because she's worth wondering about. I hope you all have a wonderful vacation!"

He is the best preacher I have ever listened to. He can drive you crazy because he is so superb and then can get carried away and go into the detail of a rape on the cold marble floor of a Harlem drugstore. Coming from the pulpit, that upsets a lot of people, especially older people. Bill's critics say he is an egotist, that he is more interested in a spectacular performance than in the essence of what he is saying. That just is not so. He is a deeply thoughtful and concerned man, with a showman's gift. I agree with Jack Stevens, who once said, "Bill Coffin is the only practicing Christian I know."

I told Coffin we had to have drownproofing at Arecibo. I told him about Freddy Lanoue, whom we would have to shake loose from Georgia Tech. The minute I mentioned Georgia, his hackles rose. "We're going to have blacks in Puerto Rico. We can't be subjecting them to any redneck prejudices." "Come off it, Bill," I said. "Anyway, Fred's a Canuck from Worcester, Massachusetts, and Springfield College, and everybody loves him." Coffin was unconvinced, about Lanoue and about drownproofing. "Get him up here," he said, "I'll have to talk with him." It was already evening when I reached Lanoue at his home in Atlanta. He greeted me with a string of affectionate expletives. I said,

"Fred, what are you doing tonight?" "What do you mean, what am I doing tonight? It's eight-thirty." I said, "How fast can you get up here to Washington?" He said, "I can be there at quarter to twelve. I often make that flight," and he gave me the flight number.

I called a member of our Peace Corps team, Sally Bowles, daughter of Undersecretary of State Chester Bowles, at her parents' home in Georgetown. "Sally, I need your swimming pool tomorrow morning. Can we borrow it?" "I don't think you can," Sally said. "Mother's giving a lunch party for the African envoys, and they've been invited to come early for a swim." I assured Sally we would be there early and only needed an hour. We were given permission to use the Bowleses' pool with the understanding that we would be gone before the first guest arrived.

Coffin and I were waiting for Lanoue when his plane came in. I lost track of how many people stopped us between the gate and the car. ("Coach Lanoue, you don't remember me, but—" "Sure I remember you. You're such a dumb son of a bitch you nearly drowned.") It just seemed that every tenth person at National Airport was a friend of Freddy Lanoue.

In the morning, poolside at the Bowleses, Coffin was looking dubious. "All right now, Reverend," Fred said, "just put your hands behind your back and cross your wrists, that's a good boy. Let me tie 'em up tight. That's it. Now your feet. Not too tight? O.K. Usually we take twelve hours to get to this tie-up phase, but time is short." He pushed Coffin into the pool. "All right now goddammit, Reverend, you do as I say, or I'm going to drown you. Trouble with you reverse-collar so-and-so's is you never listen to anybody else. I got you trussed up real good, so now you better listen up, hear?"

Coffin was wild. He was so mad he could not talk. Lanoue began to teach him the basics of drownproofing. Every time Coffin made a mistake, Lanoue put a foot on his head and drove him down to the bottom of the pool. Bill would float up so mad that if he could have gotten loose, I think he would have torn Lanoue apart. When he surfaced, Fred would say something like, "For God's sake, Reverend, relax! I thought you were a man of faith!"

Pretty soon Coffin was getting the hang of it. "That's fine, rend, you got the rhythm just fine." He did the travel stroke to the shallow end, where I untied him. His wrists were bleeding; apparently he had panicked a bit in those moments on the bottom of the pool. We sat on the pool's edge while Fred gave us a fascinating discourse on the theory and practice of drown-proofing. He finished just as the first of the Bowleses' guests arrived poolside. Recognizing Arthur Schlesinger, Jr., the historian and at that time a Kennedy staff member, Coffin introduced us. "Glad to meet you, Art," Lanoue said. "Put your hands behind your back." Before Schlesinger knew what was happening, he too was bobbing in the pool. In his case, however, Lanoue only tied his hands.

Now I spotted one of the African envoys coming out, a flowing white robe over his bathing suit. Lanoue walked up to him and held out his hand. "My name's Fred Lanoue, Ambassador, mighty pleased to meet you. Put your hands behind your back like a good boy and do exactly what I tell you." Soon he had the plenipotentiaries of a dozen African countries bobbing up and down with their hands tied. "Goddammit, Ambassador, I'm not going to tell you four times." Pow—he would reach out a foot and push the man under. Sally's mother came out, and I could see she was beside herself with anger. I was mortified. Then, watching, she began to smile. Her guests were having the time of their lives. Afterward Mrs. Bowles said it was one of the most successful luncheon parties she had ever given. Nobody in the world but Freddy Lanoue could have pulled that off, nobody. Coffin hired him.

The summer was a primer lesson in the uses of power. For Shriver, Haddad, and the rest, anything was possible. Who's the best guy for this or that? Get him! Coffin had hired Jack Snobble to be an instructor and to help him set up the Puerto Rican operation. Then Snobble told us he could not make it; he had to go on army reserve duty. When Haddad learned we were looking for someone to replace Snobble, he gave us what-for: "When are you guys going to catch on you're working for the U.S. government? Call Adam Yarmolinsky in McNamara's office and tell him the Peace Corps wants Snobble." It was that simple.

In August Coffin took off for Arecibo to rendezvous with Freddy Fuller, who had agreed to help make the project authentically Outward Bound. They had a scant six weeks in which to transform the scorpion- and tarantula-infested remnants of a lumber camp into a habitable "advanced training" base for Peace Corps volunteers about to go abroad on their appointed missions. Coffin and Fuller were joined by Snobble, Reagh Wetmore, who had signed on to work with Lanoue, and Ray Slawson, an ex-Navy officer.

Snobble, recalling the masterful liaison-and-scrounge technique that brought the camp into being, says that while the Peace Corps may have been strictly nonmilitary, it would not have gotten off the ground in Puerto Rico without the gracious cooperation of all branches of the military service on the island, who loaned and gave to the camp vehicles, equipment, stores, and even manpower assistance. When Jack succeeded in cadging an overage bus and station wagon from Ramey Air Force Base, the motor pool there added a touch of class to the wagon by painting it with surplus off-color blue paint and emblazoning its identity in white letters. This seems to have been how the Peace Corps got its official colors, blue and white.

Coffin, happily aware of the direct power line into the White House maintained by his Washington superiors, refused to deal with anyone under the rank of general or admiral. On one occasion he went to the mat with a three-star official who was trying to withdraw a promise of four trucks. "General," he said, "if you welsh on those trucks, I'm going to wire our man in McNamara's office that you deserve a court-martial, disgrace, a firing squad, and an unmarked grave." Bill got the trucks. He made a frequent point of referring to "our man in the Pentagon." Fortunately no one ever asked for the man's name.

Meanwhile, I was combining a family-vacation pack trip in Montana with my recruiting task. We came back through Jackson Hole, Wyoming, which was headquarters for Glen Exum's climbing school in the Tetons, where I had hired two of his guides. We drove on down to visit the Outward Bound site above Marble, where Tap Tapley was directing the building of the Colorado school. Chuck Froelicher, operating on a shoestring, had moved that project resolutely forward since our exploratory visit with Captain Fuller in March. Before deciding to buy the Marble property, he had sent Tapley out in his jeep to see if he could find anything better. Tapley had reported back in favor of the Marble site: It was isolated from resort areas. It was safe from fire, flood, and landslides. The water supply was adequate. It had a southern exposure. The access was satisfactory. And it was fantastically beautiful.

Tapley and Stroud had surveyed the area, marking off 45.2 acres. Tapley mapped out a plan and gave the map to Froelicher. With Stroud's permission—there was no money for the purchase yet—Tapley and a man named Al Kirsch started cutting aspen. Froelicher, who was giving all the time he could spare to lining up a board of directors and getting pledges, would visit the site and take pictures, which he then used to help raise funds. An access road had to be built, power lines put in, ditches dug for drainage and sewer lines, a large sewer plant installed, the building foundations put down, a ropes course built. Chuck recalls: "We would O.K. a project and then we'd have to find the money to pay for it. That can be motivating."

Tapley hired a backhoe man and a bulldozer operator, and later carpenters and men to pour concrete for the sewer leaching beds. In June a volunteer work brigade of fourteen youngsters from Colorado Academy arrived.

We found Tap running an easy ship, yet everything shipshape. The boys lived in tepees they had put up. Tap had built a marvelous tepee for Lee and himself. There was an excellent outdoor cooking arrangement. Running spring water was being piped in. There was an archery range and a horseshoe pitch. It was the tidiest work camp I have ever seen. The boys worked mornings, and in the afternoons Tap gave them a course in mountaineering. In midsummer they put on a rock-climbing exhibition for parents, and Froelicher used those photos to raise more money.

Tapley, I was discovering, was a contemporary mountain version of renaissance man. He could live in the wilderness with nothing but a knife. He was a skilled hunter, tracker, trapper, fisherman, an expert axeman, a fine outdoor cook, a virtuoso with ropes and knots. A master of all trades, he could make anything and engineer anything. He had the greatest manual intelligence I have ever seen, could do the most minute things with his hands. He was a forester, fire fighter, mountaineer, canoeman, mule skinner, dogsled-team driver, navigator, meteorologist, avalanche expert, cliff evacuation expert, survival adept. He played the violin, and painted. He was a born athlete, a deadly horseshoe pitcher blindfolded. On that visit I learned his life story.

Ernest Tapley grew up in Amesbury, Massachusetts, son of the town baker, one-eighth Passamaquoddy Indian. In the winter of 1941, when he was seventeen, he had a job in North Conway, New Hampshire, as a busboy at the Eastern Slopes Inn, which was a social center of the great skiing boom that had recently come to the country. Whenever he got off from work, Tap skied. On a day in the early spring of 1940 he was in Tuckerman's Ravine on Mount Washington when Lowell Thomas, then at the peak of his fame as an author and radio commentator, was also skiing there. At that time few skiers had the combination of courage and technique to make a successful descent of Tuckerman's famed headwall; Tapley was one. Dining at the inn that evening, Thomas spotted him. If Tapley ever came out to Sun Valley, Idaho, Thomas told him, he would introduce him to the head of the ski patrol. A year later, without waiting to graduate from high school, Tap sold his bicycle and hitchhiked west. In Leadville, Colorado, he got a construction job, worked double shift until he had $300, and completed his journey to Idaho. In the fall he joined the Sun Valley ski patrol, one of the country's first paid patrols. In December the United States declared war on Japan and Germany. The following spring Tapley returned to Amesbury to get his diploma, so that he could join his Sun Valley buddies who were enlisting in the Tenth Mountain Division at Camp Hale, Colorado, to serve as winter skills instructors. Paul Petzoldt, a top U.S. mountaineer who was there as a civilian adviser, remembers spotting the youngster: "I thought, my gosh, he would be the guy to send to the Himalayas, because this guy had everything—strength, coordination, terrific intelligence and ability." The war and the ensuing years would separate them, but they were destined to have a partnership.

Tapley was one of a cadre of ten who were detached and sent to the Aleutian Islands to staff the North Pacific Combat School. At one juncture he was located at an outpost near the Arctic Circle, where it was his duty to brief visiting brass on a proposed air-base site. The base was to be developed as a precautionary measure against the possibility the Russian status might change to something other than ally.

Coming back to the "lower 48" after the war, Tap went into a partnership breaking wild horses. He helped develop the White-fish Ski Area in Montana, operated his own ski school in Tele-mark, Wisconsin, then signed on as a U.S. forest ranger at Big Fork, Montana. The forest service was the finishing school in which he became the complete mountain man. After five years he left the service to help his mother, who was running a lodge at Redstone, Colorado. Jack Snobble, ex-Dartmouth skier and assistant headmaster of Rocky Mountain School in Carbondale, was a ski instructor at the lodge. It was Snobble, we have seen, who brought Tapley and Colorado Outward Bound together. "I'm always interested in trying something new," Tap told me.

He related the troubles he was having with Charlie Orlofsky, the sheriff of Marble. This was the beginning of a semi-epic feud between that officious gentleman and the Colorado School. In their long battle of wits Tapley usually managed to stay two steps ahead of the sheriff. One day that summer he got word that Orlofsky had lodged a complaint with the Marble Board of Health that Tap had a resident work crew and no refrigeration on the premises, which violated the code. A few days later the health inspector showed up. It was a hot day; after hiking up from his car, he was in a heavy sweat. "Have a seat," Tap said. "How about a glass of iced tea?" The inspector did a double take. "Iced tea! Up here?"

Tap went over to the aspen grove where the ropes course had been built and threw back the tarpaulin covering the camp's kerosene-operated refrigerator. He came back with two tall, moisture-beaded glasses of iced tea, cubes clinking, and handed one to the perspiring inspector. As the two men sipped their drinks, the inspector's gaze roved over the site. "Where do you put the garbage?" he asked. Tap pointed to the fire pit. The inspector walked over to the pit and poked with a stick. Nothing but clean ashes. He wandered around the camp and came back. He said, "This is the cleanest place I've inspected all summer. I don't know what the complaint is." Tap said, "I won't ask you who made the complaint. It isn't worth knowing." Charlie Orlofsky, who had not checked under the tarpaulin in the grove of aspen, never forgave that.

We went on to Denver and visited with the Froelichers. Gil Burnett was there. He was spending the summer at Marble and Denver, working on promotional material for the new Colorado Outward Bound School. The first Colorado course was still ten months away, but already that was beginning to seem close.

Hectic Year

Action is eloquence.

—Coriolanus

The school year of 1961–62 raced by. I had a full load of teaching and admissions duties and was doing my work for the Atlantic Foundation. In addition to his full-time job running Colorado Academy, Chuck Froelicher was steering the Colorado Outward Bound project and raising money for it. He had put together a strong board of trustees and been made chairman. The board hired a school director. He was William McK. Chapman, a former journalist who at that time was headmaster of a school on an Indian reservation. The construction work under Tapley went forward until winter closed in. It was a tight time. The work was barely on schedule, and there were payrolls and material and equipment costs to meet. The Atlantic Foundation was having difficulty raising the money it had pledged. The course had to be designed and staffed. The all-important task of enrolling the students had yet to be accomplished. Maybe nobody would come to the party. At the annual meeting of the National Association of Independent Schools, Froelicher, John Holden, and I made a panel presentation of the Outward Bound story. Very few of the school people there had previously heard of Outward Bound. We were encouraged by their positive response.

Through the fall the money problem hung in the balance. I began to learn about the wonderful world of foundations. People with lots of money to give away but difficult to persuade that you could put it to work worthily. On one of Froelicher's trips east I was happy to have him join me in the New York money quest. We went to see Frederick Warburg, Eric's cousin, at the offices of Kuhn, Loeb and Company. We told him about Outward Bound and the plans for the Colorado school, about the construction work in the Rocky Mountains, and the immediate critical problem of $7,000 for payroll and equipment rentals due the following week.

Warburg was a great activist in the Boy Scout movement. He was furious that we were starting a new outfit. We told him how Sir Robert Baden-Powell, the founder of the Boy Scouts, had been a strong supporter of Hahn's work. We talked some more, and I did not feel we were making progress. Suddenly he asked, "Who sent you here?" I told him it was Mrs. John McCloy. He dialed her number without having to look it up. "Ellen? Why aren't you here with these two young fellows who are asking me for money?" He kept his fierce glare on us. "Well, you should be here, because they remind me of a high-school team being sent in to play Notre Dame without a coach." That was unfair to Chuck, who had won his money-raising spurs getting his school back on its feet, but it fitted me. When Warburg hung up, he said, "Look, I won't give you one damn penny. Not until you have raised all you need except for five thousand dollars. Then come and see me, and I'll cap it off." Eventually he gave us more than that.

Friday afternoon came, and we were still scratching for that seven thousand. It was raining, and I had no raincoat. We were wet, tired, discouraged. As a last resort we called at the Taconic Foundation without an appointment. I had stayed in touch with Steve Currier after he sent us to talk with Harris Wofford in Washington the previous spring. Now, with my naive concept of how foundations functioned, I had the desperate idea that maybe we could get the Taconic Foundation to spring some money loose for us. In Currier's office the rug was ankle-deep. It was dry, warm, cozy. Currier could not have been more thoughtful. He said, "You guys sit down, you look beat! I bet you need a drink." After the drinks were served we told him our story. He said, "Look, I can't possibly get foundation money for you, but here's a personal contribution." He wrote a check for $5,000 out of his own pocket. It was one of the critical checks in Outward Bound history.

The fiscal problem continued serious. In December a crisis was averted by a loan of $20,000, personally guaranteed by Jack Stevens, from Phillips Academy to the Atlantic Foundation. At the same time, John Kemper agreed to coordinate the fund-raising activity.

Bulletins came from Puerto Rico. The camp opened in early September, on schedule but not altogether propitiously. The first group of volunteers, twelve surveyors and road builders bound for Tanganyika, arrived with a collective chip on their shoulders. They had been told only two days before that they had yet to undergo a month's "capstone" training experience to qualify for Africa. At six the first morning, Coffin led them on a four-mile run along a route he personally had hacked out. Only three volunteers finished with him; the rest straggled in during the ensuing half hour. Sensing the mutinous tone of the breakfast muttering, Coffin made a kind of welcoming speech. While he could sympathize with their resentment at being there, he said, he thought they could profit by the training. In any event he and his associates could profit by their taking it, for changes were bound to be needed to make the program as helpful as possible to later volunteers. If there were some who felt they could not put themselves out for others, he would not hesitate to recommend their dismissal from the Corps.

The volunteers' grudging response gradually grew more positive toward the Outward Bound elements—morning run, ropes course, rock climbing and rappelling, drownproofing, jungle and mountain treks, overnight jungle solos—that Freddy Fuller had designed into their training regimen. But even though he earned the instant respect of instructors and students, Puerto Rico cannot have been Captain Fuller's favorite billet. The volunteers, with their mix of maturity, high motivation, and American inability to take orders without knowing the reasons why, constituted a rather different kind of human material from the younger, more respectful Britishers he was accustomed to. Jack Snobble, who with Coffin was better equipped to understand the Americans, says that ultimately "Outward Bound's inherent flexibility and ability to adapt to a variety of needs" proved its strength.

One innovation in the American program that Fuller wholly

approved was the drownproofing; when he returned to England, he added it to his Aberdovey curriculum. Coffin's autobiography provides a nice picture of Lanoue striding up and down in his red trunks, explaining to the volunteers the parallels between swimming under water and dancing at the high school prom:

> Lanoue told them, "You remember, you had to go to the bathroom, but the music wouldn't stop. So what did you do? You kept on dancing. It's the same principle here. The human will can postpone bodily gratifications far longer than you think. Just remember: whenever you think you have to come up for air, at that moment swim for the bottom." The rest of the afternoon he paced alongside the pool screaming, "Deeper, deeper!" till every volunteer had done what only one had originally thought he could do. That was really what we were after in all our camp training—to see how many times a day we could get volunteers to say, "I never thought I could do that."

Coffin and I had been told that Puerto Rico had one of the world's finest community-development programs. The program's codirectors, Fred Wales and his wife Carmen, arranged for Bill to go out in the hills with one of their workers, a third-grade schoolteacher named Juan. In a pickup truck loaded with a movie projector, a gas-driven generator to power the projector, and a big screen, they drove to a tiny *barrio*, where Juan showed a film and conducted a village meeting. The villagers decided their greatest need was a deeper well and with Juan's help initiated a project to get it. That night, lying on a straw pallet in a tiny but spotless hovel, Coffin decided he had chanced on the most important part of the training program. Every volunteer spent three days in a remote *barrio* with one of Fred Wales's workers. Fred was so impressed by the volunteers that he came twice to the camp to spend an evening. Bill says, "I've never heard anyone speak about poverty-stricken people with more compassion and less sentimentality."

In January and March the Atlantic Foundation's financial commitment to the new Colorado school was covered by grants of $25,000 each from the Old Dominion Foundation and the Avalon Foundation. These grants proved to be a highly significant precedent. The two foundations, both Mellon family funds, were subsequently merged into the Mellon Foundation, which over the years has provided $300,000 in start-up dollars for new Outward Bound schools.

Bill Chapman went to England for his Outward Bound indoctrination. Tapley, who was to be chief instructor, followed. After visiting Aberdovey, Tap took the course at Eskdale. Toward the end they asked him to help instruct the rock climbing. Eskdale brought him into contact with the school's warden, Tom Price, one of the outstanding figures in the British Outward Bound movement. Among the instructors there, Tapley especially liked Ralph Clough, who had taught at several of the British schools and played a part in starting Outward Bound in Nigeria. He arranged for Clough to come to Colorado and help shape the course the following summer.

On his return Chapman began to make the rounds, speaking to schools and parent groups. Both the Denver group and I promoted scholarships. As the long mountain winter yielded to spring, Tapley got his construction people back at work. The staffing was completed. The enrollment applications came in, slowly but steadily. Enough were coming to assure a party.

Through April and May and into June the push to finish the school buildings—a large dining hall with a balcony library, a washhouse and a smaller facility for women who were coming in a Peace Corps group, a small administration building, an equipment house, and houses for the director and the chief instructor—was a race against the calendar. The last few days before the school opened were intense. Tapley and Clough were putting the instructors through their final training paces. The late equipment deliveries were being sorted and readied. Frank Menendez, the chef, was laying in the food supply. Tapley was riding herd on the construction wrap-up. He remembers: "Everyone was for us. The forestry people, the fish and game people, the power company people, they all liked the sound of what we were planning to do. On the day we were to open up we were putting the finishing touches on the power line and the hookup. In the morning it looked as though we would have to cook the first meal that night outdoors. But two hours before the students arrived, the power company crew cut in the electricity."

C-1

*I am very glad to have taken this course, and I can
think of no substitute. My job now, and a continuing
one, is to live up to what the school has revealed to me.*

—From a Colorado School student's
course impression, first summer

The Colorado Outward Bound School opened on June 16,
1962. C-1,* the first course, had thirty-five students. The three
courses that summer had a total of one hundred regular students,
with forty-six in C-2 and nineteen in C-3, which was primarily
a contract course for seventy-six members of a Peace Corps group
that was going to Nepal. The one hundred regular students
came from twenty states. Fifty-one were on scholarships. Denver
businessmen provided twenty-five scholarships for local boys, four
from the jurisdiction of the Denver Juvenile Court, and the
remainder came through the Eastern effort. To get as wide a
social and geographical selection in each patrol of ten boys as
possible, applications were examined and the students assigned
before they arrived. As Bill Chapman noted in his director's
report, "No one knew another's background, and the boys
plunged into the strenuous course together with little time for
introspection or comparison of notes. This way they frequently
found out each other's worth before they learned of each other's

* The system of designating courses by letter and number was subsequently
picked up by all the U.S. schools. Hurricane Island prefixes course numbers by
H-, Minnesota by M-, North Carolina by NC-, Northwest by NW-, Dartmouth
by D-, Southwest by S-.

backgrounds and, in a number of instances, boys of less fortunate backgrounds than others were soon able to establish their leadership on a basis of true equality."

Under Ralph Clough's guidance, the twenty-six-day course closely followed the Eskdale model. A distinctive difference was that Colorado reflected considerably less of Hahn's "dunk 'em and dry 'em" operating philosophy. Some of the contrast was between the comfortable living quarters and other indoor amenities at Eskdale and the eight-man tents the students lived in at Marble. But the marked difference lay in the Colorado plan of operating much of the course, after basic training was completed, away from the main base altogether. A base camp was established in a meadow about six miles north of Lead King Basin, at close to 10,000-foot elevation. Surrounding this area were several snow-capped mountains in which major expeditions were carried out.

The initial training included physical conditioning and instruction in needed skills: "circuit training," map and compass reading (we were not yet calling it orienteering), campcraft, backpacking, first aid, axemanship, knots and rope handling, rock climbing and rappel technique, fire fighting, mountain rescue. Circuit training was a form of physical conditioning for mountaineering that British Outward Bound had devised to replace the athletic events (essentially the old Gordonstoun Break program) that were part of the original Aberdovey curriculum. On the first day, each student was put through a "circuit course" —a series of press-ups, deep-knee bends, chin-ups, and sit-ups done in rapid succession in thirty- or sixty-second spurts—and his maximum capacity was measured. Half his maximum became his "daily dose," which he did three times a day throughout the course. Near the end, maximums were tested again to measure improvement. Everybody also did a quarter-mile uphill run before the mountain climbing started. In addition to the skills instruction, the students were given an elementary review of the geology and the flora and fauna of the area.

Central to the basic training were a set of initiative tests and the aerial ropes course. The primary purpose of the initiatives was to build group cohesion and esprit. They included the wall and beam, two tests that have become virtually standard elements in the Outward Bound curriculum. The wall in particular is a highly effective means of taking a collection of individuals, strangers to each other, and transforming them into an instant group. Typically, a cadre—at Colorado a patrol—of students is being led on a first-day orientation tour of the base camp area when they come to a vertical board construction, normally thirteen to fourteen feet high and eight feet wide. This wall is used to transform the casual tour into an intensive test of the raw group's ability to tackle a problem together. They are told they have so many—usually five—minutes in which to plan how they will get all their members over the wall. During that time and the ensuing effort, the group learns a lot about itself and its component strengths and weaknesses. The working out of the problem becomes an exercise in group dynamics. Good and poor leader and follower qualities reveal themselves. To some in the group the problem appears impossible. Others jockey for leadership or prestige in the immediate hubbub of counsel. The more thoughtful, who may be slower to speak, may or may not succeed in carrying conviction. Some will have nothing to suggest, waiting the group decision with varying degrees of positive or negative attitude. Carrying out the decision engages a new set of dynamics. Leadership emerges through action. As important as the effort itself is the action's effect in bringing all into close, coordinated physical contact—touching, holding, giving a lift up, clambering over bodies, seizing a down-reaching hand, in turn offering a hand down to others. The final success is a shared success; everyone senses that something significant has happened in the alchemy of the group. Usually the group will go directly from the wall to the beam, which is a log nine or so inches in diameter supported horizontally some nine feet off the ground. Again, the assignment is to get everybody over the beam. Now the group is reenforced by the experience of having solved one problem together. The second success produces a further synergistic flow.

The ropes course is a personal test, a confidence-building trial that British Outward Bound originally borrowed from the military. The course is a complex of rope and timber pathways, much of it constructed at considerable height, that must be negotiated in a series of climbing, traversing, and balancing maneuvers. In the "postman's walk," for example, the student slides feet sideways along one rope while holding onto a second. The ropes

course is the part of Outward Bound experience that, except for
rock climbing and rappelling, causes most students the most
apprehension. The course that Tapley had built in a grove of
aspen called on them to start by climbing a thirty-five-foot rope
ladder. They had ample occasion to look up at the course prior
to the day they essayed it. As they eyed the apparently insubstan-
tial footing and bodily support high in the air, the trial ahead
grew fraught with mental hazard. Negotiating the course combined an exorcising of fears with a test of coordination, timing,
balance, and arm and shoulder strength. The experience was
invaluable in helping a youngster to deal with his fear of heights
and to make an essential Outward Bound discovery—that with
resolution one can do what one has thought or feared one could
not. Success was all the more powerful when it followed on failure.

Shifting to the camp above Lead King Basin, a patrol promptly
moved out on a three-day training expedition. This was a time
for breaking in boots, getting used to a heavy pack, learning to
cope with the exigencies of group living on the move. How to
select safe, comfortable campsites. Building a fire in the wet.
System and logistics of cooking, eating, clean-up, sleep, and moving on. Dealing with the wide day-and-night temperature swings
and the vagaries of mountain weather. The theory of map reading, compass bearings, and route finding becoming the hard
question of just where one was on a timbered trail or a naked
mountainside. Getting to know one another better in group-stress
situations.

A day of rest and re-outfitting back at the main base, a rock-
climbing baptism, and then the major expedition, climbing one
of the high peaks. Now came the full test of endurance, bodily
and mental—the daylong hikes up rocky trails, traversing a great
boulder-strewn terrain, moving on up into the perennial snowfields, hacking a route across treacherous blue ice; roped together
to negotiate a steep pitch one step, one handhold at a time, wary
of loose rock; straddling the length of a mountain ridge; confronting—or bending to—the raging power of mountain storms;
blisters, hurts, fatigue. With each day's end a debriefing, a chance
to articulate experiences and feelings, to share joys, to talk out
tensions and irritations, the group growing in its capacity to make
it together. Winning finally, having surmounted the physical and
psychological obstacles, to the summits at 13- to 14,000 feet, of

Maroon Bells, Capitol Peak, or Snowmass, looking down with wonder and pride at the route traversed, looking out in elation at a sight of awesome beauty such as a young lifetime had not known till now.

Nor was the descent anticlimactic. A long traverse across a snowfield, roped together at seventy-five-foot intervals, the leader belayed lest in falling he pitch downward out of control and take others with him. Learning the art of a glissade down an incline of icy snow, picking up speed, and digging in with the ice axe to brake oneself.

Advanced rock climbing. The high rappel: the trusting lean-back off the clifftop edge, supported by two half-inch nylon lines; an act of faith to remember.

At most Outward Bound schools the marathon has come to be the final event of the course, but in the early years at Colorado it came between the major and the final expeditions. A six-mile run through mountain country from the town of Crystal, near Lead King Basin, to Marble. Few students had ever come even close to running that distance. At the start of the course, the relatively short run on rising—not quite a mile with a dip in a stream at the halfway point—had taxed most of them. For virtually all, the idea of having to go six miles later in the course had seemed an impossibility. The marathon was run as a patrol competition, counting total elapsed time of all patrol members. But as the runners spread out, often out of sight of one another, the race became very much a personal test. The decision to keep running, to try harder despite ache, pain, blisters, and shortness of breath, was one's own. Finishing, with a sense of having tried to do one's best, was another satisfaction in a time replete with successes that surprised and revealed.

The curriculum Ralph Clough brought with him included a "night alone"—one overnight when each student camped on his own, isolated from his fellows. The night alone was a successful part of C-1. For many of the youngsters it was—in retrospect, at least—a new, satisfying experience. Tapley thought it a highly valuable course element: "So many people have never been alone, completely on their own, in their whole life. Never been in a place where there was just no chance of reaching out for a telephone to say something has happened or I'm sick."

In C-2, on the day preceding the scheduled night alone, chef

Frank Menendez came to Tapley in a panic. The school was running out of food, and the supplier had just called to say he could not make a delivery up the mountain for several days. Tapley perceived the crisis as opportunity. "If you have three days without having to feed anybody," he asked Frank, "will you be all right?" Frank said he would. "What we can do," Tapley said, "is something I've been wanting to try anyway. Tonight we'll get the group together, and I'll give them a talk on edible plants and berries, and what kinds of game and fish they can find to eat, and we'll tell them they're going on a three-day solo survival."

Tap remembers, "That was when we began to find out about a lot of things. First off I told the kids they didn't have to eat anything, they could get along fine on nothing but water for three days. I told them how I'd gone several days without food, just drinking water and picking plants like miner's lettuce and brook sassafras, pond-lily roots, things like that. With fire and water, they could make tea from the cambium layer of most any tree—spruce tree was especially good.* I told them about cattail roots, and fern fiddleheads in the spring, marmots, snakes, and frogs for meat, how to make a snare. We gave them a knife, a fishhook and a short piece of line, salt, matches, and a sleeping bag. We took them out and placed them at least a half mile apart, where they couldn't even see the smoke of another fire. We put them by a source of water and told them they were not to go more than one hundred yards in any direction. The instructors checked by day that they were all right, trying not to be seen. At night I made the rounds of the ones I was more concerned about, to be sure they had a fire and were by it.

"It was a great experience for the kids, and the greatest part of it was after they came in for the debriefing. We found they had got much more out of their solos than we had expected. They swapped confidences and learned of bad and good experiences. It was a tremendous release for a boy to learn he wasn't the only one who had been scared. I told them, 'I've been in the hills for twenty years. If I wake up and hear something like a porcupine walking right over my head, and I can't see him, it scares me. Staying by yourself out there all alone, you see how

* Conservational proscription no longer permits this.

a human being just isn't equipped to take care of himself as an animal does.' "

That was how the solo, which more than any other feature of the program has brought Outward Bound its fame in the United States, came into being. The following year Colorado extended the solo's length from two nights to three, and when other American schools opened, they made the three-night solo standard to their courses as well. There has never been doubt of the high value of the solo experience. But ironically, the publicity it has received is responsible for a widespread misapprehension about Outward Bound—that it is a survival school, which it emphatically is not. Today most students on solo simply fast. The "survival" aspects, never intended to be physically rugged, have become incidental to the solo's primary purposes, which are the experience of solitude in the wilderness and an opportunity for contemplation. For most young people those experiences may well be more stressful than being hungry or cold.

Near the end of the course the students were reorganized into four-to-six man patrols for their final expeditions. This time they were on their own for four days, without an instructor to turn to. The patrol planned and executed its own undertaking as a team, each man carrying a forty-pound pack through forty to seventy-five miles of unfamiliar mountain wilderness. The final expedition, with its ultimate discovery by each individual that more than anything else Outward Bound is a revelation of people's interdependence and a challenge to their ability to work things out together, was a kind of rite of passage.

An unscheduled event of that first summer was U.S. Outward Bound's affirmation of the powerful rescue tradition that, deriving directly from the consuming commitment of Kurt Hahn, Outward Bound schools had already created around the world. Since the preceding work summer, it had become well known in the surrounding mountain area that the school was on twenty-four-hour rescue call. During the second course a call came in that a man was ill at 13,000 feet on Snowmass Mountain. Three instructors and eight students took off immediately, making the climb through the snowfields and up a steep rocky trail to the ledge where the ill man lay in a coma. They revived him, fed him hot soup, wrapped him in blankets and secured him to a Stokes litter, and tied themselves together for the long, difficult descent. Four hours later they placed him in a truck that rushed him from Marble to the hospital thirty miles away. The students were euphoric, on a rescue high. One said, "Two weeks ago I couldn't have gotten myself out of the mountains, let alone a sick man." The grateful evacuee made the school a gift of a slide projector and screen.

The summer's health and safety record was exemplary. No broken bones. A normal incidence of cuts, bruises, blisters, sprains, a few sore throats. Two cases of tick-bite fever, the duration of each about six days. Nurse Bonnie Condon kept arrival and departure charts of blood pressure, weight, and pulse changes to determine the effect of altitude (8800 feet at the main base camp) on boys from sea level and other parts of the country. The students apparently acclimated more readily than had been foreseen; mountain sickness was almost unknown. The records revealed one remarkable health phenomenon, bearing out Hahn's contention that asthmatic youngsters should be encouraged to run. The students who had a history of asthma did the full normal course, including the marathon, with no symptoms of their affliction appearing.

At summer's end there was no doubt that the Colorado Outward Bound School was here to stay. Most of the students departed in various stages of outward and inward euphoria. Their journals and the evaluations they wrote on the final day attested to intense, memorable, highly valued experiences: "I am very glad to have taken this course and I can think of no substitute. My job now, and a continuing one, is to live up to what the school has revealed to me" . . . "I learned to get along with people that I really disliked at first. Perhaps the most amazing thing to me was the different perspective with which I seemed to begin to look at things up here" . . . "The greatest single thing which helped me the most was the solo survival. Here I started to find myself." Afterward came letters from both students and parents—the first batches of the thick testimonial accumulations now in the files of the seven U.S. Outward Bound schools. The parent letters were usually variations on the theme of "We sent you a boy and you returned us a man": "When he returned early this month, we saw a new boy, fit, with muscles he never knew he had before. But more important than the physical changes were the self-confidence and pride that he showed. I am sure that he was not aware that he frequently used the word 'challenge' in referring to his forthcoming freshman year at college, but I think his Outward Bound experience has taught him to meet challenges with an assurance he never had before."

The school's fame was spreading. In Lander, Wyoming, Paul Petzoldt, one of the country's great pioneer mountaineers, who had directed the Petzoldt-Exum School of American Mountaineering in the Teton range, was intrigued by what he heard. During C-3 he came to see the Colorado school at first hand. A result of his visit was his appointment to be the school's mountaineering adviser the following year.

Petzoldt's visit brought him to a reunion with another great American climber, a former student and longtime mountaineering companion-in-arms. This was William F. "Willi" Unsoeld, who was in charge of the Peace Corps group for which C-3 had been set up. Since this group of volunteers was headed for mountainous Nepal, it had been sent to Colorado rather than Puerto Rico. Unsoeld, who was to be deputy director of the Peace Corps in Nepal, had a special interest in going there. He was one of a group of Americans planning to attempt an ascent of Mount Everest—on the Nepal-Tibet border—in the year ahead. While at the time his contact with Outward Bound seemed only a passing encounter, it proved to be the start of an important liaison.

1962-63

Not fare well
But fare forward, voyagers.

—T. S. ELIOT

Among the outstanding instructors in the Colorado School's first summer was a social science teacher from the Midwest named Joe Nold. The trustees, in agreement that Joe had the qualities needed for long-term leadership, offered him the post of school director in the summer of 1963.

Joe Nold was born and grew up in Saskatchewan, Canada. When he graduated from the University of British Columbia, he had two goals—to become a teacher, and to experience the wilder and higher parts of the world. Going from one overseas teaching post to another, he spent his vacations climbing mountains, ski touring, and generally beating about remote parts of the globe. Along the way he heard about the British Outward Bound movement. His quest for more information brought him into contact with the Gordonstoun School, and in 1955 he went there to teach for a year. Immediately congenial with the Gordonstoun tradition of exposing boys to outdoor experiences, he took students on weekend backpacking trips and during the holiday periods led them on climbing expeditions in the Spanish Sierra Nevada and Morocco's Atlas range. Gordonstoun helped him get a post at a school in India, and there he trekked with youngsters in the foothills of the Himalayas.

Eventually Joe wound up teaching at the North Shore Country

Day School, in the Chicago suburb of Winnetka. Nathaniel French, the school's headmaster, was a friend of Chuck Froelicher. One day in the fall of 1961 he said to Nold, "Here's something that should interest you," and handed him a mailing piece from the new Colorado Outward Bound School. Joe promptly wrote Froelicher. One of the first instructors Chuck hired, he would become a key participant in the flowering of the U.S. Outward Bound movement.

Even with Nold's year at Gordonstoun and the enthusiasm for the Outward Bound movement that he brought with him, the effect on youngsters of the first Colorado courses was a revelation: "Before Colorado I had not experienced Outward Bound in the one-month impact kind of thing. I was deeply impressed by the whole quality of lifting a group of kids from their familiar environment and creating a new society in the mountains. There was a dynamic to it that had an impact like no other I had ever known. When Nat French asked me how the summer had gone, I told him, 'I've been teaching for you for three years, and I really think I've done more teaching in the last two months than I've done in three years in the classroom.' What excited me most was the extent to which Outward Bound spoke to the whole sense of being and meaning and values and purpose of life. That's the basic structure into which we have to fit academics. I felt that this was the most deeply educational involvement I'd ever had as a teacher with young people."

For Nold and others like him there was something else. "A penalty of teaching in one of the country's finest independent day schools in that well-to-do suburban environment was that we young teachers felt cut off from the mainstream of American life. We had come into teaching with the idea that it was a service-oriented profession. It was the early Sixties, Kennedy was newly in office, the national social conscience was waking, and we couldn't help feeling dissatisfied. At Colorado we not only had a chance to work with disadvantaged youngsters; we were able to mix kids from affluent families with kids from the ghetto. Part of the beauty of that was that the highly motivated, upper-mobility type of middle-class and rich kid got so much out of the social interaction. I had the feeling that Outward Bound was in the marketplace."

Nold accepted the directorship offer with a qualification. He could only be at Marble for C-4 and C-5; someone else would have to take over for C-6 in August. I was nominated. I was not keen on taking charge of a mountaineering program when I had no big mountain experience. But partly from a sense of responsibility, partly out of a realization that the experience would be valuable, I assented.

Applications were coming in slowly but steadily, and the number of scholarships mounted encouragingly. It looked like the second summer's enrollment would hit at least one hundred and fifty. We were not concerned about the Colorado School's ability to survive. Froelicher had done a fine job. He had a strong, enthusiastic board, and the school was getting valuable word-of-mouth advertising as a result of the first summer's success. Our thoughts were on expansion. The Atlantic Foundation now saw its primary mission as fostering the growth of Outward Bound throughout the country. The winter and spring of 1963 brought definite indications that we had the beginnings of a national movement. One such indication was the intense interest of Peter Willauer, a former Andover colleague then on the Groton School faculty, in starting a school on the Maine coast. I encouraged Peter in his quest for a strong board chairman and board, and a site. As publicity about the Colorado Outward Bound School spread, we had a number of other inquiries from people wanting to start a second school. I wrote Sir Spencer Summers, chairman of Britain's Outward Bound Trust, requesting that the Atlantic Foundation be authorized to grant, with appropriate discretion, the use of the title "Outward Bound" in the United States. The trust's management committee instructed him to inform us that the trust would be agreeable to this arrangement as soon as the Atlantic Foundation had appointed a permanent secretary. This coincided with the foundation's thinking that the time had come to set up an office headed by a foundation officer devoting full time to Outward Bound affairs. My sabbatical year was coming up, and it was decided that I should take on the assignment for a year, starting with the coming summer of 1963.

One of the more promising letters of inquiry came to John Kemper from a fellow schoolmaster named Robert Pieh. Bob Pieh (pronounced *Pay*) had been running a summer camp for boys at the edge of the Superior–Quetico Wilderness in northern Minnesota and Canada, which is great canoeing country. He had headed the department of physical education, health, and recreation at Antioch College and was currently headmaster of Anniston Academy, a boys' school in Anniston, Alabama. Pieh wrote Kemper he had long been an admirer of Kurt Hahn and his educational philosophy and an interested follower of the British Outward Bound movement. He thought his northern Minnesota facility offered an ideal, ready-made setup for an Outward Bound school.

Pieh and his son Jerry, who was in the master of arts in teaching program at the Harvard School of Education, came to see us in Andover. They were an impressive pair. Bob was a striking physical specimen, the very image of a woodsman, articulate, a philosopher. At Antioch he had been a highly creative physical educator. We were impressed by his staunch confidence that he and Jerry could create a successful Outward Bound school in the Minnesota–Canadian wilderness. It was arranged that I would visit their camp in June. Kemper quickly perceived that Jerry had the makings of a fine teacher; the following year he put him on the Andover faculty. What he did not know was that Jerry would become his son-in-law.

Early in the spring came our first big national publicity break, an event that dramatically stepped up the pace of U.S. Outward Bound's growth. The preceding summer I had given a talk in New York. One of my listeners was Donald Watt, son of the founder of the Experiment in International Living. After hearing me tell the Colorado School story, he told Lydia Ratcliff, a writer friend, about it. Intrigued, she came to see me in Andover, and the upshot was that the March 1963 issue of the *Reader's Digest* carried her article on the Colorado school entitled "Outward Bound: Rugged Challenge for Teen-Agers."

Bonanza! The issue was hardly out in the mails and on the newsstands when a torrent of letters and applications, sometimes with money enclosed, poured into the small school office that Froelicher had established at Colorado Academy. Helen Rawalt, who was operating the office, had to be given additional help just to handle the mail. Within a month all the courses were filled and had waiting lists. Applicants turned down for lack of room were offered places in a 1964 course, and most enrolled. A steady flow of mail continued through the summer and did not tail off until the new year.

School closed, and I flew to Ely, Minnesota, to see the Pieh camp and get an idea of the terrain. The camp was called Shining Trails, derived from the Ojibwa Indian word for "spirit roads." Jerry Pieh and I took off in an outboard motorboat, switched to a canoe, and paddled for hours to an overnight bivouac. I got a feel for the mode of travel, the country, and the climate. The Superior–Quetico Wilderness is a vast latticework of lakes, streams, and forest, with virtually impenetrable bush, extending well up into Canada. Wild, beautiful, dramatic country. Reporting back, I noted that the Minnesota–Canadian terrain differed greatly from that of Colorado. At that time no rocks suitable for climbing had been found. (In the end, that was not a problem; there is good rock climbing in the area.) Developing a school program based on canoeing expeditions in that unique wilderness would call for a creative new adaptation of the Outward Bound method. I gave my opinion that the Piehs had the understanding, expertise, and creativity needed to establish an Outward Bound school. Soon afterward Jerry visited Marble, where he had a good look at the Colorado program in action. He did his first rock climbing, under Tapley's tutelage, and rappelled a 300-foot rock face. He got advice from Nold, Tapley, and others. The plan was to apply for a Minnesota Outward Bound charter in the fall.

At Colorado, C-4 had opened with more than double the 1962 enrollment, and a considerably enlarged instructor staff. I arrived at Marble in July. Anxious to upgrade my qualifications for taking over the directorship from Joe Nold, I went early to participate as an observer in the C-5 course. Joe was spending much of his time in the field, giving top priority to directing the mountain program, and I assumed I would be expected to do the same. Having hiked and camped through the mountains of New England for years, I considered myself a competent outdoorsman, but the Rockies were something else. I had never been on a really big mountain, had never climbed a rock face, or rappelled, or been exposed to the risk of a precipitous fall, or scaled a high peak. I had the average person's fear of heights. I was forty-three, and not in the best of shape. I went to my Marble assignment with considerable apprehension. But I was set on being a participant as well as observer with that patrol of teenagers, on having my own successful Outward Bound experience.

It was, indeed, not easy. Things like the ropes course I could handle. What I did not have was the endurance to stay with those youngsters. The morning run was agony. I very much minded the thinness of the oxygen supply at 9,000 feet. I was getting up at 5:30, a half hour before the school, to gain a head start on the run and dip. When I was part way at my own pace, the kids would pass me. I would stop behind a bush to vomit. My lungs were raw, my head ached, my teeth ached. Through the day's drive, drive, drive, I was miserable. Worst of all was the climbing. We were practicing for our first alpine expedition. The higher we went, the harder it was for me to keep up. I wondered about my ability to stay with the patrol for five days when we climbed to fourteen thousand feet. But I was determined not to appear inadequate.

The evening before the expedition was to take off, one of the instructors came into the mess hall and said, "I'm going on the alpine tomorrow. I wish I could go into town and spend the night with my family, but I have the duty." Town was Glenwood Springs, thirty miles away. I said, "What's involved in the duty?" He said, "All you have to do is be there, tend the phone, and at ten o'clock turn out the lights in the tent area." I said, "I'll take the duty for you. Show me how to turn out the lights." He took me up to the students' tent area and showed me where the switch was located on an aspen tree. When the time came, I walked the sixty yards or so from the first-aid tent, where I had been talking with Paul Petzoldt, and pulled the switch. Not having thought to bring a flashlight, I found myself in complete darkness. Feeling my way back, I stepped into a hole that had been dug that day for a new water line. As I hit bottom, pain stabbed through my left leg. Getting up on my right foot, I found I could not put weight on the other. I worked myself out of the hole and lay on the ground with the hurt leg raised, to check any internal bleeding and hold down the swelling. After a while I was able to hail someone headed for the latrine, who went for help. They carried me to the aid tent. By then the leg was considerably swollen. The consensus was that it was broken.

I lay on the tent floor with the leg propped up on a cot. Petzoldt packed it in ice and gave me a shot of morphine. He asked if I had any whiskey. To mix whiskey and anesthetic, he said, violated every canon of first aid, but maybe it would cheer me up. I told him where I had a bottle cached. He sat and talked with me for hours, and we finished off the bottle. I was flat on my back, looking up at the ridge pole of the tent, and at about 1 A.M. the pole started to travel. It moved from right to left at a forty-mile-an-hour speed without stopping. Strangely, it never reached the side of the tent.

In the morning they took me in a jeep to the hospital at Glenwood Springs. The X rays showed a broken tibia about eight inches above the ankle. The hospital was Amish; they took good care of me. Two days later I flew to Eugene, Oregon, where a Peace Corps group that was coming to Marble later were in training at the state university. They were gathered in an auditorium to hear me, and when I came out on the stage on crutches with my leg in a cast, they greeted me with groans. I was not the most propitious image that Outward Bound could have sent to brief those volunteers.

In the end the accident proved serendipitous. When I took over at C-6, I could not be out in the field, where I would not have been any good anyway. Except for forays on horseback, I had to stay at the base and be an administrative type, which was a useful thing for the program at that point. The rapid expansion from the year before had made for logistical, personnel, and other organizational problems, and someone was needed to run things from an overall vantage point.

That second summer the school was in process of finding its own identity. Ralph Clough was still on hand, helping it to hold to the basic Outward Bound scheme, and it still closely resembled the British model. That was desirable as a foundation, but in the nature of things, with experience and time, U.S. Outward Bound was sure to acquire its own distinctive character. This was beginning to happen, particularly as the second-year members of the staff increasingly got their own feel of the Outward Bound dynamic.

Petzoldt's presence as mountaineering instructor was a valuable addition. In Petzoldt and Tapley the Colorado school had two of the country's finest outdoorsmen. While Petzoldt himself defers to Tapley's sheer versatility, Paul brought to the school a superb expertise in his mountain expedition specialty. This was not simply because his involvement exposed instructors and students to the experience-garnered wisdom of a veteran mounaineer of the first rank. It was more particularly due to Petzoldt's having massaged that experience with an analytical turn of mind that, together with his fervor for communicating his love of the wild outdoors and a gift of communication, made him a fine teacher of wilderness adventuring. He was then fifty-five years old, a big bear of a man in full vigor. Even today, when he has done his three score and ten, were I on a mountain under conditions of dire hazard, there is no one I would rather be with. As a youth Paul was the first person to climb Wyoming's Grand Teton in the winter; the mountain still often turns back efforts to duplicate that feat. Paul has never forgotten that in that successful trip of his youth he almost lost his life. At the heart of his attributes is a deep understanding, gained in a long companionship with risk, of the hard realities of safeguarding others and oneself in undertakings that are inherently dangerous. Coming out of his own particular environment, he was not wholly sympathetic to the British course model. But he had a wholehearted commitment to the Outward Bound concept of challenging young people to stretch their capabilities.

I recall a time in Lead King Basin (perhaps it was the following year) when I took a teaching lesson from Tapley. We were at supper with two patrols. It was raining, on the verge of freezing, and the students had had difficulty starting a fire. Some of the rain was coming down snow, and it was so cold and miserable that we stood up to eat. Sucking on his pipe as he and I chatted, Tap took a knife from his belt. Holding the blade between thumb and forefinger, he winged it across an open space into a log by the cook-fire. At the *thk!* sound of the knife point driving into the log, the kids perked up their heads. Tap walked over, pulled the knife out, came back, went on talking and sucking on his pipe. Pretty soon he threw the knife again, stuck it in the same place in the log. This time, as he came back, one of the kids asked, "Tap, have you ever killed a deer with a knife?" "Yes." "How did it happen?"

"Matter of fact," he said, "it was a night pretty much like this, cold and rainy. When you camp out on a night like this, your problem is fire. How you going to start a fire? It's easier if you're prepared. You all know about snapping off the dry dead wood under the branches of the hemlock or the Engelmann spruce. That's the first thing you do." He reached into his pocket. "You get real small wood in three different sizes, like this. But if you're really prepared, you never go into the woods without a mouse's nest, like this." Out of another pocket he took a mouse's nest and blew into it. "A mouse's nest is very flammable. You puff it out, so there will be a lot of air circulation through it."

"Hey, Tap, how about that deer?"

Tap was down on the ground now. "You put the smallest wood on top of the mouse's nest. Then the next size, but you hold the third. When you light the nest, your head should be at ground level so you can blow just a little bit." He had the fire going and was adding the larger pieces. "Just as I had my fire started, this buck walked into my camp and stood there. I moved my hand slowly and got my knife out. Slowly I raised my hand like this." Wow, he stuck that knife in the same place in the same log for the third time. Then he said, "I dropped my head to the ground and didn't move a muscle."

The kids were all questions. "Why'd you do that, Tap?" "Were you afraid to move?" "Were you afraid the deer would run and you'd have to chase it?" Tap said, "And then the deer's head sagged. Sagged. Sagged and dropped, and his legs buckled and he went down." The fire was burning briskly in the rain as he arose. "You want to remember the whole thing is one of air circulating through dry material." I doubt that any of us who were there have forgotten how to build a fire in the rain.

That summer Tapley's solo innovation had been extended to three days and three nights. When the C-6 solo was coming up, we held a staff meeting to prepare for it. Going around the circle to get ideas from each instructor, I happened to ask one if he had ever had that kind of experience. He said he had spent many hours in the woods. I asked him if he had ever spent seventy-two hours completely on his own, out of sight and sound of humanity, and he said, well, he had been in the woods all his life. I quizzed the others and got similar answers. Not one had ever had three days in the wilderness entirely by himself. I said, "I'll tell you what we're going to do," and someone said, "Oh, no!" There was a groan, and I said, "Yes," and they said, "How about you?" I said, "That means me too." On the day the solo started, Frank Menendez loaded me, my pack, and my crutches on a horse and led me on his horse up into Fravert's Basin and dumped me off, to live with myself for three days and three nights.

The great discovery I got from that experience was that on a wilderness solo you become very much in tune with your environment in a way that makes you realize how out of tune you are with your everyday environment. I was picking wild currants. I would pull them off the bush with one hand and pop them into my mouth, and every now and then my head would lift up, and I would be listening to things, or for things, that I had never listened to before. Maybe a breeze stirred, or a change in the wind's direction suddenly brought tree noises or amplified brook sounds, or perhaps there was an animal or insect sound or a bird song. Whatever it might be, my head would lift up, and I would open my mouth to hear better. At the same time I would stare; with my eyes stationary, it was easier to catch sight of anything that was moving. It hit me that I was far more aware of my environment than ever before in my life, acutely tuned in to everything around me. Then I got to laughing at myself, because I realized I was behaving just the way a deer does. I would browse a bit, and my head would lift up, and turn; I would stare, then go back to browsing. At no time was I startled; I was just intensely responsive to the matrix in which I was living.

Then I remembered Bill Coffin's story of his experience on the rock face. When he visited Eskdale, they introduced him to rock climbing. Like many of us, Bill has a great fear of heights. In the O.S.S. he had made parachute jumps with few qualms; it is when you are connected to the ground, he tells you, that heights can be psychologically formidable. He was well up the rock face, and above they were calling (no doubt with a dash of British glee), "Come along, old chap. Come along, Yank." Not finding a new hold to come along by, Bill says, he was in a state of terror, his face a burst of sweat. As he clung there, the granite rock suddenly jumped out in startling focus. He saw the crystalline structure, the color and composition of the individual grains, the marvelous way they interlocked. He had never looked at a rock in that way before. He found himself wondering what else he had been missing by failing to see. And then, he said, Outward Bound hit him. Because he wondered what he had been missing in the faces of the parishioners he had counseled.

Browsing like a deer on currants, my head popping up, tuned into my environment, I wondered in turn, as I recalled Bill's story, what I had been missing in my Andover environment, my family environment. It made me wonder what it takes to enhance sensitivity to that degree. As Coffin had, I got a new, revealing message. It was worth its weight in gold, for it made me realize how meaningful the solo could be. I became a persuasive advocate of incorporating the three-day solo in all Outward Bound courses.

Toward the end of the summer we had a visitor whom I was glad to get to know. Bill Byrd, an Oregon educator, had just finished a twenty-month stint as director of the Peace Corps training camp in Puerto Rico and was returning home. Coming away from Arecibo with a continuing interest in Outward Bound, he stopped off at Marble to learn more about what we were doing. I had pretty much lost track of what was happening in Puerto Rico after Bill Coffin, having fulfilled his commitment to see the Peace Corps undertaking through its first two training cycles, returned to Yale. Byrd's visit was my first good chance to catch up on the Arecibo story.

Soon after Coffin's departure the training center closed down for a month of breath-catching. It reopened in January 1962 under the directorship of Grant Venn, who had been president of Western State College in Gunnison, Colorado. Byrd was a new staff member. Shriver's charge to him shows that his thinking about the purpose of the Puerto Rican operation had not changed since the day of our first meeting. He told Byrd: "Somewhere in the training program we have to do two contradictory things. We have to test them at the same time that we build them. In one and the same program you test an individual's ability to face up, and you reenforce his ability to do so. That's what I want you to go down there and do." A few months later, when Venn became ill and had to resign, Byrd was appointed director.

For a time Byrd and Fred Lanoue were roommates. The two men hit it off beautifully; Freddy was one of Bill's happy memories. Lanoue had his critics, but Byrd was not one of them: "A lot of our own staff objected to Fred's tactics as overzealous. He would pin his critics right to the wall. He'd say, 'You son of a bitch, you do that person a disservice to allow him to go away fearing the water.' And he was absolutely right. That was our obligation there. If we didn't meet it, we were sentencing those people to a lifetime of fear. Lanoue's uncompromising commitment was a great lesson for the staff people who were perceptive enough to catch on. I fought the same thing on the rocks. A lot of people have the same fear of heights that they do of water, and they wouldn't rappel. I stayed out there on the rappelling cliffs for nine hours, to get them over that cliff. We got them over. There wasn't a single person who came to the Puerto Rico center who didn't rappel. You let people be conquered by their fear, and you sentence them to loss of a part of their lives they're never going to realize. You can enrich a person's life a hundredfold when he gets through with this hang-up. That's what you have to keep your sights on—not the immediate small trauma that he has to go through to get there." Byrd made that statement much later than 1963, after years as director of an Outward Bound school. There are those in Outward Bound who would agree with it wholeheartedly; there are others who would disagree that there is no productive alternative to dealing with an individual's fears by immersing him in the feared element.* The issue makes for keen debate when both proponents argue from thoughtful conviction. It is perhaps one of those moot issues where personality, temperament, and subtleties of method may decisively influence the rightness or wrongness of an action principle.

---

* For a differing, also authentic Outward Bound view, see "A Gestalt Conundrum: Lady on the Rocks or Rockclimbing as Self-Discovery" by John Huie, director of the North Carolina Outward Bound School, in *OBA News*, Summer 1977.

A School in Minnesota

≡≡✕≡≡✕≡≡✕≡≡✕≡≡✕≡≡✕≡≡✕≡≡✕≡≡✕≡≡✕≡≡

*My son attended Minnesota Outward Bound two years
ago. . . . He arrived in Duluth airport a little boy,
frightened, lacking self-confidence, angry with the world,
and with no ability to persevere. He bombed out of
high school in his junior year. His month with MOBS
produced all the miracles one might wish for, and on a
lasting basis. He knows he's someone special . . . even
changed his posture to be more erect. He has forgotten
the words "I quit," persists in difficult tasks until he is
on top of them. He has staying power to reach for
distant objectives. He has tolerance for the flaws in
others. He has accepted society as necessary and stimulating. He has learned his real limits are much greater
than he ever thought possible. Ben graduated in June
from high school with honors. May you continue to
supply others those conditions that stimulate people to
reach their potential.*

—Letter from a Minnesota student's parent

I returned East to open up the new Outward Bound headquarters in New Haven, Connecticut. Bill Coffin, now an Atlantic
Foundation trustee, had made office space available in Yale's
Dwight Hall. Helen Rawalt came with me on a two-month loan
from the Colorado School. My charge from the Atlantic Foundation trustees was to see that the Colorado School opened with
a full enrollment the following June, to guide establishment of

118

additional schools, conduct public relations, raise scholarships, and develop an alumni organization.

During the summer Johnny Kemper and Coffin had followed up my visit to the Pieh camp in Minnesota. They saw Shining Trails in operation, did a canoe reconnaissance and got a dunking, had a good look at the Quetico Wilderness from the air, and discussed an arrangement for leasing the facilities from the Pieh family. The aerial reconnaissance northward into Canada gave them an awareness of the utter wildness of the country, where an expedition could go days without encountering another human.

Coffin also had another matter on his mind. Before becoming headmaster of the Anniston School, Bob Pieh had taught at the Indian Springs School in Alabama, which had been founded with money left by a Birmingham industrialist to create a model for secondary education in the state. Coffin was aware that the terms of the will originally restricted attendance to "white Caucasians." He had no sooner arrived at Shining Trails than he put the question to Pieh: What was a Yankee like him with his humanistic Antioch background doing in a school that placed such restrictions on its student body? Bob could satisfy him on that score because diligent efforts by trustees and faculty had succeeded in getting around the restrictive covenant, first for Jewish youngsters, and eventually for blacks.

Kemper and Coffin came away satisfied that the Pieh proposal was sound. Kemper made a second trip, to Minneapolis and St. Paul, where he undertook to interest a group of Andover alumni and others in helping to form a board of trustees for the proposed new school. Among them was Louis F. "Bo" Polk, one of the Twin Cities' brightest young businessmen. At thirty-two Polk was a vice-president of General Mills.

On October 7, 1963, the Atlantic Foundation approved formation of the Minnesota Outward Bound School, to be opened the following summer. At a meeting two months later the Piehs made a progress report that included the names of the fifteen men comprising the school's board of trustees, with Polk as chairman. In addition to his own dynamic energies, Polk was able to involve other resources at General Mills. One of the people he brought on the board was John Burger, a member of the company's public relations department. Although Pieh was resigning his school post in order to be a full-time director of the Minnesota School, he had to finish out the school year in Alabama. Polk, Burger, and other members of Polk's staff became the *ad hoc* staff for the school in the months before it opened, responsible for publicity, promotion, scholarships, and recruitment. Burger, working at the task virtually full time, did a splendid job in getting out publicity and literature and building community support. I would go out to the Twin Cities, and John would have a staggering schedule of meetings set up for me, as many as four in a day. John would always be in the back of the room when I talked, giving me a three-minute sign, two, one, and then the cut gesture. He was a tiger on preventing overkill of an audience.

An Andover alumnus and former Andover teacher in Minneapolis whom Kemper had had no difficulty in proselyting was A. Lachlan Reed. Because a relative had married a former Gordonstoun student who idolized Kurt Hahn, Lach was already well aware of Hahn's work. He took on with Polk the task of raising funds to cover needed capital expenditures for construction and equipment. General Mills also helped by putting up $7,500 for scholarships for sons of their employees around the country. The Avalon Foundation and the Old Dominion Foundation each made a seeding grant of $25,000; $10,000 of the total was to help support Outward Bound Inc., which had just been established, the balance of $40,000 going to the school's scholarship fund.

During the spring school vacation the Piehs flew overseas for a round of visits to the British Outward Bound schools. They signed on Ralph Clough and Colin Bolton, an instructor at Ullswater, for the Minnesota staff. The Minnesotans too recognized the value of using British instructors to facilitate transplant of the Outward Bound philosophy and method to American soil. In June the Minnesota Outward Bound School opened the first of the summer's two courses with an enrollment of ninety-six students comprising eight twelve-man "brigades."

For Bob Pieh the Minnesota beginning was the "catching of a train for perhaps an infinite journey" that he very much wanted to be on. He had grown up in Madison, Wisconsin. A natural athlete, he played all sports avidly. Also, from when he was very young, he nurtured his growth on an affinity for the out-of-doors.

"I found a lot of religion in natural phenomena," he says. "This grounded my concepts of God and ethical development." The Pieh family was hit hard by the Depression. After his father's death during his senior year of high school, Bob attended the University of Wisconsin part-time while working for the city of Madison. He was made assistant to the city's recreation director, became involved in adult education, worked nights on a newspaper sports desk.

Browsing in the university library, Bob happened on something Kurt Hahn had written. Impressed, he continued to collect Hahn items. When he graduated from Wisconsin with a B.S. in biology, he had enough other credits to qualify him also to teach English, history, or physical education. A few years after joining the faculty of Antioch College in Ohio he was made chairman of its health, physical education, and recreation department, directing the academic program for students in the field and coordinating physical education for the student body. In the latter role Bob extended the available electives far beyond conventional sports. He encouraged students to play the games of other nations as a way to gain insight into foreign cultures. He developed an "open country" program, a mix of trekking, campcraft, canoeing, and other outdoor activities, that became more popular than any of the standard sports. There were also teams organized as clubs that represented the college, sometimes students and faculty together. Bob played on the soccer team. He sought ways to use physical education to help build a genuine college community:

"We encouraged the faculty to play too, and made sure they didn't feel inferior if they needed to learn skills or improve themselves physically. Our conditioning program included Swedish and Danish free exercises and some yoga. We were interested in why the Eastern yogi advocated physical purification before advancing toward the spiritual. At that time there wasn't much in print on yoga—I had to write the universities in Calcutta and Bombay. So we had a healthy mix, a crazy quilt of experience that I think Kurt Hahn would have approved."

In 1957 Pieh went to Alabama. Summers he ran wilderness outposts for private camps, leading their youngsters on canoe trips into the Quetico. He bought the Minnesota property, where the Pieh family developed a camp-and-canoe expedition base for families and student groups. Continuing to glean Kurt Hahn material, he became aware of the roots of Outward Bound in England and felt he was using a kindred approach in his own educational efforts. Then one day he read in *Time* magazine that a U.S. Outward Bound school had been started in Colorado. Suddenly events seemed to be passing him by. "I had this strong feeling that the train was starting to leave the station. I told myself, if this really represents what you most want to do, you'd better act." That was when he wrote to Kemper.

In that first summer of 1964 the Minnesota School operated under physical handicaps. New construction was incomplete. A generator provided limited electricity. The water system, while approved, was improvised. Meals had to be cooked in the old resort main building and carried up to the unfinished dining hall during the first course. Pieh gave the students a sense of belonging by making the unfinished tasks part of the curriculum.

None of these physical shortcomings at Homeplace—the name the Piehs gave to the school base at Ely—diminished the positive aspects of the program. The students received a ten-day basic training in canoe fundamentals, swimming, drownproofing, water rescue, camping and cooking skills, map and compass route-finding, fire fighting, and survival technique, and took short training expeditions. A spectacular ropes course and a variety of initiative tests built positive attitudes and teamwork. An inter-brigade competition was built into the activities. After the training period each brigade took off on a long canoeing expedition, heading up into the Canadian wilderness. Two men to a canoe, six canoes per brigade, and a seventh for the instructor and his assistant. The routes threading a maze formed by rivers and lakes. The portages often exceedingly difficult, the dense bush testing determination and endurance, the arduous day's run sometimes extending into the long northern twilight. A three-day solo, followed by a final expedition, the brigade making its way back to Homeplace on its own. The marathon, the students writing their course impressions, and home.

The shaping process I observed at Minnesota renewed my awareness, acquired in my British exposure, that each school, while adhering to the essential concept, develops its particular personality and ambiance. This is partly a matter of geography and environment, but mostly, I think, the product of the leadership. The Piehs put their own mark on Homeplace and the wilderness activities. In a later time Jerry Pieh was to think back: "U.S. Outward Bound was then heavily into the challenge issues. There was a heavy emphasis on that in the beginning, and I think rightfully so. We also had a hidden agenda. We wanted to emphasize as much the beauty of nature and the importance of human relationships and caring for other people as we did the physical side of the program. We consciously did things that were intended to help kids appreciate natural beauty, and to emphasize humanistic kinds of values."

Among the students in M-1 were Lach Reed's eldest son and a school friend. Lach remembers: "The friend was the son of a millionaire, handsome, bright, a good athlete, and obnoxiously conceited. A spoiled rich kid. I'll never forget picking up those two at the Greyhound station when they came back from their course. My son said, 'Gee, Dad, it was a great experience,' and he and this boy got in the back seat. I said to his friend, 'How was it for you?' 'Mr. Reed,' he said, 'it's the greatest experience I ever had. For the first time I realize what a horse's ass I've been all my life."

Lach, who was with the Honeywell Corporation, got a second insight that first year into the salutary influence Outward Bound could have on a youngster. James Binger, Honeywell president, gave money for two scholarships and told Lach to select the recipients, preferably from a Honeywell family. "Just about then a toolmaker in my department came to me and said, 'I hear you're helping to start a survival camp or something up north. I have a son who's not worth the powder to blow him up. He's sixteen, he quit high school at fourteen, he lies in bed all day smoking cigarettes and is out all night. I've tried everything, and he's just a mess. Would you take him?' I called Bob Pieh and told him about this kid and the scholarship, and Bob said, 'Sure.' I saw the boy up there at the start of his course, and he did bear out his father's just-a-mess description. The boy completed that course, came home and got a job right away, and enrolled in high school at night. His father said to me, 'Lach, it's absolutely unbelievable how that kid has changed!' I kept track of him for several years. He finished high school and the last I knew he was still doing fine."

*   *   *

On January 9, 1964, incorporation papers were drawn up creating Outward Bound Inc. They provided for OBI, as it would come to be known, to take over the Outward Bound responsibilities that the Atlantic Foundation had been discharging. The incorporators were the Rev. William S. Coffin Jr., John M. Kemper, Mrs. Ellen Z. McCloy, Joshua L. Miner, John P. Stevens Jr. These five were named trustees, along with General Bruce C. Clarke, H. Wentworth Eldredge, F. Charles Froelicher, Thomas B. Hartmann, and Fred I. Kent II. At the first trustee meeting I was elected president of OBI. It was a full-time salaried position; I was now wholly committed to Outward Bound and its future growth and welfare.

In June we returned to Andover, where the Outward Bound headquarters would be located for the next six years.

A Tragedy

For sorrow ends not when it seemeth done.
—RICHARD II

Seeing the Minnesota School in action, getting feedback from students and parents, made it clear that the Outward Bound dynamic worked as aptly in lake as in mountain country. There was, however, a distinction. The high mountain vistas proclaim their hazards. The dangers implicit in those soaring peaks are all too apparent; one needs no special warning to know they are there. The Quetico, on the other hand, its placid waters set like jewels in the endless bush, has an illusory benign quality. One forgets that of all the earthly substances, water is the most inimical to man. It was in that seemingly kind northern country we suffered our first fatal accident and were taught our first harsh safety lesson.

In August I was visiting the Colorado School when I received a telephone message that hit like a blow to the head. A student in Minnesota's M-2 course had drowned. When I reached Ely the next evening, I heard the story of what will always remain an unexplained tragedy. After a day of paddling on the ninth day of the course two students, Dan Lucas and Larry Hanson, had been placed by their instructors on the shore of a fairly small lake for an overnight "duo," as a preparation for their forth-coming solo experience. While Larry made shelter and other preparations, Dan went out in the canoe to try to catch fish for supper (an action not in accord with the school's strict rules governing one-man canoeing). When he was two hundred yards

125

or more offshore, he either fell or jumped from the canoe. The only witnesses were Hanson and another student on the opposite shore. They both agreed they saw Dan in the water but differed as to the circumstances. Hanson said that he heard a banging noise and saw Lucas kneeling in the canoe and clutching something "black and white and looked like a loon," and that Lucas then fell out of the craft. (On the way to the duo site, according to Hanson, Dan had suggested they might catch a loon.) The other student said that Lucas seemed to get in and out of the canoe several times, that he suddenly was in the water with the canoe drifting away. Both agreed there was a yell and a whistle but that they sounded more like cries of triumph than calls for help. They agreed, and this was confirmed by others, that later a loon was swimming in the water near the empty canoe.

When Hanson realized that Lucas was in trouble, he gave the distress call of three shouts. Three youths who heard the call paddled to where the canoe was drifting, but found no sign of Lucas other than his floating paddle. A search of the water directed by the instructors proved fruitless. Early the following morning Jerry Pieh arrived at the lake to organize an ongoing search. Scuba divers of the Silver Bay Rescue Squad were flown in and continued for days to look for the body without success. Other searches were conducted in the woods around the lake.

As the days dragged by with no positive result, I spent considerable time with Joseph Lucas, Dan's father. In the timeless setting of lake and forest we talked about life and its uncertainties, about parents and children, their hopes and aspirations, and the cruel forces that can suddenly, brutally take charge. A splendid man, he bore no ill will against the school for what had happened. Dan was a husky, athletic boy and had been a leader in looking out for other boys in his brigade less naturally able than himself. He had been ranked a competent swimmer of average ability and had successfully undergone the school's drownproofing and water safety training, including the test of remaining afloat for forty-five minutes. He had been taught what to do if a capsizing or loss of balance put him in the water—the first principle being to stay with the canoe, which is a natural life raft. There seemed to be no logical reason for his having drowned.

It is possible, we knew, for a person to inhale only a few drops of water into his windpipe and have his breathing automatically shut off. Virtually everyone has had the experience of a drink going down "the wrong way," precipitating a fit of gasping and coughing. The cough is the body's effort to expel any foreign body from the windpipe. Unless water that has entered the windpipe is dislodged, a person who has gone overboard can be asphyxiated in two to five minutes even while remaining at the surface. But the prevailing placid conditions and Dan's natural abilities seemed to cast doubt on that possibility. There was the strange suggestion that Dan had been grappling with a loon and that this somehow accounted for the accident, but the weight of the evidence was against that hypothesis as well. It was because the drowning was so hard to explain that we also combed the land areas.

Dan's body was finally discovered by state fish and game personnel twelve days after the mishap. The autopsy concluded that death was due to drowning, that there was no other finding to explain the death, no evidence of a major injury or trauma. I had concluded that it was OBI's responsibility to have the accident investigated by a committee of persons not associated with the school, and Bo Polk and Bob Pieh concurred. I named a three-man team—Philip Allen, an Andover neighbor who was a Hurricane Island trustee, William Dabney, a trustee of the Colorado School, and John McLane Jr., an attorney from Manchester, New Hampshire, whose son was enrolled at Colorado that summer. Assembling the evidence, the investigators rejected the possibility that young Lucas had caught a loon—on the grounds that loons are almost impossible to catch from any kind of a boat, that they are extremely dangerous birds to fool with, capable of inflicting serious injury with their powerful neck and sharp beak, and that there were no injury marks on Dan's body. They concluded that he accidentally fell out of the canoe for some unknown reason, was inhibited by the weight of his clothing, and inhaled water and became asphyxiated within a few minutes, thus preventing him from making any attempt to save himself.

Subsequently I had a letter from Fred Lanoue, in response to the copy of the investigating committee's report I sent him. I cannot know whether any of Fred's theorizing was correct with regard to the Lucas boy's death, but the points that he made are certainly cogent to water safety. He did not agree that the hampering clothes, including leather boots, were a major factor contributing to the drowning and suggested the possibility of three additional factors. One, which would account for Dan's gyrations in the canoe, was cramps—quite common, Fred said, at the end of the first day of a canoe trip with relatively inexperienced paddlers. Another factor he thought could have played a part was an attempt by Dan to remove his shoes. "When one feels the hampering effect of full clothes," he wrote, "the inadequacy of the kick contribution is immediately obvious, and so the first effort is always made to kick off the shoes. Using hands to remove shoes is lethal because one may be sinking all the time, whereas when attempting to remove clothes the legs are working all the time to remain at the surface. I have personally rescued a number of fair swimmers in pools and lakes from this specific situation." A possible third factor, he suggested, was the complication of expelling water from the throat: "With no other complications present, a certain amount of success is probable by the usual orthodox up-hill coughing with the head out of the water and face up. Down-hill coughing with the head in the water is the only sure way to clear the throat."

U.S. Outward Bound's first fatal accident made us aware, in a way nothing else could, how simultaneously important and difficult the problems of safety in our program were going to be. The tragedy's many lessons included one of the most basic—that it is when the hazard is not obvious, or does not appear to exist, that it may most readily exact its toll. Unfortunately, this is not a lesson that any of us tends naturally to absorb from the experience of others; it is among the most difficult to teach and so save the learner the cost of having to learn it through personal experience.

One of the services performed by Ralph Clough and other instructors who came from England to help launch U.S. Outward Bound was to make the school staffs conscious of the fine safety tradition they were inheriting from the British movement. The schools gratefully accepted from the British Outward Bound Trust that body's safety policy, which provided a well-articulated set of guiding principles. The policy statement opens with the explanation that since Outward Bound students are encouraged to engage in activities where the risk of accident may be greater than in their normal way of life, those charged with their train-

ing have a special responsibility to take adequate, continuous
care to protect them against accidents. The principle, it continues, is not to avoid activities involving danger but to prepare
students, both by technical training and physical fitness, to deal
competently with the risk. But hazards should not be sought for
their own sake; they should be forestalled as far as possible, mastered through competence if they come. Safety, the policy states,
is an integral part of Outward Bound's training and experiential
process, exemplified by the words and action of each instructor.
It involves not only overt precautions to prevent accidents but
also a "what if?" attitude toward every experience. At its heart
the policy states: *"The aim is to teach that the more adventurous
an undertaking is, the more care and prudence it calls for if it is
to succeed."*

Each school implemented these principles by prescribing safe
practices for its particular environment and courses, and by diligent instructor training and student instruction. Increasingly
with the passing years, the directors coordinated their safety
thinking and policies, and the schools exchanged information
about their experiences of encountering hazard and the knowledge they gained in dealing with it. In time this led to the formulation and servicing of a national safety policy that has been
much admired in the outdoor-pursuit and education communities.

A Sea School

The sea, the granite quarries—nature herself—was seen not as something to be feared as the enemy but to be respected and even loved. You were taught to be in concert with nature. The sea, the rocks, the physical elements of nature were the training tools. You were not being trained to be an expert sailor or rock climber but rather how to use your knowledge and respect for them to make you a better person.

—From a sermon based on his Hurricane Island experience preached by the Rev. Thomas B. Kennedy in Trinity Church, Boston

It has been said of Peter Willauer that had he been born one hundred and fifty years sooner, he would have been a whaling captain. His mother was a great-niece of Winslow Homer and had grown up in Prouts Neck on the coast of Maine. Like his architect father before him, Peter spent his boyhood summers at Prouts Neck. He learned early to handle small boats, won three national junior sailing championships and competed on the U.S. Olympic sailing team. At Princeton he did Navy ROTC; for his required two-year service duty following graduation, he was appointed sailing instructor at the Naval Academy in Annapolis. He lived aboard a barracks ship where he supervised the black and Filipino sailors who, in the Navy's way at that time, were mess stewards at the Academy; here he acquired some insights into race relationships.

His duty completed, Willauer went back to Princeton to work

in the admissions office, decided to be a teacher, and won a teaching fellowship in mathematics at Phillips Academy. That was a good trick, since his college major had been international studies. At Andover he was much taken by the enthusiastic talk about Outward Bound from Reagh Wetmore and me. In particular, he was entranced by the fact that the original school at Aberdovey was sea-based. He spent the 1960–61 year at Harvard, earning his master's in education, and took a teaching and admissions job at the Groton School, where he also coached football, hockey, and crew. He had come out of Harvard not sure whether he wanted to teach in a public or private school. What decided him on Groton was the chance to work with John Crocker, one of the century's great headmasters. "Jack was an inspirational character for Betty and me," Peter says. "He was a unique, special human being. His teaching and example as a terrific Christian and wonderful person were very much a part of why we were there."

During school vacations Willauer worked at Prouts Neck as manager of the yacht club's summer activities, coaching junior sailing and running the club's boatyard. Now he began to be uncomfortable about a sense of blandness in his life: "I was getting a little uptight with the summer bit of the social community, and finding that the year-round program had a sameness that made me conscious of how remote it all was from the rest of the world." In the 1962–63 school year he was director of admissions at Groton. I ran into him at a conference of admissions officers, and naturally I had to fill him in on the exciting developments on the Outward Bound front. When I told him that we were hoping to see a school get started in the East, he said, "Why don't you have a sea school?" We spent a good part of the conference kicking that around. In the spring he came over to Andover to tell Kemper and me that he was seriously interested in starting a school. We told him to get himself a board of trustees and a site and come back.

In Prouts Neck that summer, he read Kurt Hahn and did a lot of thinking about the kind of school he might create: "I knew I wanted a school based on a vessel that students could be independent in without having a captain aboard, so I discounted the large-vessel approach. That pointed to some kind of pulling boat that a dozen or so people could sail or, if there was no wind, could row. My thinking was influenced by a friend at Prouts

Neck named Fritz Osther, a brilliant young scientist who had had a great career at Harvard and was working for Avco. He was a fine person to bounce ideas off and he helped me research the pulling-boat idea. Another who guided me was Seymour Alden, a friend who had had my job at the yacht club before me, and who would be with us at Hurricane Island until he died. Seymour was a good listener and a steadying influence on a brash young man. Dan Bickford, whom I had known at Annapolis, and Rog Sherbrook, a Princeton sailing friend, helped to think through a program, and I had help from other Navy and sailing friends. Dick Homer, an architect friend of my father, got intrigued. Jack Crocker, who knew Kurt Hahn—Hahn had visited his school a couple of times—was giving me lots of encouragement. It was Crocker who gave us the key lead to a site."

Peter was envisioning an island as probably the best kind of location for his school. The coast was getting built up, and he liked the idea of the dramatic separation an island would give both mind and body. "The mystique you have in being isolated. Also, I realized we couldn't put a nonsailor in a boat all day, that you had to start out slowly and learn skills, leading up to expeditions at sea. So we would need a solid program on land as well as on water. I particularly liked the idea of drownproofing, which I had learned about from Reagh Wetmore. I thought it would tie into the curriculum nicely, and that it was a wonderful activity for the individual, as against the group stress experiences we were sure to get in a boat. I didn't know anything about rock climbing, but I recognized it was virtually a standard part of an Outward Bound program, so I felt we would want access to suitable rocks. I knew about the solo idea they had come up with in Colorado, and I bought that."

Jack Crocker summered at Vinalhaven, an island in Penobscot Bay off Rockland, on the central Maine coast. He suggested to Peter that Hurricane Island, a small island south of Vinalhaven, ought to meet his specifications. Hurricane had once been the location of an important granite-quarrying community; the Library of Congress building is one of the structures built late in the nineteenth century of Hurricane Island granite. The stone had run out, the stoneworkers had left, and the island had been uninhabited for decades. Because the excavated quarry was a natural catch basin for rainwater, it was well known to yachtsmen cruising in Penobscot Bay, who often put ashore to do laundry and take fresh water aboard.

In September Peter and Betty Willauer sailed from Prouts Neck "down east" to Hurricane Island. "It was blowing like hell from the northeast," Willauer recalls, "and we couldn't get ashore on what's now the main pier and Valley Cove side. We anchored over on the opposite, stone-beach side, off the quarry. We couldn't keep the anchor down, so Betty stayed with the boat while I rowed ashore and did a ninety-minute reconnaissance. I saw these granite cliffs and the fresh water, and the foundations of the old quarry village, and the mostly wooded island with the good harbor, and I thought, 'Gee, this is a natural!' and rowed back to the boat. I went down to Andover and told Josh I'd found the ideal site. We got a few trustees together, and they gave some encouragement. That fall with Dan Bickford I began negotiating with Jim Gaston, the owner, to lease Hurricane Island. The negotiations went on all winter before we finally worked out a deal."

All Peter needed now was money. At Andover's alumni weekend in the spring of 1964 I was in the rooms of Fred Peterson, a faculty colleague, when he introduced me to William Shallow, his visiting classmate. Bill Shallow was a New York advertising executive. Not surprisingly, with me in the room, the talk turned to Outward Bound. Shallow was for it immediately. I told him about the Hurricane Island possibility, and he asked, "What does it take to get it going?" and I said, "Cash." He indicated he did not think cash was the world's biggest problem. I told Willauer about him, and he drove down to Connecticut to the Shallow home. It was his first fund-raising effort: "When I got there, I learned all the Shallow kids had some communicable disease like chicken pox, and I couldn't go in. Bill Shallow talked with me from a window. I told him about our plans and needs, and he said, 'It sounds good to me. I'll send you a check for five thousand dollars.' The next week the check came, and it was for ten thousand. That money enabled us to move ahead on our plans to build the school that summer. Also, the occasion gave us one of our very good early trustees. Shallow came on the board and was a real asset. Good judgment, tough-minded, willing to go out on a limb, and—obviously—generous."

Dick Homer drew up a plan for the school, and Peter, working through friends and friends of friends, lined up forty volunteer young people, most of them from secondary schools, to spend the summer of 1964 on Hurricane Island with him and some Princeton friends and build the base. The advance group went ashore on June 20, and the work moved forward from then until Peter had to return to Groton in mid-September. The work crews lived in platform tents. They built a pier, put up several buildings, including their own mess hall—now the laundry and generator building—and framed the big main structure that was to become the school mess hall and office. They cut roads to the quarry and hauled rocks. An electric generator was brought in on a barge; with special rigging and a lot of arm and leg power, they got it ashore and in place. Power was turned on on August 20.

Tap Tapley, having completed the instructor training courses he gave in Colorado that summer, came on to consult and supervise the building of the ropes course. Another who showed up to help him was a twenty-three-year-old New Jerseyite named Phil Costello, fresh out of the Marines and preparing to start teachers college in the fall; for Phil this was the beginning of a long Outward Bound association. Tapley's coming added a new dimension to the island activities. It was interesting for a bunch of sailors to get with a mountaineer for the first time and exchange knots, navigation and orienteering technique, and the like. For the youngsters, whose recreation up to then had been largely on the water side, Tap was the start of a new chapter. He got them up early each morning for a run and dip. He taught them how to build a fire and cook when it was wet in the woods, how to hunt with a bowie knife. He introduced them to rock climbing and rappelling and cliff evacuation in the quarry. With the kids, he took Wetmore's drownproofing course. When the ropes course was finished, he put them through it. He gave them fire-fighting drills, and did a ship-to-shore rescue drill with a kind of Tyrolean traverse arrangement. Each youngster also had a two-day solo on a Penobscot Bay island. Seymour Alden, a self-taught naturalist, briefed them on the edible foods they were likely to find.

During the summer Willauer experimented with possible models for a pulling boat. When fall arrived, the design of the vessel that was to be the heart of the Hurricane Island program the following June was still an open question. Homer brought

Willauer together with Cyril Hamblin, a Rockland yacht and commercial-fishing-boat designer and an expert in lightweight wood construction. The two decided that no boat then existed that could be sailed and rowed and had the sought-for simplicity and margin of safety.

The nearest thing to it they could find was the thirty-foot whaleboat that the U.S. Navy had used in the 1920's and '30's off the old four-stacker destroyers. Part of the midshipman training of that time was to be put overboard in the whaleboats and row around the mid-Atlantic for a day. Cy Hamblin took the Navy's old plans and reworked them against Willauer's demanding specifications. He added sheer for Penobscot Bay's steep seas. For sailing he designed a split rig, i.e., two masts, with a low center of effort—short masts and a minimum heeling moment. The boat had to be able to carry fourteen—a full "watch," as the school's twelve-man cadre was to be called, plus an instructor and assistant—and gear for an expedition. Since it was expected there would be some sailing off beaches, it had to be light enough for a crew to launch. It had to have enough flotation so that even if it filled in the cold Maine waters, it would not sink, and even if it capsized, it could be righted. Willauer felt strongly about a boat for inexperienced sailors on the Maine coast having this built-in flotation. He had helped to design the Explorer class, which has a double bottom plus solid flotation in the wooden seat and bow, one of the early boats that could be capsized, righted, bailed, and sailed. The Hurricane Island pulling boats, in addition to their wood construction, have thirty-two cubic feet of styrofoam built in the bow and stern and side thwarts. Every watch learns how to right a capsized boat.

For Willauer the collaboration with Hamblin was extremely happy. Years later he would say: "I was trying to get something that was sea kindly and also kindly to an inexperienced crew, with a gigantic margin of safety—even though the people in it would not be aware the margin was there. Cy came up with a design that gave us what we needed. When we had our second set of boats built in 1969, we made sixty small changes in design and construction detail, but it was still the same boat. All told, that boat has been sailed and rowed by close to eight thousand students the equivalent of four circumnavigations of the globe, with no mishaps more serious than one capsize, which proved routine, and two swampings when a boat broached on a jibe and filled in heavy seas."

February came, and the opening of the Hurricane Island Outward Bound School was less than five months away. Willauer had his designs for the boats but no money to build them. Dick Preston, the trustees' president, was on a business trip. Peter caught him by phone in St. Louis. He said, "You know, we're not going to have a sea school if we don't have any boats." Preston told him to order one. He ordered five. They were delivered just before H-1 opened.

H-1 and H-2, in the summer of 1965, had 170 students, half on full scholarship. The planning in the building summer paid off; the curriculum worked smoothly, with few changes. The students were in twelve-man watches instructed by a watch officer and an assistant. Hurricane's run and dip was an 0545 call, a two-mile run up and down root-snagged paths through the woods and across great granite boulders along the water's edge, ending with a plunge into the icy ocean (48°F). For their first-day waterborne experience the students were towed in a pulling boat a mile out to sea and told when lunch was—a fast lesson in the importance of self-discipline and teamwork that made for attentiveness during the subsequent instruction in seamanship and navigation. The students were on the water virtually every day. Practice in two-man peapods and seventeen-foot Marconi-rigged Explorers supplemented pulling boat instruction in rowing and sailing. A two-day cruise under instructor supervision—extended to three days in later courses—completed the training. For the final four-day expedition, the watch was on its own, usually sailing in convoy with two other watches. Instructors aboard a power boat followed within emergency-aid range. Each expedition included a service phase.

A single season provided all the evidence needed to prove that in creating the Hurricane Island pulling boat, Hamblin and Willauer had devised a stress vehicle par excellence. A student on a mountain or desert expedition who wants to separate him- or herself from the interpersonal stresses of the cadre can drop back fifty yards on the trail for at least temporary isolation. But for twelve people in what is essentially a twelve-person boat (with two instructors also aboard, it's really tight) there is no escaping one another. Some may withdraw by occasional dozing, but enough must remain awake to man the helm, navigate, stand bow watch, assist at every change of tack, row when there is no wind, and prepare a meal for a hungry crew. Inseparable from the situation in the boat are the elements in which it is operated—the sea and the Maine weather. No two days are the same, conditions ranging from flat calm through fog, wind, and rain, to whole gales.

Among the watch officers were Adrian Middleton, an experienced Australian seaman and former instructor at the Fisherman's Point Australian Outward Bound School and Aberdovey; Barry Crook, a British instructor who had led thirty-five courses at the Ullswater, Aberdovey, and Devon Schools; and Jay Evans, who had taught at Colorado the previous two summers. Those without specific Outward Bound experience had equally fine credentials. The watch officers were assisted by specialists in seamanship and navigation, rock climbing, drownproofing, first aid, and fire fighting. Knut Smith, former Colorado as well as army and marine rock-climbing instructor, was in charge of the climbing in the old quarry. Euell Gibbons, famed writer-authority on edible wild foods, conducted a course in ecology and briefed the students on how they might eat well on solo.

Reagh Wetmore taught drownproofing—a ten-part course in the cold waters of the quarry pool, through to the final trials with hands and feet tied. The mile swim with clothes on tested mastery of the travel stroke. The fifty-yard underwater swim was an exercise in resistance to rising panic and fear of the unknown. Reagh's life-saving instruction included a one-hundred-yard carry of a victim whose hands were tied behind his back—a surprisingly realistic experience for both rescued and rescuer.

"In an Outward Bound program," Willauer declared, "the place of honor must be held by the Rescue Services." He cited the heart of Kurt Hahn's programmatic thinking: "The experience of helping a fellow man in danger, or even of training in a realistic manner to be ready to give this help, tends to change the balance of power in a youth's inner life with the result that compassion can become the master motive." From Hurricane Island's beginning, each watch in a standard course has been required to do several twenty-four-hour tours of duty at the island's Rescue Station, which maintains a continuous radio watch for distress calls, fire alarms, and other emergency messages. Duty includes instruction in use of the school's fire-fighting equipment. The duty watch is charged with making the appropriate response to all emergency calls, under staff leadership.

For Willauer it was providential that on the final day of H-1, during the last tug-of-war in the interwatch competition, the general alarm sounded. Twenty acres of woodland were ablaze on Marshall Island, eighteen miles to the east. In a swift execution of emergency procedure the duty watch, twelve students and two watch officers led by fire-fighting specialist John Pingree, were en route in the Rescue Unit *Penobscot* and in forty-eight minutes had water on the fire. The Coast Guard arrived soon after, and two other watches followed in smaller boats. Fifty men fought the fire until it was under control at 3 A.M. All hands returned exhausted to Hurricane Island, ate a late dinner during a predawn awards ceremony, packed, and at 0800 were aboard the ferry for Rockland, headed home.

The Disadvantaged:
Experiment with Delinquents

≡≡✕≡≡✕≡≡✕≡≡✕≡≡✕≡≡✕≡≡✕≡≡✕≡≡✕≡≡✕≡≡✕≡≡

I prefer the lawless to the listless.
—KURT HAHN

Because so many of us involved in the start of U.S. Outward Bound were connected with independent schools, we were concerned lest the movement acquire a "preppie" stigma. We knew it would be fatal for Outward Bound's purposes if people came to think of it as available just to the affluent. We wanted a broad socioeconomic mix. Early on, therefore, it became Outward Bound policy that one-half a school's enrollment should be scholarship students. Some of these had partial scholarships, but many were economically and culturally deprived youngsters receiving full stipends. Most came from what a few years later would be called the inner city.

At that time Andover enjoyed a close relationship with the Boys' Club of New York, a liaison that had come about through an alumnus named Peter Capra. Peter grew up as one of an immigrant family in New York's tough Little Italy. Before joining the Army in World War I, where he served as an orderly to a colonel, he had fought his share of fights on the streets, and he aspired to be a professional fighter. Just before Peter's discharge at war's end, his colonel discovered this ambition. He was wild. "You're going to make something of your life," he told Peter. "You're going back to school, to Phillips Academy and Yale like I did." So Peter took the train to Andover and spent his last fifteen cents for a cigar that he smoked while parked on the front porch of the headmaster's house. The maid tried to send him around to the back door, but Peter just did a sitdown until Al Stearns, who was headmaster then, found him there and took him into the school. The other students gave the New York kid a hard time. Finally Peter had to use his fists on a big jock who tried to bully him. After that his peer relationships were much improved. He went on to graduate from Yale, became head of the Boys' Club of New York, and chairman of Yale's Scholarship Committee. When we were getting ready for Colorado's first year, I went down to see Charlie Sikoryak, who headed up the club's educational program, and told him about Outward Bound. The club put up scholarships for ten kids a year. It was one of our early scholarship bonanzas.

Among the buses arriving at Marble for C-2 in 1962 was one carrying the first New York Boys' Club contingent. The students had to walk two miles from where the buses dropped them to the assembly area where they lined up to get their gear and tent assignments. One of the New Yorkers was a sixteen-year-old black youth with an ebullient grin named Arthur Wellington Conquest III. As Arthur arrived at the assembly area, he took a wide-eyed look at the surrounding peaks, drew a knife from his belt, and with a whoop threw it high in the air. The assembled students scattered, leaving Arthur alone as the knife came down at his feet. Joe Nold, who had Arthur in his patrol, still relishes the incident: "It was Arthur's way of saying, 'Look, man, I'm here. I'm Arthur Wellington Conquest, I'm from New York and I'm black, and them mountains don't scare me!'" That was the beginning of a liaison between Arthur and Outward Bound that is still going strong.

The fact is that for all his clowning and bravado, Arthur was somewhat daunted by the mountains. Agile, he did well on the ropes course. The heights did not faze him. But he took less kindly to the grueling expeditions, the rock faces, and the strangeness of the high peaks. While he was able to absorb the culture shock that overwhelmed some of his peers in the abrupt transfer from city streets, his relationship with the mountains was an encounter rather than a love affair.

It was George, a patrol mate, who perceived that at times Arthur's clowning was a cover for his concerns. George, who was a good athlete and accustomed to the mountains, came from a well-to-do family. He tended to stay aloof from the group, and the others resented his indifference to the patrol's welfare. That changed as George and Arthur developed a warm friendship. On the expeditions George helped Arthur past the rough spots, and the day came when Arthur stood atop Snowmass Peak at 14,092 feet with the world spread about him. Back at Marble he recalled the moment: "It was then that I first woke up to life."

Later, on a visit to Bill Chapman, George reminisced: "It had never occurred to me that I would be needed to help somebody else. When I realized Arthur needed help, and saw what my help could do for him, something inside me changed. I found I was thinking about him and the patrol. That was a complete reverse for me. I'm a different guy now."

Today that sort of thing has happened often enough in Outward Bound that no one thinks twice about it, but to us in the early days it was an exciting social phenomenon. We used to say that if you had an Ivy Leaguer belaying an Urban Leaguer on a rock face in the morning, and in the afternoon the Urban Leaguer belayed the Ivy Leaguer in turn, and that night they shared a polyethylene tarp for a shelter, something happened! It was a dramatic discovery that you could take two youngsters with little or nothing in common beyond their youngsterhood and give them an experience that created a meaningful, perhaps even poignant, bond.

Something of the same sort happened to the instructors as well. Thinking back to that first summer of instructing at Marble, fresh from his teaching at suburban North Shore Country Day School, Joe Nold says, "I had never worked with Arthurs before. That part of the experience was a great awakening of one's own awareness, and one's own self as a teacher. This is one of the things that is exciting about the Outward Bound involvement—that all of us in it have had to grow, and have grown."

Not that the socioeconomic mix always worked well. Not all those early New York Boys' Club kids and disadvantaged kids from Denver and elsewhere, some of whom were sent by the Juvenile Court, were having a gratifying experience. The difficulty was that if inner-city youngsters were recalcitrant or disruptive, we did not know how to work with them. When they created problems, there would be flack. Somebody would say,

"Don't send us any more of those ghetto kids. They were trouble-makers."

That attitude began to filter up to the school trustees and to the national trustees. Some of them began to say, "Why should we bother?" The man who took the decisive stand, who made Outward Bound history at that time, was Bill Coors, a leader among the Colorado School trustees. There was a trustee meeting where the sentiment was voiced in a policy-making session: "If the kids of that type are going to respond negatively, why do we have them? Why let them spoil it for the others?" Coors stood up and socked it to that meeting. He said in essence, "Listen, helping kids like this who have socially negative attitudes is part of what Outward Bound is all about." Nobody argued with him. It was a powerful piece of leadership at a time when resolute thinking was needed. Coors's stand influenced the entire movement. Awareness of it spread to the trustees of other schools, and in a remarkable way the precepts he stated became organizational policy.

In 1964 I read an article in the *Boston Globe* about the corrections institutions of the Massachusetts Division of Youth Services, which was part of the state Department of Education and carried out policy set by a Youth Service Board. The conditions the *Globe* reporter described were so bad I could not believe them. I called the director of the division and asked if I could come to see him. Dr. John Coughlan had taken this post years before, an able man who had established a reputation as a humane corrections specialist. Now he had white hair and a heart condition and lived with the fear that if he got too angry or too frustrated, he would have a relapse. Nevertheless, I would learn he was a brave man.

I said, "Dr. Coughlan, I can't believe that what you're running is as bad as this article says. I deal with young people, and I need to learn how to deal with the kind of young people you have to deal with. I'd like to look around." He said, "I let this reporter look around on condition he show me what he wrote before it was published, which he didn't do. He's grossly distorted the facts and got me in serious trouble." I said, "I'm not here to muckrake. I'm here to be educated. Maybe Outward Bound is something that can help. I'm not sure how, but I'd like to have a look at your institutions, and maybe we'll come up with some ideas." He gave his permission and turned me over to Herb Willman, one of his officers.

Willman first took me to the Roslindale Detention Center, where male offenders were taken when the court remanded them to the Division of Youth Services, usually referred to as DYS. A boy remained there while a sociopsychological diagnostic evaluation was made and his case was presented to the Youth Service Board for disposition. The building was intended to house about one hundred inmates for a few weeks, but the caseworkers and the system were so overloaded that as many as three hundred to four hundred boys were there, some for as long as six months.

It was a sight I shall never forget. Kids were scarcely treated as humans. Underfed, no furniture, bare floors, no recreation, no reading matter, no television. Defecating and urinating without toilets. The center was understaffed, the inmates frequently brutalized, the whole scene dehumanizing. It was unbelievable that this existed in the present day.

The Worcester Reception Center for girls was even worse. We visited the DYS training schools. In many dormitories bodies outnumbered beds—a violation of sanitary and safety laws. I found kids—recaptured runaways—in cages. Their heads had been shaved and they were kept on exhibition as object lessons.

I went back to Coughlan. "You know all about this," I said. He said, "Yes, I do." "What are you doing about it?" "I'm doing the best I can. First, I'm trying to keep kids from coming in here. Then I'm trying to keep them from getting back in. There's very little I can do while they're here." He had an educational counselors' program—specially trained and qualified counselors at good pay circulating through the schools, working with kids before they got into trouble and after they were released from incarceration.

I said, "Give us five of your youngsters. You pick them. I'll find the money, and we'll send them to the Colorado Outward Bound School. And we'll see what happens to them."

"Impossible," he said. "In the history of the Commonwealth of Massachusetts we have never sent an incarcerated person outside the borders of the state. Suppose they run away?" And he said, "My reappointment is coming up in January." And then he did it—he gave us five kids. It was a big gamble for him. It took courage.

As it happened, the Youth Service Board had its offices in the building of the United Community Fund, which was placing our Boston area scholarships. Dr. Francis J. Kelly, a young psychologist who was on the board's staff, was in his office when the fund lady from upstairs looked in and said, "I have five scholarships for a summer camp called Outward Bound. Do you have five boys?" To Frank that was "like asking the Pope if he's a Catholic. I had two thousand boys under my care. Then she told me that this 'Outward Bound camp' was in Colorado, and I thought, oh-oh, that means sending Massachusetts-committed delinquents to another state."

On Kelly's advice, I went to see Lieutenant-Governor Elliot Richardson. He gave the needed authorization. Coughlan managed to get the support of his fellow board members, and Kelly steered us through the paperwork. The more Kelly and his people learned about Outward Bound, the more interested they became. They were professionally intrigued that it was not a camp, but a school with a curriculum based on wilderness challenges. They handpicked five boys they believed would respond positively to the experience.

Reports came back from Colorado that all five were doing fine. One was doing so well that Joe Nold asked to keep him on as a "sherpa" (a logistics helper) in the next course. The day the others were due back I went with Coughlan to the airport. The kids had flown out with escorts, and they returned with escorts. Watching as they came out of the aircraft, Coughlan blanched. "There are only four!" he said. I thought he was going to have that second heart attack. "Didn't you get my letter?" I asked. "What letter?" "I wrote you that they hired Robert Wilson * as a sherpa. He stayed on."

The next day Kelly called, excited. He had been talking with the four scholarship boys. "I'm impressed by their elation, their strong sense of well-being," he told me. "They're high as kites."

It was the same with young Wilson when he returned. He was a black youth who had run away from home in Ohio when he was

---

This is not the boy's real name.

just into his teens, had stolen money from a Massachusetts gasoline station and been caught. With no family to be sent back to, he had been kept in DYS institutions for four years, going to school. It was just a holding operation for him; he could not read or write. When he returned from Colorado, he got a dishwashing job in Boston and was living in a state police barracks. The next year the Colorado School wanted to rehire him. I went to see Robert where he was working. He was standing at a sink, his arms in suds up to the elbows, with his back to me. I told him about the job. He did not reply. I came around to where I could see his face. He was crying. "What's the matter?" I asked. He said, "I can't take the job." "Why not?" "Because this is the first job I've had in my life and I don't want to quit." I went to Willman and Coughlan, and we arranged for him to leave that job with honor and move to Colorado.

The next summer DYS sent forty boys to Colorado and Minnesota. Again they were handpicked. All but three completed the course, and nearly all of them had the same positive experience. Kelly followed these boys on parole, along with the original five, through the fall and winter and found they were compiling a remarkable record of keeping out of trouble. (Even several years later only five of the forty-two, twelve percent, had been returned to a correctional institution—a figure strikingly lower than DYS's expectancy rate of forty-five percent for this age group.) By now Kelly was so high on Outward Bound that he was anxious to do some significant research. We helped him write a grant application for a demonstration study to the Office of Juvenile Delinquency in the Children's Bureau of the then U.S. Department of Health, Education, and Welfare. The proposal was that one DYS group—randomly selected this time—would take Outward Bound courses in the summer of 1966 while a matched group received routine treatment. Kelly and his associates would then make a study to compare recidivism—defined as return to a juvenile institution for violation of parole, or commitment to an adult institution for a new offense—of the two groups. Funding came through, and DYS contributed about $20,000 for tuition and other costs. We were excited. Here was to be a real test, the first anywhere, of whether or not Outward Bound had a substantively salutary influence on behavior.

One hundred and twenty adolescent delinquent boys were selected for the study from the Roslindale Detention Center and two resident institutions. The criteria for selection were: (1) fifteen and a half years and older; (2) good physical health; (3) absence of severe psychopathology; (4) minimum IQ score of seventy, to exclude severely retarded boys; (5) no history of violent assaultive or sexual acts; (6) voluntary participation. Sixty of the selectees were randomly chosen for the Outward Bound experience, to be paroled at the conclusion of the course. The other sixty went through the normal detention-center procedure or continued their institutional sentences.

The Outward Bound students were assigned to courses at Colorado, Minnesota, and Hurricane Island. Prior to the courses, the boys in both the Outward Bound and the control groups were tested to assess personality and measure self-concept, and these tests were repeated at the course's end. Relevant information such as background and school and court records were recorded from their social histories, and each subject completed a biographical data questionnaire. Scales were developed for use by the Outward Bound instructors to rate the delinquent youths in their patrols.

The project employed three doctoral level social scientists as participant observers. They were Dr. Richard Katz of Harvard, Dr. David Kolb of Massachusetts Institute of Technology, and Dr. Thomas D'Andrea, an assistant professor at Haverford College. Each observer attended at least one course; Dick Katz did one at each school. The participant observers completed the full course, recording their daily impressions of its impact on them and the boys, and of the interaction of the boys with staff. They interviewed each boy at the conclusion of his solo experience and trained the instructors to use the rating scales.

Every boy finished his course; that promise of immediate parole was a powerful carrot. Upon their return to Boston, the boys were retested, interviewed, and released on parole either to their own homes or community placements, and the recidivism check was started. However, since the paroles of the control group members, who were still in institutions, would not start until their normal release time, all returns would not be in until 1968, two years hence.

The Mainstream Policy

≡≡≍≡≡≍≡≡≍≡≡≍≡≡≍≡≡≍≡≡≍≡≡≍≡≡≍≡≡≍≡≡

I have multiplied visions.
—Hosea 12:10

The minutes of the May 1965 meeting of the OBI trustees read in part:

> The remainder of the meeting was devoted to a discussion of the broad purposes of the Outward Bound idea. It was the spirit of the meeting that a new stage had been entered. The establishment of new schools is one aspect of this stage, but the broad application of Outward Bound techniques as well as its philosophy is being asked by a multitude of agencies, both public and private . . .

The board was taking cognizance of developments that were giving me growing concern. My mail and telephone were constant reminders that we had given substance to an idea whose time indeed had come—and that we were not up to reaping what we had sown. We were getting a steady flow of queries asking, "How can Outward Bound help us?" A lot of these came from more or less local programs—for instance, Montgomery County, Virginia—asking what we could do for their public-school system. But not a few of the letterheads or the signatures prompted a whistle of surprise. Commandant, United States Naval Academy. How might the Academy work Outward Bound into its curriculum? The U.S. Army's STEP (Special Training Enlisted Personnel) program. About forty thousand potential draftees a year failed to qualify. All they needed was a little push, physically, attitudinally—to make them eligible. The Army had looked at all the youth movements in the country and decided that Outward Bound was their most likely source of help. Could we take on forty thousand kids a year if they paid for it? The Marine Corps' Mustang program, which selected outstanding noncommissioned officers who had been in the corps for ten to fifteen years and sent them to officer candidate school. The program was experiencing a heavy attrition. For some, the idea of making the leap to an officer's commission created a strong psychological barrier. Would Outward Bound care to look into the possibility of its playing a helpful role? The Boy Scouts were making interested inquiries. So were various YMCA's.

Already one Job Corps Center had enlisted the Colorado School's advisory services. The Massachusetts Youth Service experience was producing a strong indication that the Outward Bound dynamic could be used for positive influence on the self-esteem and values of adjudicated youth. An experiment with disadvantaged high-school youth in Trenton, New Jersey, financed in part by the Ford Foundation, was just beginning. Inquiries from schools and colleges were coming in every week. We were getting all kinds of calls for which we had neither a program nor resources with which to respond. With two or more additional Outward Bound schools in prospect, I felt I was carrying the organization about as far in expansion as was practicable. I was feeling half-submerged by the rising tide of demand for our services.

The upshot of the discussion at the May meeting was a special trustee meeting in September, called to discuss "The Future of Outward Bound in the United States." Jack Stevens was in the chair. He was carrying a bombshell and lost no time in tossing it on the table. Outward Bound, he said, had been extraordinarily successful to date. We had established three schools, had put 2,000 youngsters through the program, and the schools were now enrolling 1,000 students a year. The feedback—from the students, their families, their institutions—was highly gratifying. We had reason to be pleased with our results. But we should not fool ourselves. Our success to date was no more than a demonstration. A thousand youngsters a year against the several million who could be helped by an Outward Bound experience was a mere drop in the bucket. Even if we were to increase the number of schools tenfold, which was not possible, and put through 10,000 a year, that would still be but a small drop in a big bucket. For Jack, all this pointed to a clear conclusion: The future of Outward Bound lay in making its way into the mainstream of American thought and American education, and the central question facing us was how could we best do it? How best to shift from demonstration to full production?

The board was not, I think—any more than I—prepared for the force and sweep of Jack's remarks. His blunt how-do-we-get-into-production approach took the wind out of the sails of some of us. No one, however, quarreled with his logic or his mainstream thesis. The ensuing discussion produced a potpourri of ideas for implementing the mainstream idea that served to underscore how ill-prepared we were: Outward Bound must build an adequate headquarters staff. It should provide a pool of counselors and instructors. Facilities and programs had to be created for training instructors. Pilot courses should be made available to community leaders, government officials, school administrators, and welfare personnel, to give them an understanding of what Outward Bound was about. We should have our present program evaluated. We should bring experts together to plan a conference. We should establish a counseling section at headquarters. A training center, with mobile training cadres working out of it. Through all the brainstorming, Stevens stubbornly reiterated a single thought. We did not yet have a policy; we must come up with a well-defined policy, and the broadest feasible program based on it, before we let ourselves become involved in the specifics of any programmatic area. That program should have one overreaching objective: effective ways to project Outward Bound into the mainstream of American life. Nothing less would do. It was agreed that as a way of proceeding, I should prepare a preliminary planning paper and submit it to the trustees for reactions and suggestions.

Of the original Atlantic Foundation group who kept the U.S. liaison with Kurt Hahn alive by supporting his work abroad and ultimately attending U.S. Outward Bound's birth and growing pains, two in particular earned the everlasting gratitude of Outward Bounders everywhere. One was Johnny Kemper. The other was Jack Stevens. A successful businessman, Jack was equally successful in various endeavors for his fellow human beings. He was a born analyzer, a great person to take a problem to. He had a way of listening and then saying, "Now what is the problem?" You discovered you had not defined it, and that the defining pointed to the solution.

Jack was an enthusiast, in the sense that he put his energies where his enthusiasms were. An inveterate birder, for a time he served as a trustee of the Audubon Society. He was a musician, an omnivorous reader, a great Civil War buff. He enjoyed giving; he considered himself a sophisticated donor and took pride in giving intelligently. When the Atlantic Foundation voted to support the proposed school in Colorado and he immediately contributed $10,000 to get the project rolling, it was not a spur-of-the-moment decision. He had been awaiting that moment for more than nine years.

Jack first met Kurt Hahn when he and my mother-in-law visited us at Gordonstoun. The two men, so widely different in background and experience, respected each other. When Jack asked him what he would think of a school that admitted youngsters primarily on the basis of their mental ability, Hahn said, "I would think that was as immoral as admitting them on the basis of how much money their fathers had." Jack understood and agreed. Another time Jack asked, "How important do you think brains are?" Hahn replied, "I think they are as important as your arms and legs. They're useful to you." He meant, Jack explained, that brains don't make the man. One of Andover's mottos is *"Non sibi"*—not for oneself—and Jack had always said that Andover should teach more *non sibi*. It seemed to him that was what Hahn was doing. He was deeply sympathetic to Hahn's goals and saw them as too important to pursue in a limited way. Production!

Because I did not really understand the Stevens demonstration-production analogy, the next six months were as difficult as any half-year of my life. I had thought we were in production. No one was more aware than I of the evidence that Outward Bound had a greater potential than it was realizing, but I had assumed it was to be regarded as a potential, not a near-term objective. I had just succeeded in getting my first staff assistant, and our minuscule headquarters in Andover hardly seemed ready to attempt a massive infiltration of the American mainstream. I went to see Jack a couple of times to get a better understanding of what he was after. I talked with Kemper at great length. What I eventually did was go back to the correspondence files, to all those requests for help that had come in and were still coming in, and make an analysis. I found they divided into three categories. One was education. The second was government agencies. The third was organizations such as the Boy Scouts, the YMCA, Boys' Clubs, church groups. A fourth category was conspicuous by its absence: industry. In contrast to British Outward Bound, where industry was the primary source of enrollment, we had had no calls for help from American industry. Nevertheless I included it with the other three as a mainstream component, a potential to be worked on. I drew up a paper that proposed a Mainstream (with a capital "m") policy of (1) endeavoring to persuade institutions and organizations in those four areas of the values inherent in the Outward Bound dynamic of utilizing challenge to develop self-growth, foster salutary interpersonal relationships, and nurture compassionate concern for one's fellow beings, and (2) seeking the means of helping them to weave Outward Bound methods into the fabric of their own programs.

Looking back from today's perspective, that special meeting of the trustees in September 1965 was a watershed occasion. It was the time when the organization first made the commitment to what, some years later, it came to call "Outreach," the policy of venturing beyond itself to proselyte institutions capable of multiplying its influence. It was a positive commitment that had positive results—even though no policy or program as cogently articulated and pursued as Jack Stevens asked for ever fully materialized.

All sorts of bedevilment of our effort to implement Mainstream lay ahead; all sorts of forces of circumstance would thwart an orderly growth of the implementation. We were not prepared, for example, for the mixed reception the Mainstream idea would, in the crunch, get from the individual schools—although we should have realized that the first concern of each school would have to be its own viability and the quality of its own program. We failed to face squarely the hard facts of how much in staff, resources, and money would be needed to implement a comprehensive Mainstream activity, or how difficult it would be for OBI and the schools to make the Mainstream effort pay for itself. We did not reckon with how precarious would be the status of adaptive programs born of Mainstream when they lost their original leadership and with it the enthusiasm, faith, and energy that launched them, or when their initial funding from a government or foundation grant ran out. We were comfortably unaware of the organic frustrations inherent in any undertaking to transplant new philosophy and method from a seminal to an established institution—and that those difficulties would exact a protracted amount of learning by doing, much of it harsh lessons in what not to do. Buoyed by our sense of mission, we did not stop to reflect that at a time when the new schools were still being formed and so much was needed in the way of strengthening the organizational mainframe, the attempt to pursue a vigorous Mainstream program might be premature.

Thinking negatively, one could say that even though the trustees supported my 1966 position paper, Outward Bound has never had a clearly defined, resolute Outreach policy. One would have to acknowledge that there continue to be those whose vision stops with asking why we should create competition for ourselves. Yet, again seen from today's vantage point, the remarkable fact is that the potential of Outward Bound for a positive influence on American life foreseen by Stevens and others has materialized in substantial measure. Mainstream did happen—successfully. Outreach is happening—successfully. It is a fact that Outward Bound has become a significant part of, and catalyst in, the educational mainstream across the gamut of elementary, secondary, college, and graduate-school levels. Virtually to its own amazement, it found itself spearheading a vigorous national experiential education movement, and has played a key role in the formalizing of that movement. It is being employed as a vehicle for helping a diversity of groups victimized by misfortune—the economically and socially deprived, the physically handicapped, the mentally retarded, the mentally ill—to deal positively with their disabilities. The successful employment of its methods as an alternative to conventional penal practice in dealing with delinquent youth, and to a lesser extent with adult offenders, has earned it a growing influence in the corrections community. Having removed all upper age limits in its own enrollments, and having outgrown its maleness, its influence now reaches into the worlds of educators, managers, career women, housewives, and the adult world generally.

While the degree of success of a particular adaptive program may vary with a dozen factors, and the lessons of experience continue as a check on easy optimism, and while organizational policy may shift from one period to the next, the record is graven that within the Outward Bound experience there is a dynamic that will out, even when no one proselytes. The experience creates its own missionaries. When, to go all the way back to Dr. Zimmerman's happy phrase, "the bug has bit," there is no knowing how the "infection" may spread. Looking back to when Mainstream was given its initial amorphous shape, one is startled into an awareness of how extraordinarily far the movement has come in a mere fifteen years. Jack Stevens's vision is being realized —however impatient with the rate of realization he remained until the day he died in 1976.

Young Women

≡✕≡✕≡✕≡✕≡✕≡✕≡✕≡✕≡✕≡✕≡✕≡

. . . These differences may be more of an artifact of social or cultural restrictions imposed on the female rather than a result of true biological differences in performance potential. . . .

—DR. JACK W. WILMORE

Since the student body at Kurt Hahn's school at Salem included both boys and girls from the time of its founding in 1920, I once asked Hahn why he had not made Gordonstoun coeducational. The blue eyes twinkling, he replied, "You don't try to grow dates above the Arctic Circle." The British, he had realized, were not ready for coeducation in 1934. His judgment that it was only a matter of time before they would be was confirmed later when Gordonstoun began to accept female students.

In this country things took a different tack. It was Bob Pieh who in 1965 broke the sex barrier in U.S. Outward Bound. On the heels of the Minnesota School's first season, he announced that he planned to put a "pilot group" of young women through the same course the following summer. Gene Caesar, a writer who had observed and written about the Minnesota course, tried to dissuade him. "I did my best to reason with him," he wrote. "I reminded him that everyone, from the President's Commission on Physical Fitness down through the cartoonists who draw the junior-miss comic strips, has agreed that the country's teenage girls are soft, pampered creatures. But Bob Pieh is an idealist, and idealists can be incredibly stubborn."

The first girls' course, designated MG-1, had two twelve-woman brigades. Most of the students were sixteen and seventeen, a few eighteen; there was one twenty- and one twenty-three-year-old. The young women in MG-1 had to meet essentially the same challenges the boys encountered that summer. They had the same training in canoeing, drownproofing, map and compass, rescue and first aid. They did the same run and dip, the same ropes course and initiative tests, ran the same obstacle course, climbed and rappelled the same rock faces, penetrated the same total wilderness on their expeditions, portaged the same sixty-five pound canoes and heavy packs, and dealt with the same deprivations on equally lonely solos. While the pace of the expeditions naturally accommodated to lesser female strengths in paddling and portaging, the Quetico wilderness did not mitigate the rigor of its challenges.

The first female course is well documented, for it was covered by writers for two national magazines. Gene Caesar wrote for *Seventeen* an informative reflection of an adult male response to a young female phenomenon that is enriched by his access to the journals of a number of the students. Barbara La Fontaine, one of *Sports Illustrated*'s top staff writers, did a two-part piece.

Caesar found his first sight of the student body, descending the bus from Duluth, a shock: "I had expected an assortment of muscle-molls, a native version of the Russian women's Olympic track team. Instead, I saw two dozen feminine young women, several of whom, as a north woods guide would say, wouldn't have weighed a hundred pounds wringing wet—which they were destined frequently to be." He had several occasions to note a kind of blitheness under stress recognizable by anyone who has known teenage girls in an Outward Bound environment. Going along on the "Quiet Walk" that was the Minnesota staff's welcome to the group—two hours of struggling through heavy bush and soft swampland in alternate spells of brisk striding and running, with crossings of the South Kawishiwi River in progressively swifter and deeper (but still safe) stretches of rapids—he was surprised by the contrast to the male behavior he had previously observed. Where males had wallowed through waist-deep muck "like soldiers but griping and occasionally cursing like same," the young women grinned, giggled, and made remarks about "lolling around in a lot of gook." Of another occasion, at the end of a day of rock climbing that had been followed by a hike "with singing and laughing in a kind of triumphant exhaustion strongly suggestive of drunkenness," he wrote: "Long hours later, after taps had been sounded, high-spirited laughter was still ringing out in the tent village." Then he added, "There were almost certainly moments of despair as well in the privacy of that village. From the several diaries that were later shared with me in confidence, I'm certain that there was some sobbing too. But I wasn't permitted to hear it. The fellows had treated me like an unofficial chaplain with their complaints. The girls put on instant grins and brave smiles like magic make-up jobs."

Barbara La Fontaine participated in the entire course. Her *Sports Illustrated* report tells something about how it was for a thirty-four-year-old woman as well as for adolescent girls:

> [On the long final portage of the first day] I think it was disbelief that sustained us. Betty started off with a canoe, missed her footing and subsided, with loud cries, into the mud. Carrying pack, paddles, and an armful of life preservers, I went in only up to my shins, but it seemed enough and my temper was very bad. My character, I felt, was not developing; it was shrinking to the size of a pea, a small dry pea. And it turned out to be a long portage, about a mile and a half of mud and treacherous footing. We didn't know how long it was—for all we knew it was endless—and at one point I felt almost panicky with weakness. As Polly was to say much later, "You just try to keep from screaming or crying or anything," and so you do—a matter of what the boys call "gutting it out." It turned out there was an end to the trail, and all the first girls who got to it turned back for extra packs . . .
>
> The boys had commented on how the girls carried packs, going slowly, watching their footing; I think they didn't see that if we lost our footing, we were down and could not get up again. The mud, underbrush, hills, rocks, and fallen trees made it difficult to keep our balance and with The Monster [the biggest pack of all] I couldn't keep mine . . . I fell one day and had to crawl on my hands and knees to a tree and pull myself up, gasping for breath. I had seen Polly leaning against a rock, almost in tears—"This isn't even Out-

ward Bound, this is just torture," she had said. At this moment I could only agree . . .

It had been raining again and, besides, we had all got the idea by now that there was no keeping dry, and we slopped briskly into the water at all the portages. The flower of American girlhood, brought up on, "Get out of those wet clothes!" had learned a marvelous truth on this trip. When soaked to the skin, keep all that wet stuff on, and with body heat, a fire, and any luck at all you may be dry by the time you have to try to sleep on the ground.

From day to day each girl carried within herself the apprehension of solo—three days and nights in that utterly wild country, alone except for possible animal visitations, without tent, sleeping bag, food, and insect repellent. For some—a matter of competence and temperament—the actuality proved pleasurable. A few did well in the culinary department, preparing varied menus of fresh water clams, crab, cattail roots, and leaf tea. For some the actuality was as miserable as they had feared. Most were content and miserable in turn.

All of the girls had stuck it out, most of them without eating, though Joan had had two pairs of frogs' legs, some berries, and "the inside of a tree," and Cathi had eaten 12 ants, in groups of four. Genie had constructed an obstacle course and spent her days running it and had memorized the label on her survival can and the whole of her last letter from Bill (which, strictly speaking, I don't think she was supposed to have with her at all). Max said she had sat and sung to herself every song she knew. Sandy had built what sounded like an exquisite ant trap, with a lid. She lured ants into it and squirted them with antiseptic cream. We were all of us somewhat enfeebled, and the girls looked more wan and spiritual than they will probably look again for 30 years.

"Survival" over, the brigade settled into the expedition's final days. Fed again, they were stronger "and rather competent."

Darcy took to carrying two packs, one back, one front, now that the food packs were lighter. On long portages

Sandy's interest was in carrying the canoe the whole way without a rest, not just in whether she was going to live or die. One day several of the girls double-portaged a mile-and-a-half trail, thus making the trip with packs three times, and then walked a fourth and fifth time, in the rain, to help a vacationing couple they had met. I myself had shaped up and could swim more than a mile and not feel winded.

Bob Pieh had told them that there was a rhythm to the wilderness that would catch them, and now they found it to be true.

We had no watches, and we just went along, getting up after the sun rose, going to sleep after it set. When we were thirsty we dipped a cup over the side of the canoe and drank, or we drank from our paddles. When we were hot we took off our clothes. When we wanted to bathe we jumped into the lake. I brushed my teeth in pools with minnows gathered to nibble at the cloud of toothpaste, and I hung my clothes on a tree. Life was very simple. We got tired, but that is a simple matter, too, and most of us became very tranquil —even those of us who were most miserable were tranquilly miserable.

Nearing the end, a student wrote in her journal: "We paddled all day and made some hellish portages—over beaver dams, through swamps, etc. Early in the afternoon, we reached the river that divides Canada and the United States, so we went ashore and kissed the huge rock on our side. I have never known such close friendship as with these girls." La Fontaine came out of the wilderness a day ahead of the students. Up on Birch Lake the same evening a student reflected: "Now we are sitting in our leaky tent as it rains buckets. A fitting last night for this little expedition! But I have been thinking. A bar of soap would be a luxury now. So would an orange. A little brown sugar to put on the Bisquick we bake over the fire would be a real treat, if we had any left. If only there was some way to go right on appreciating things! Wouldn't it be cool if one could always get excited over something like brown sugar and Bisquick?" The next day La Fontaine watched as the girls came out.

They were sick of the wilderness, and they wanted to go

home. In spite of this, their manners and their tempers had done nothing but improve. If they looked a little gritty as they finally emerged, they were more thoughtful, more gentle, and more ladylike by far than they had been when they went in (something the so-called "best" girls' schools in this country might ponder—that the Canadian woods succeed where they too obviously fail). The girls had gone into the wilderness teenagers and had come out human beings—no small transformation. It had happened, and I had failed to see it develop. Having made a point of going all the way to watch for it, I had even missed the moment when it began. However, I am sure the cause was partly pride. The girls had done a good job; they were properly proud of themselves, and the dignity of their pride did for them just what Kurt Hahn used to explain that it would do.

Months later, when queried, a number of the girls wrote of their feelings as they had crystallized with time. Some called the course a turning point in their lives, and at least two were ambitious to return as instructors. Several for whom much of the experience had been a hated ordeal were in retrospect among the most enthusiastic. One of these articulated the nub of the retrospect thousands of Outward Bounders have known: "Nothing seems as bad as it really was." (Twenty years before a youngster had expressed the same idea to Hahn: "Magnificently, sir, except at the time!") One mother, however, took issue with La Fontaine's "ladylike" finding: "I sent a graceful young lady with a beautiful skin and a lovely figure to Minnesota. I got her back with her feet and ankles swollen double, legs scabbed by mosquito bites, and talking like a lumberjack. There *must* be some easier way to find one's inner self!" But her daughter saw it differently: "It's true that I was never so terrified and never pushed half so hard. But I never felt so *alive* before either."

Intriguingly, it was Barbara La Fontaine—then years ahead of her time as "a woman over thirty" taking part in an all-female course—who stated about as well as it can be stated the essence of what Outward Bound is all about: "None of us, I suspect, who was not an outdoorswoman before all this has become an outdoorswoman because of it, but that was never the point; in fact, whichever girl liked it the least has probably come off best, having learned more than any of us what she is capable of. And that *is* the point. We are better than we know. If we can be made to see it, perhaps for the rest of our lives we will be unwilling to settle for less."

The following summer Minnesota offered two female courses and enrolled close to one hundred. There remained the interesting question of how the other schools would respond to the precedent. One by one they came along: Colorado in 1967, Northwest in 1969, North Carolina and Hurricane in 1971. Due to the Dartmouth Center's early focus on college students and teachers, its public courses were coeducational from the start.

I happened to be at the Northwest School the first morning of NWG-1. Wanting to get his own sense of the group—and perhaps to deliver the message early that Outward Bound would be no brownie bake—Director Bill Byrd personally led the run and dip. The run ended at a stream whose source was in a melting Cascades snowfield. Bill plunged into the icy water and was out in a flash. "All right," he said to a group of girls, still breathing heavily from their run, "everybody in!" He waited, with a pleased this'll-give-'em-the-idea expression, for the first female scream. Seventeen-year-old Cinda Kittredge dove in and came up, shaking the water from her head. Instead of heading for shore, she slipped into a smooth backstroke, gave an exultant cry, and called to her companions, "Oh, it's great!" Bill's face was a study.

Experience has demolished early concerns about the wisdom of introducing the female element into Outward Bound. One apprehension was that women were not up to hard physical stress or to meeting traditionally male kinds of physical challenge. Another was the "Amazon syndrome"—a concern lest Outward Bound have a defeminizing influence on girl students, or attract "Amazon types" to staff jobs. Some of the schools responded to these concerns by making girls' courses easier, but this did not last long. Male instructors and students were treated, often to their bafflement, to demonstrations that, age bracket for age bracket, women are competent to meet the same physical challenges as men. It was highly disconcerting, for example, for an adolescent youth to be shown, as not uncommonly happened, that his female peers were better natural rock climbers. That sort of realization is less surprising today, in a time of superb female athletes, women team sports, coed volley ball at the "Y" and the like. Already it is difficult to believe that the discovery females need not be Amazons to lead or come through an Outward Bound experience with flying colors was then cause for wonder.

There was another concern. Bob Pieh recalls some of the responses to his pioneer course: "Reactions in the Outward Bound community were mixed. There was strong feeling at that time among those valuing and cultivating Outward Bound's machismo image that the success of women in similar experiences would diminish that image. Regular Minnesota male staff felt the presence of mere women would cause 'changes.' That local resistance diminished rapidly when the willingness of women students and overall readiness and courage of both women staff and students became evident."

The fading of the machismo concern was a subtle matter. It is frequently described in terms of one of its aspects—that the Outward Bound influence transformed male attitude from one of regarding women as sex objects to one of relating to them as persons. The female incursion, Pieh says, "may have been a threat until it was lived with." In the long run the entire Outward Bound community has shared the same lesson: Don't worry about the women; they can take the physical challenge, and will be no less women for the experience; and the men will be the better for it. In retrospect it is ironic that there was any hesitancy to offer distaff courses, for today the schools could not be viable without women students. More than forty percent of the current U.S. Outward Bound enrollment is female.

New School in the Northwest

═══×═══×═══×═══×═══×═══×═══×═══×═══×═══×═══

It's not that I'm not scared anymore; it's just that I know I can function when I'm scared.
—From a Northwest student's course impression

In the early winter of 1965 I made a presentation in Portland, Oregon, at a meeting sponsored by St. Helen's Hall, an Episcopal private school. Samuel McKinney, the school's development officer, was much interested in the idea of an Outward Bound school in that area. Since we especially wanted to see a school founded in the Far West in order to achieve a continental span of activity, and since the Cascade Mountain range, running from British Columbia down into Washington and Oregon, offered dramatically beautiful and challenging terrain, this was a potential of strong appeal. Among the thirty or so persons present at the St. Helen's Hall gathering was Donald Vetterlein, a Portland businessman. In Maine the preceding summer Don had run into an old friend, Hugh Latham, who was an enthusiastic supporter of the new Outward Bound school being built on Hurricane Island. The two men sailed out to the island, where they had a look at the building activity and talked with Peter Willauer. Vetterlein came away impressed; months later learning of the meeting at St. Helen's Hall, he got himself invited.

The occasion produced a core group of a dozen or more who were willing to pool their energies to investigate the idea of starting a school in Oregon. By spring the sentiment was strongly affirmative, mixed with uncertainties about costs, start-up problems, and the like. Vetterlein, who was going east again in the

162

Kurt Hahn

Jack Stevens

John Kemper

Colorado Outward Bound in the Canyon Country of Utah (Spring and Fall courses). PHOTO: CHRIS BROWN

Winter mountaineering courses (December through May).
PHOTO: RICK TAPCA

". . . the full test of endurance, bodily and mental . . ."
PHOTO: ROBERT GODFREY

Learning new skills.
PHOTO: GALVIN

Minnesota Outward Bound group getting acquainted during a "quiet walk in the swamp"

Portaging the "North Canoe" voyageur-style

The high Burma bridge of the Minne-sota ropes course

Getting the last person over the wall

At the Hurricane Island Outward Bound School the crew and instructors of a thirty-foot pulling boat eat lunch while under sail.
PHOTO: KARL ZEISE

A Florida "watch" gets to know the seas above and below their craft.

The island solo leaves students alone to meet themselves and their environment.

A "watch" gets the last rays of sunset in Penobscot Bay.

Northwest Outward Bound expeditions in the Cascades.
PHOTO: ROBERT GODFREY

On the summit of Middle Sister

Crevasse rescue practice on Glacier Peak. PHOTO: JIM HOSMER

Hawksbill rappel of the North Carolina Outward Bound School.
PHOTO: BARRY CARDEN

Linville River crossing.
PHOTO: DAN MADDEN

Completing the third pitch on Table Rock Mountain.
PHOTO: JEAN MACGREGOR

North Carolina Outward Bound instructor conducting a course for deaf students. PHOTO: DAVID HENDRICKS

Dartmouth Outward Bound Center expedition in the Presidential Range of the White Mountains. PHOTO: ROBERT GODFREY

Evacuation of injured Living/Learning student in the Carter-Moriah Range. PHOTO: NAT MEAD

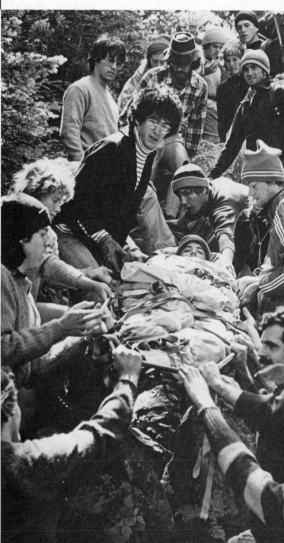

Laboratory conducted by Dartmouth Outward Bound in psychology course in helplessness—improvised raft to escape an island.

Photos: Scott McGovern

A Southwest Outward Bound School expedition in the Grand Canyon.

PHOTO: JOHN RHOADES

Rafting the Taos Box on the Rio Grande

Truchas Peak in the Pecos Wilderness. PHOTO: PEGGY WIER

Rock-climbing in Mateus Canyon, Gila Wilderness. PHOTO: PEGGY WIER

Prince Philip bestowing doctorate on Kurt Hahn

Early Colorado Outward Bound high-altitude camp

summer, volunteered to make inquiries en route. He revisited Hurricane, where Willauer gave him helpful advice and data. When he came to Andover, my most useful counsel was probably that the Portland group had only to journey one hundred miles south to the city of Eugene to find a ready-made school director—Bill Byrd.

After my meeting with Byrd in Colorado two summers before, at the time he was returning to Oregon from his Peace Corps duties in Puerto Rico, I had made a point of keeping track of him. In the spring of 1965, in the course of discussing some Colorado School matters, I suggested to Joe Nold that he get in touch with Byrd. Bill was living in Eugene where, instead of going back to teaching school, he had set up a trial-preparation practice as a service to the city's plaintiff lawyers. Talking with him, Nold mentioned that one of the Colorado's School's problems was the physical limitations of the Marble base, which were limiting enrollment.

Byrd suggested that Nold experiment with a mobile course operating without a base. "Take advantage of the out-of-doors," he said. "It's there, you don't have to do anything to it. All you have to do is get out there, equipped. Run students out in buses, introduce them to the staff, provide them with their equipment, resupply them at designated points and times, and run your courses. Why fuss around with a big base facility?" Nold saw the merit in the suggestion, and the upshot was that Byrd agreed to come on that summer and direct an experimental mobile course in Colorado. While he ran it out of a tented training-and-supply base near the ghost mining town of Ruby, it approximated the fully mobile model that later became his particular style.

When Vetterlein stopped at Marble to observe the Colorado program and get counsel from Nold, the latter likewise suggested that Byrd would make a good school director. Don drove over to Ruby to meet him. Byrd remembers, "Vetterlein said, 'Why don't you look me up in Portland when you get home?' But I just went back to Eugene and went to work. I was making money with this business I'd set up, and that was kind of fun for a schoolteacher. Then Vetterlein and a whole delegation came down to see me. By that time I was getting up to my eyebrows in the legal business. It was fun to make money, but I was getting completely out of touch with my family. I was thinking this is kind of silly—making money can't be all that important. So I said. 'You guys want to start an Outward Bound school, and you know damn well I do too. Working with kids is apparently my life, so how do we do it?' We had it going in six months."

Bill Byrd was a platoon sergeant in Charlie Company, 161st Regiment, in New Caledonia in 1944, taking part in General MacArthur's preparations to invade the Philippines. Finding he enjoyed instructing his men, he decided he wanted to be a teacher. "Even though it was the art of war, it was teaching. We'd lost so many guys we were full of new recruits, and for them there was an immediacy to the value of learning. You didn't have much trouble with attention span." The 161st Regiment still has the record for continuous front-line duty; in the Philippine campaign they were in contact with the Japanese for 178 consecutive days. Bill's platoon was turned over about four times.

But when he went back to college, at the University of Oregon in Eugene, got his B.A., and went on to graduate work in education, Byrd found himself in a confrontation with the establishment. "It was disillusioning for me to see the price I had to pay to become a teacher, since I was already a proven teacher in the field under the most difficult of conditions. I got a sampling of some of the courses and thought, what a way to breed incompetence in the classroom." He switched to the law school. In his second year there he became involved with a group who felt the university was not meeting students' educational needs, especially those of returning veterans. The dissidents lost their fight—at least in the short run; eventually their chief faculty supporter became president of the university—and Bill dropped out. He went abroad, climbed in the Alps and Dolomites, and toured Europe on a bicycle until his money ran out. Back in Oregon, he worked in a logging camp, then got a job teaching at a small high school in the wheat country of central Oregon. Summers he was a mountain-climbing guide in the Petzoldt-Exum School of American Mountaineering in Wyoming. With some of his fellow guides he took two summers out to start a mountain-safety program and establish a rescue service in Teton National Park. Following his marriage in 1953, he returned to the university and "paid the price," getting his master's degree in education.

Byrd was appointed an English teacher in the McKenzie High School, a small regional school serving a group of unincorporated communities along the McKenzie River. The district school superintendent was a remarkable educator named Ben Huntington, whom Bill admired greatly: "Ben encouraged innovation, however far out, so long as it was based on solid teaching, control of the classroom, and genuine communication with the students. The students were mostly the children of loggers and laborers and they got virtually no encouragement to higher education at home. Ben's idea was, How can we change this for the kids in school? How can we take advantage of what curiosity is there and sustain it and help it grow? How can we get a few of these youngsters into higher learning; if they have no aptitude, how can we get them the best skills training possible, so that they can function as resourceful, independent folk in society and have a little bargaining power with the system?"

With encouragement from Huntington, a fellow teacher named Bob Cooley and Byrd came up with a radically new plan for adapting the school's resources to the individual abilities of the students. When the faculty voted it down, Huntington gave the pair one end of the school building and authorized them to use the plan with their junior and senior students. One of the first things they did was have the students make a community resource study. The youngsters discovered that along the McKenzie River were an assortment of retired people rich in experience—businessmen, professors, writers, artists, and so on. Byrd remembers, "We got these people down into the school. We had loggers teaching in the classroom because some were history buffs, or were great on local folklore. Some of them were artists, but didn't want anybody to know it. We had a great year. Kids who had just sat dumb for years were on their feet taking part. At first the parents were all over us, calling us left-wingers and Commies, but after a while they came around."

The second year the state people came in to evaluate what Cooley and Byrd were doing and decided to fund it as a "gifted child" program. Although the two teachers considered it an "all kids" program, they welcomed the endorsement. Byrd, however, found his concerns centering increasingly on the youngsters

at the "non-gifted" end of the spectrum. He volunteered to take
all the school's "rejects"—the students the teachers had fingered
as troublemakers—into a single class. In the mornings he, or
other teachers with whom he swapped classes, worked with the
youngsters on the basics they had never mastered. He also spent
time with them on a kind of "consumer education" that dealt
with practical problems of living they would have when they
left school. In the afternoons they were given a work release to
part-time jobs, and in the evenings those who wished came back
to the school for additional tutoring. This plan also won state
approval and funding. It became known as the McKenzie Plan
and was adopted as a model by the federal Job Corps.

When I was recruiting staff for the Peace Corps in the summer
of 1961 and spoke with the Teton guides, Bill was more interested
in getting back to teach his rejects. But he had a rendezvous with
Outward Bound. The following November the school secretary
took a call for Mr. William Byrd, "the White House calling."
The caller was one of President Kennedy's assistants, who several
summers earlier had been in a Teton climbing party with Byrd
as guide. He told Bill he had just come from a top-level Peace
Corps meeting concerned with staff needs where Shriver had said,
"What we need down there in Arecibo are people who know
the Outward Bound type things and also are educators." He had
said, "I know a good one," and told what he knew about Bill.
Shriver had said, "Get him!" Would Bill please come to Washington for a meeting? In January Byrd went to Arecibo to
partner his old Teton buddy Al Read as a rock-climbing instructor. A few months later came Grant Venn's illness and
resignation as director of the training center. Venn recommended
Byrd to be his successor, and Shriver appointed him.

Byrd arrived at the training center just before Freddy Fuller
returned to England. When he became director, he took over an
evolving program that by then was staffed by people with no
Outward Bound affiliation. Nevertheless, he recalls, the program
continued to carry the Outward Bound stamp: "From talking
with Fuller and with some Englishmen who stayed on, we still
thought of ourselves as doing a heavy adaptation of Outward
Bound. A lot of our off-hour discussions were about how nice
it would be if we could do it pure some place—which we couldn't
do there because of the special demands of the Peace Corps

training. And wouldn't it be great, we said, to run it parallel to the American classroom type of education, to expose kids to this kind of challenge and self-discovery. Most of us, being educators anyway, couldn't help but explore the hypothetical limits of the particular philosophy we were trying to implement there."

The Oregon organizing group incorporated in the fall of 1965 and was chartered as the Northwest Outward Bound School, with Don Vetterlein as president. In January I went to Portland to help launch a fund-raising campaign, and by February the recruiting for courses NW-1 and NW-2 to be offered that summer was under way. The Forest Service granted the school a use permit in an area of mixed old-growth timber in the Willamette National Forest, at the base of the Cascade Range about seventy-five miles east of Eugene. Byrd set up a tented training base under a stand of magnificent Douglas firs—pyramidal two-man miner's tents for the students, large tents for staff headquarters and cooking, no plumbing, and a ropes course. The site was on a small stream called Kink Creek near the headwaters of the McKenzie River, five miles from the nearest settlement, a mile from Robinson Lake, a body of water fortuitously situated for the morning run and dip. A dozen or so hiking miles away were Mount Washington and the Three Sisters, the latter a group of three 10,000-foot peaks, the highest in the more southerly Cascades.

Forty-odd boys hailing from all parts of the country, half on full or partial scholarship, completed each of the two 1966 courses. After five days of training at the base, virtually all the rest of the course was carried out in a mobile mode. The students linked a basic expedition, an alpine phase of rock climbing and peak ascents, and a solo in a thirteen-day stretch. They returned to base for two days of interpatrol competition, including the marathon, then broke up into groups of four for a four-day final expedition on their own. Some of the final expedition feats in the second course, undertaken in response to challenges set in NW-1, were prodigious. Two of the groups covered routes just short of one hundred miles in the allotted four days.

In his final award-night talk to the students Byrd addressed the theme of "Know yourself, know where you're going, and be of service to mankind." From its beginning Northwest was among the staunchest of the schools in its commitment to service. The senior staff that Byrd assembled were skilled in mountain rescue and stressed it in their training. The Oregon Mountain Rescue and Safety Council designated the Northwest School rescue team as the ready unit for the Three Sisters area. The Forest Service designated the school a fire-suppression team. In the second summer, which was exceedingly dry, the students contributed 1800 man-hours to forest-fire fighting. The first-year students built a well-marked trail from the Kink Creek roadhead to Robinson Lake to keep fishermen and other recreation seekers from getting lost. In the two years, students removed some seven hundred and seventy pounds of litter from public shelters, campsites, and picnic grounds. Other projects included rebuilding of a foot-bridge and a miscellany of brush removal, grading, clearing, excavation, and barrier work. Altogether, service projects totaled 3754 man-hours the first two summers.

In 1968, Northwest's third season, the school combined two weeks of staff training with a Wilderness Workshop open to teachers and others interested in gaining firsthand knowledge of Outward Bound educational principles and techniques. The workshop was led by Willi Unsoeld and Dick Emerson, Unsoeld's west ridge teammate in the successful 1963 American Mount Everest expedition. Another Northwest innovation took place in September, when the school offered a ten-day senior course, dubbed "Rebound," for men thirty and over. It was one of the first adult Outward Bound courses offered the general public.

The Northwest School was the first to function without costly construction of a permanent base. In 1967, with doubled enrollment, the Forest Service had granted permits for two new training base locations, Foley Ridge and East Fork. With enrollment again doubling the third summer, the Foley Ridge site was retained, but two other central Oregon courses were conducted in the Mount Jefferson area on a fully mobile basis. Training was conducted on the trail, with emphasis on learning by doing. The course covered 150 miles but was shortened in subsequent seasons. Also in the 1968 summer, Unsoeld and Emerson led a mobile course in Washington's north Cascades.

The collective experience of that season confirmed Byrd's faith in the mobile-course concept, and in subsequent years the school's curriculum evolved into an all-mobile program. Eventually this enabled Northwest to operate in the three states of Oregon, Washington, and Idaho. The other schools were quick to note the positive values in Byrd's example. In particular, the schools operating from permanent bases sooner or later saw those bases subjected to the strains of overpopulation; when that happened, mobile courses provided a viable alternative. Today all the schools run at least some mobile courses, and some operate entirely on the mobile principle.

The fourth school. We were growing. At Andover, OBI was beginning to look more like a national headquarters. In the early years fiscal constraints had limited me to a single staff assistant. My first good staff break came in 1966, when the Ford Foundation gave us money for salary purposes and I was able to persuade Bob Bates to take a leave of absence from his teaching at Exeter. Bob is one of the country's top mountaineers, a former president of the American Alpine Club and co-leader of the American K-2 expedition of 1953. He had helped me with advice when Coffin and I were recruiting staff for the Peace Corps in Arecibo. Subsequently he served as Peace Corps director in Nepal. Exeter gave him a year's leave to work with me. A fine person of high and versatile competence, he was an invaluable assistant.

At that time a trustee committee was searching fruitlessly for the right man to fill a new OBI post of "schools coordinator," who would work closely with the school directors. I tried to sell Bates on taking the job. He declined. "Willi Unsoeld is your man," he said. "He has the talents you want. He knows Outward Bound from his time in Colorado with his Peace Corps volunteers, he believes in it, his life-style and interests are in tune with it. And since he's about to complete an assignment for the Agency for International Development in Nepal, he's available." Bob called Unsoeld and offered the job on our behalf. Willi accepted. He came aboard in the fall of 1967 as my number two and chairman of the Outward Bound Coordinating Committee (OBCC),* the newly formed school directors group. A few months later he was named OBI's executive vice president.

* OBCC replaced the Operating Committee (OBOC), the former school directors body.

* * *

Willi Unsoeld was a twelve-year-old Boy Scout when he looked up at the Three Sisters in Oregon's Cascade Range—his first sight of mountains—and experienced an instant desire to be a climber. Following army service in World War II and two years as an undergraduate at Oregon State, he spent another two years beating his way around the world, climbing mountains as he went. In India he lived for months in a cave with a Hindu holy man, and spent time with two American missionaries whose dedication to compassionate service "opened my eyes to Christianity." Back home, he got his B.A. in a year and took up graduate study in religion, first at Oberlin, and then at the Pacific School of Religion at Berkeley. He intended returning to India as a missionary, but by the time he finished seminary, India was surfeited with missionaries expelled from Communist China. Deciding to be a teacher, Willi earned his Ph.D. in philosophy at the University of Washington and joined the philosophy department at Oregon State, where his field was ethics. Along the way he went on two Himalayan expeditions.

Although Unsoeld loved teaching, he was having doubts about being a philosophy professor when Bates asked him to be his Peace Corps deputy in Nepal in 1962. That was when Willi came to the Colorado School with his volunteers and took part in C-3. In Nepal he succeeded Bates as director after a year, but not before taking a leave of absence to join the 1963 American Mount Everest expedition. With Dr. Thomas Hornbein he was the first to reach Everest's summit by its west ridge. The price was nine of his toes and the agony of recovering from frozen feet.

One of the highlights of my life was the three years of hard work and close friendship with Willi Unsoeld at Andover. As Hahn would have said, he was the kind of fellow you like to steal horses with. He had intelligence, enthusiasm, a great sense of humor, supreme confidence, a talent for partnership. Much in demand as a witty and inspiring speaker, he brought Outward Bound considerable limelight. He was a genius in human relations. One of his greatest gifts was getting to know people quickly; he never met a stranger. The ultimate instance of that was his meeting with John Laycock.

John was sort of the majordomo of the Andover skating rink. A Scotsman, he kept the skating club kids in line with an iron hand and much love. One day between halves of a hockey game

I took Willi into the little room where John sharpened skates. I said, "John, I want you to meet a friend of mine. This is Willi Unsoeld—Willi, this is John Laycock." John looked at Willi and said, "Who sent you, Willi?" The two men stood gazing at each other. Willi said, "John, who's your guru?" John replied, "Willi, you were sent. Who's your guru?" They exchanged guru names, and there ensued a dialogue quite outside my understanding. I had not known John could spell guru, let alone that he had one.

It was just a godsend to have Willi's collaboration on so many responsibilities that up to then I had carried alone. We were a good team. He had a faculty of listening carefully and understanding the essence of what you were saying, not letting the words get in the way of his comprehension. I always knew that when I went out on a mission with him, we would both get back intact, and that the mission would be accomplished. Hahn, on one of his periodic visits, observed us and approved. I remember Hahn once advising me about fund raising. "Don't go alone. Alone, you are strident. Take Unsoeld with you. Remember, lions hunt in pairs."

Another staff member at that time was Dyke Williams, a young Bostonian who had joined us when Bob Bates left. Dyke had the indispensable zeal for Outward Bound, and talents to implement it. He spoke and wrote well and was a good fund raiser. OBI was charged with raising the money for one-half the scholarships at all the schools, and Dyke had much to do with our achieving our annual quota. He was our proposal writer until he left to join the Minnesota School staff in 1970.

James "Gil" Leaf was a valuable staff addition in 1968. After graduating from Harvard in 1963, Gil had twice worked his way around the world, instructed at Hurricane Island and at Outward Bound Schools in Australia and East Africa, taught at the Fessenden School in Massachusetts, been an assistant to Peter Willauer, a consultant to the state of New Jersey on an Outward Bound adaptive proposal, worked with Trenton Action Bound and with Massachusetts juvenile delinquents. We gave him the job of organizing Mainstream. Gil's enthusiasm, energy, and imagination together were a veritable idea factory. I had to put a sign on my door, "No one under 35 allowed after 11 A.M.," to keep Gil from overwhelming us with new ideas as we worked on those he had already given us. Outward Bound carries a debt of gratitude to both Dyke Williams and Gil Leaf.

Trenton's Action Bound

There are pitifully few channels in our society through which young men can move with dignity, success, and a sense of adventure from adolescence into manhood. Opportunities for positive, character-forming experiences are particularly limited for youngsters of low-income families. . . . They are the ones who most often sink finally into aimlessness and apathy, or who take out their frustrations on the institutions that have failed them in acts of violence and hostility. . . . They need experiences that will show them that they are not so limited as they think, experiences that will give them confidence and enthusiasm for the business of facing life, experiences that will assure them that they can make it.

    —Gregory Farrell, in the application for funding of
      Action Bound.

In 1963 Gregory Farrell, a Princeton alumnus who was working in the university's admissions office, was driving to Boston with his friend Mike Stewart when their car broke down at New Haven. Waiting on the repairs, Stewart suggested they drop in on his friend Bob Kiphuth, Yale's great swim coach. Stewart was a former Princeton end and Rhodes Scholar who had been stricken by a wasting disease while serving as a naval officer in the Far East. Kiphuth, whose competence as a physical educator and therapist approached genius, had helped him rebuild his physique. While these two were chatting, Farrell perused the bulletin board outside Kiphuth's office. His attention fastened on a quotation the Yale coach had posted:

> In present day civilization five social diseases surround the young, even in childhood. There is the decline of fitness due to the modern methods of locomotion; the decline of initiative due to the widespread disease of spectatoritis; the decline in care and skill due to the weakened traditions of craftsmanship; the decline in self-discipline due to the ever-present availability of tranquilizers and stimulants; the decline of compassion, which is spiritual death. —KURT HAHN

Greg remembers: "I was struck both by what the man said and by the spiky, nineteenth-century language. I asked Kiphuth who Hahn was. He told me the little he knew and gave me some literature from the new Colorado Outward Bound School." Excited by what he read, Farrell wrote us a letter asking if there was a way he could become involved in the Colorado activity. Subsequently I met Greg and was instrumental in Joe Nold's offering him a place in the instructors' course Tapley would be giving in the summer of 1964. Farrell, who by then was a reporter for the *Trenton Times*, snapped up the offer.

He was twenty-eight. At Marble he found that most of his course-mates had two advantages over him. They were under twenty, and they had had the basic course. "The first five days," he says, "I thought I was going to die. I felt like a thirty-three and one-third record being played at seventy-eight." After the grueling first days, things went better. "I came to feel strong and good, very light-headed. I got to love Tap and his wife, and all the guys in the course. At the end of it I was really moved." He discussed the Outward Bound idea with Tapley, Nold, Petzoldt, and others. One of the thoughts he took back with him was that the Outward Bound method would be applicable to any educational environment.

Things happened fast to Farrell that year. A series of pieces he wrote about the Community Action project in New Haven, a pilot undertaking in the new federal antipoverty program, led to his being commissioned to write a book about it. Covering Trenton meetings where a project on the New Haven model was being planned, he was frequently able to contribute helpfully to the discussion. Before the year was out he was made director of

United Progress Incorporated, the official agency spearheading action on Trenton's poverty problems.

At Colorado, Greg had seen ghetto youths responding positively to the Outward Bound experience. One of his first moves in his new post was to obtain funds to send youngsters from the Trenton ghettos to Outward Bound schools. He did the recruiting himself, making the rounds of neighborhood youth activities, telling the youngsters about his own experience, showing *Tall as the Mountains,* a new film about the Colorado School the Adolph Coors Company had made. Some thirty boys signed up, mostly blacks and Puerto Ricans, and in the summer of 1965 he packed them off to Colorado, Minnesota, and Hurricane Island.

One morning several weeks later he went to his office early. "I had hardly started working when I was surprised by a knock on the door. I opened it, and here were two kids, a Puerto Rican named Miguel Camacho and a black kid whose name I can't remember. They said, 'Hi, Mr. Farrell!' I said, 'Hey, what are you guys doing here?' and they said, 'We're back from Hurricane Island.' I said, 'But it's seven-thirty in the morning'—these guys never got up before eleven. They said, 'At Hurricane we get up every morning at five-thirty and we run around the island. So Miguel and I got up this morning and started running, and we thought we'd run down here and see how you're doing.' They were four feet off the ground. I was really thrilled, because it obviously had caught them so hard."

When the others got back, it was much the same story. Only three of the thirty had dropped out. Greg arranged for several of the youngsters to attend a meeting of the city's antipoverty committee, of which the mayor was a member. The youths told about their good experiences. The mayor asked them, "Now what are you fellows going to do?" One black lad said, "We're going to set up a rescue service on the Delaware River. We're going to patrol the river and save people from drowning." The boy saw that the mayor and some of the others were skeptical. He said, "Mr. Mayor, do you know how many people drowned in the river in the city last year?" The mayor did not know, so the boy told him. The mayor asked, "Why do you fellows want to set up a life-saving service?" The boy said, "Because then we can save Whitey instead of get Whitey."

Farrell and I talked a lot about the need for follow-up. He was responsive to my point that one person who goes to Outward Bound and comes back alone may be treated as an oddball, especially by ghetto peers; but several together have their own esprit with which to counter peer pressures to conform to the group. We discussed forms the follow-up might take, ways in which to facilitate transfer of an enhanced self-image and the new sense of what's possible that goes with it, as these youngsters returned to their street environment.

Farrell held a series of meetings with about twenty of the Outward Bound kids, looking to come up with an ongoing program with them as a core, along with a second group who would be receiving scholarships the following summer. They rapped about how they might do Outward Bound in the city, discussed things like what kind of urban expeditions they could have, whether doing a solo in the city would encourage stealing, how they might set up a rescue program. Finally, this informal activity jelled into a plan, funded by the Ford Foundation and the U.S. Office of Education under Title III (innovative programs) of the new Elementary and Secondary Education Act (ESEA), for a special program called "Action Bound" for a volunteer group of students in the Trenton City High School.

The plan called for the Action Bound students to be together in their own homerooms and to participate in a combined school-time and weekend schedule of Outward Bound-oriented activities. The Trenton Board of Education gave somewhat uncertain support. Since nobody in the school system felt threatened, and the program proposed to deal positively with some of the more troublesome students, the school people went along.

Trenton was a new kind of challenge for us—the first time an urban community sought to use the Outward Bound experience of a few as a healing force that could be brought back into the community and somehow harnessed as a multiplier. At the same time it suggested one practical way to deal with the perennial question of Outward Bound follow-up. From the educators' viewpoint, it was a pretty radical undertaking. Alternative schooling was not then as respectable as it would become; what Farrell and others were to attempt in the next several years was a pioneer effort.

Farrell asked me to find someone to take charge of the outdoor activity part of Action Bound. I nominated Barry Crook, an able young Britisher who had been an Outward Bound instructor in England and at Hurricane Island and was then helping to set up an adaptive program for New York's Horace Mann School at its nature tract in Connecticut. I had a helpful liaison at Trenton City High in Frank Nappi, the football coach, a charismatic individual whose experience accompanying some of the scholarship kids had made him an ardent Outward Bound supporter. Through Farrell I made another good Trenton contact in Warren Hill, president of Trenton State Teachers College. We helped Trenton State develop a three-part program by which students could get credit for the standard Outward Bound course. They started with a one-week precourse on campus, which I taught. Following a course at Colorado, Minnesota, or Hurricane Island, each student submitted a paper on how he intended to weave Outward Bound into his teaching practice. It was the first time a college gave academic credit for Outward Bound and, I think, the first time Outward Bound was explicitly related to experiental education theory.

A key purpose of the Trenton State scheme was to help provide Barry Crook with a staff. Half a dozen students signed on to work with him on Action Bound weekends, thereby earning additional college credits. Another Trenton State undergraduate whom Crook acquired was Phil Costello, the ex-Marine who had participated in the building summer at Hurricane Island and now was an instructor there. Also attending Hurricane that summer of 1966 was a forty-five-year-old former Flying Tiger pilot, ex-actor, and ex-nurseryman and landscape designer named Jose Gonzales, who was a special-education teacher in a Trenton junior high. The oldest individual to take the Hurricane Island course up to that time, he found it "the best challenge since my war days"—this from a pilot who had survived downed flights in three different World War II theaters. At Hurricane he met Phil Costello. Action Bound would intertwine and redirect the lives of those two.

That same summer Farrell visited a federal Job Corps Center at Camp Kilmer, New Jersey. This was one of a number of centers around the country where the Office of Economic Opportunity (OEO) was bringing together unemployed youngsters for academic and vocational training to qualify them for jobs with career potentials. The youngsters lived in dormitories, each of which had a kind of resident "cottage father" responsible for their well-being. These leaders were taught a leadership process called guided group interaction (GGI), a group dynamics technique for bringing about peer influence on the side of positive behavior. Farrell sat in on a GGI session led by a young black named Joe Moore, who had graduated from Central State College in Wilberforce, Ohio, a year previously. Impressed by the effective way Moore related to his charges, Greg offered him the post of assistant director of Action Bound, and Joe accepted.

The director's post was still open. One day a young ex-theologian turned up in Farrell's office. Bob Hanson had recently left the Episcopalian priesthood in order to resolve problems in his personal life. In his new lay status he was director of a political action committee in Cambridge, Massachusetts, doing campaign organizing work for candidates who favored ending the war in Vietnam. In New Jersey as a consultant, he learned that the Trenton antipoverty program was seeking someone to head up an educational program. He went to see Farrell, who—with Moore and Crook's approval—hired him.

Some eighty-five students, sixteen to eighteen years old and primarily a mix of juniors and seniors, made up the three homerooms comprising the Action Bound enrollment. In addition to most of Farrell's Outward Bound bunch, there was a broad mix of others who were recruited—or "selected"—for the program. By and large they were youngsters who in the eyes of the school staff "didn't fit." Many were considered disruptive. Two-thirds were black or of Puerto Rican descent. Most were regarded as "problems"—discipline problems, learning problems, problems growing from family situations. They were problems in that the school did not know what to do with them.

In its first, tentative year, Action Bound had two primary components—one on weekends and the other at school. On alternating weekends, Barry Crook and his staff either trained the recruits in outdoor skills, first aid, and rescue, and led them in community service projects, or took them on expeditions. Winter and spring vacations were times for rigorous weeklong expeditions. During the week the students met with Joe Moore in an adaptation of his GGI process and for personal counseling. In evening meetings they explored leadership concepts and techniques with Barry and Joe.

Coming to Outward Bound out of the priesthood, Hanson had no difficulty with the concept. "I think I was convinced from the very beginning," he says. An incident that sticks in his memory occurred early, when the students were doing their first rappel, on the spillway of a frozen dam. "There was a great big kid who was something of a bully, overwhelming the others with his mouth, and particularly intimidating one small boy. On the rappel the big guy came first, scared to death. He couldn't bring himself to take that first step. For all their dislike, the others, including the intimidated one, were giving him moral support. 'Come on, take it one step at a time, you can do it.' But the bully never went down that day. The next in line was the intimidated lad. He rappelled down like a pro. From that time on the relation between the two changed markedly. The big guy no longer bullied. The little fellow, who had had no sense of being able to accomplish anything, suddenly in his own mind became a giant. And the two became friends. That kind of productive use of the environment helps to make a person whole."

Hanson's perception of the wilderness component came partly from his own experience. "I had been strictly putting on my suit and tie, getting in my car to go to work. All of a sudden one weekend I was running around the rocks of Stokes State Forest. The next I was in the Pine Barrens, which petrified me, because I knew there were rattlesnakes there. And the next I found myself paddling down a river in the freezing cold rain. My apprehension level remained high until we started to have problems, like an overturned canoe, or being stranded overnight in the Pine Barrens without food and freezing our butts. After I'd come through several of these, I really began to relax, and a lot of my whole sense of apprehension about what was happening in all of my life began to diminish."

Joe Moore took part in the weekend activities, then used them as "impetus" for his supportive services. He recalls, "During the week we would meet in the students' free time and discuss what the weekend experiences might mean to each individual. At the same time I was finding out what kinds of counseling needs they had, what their group needs were, and getting a line on their academic problems. Getting the kids to realize that we were really interested in what was happening to them, I was building a constituency."

At one point there were so many youngsters coming to Moore's sessions that the school library was the only room big enough for them. Hanson was impressed by how well Moore's work supplemented Crook's: "Outward Bound and guided group interaction were a beautiful marriage. It was not enough that a kid have a really good experience on a weekend. The experience had to be translated into feeling through articulation. Joe had those skills in spades."

By the end of the school year good reasons for confidence in the essential soundness of the program had been established. Particularly impressive was one research finding * that showed how teachers perceived change in the students. Rating "blind"—knowing neither the purpose of the inquiry nor to which group an individual belonged—they perceived a marked degree of positive change in the Action Bound students that they did not find in a control group. But it was also clear that Action Bound's success would be limited unless the school accepted it as an integral part of the institution. Ironically, despite the favorable blind findings, the institution did not respond favorably to the program. Hanson feels that much of the difficulty lay in a failure of understanding. "Here was a classical educational problem," he says, "that of kids coming into an institutionalized educational setting with a strong self-concept and being *penalized* for it. When you get a kid who says Hey, teacher, (and let's assume he's doing it politely), I've been through this unit in some other kind of experience, could I go on to the next chapter, or could I do an individual study project, the teacher says No, we're all going to be on this page doing this thing at this time. There are hundreds of gradations of that same problem. The kids would come back from the weekend feeling much better about themselves. They would go into class. They would see the old behaviors imposed on them, and bingo—right back to ground zero."

The rest of Action Bound's history was to be an effort to create a "school within a school." Sarah Christie, the assistant superintendent of schools, an old-timer not far from retirement, understood Action Bound and perceived its potential. It made sense to

* See *Final Report: Effect of Outward Bound Training on Urban Youth*, Harold M. Schroder and Robert E. Lee, Princeton University, Princeton, N.J., 1967. See also Arnold Shore's critique of this study in *Outward Bound: A Reference Volume*, Outward Bound Inc., Greenwich, Conn., 1977.

her to try to integrate the cognitive side of school with the weekend experiences. She assigned three teachers to serve half-time on the program staff. In its second year, 1967–68, Action Bound had its own classes in social studies, earth sciences, and history, with experiments in using the Outward Bound component as a learning resource in support of the classroom. Hanson was made acting assistant principal. There was now a small group of sympathetic teachers, but to the staff at large Action Bound remained "that project."

On my periodic visits I found the program functioning more and more on its own. The ties with those of us who had originally sparked it were increasingly tenuous. Farrell's promotion to head up the state antipoverty program took him out of touch. Barry Crook was drafted into the army. Another Britisher, Jeff Evans, took his place but stayed only a short time before moving on to be chief instructor of the Minnesota Outward Bound School. He was replaced by Herb Kincey, who came from Colorado Outward Bound and at the year's end would go to the new North Carolina School.

Joe Moore, whose growing administrative duties were leaving him little time for guidance and counseling, had come to be the one to whom the outdoor staff and the classroom teachers brought problems they were having with the youngsters. There were more problems than ever. Most of the gung-ho core kids who had helped Farrell dream up Action Bound were gone. While the recruiting effort continued to try for that kind of youngster, the "regular" school had found Action Bound a convenient repository for students it could not cope with. "One of the recruiting problems we always had," Hanson says, "was that the staff should not think of this as a program for dumb kids or troublemakers. But every time the counselors got a kid they couldn't handle, they would direct him to us. That would be the last the kid would ever be in trouble, the last time he'd ever be referred for discipline. His attendance would suddenly skyrocket. Nobody ever said this is terrific—we just kept getting all these referrals. Until finally Joe Moore had to say, Look, you guys are giving us kids nobody can handle, lay off."

Then the program lost Moore. Following a serious race riot at the school, the leaders were suspended. Sarah Christie turned them over to Joe, who started a school in a factory basement.

Moore regards that school as "probably the most powerful experience" of his life; students from the regular school were begging to get in. But this work took him from Action Bound for the rest of the year.

Remarkably, for all its vicissitudes that second year, the program actually grew stronger. The weekend expeditions continued to produce their catalysis. They became more educationally significant through being related to classroom activities. Hanson, growing skillful in the arts of grantsmanship, was bringing in new federal funds to enlarge the academic staff and pay for staff training. Now too, in that time of racial tension, the program was beginning to be seen as a kind of safety valve. Action Bound never had serious racial problems.

In its third year, 1968–69, the program was switched to a sophomore activity, formally sanctioned as a dropout-prevention undertaking. No longer could teachers and counselors be discouraged from steering the troublesome students into it. Many of the sixty or so youngsters had been put out of school at least once, and all of them were rated disruptive. That year the school-within-a-school was fully realized, embracing all required subjects and foreign languages except for the science labs. Before the year started there was an intensive week of staff training that included a wilderness expedition. Phil Costello, now a graduate student, was heading up the outdoor activity and also teaching. Moore was back, putting in a good deal of time training staff in the ways of working with ghetto youngsters: "We had a sensitive faculty, people who could understand some of the nuances where those kids were coming from. We concentrated on bringing out the kids' strengths rather than on their weaknesses." The staff included several paraprofessionals—black women, some of them mothers of students, capable women who believed in the program and could relate well to the youngsters. They counseled, helped with personal problems, assisted the teachers. Some of them visited the students' homes to explain the program and its philosophy to their families. Action Bound began to build a parent constituency in the ghetto communities.

Costello got most of the staff to go out on many of the weekend expeditions. "That was important," Moore says. "If you had that teacher who taught you sharing the same pot of dehydrated food, things were on a different dynamic when you went back to class the following Monday. The response was different, the whole aura was different. It was extremely positive." In March Moore resigned to accept the offer of a deanship at Princeton. He could leave with a sense of accomplishment: "It wasn't the smoothest of operations, but it had good attitudes and feelings on the part of the kids. They enjoyed coming to school. They took to our nontraditional approach. It was very intensive. The twenty-four-hour, seven-day-a-week situation was a powerful experience for them."

Worried about the program's fourth-year funding, looking for other models with which to strengthen it, Hanson found the Philadelphia Advancement School, itself modeled on a successful experiment in North Carolina. He worked up an elaborate proposal to the federal Health, Education, and Welfare Department for a merging of the Action Bound and Advancement School concepts into an independent school within Trenton Central High. The Outward Bound elements were central to his proposal: "I felt then and I feel now that public education artificially separates the learning functions—that we somehow pretend that the youngster is a disembodied mind—a blank slate we can simply write on without being aware of how he feels, or without being aware that he learns with his body as well. Outward Bound was the first serious attempt that I heard about to try to look at what happens to a youngster as he learns physical skills that he thought he was not capable of, as he changes his concept of himself, and with that changed concept of himself comes to a learning situation in the school that is integrated with the physical learning experience he had been having."

The proposal was an ambitious, daring venture, calling for a budget of a million dollars a year for five years. By then H.E.W. had become highly sophisticated in what it required of grant proposals and in its evaluation of them. They rejected Hanson's first submission for technical deficiencies. He went to Washington for a week's briefing and started over. But in funding terms, a year was lost. In its fourth year Action Bound was scraping the bottom of the support barrel.

Yet the program had what in many respects was its best year. The teachers and paraprofessionals had acquired a surer sense of what they were about. While Moore was gone, Gonzales was back with Costello after a year of teaching in a storefront school. Felix

Pace, a teacher fresh out of Yale, was a welcome recruit to the outdoor activity. Morale was good; the program matured. Part of the maturing process was a missionary effort to reach out to the rest of the school. Action Bound teachers offered to team up with "regular" faculty members to design and teach a course cooperatively. Costello offered the services of his outdoor activity to any team or individual teacher who wanted to use wilderness adventure in support of a classroom study. While the science and other departments did take considerable advantage of this offer, and a number of teaching teams were formed, the missionary effort met with considerable resistance. The communication lines were in too poor repair to deal with the frequently voiced suspicions that "that project" was trying to take over the school.

Still, the successes were impressive. Costello estimates that, in addition to working with sixty Action Bound students throughout the year, he and his staff took three hundred fifty others on one or more expeditions. By way of example he likes to tell the Freddy Burke story. Freddy was one of the least involved students in a largely uninvolved English class taught by Mary Ann Springle. In desperation Mary Ann asked Costello and Gonzales to take the class on a weekend expedition and try to motivate them. The youngsters were dropped off in groups of four in Stokes State Forest in northwest New Jersey. Each group received a bag containing a miscellany of items and a letter. On opening the letter the group learned they were the survivors of a plane crash on an island, cut off from the rest of the world, and they had to create their own society. The contents of the bag were all they had been able to salvage. The letter gave them a list of ways they could earn points—building things out of natural materials, inventing a new game, and so on, and a list of things they could make to trade for food. The youngsters had a fine time; an anthropologist passing through Stokes Forest would have been intrigued with the variety of cultures flourishing there. Two weeks later Mary Ann came into Costello's office holding a notebook. She said, "I've taught Freddy Burke for two years. He's never written a sentence for me. He went on that one weekend expedition with you and wrote a journal thirty pages long, and it is one of the most incredible stories I have ever read!"

Freddy, it seemed, had been the captain of the TWA charter flight that crashed, and his journal was being written twenty years later. He told everything that happened in the twenty years. He included a Christmas poem the foursome had written together on their fifth Christmas marooned on the island. Years later Costello still gets excited when he recalls it: "Talk about a creative mind, an imagination! This kid blew his teacher right off her chair! She said, 'I'm going to go out with you next weekend with ten other students and see what you do,' and she did. I started team-teaching with her, and we did a whole slew of things with that class. A lot of them came out of my happening on a paperback book called *Hooked on Books* * that gave about a hundred ways of getting kids into reading. Essentially they were techniques for finding out what a youngster was interested in and then giving him books about it. We took that idea and made it work. Kids Mary Ann had never been able to get to open a book, we would find out what interested them, what they cared about, we'd go find a paperback on it, and that kid would be reading. It was great for us because it tied Action Bound into the English Department. Mary Ann sold us to the others."

The staff persuaded people in the Trenton business and civic communities to sign up Action Bound students for various projects. Youngsters in the math classes had part-time jobs in a bank; others dug for Indian artifacts at an archaeological site on the Delaware River and helped set up exhibits in the state historical museum. One of the most successful projects was in a hospital across from the school, where a team of six students were given jobs in the emergency room. Action Bound taught them advanced first aid, and the hospital trained them in handling patients and emergency-room procedures. They worked in pairs after school, nights, and weekends. For the youngsters it was a dramatic way of being useful. A decade later two of them were still on the hospital staff.

With the support of a $1,000 grant from the state, Action Bound did a series of joint expeditions with a racial mix—black and white—of police officers and youngsters. After six months there was a plan afoot to set up an "advisory board" of inner-city youngsters who would work with the police on their youth prob-

---

* *Hooked on Books: Program and Proof* by Daniel N. Fader and Elton B. McNeil, G. P. Putnam's Sons, New York, N. Y., 1968.

lems. Unfortunately, by then the year was running out. And so was Action Bound.

The program had a dramatic high point when word came from Washington that the "advancement school" application, with its million-dollar-a-year budget for five years, had been approved. But the euphoria was short-lived. Soon after came the crushing news that Congress had failed to fund the supporting legislation; no money was available for the upcoming year. It was a death blow. Action Bound did not wither away; it was struck down in its prime. On the heels of the bad news, Hanson resigned. For Costello and Gonzales, it was a career crisis. Costello says, "We felt the things we were doing were the greatest things we had done in our lives in the way of making contributions to kids and education. We weren't about to give them up." He, Gonzales, and Pace resigned from the school system to start something they called Project USE—Urban Suburban Environments—a kind of Jersey-oriented Outward Bound. Project USE is still going strong.

There is an ironic postscript to the Action Bound story. The following year, in the winter of 1971, Washington informed Trenton that $800,000 was forthcoming to fund the proposal approved the year before. Project USE offered to help implement the program; the school said Thanks, we're going to do it our way. Gonzales sat in on one of the "our way" meetings. "I couldn't believe my eyes or my ears," he says. "They were arguing about things we had worked out three years before. They dropped the Outward Bound adventure component, they dropped the paraprofessionals and the idea of liaison with the families, they dropped the part-time job experiences. They just about dropped Action Bound!"

The substitute program did wither away, with H.E.W. dropping its support.

Historically the Trenton experience broke trail for Outward Bound's incursion into the educational mainstream. It remains a model both for what can be accomplished and the pitfalls that waylay efforts to effect institutional change. But when Trenton was happening, we did not know it was that significant. Nor had we yet discovered that introducing an Outward Bound adaptive program into an institution is analogous to an organ transplant in a human being. The reflexive action of the institution is to reject the foreign element. To counteract the reflex forces calls for a high degree of management skill, particularly in human relationships.

In the New York office where he is executive director of the Fund for the City of New York—and a much-involved national trustee of Outward Bound—Greg Farrell thinks back across a decade to his launching of the Action Bound experiment. "Outward Bound does present and make real and quite palpable another possibility for behavior, a set of possibilities which it is quite energizing to discover. Out in the wilderness, under these changed circumstances, a youngster takes on a new role for which he may have had very little preparation or model, and all of a sudden he realizes, my God, I can be this, I don't have to be that. The possibility that emerges is often a shock and a delight. Those kids who were so high when they came to my office in Trenton that morning were experiencing just that. The thrill of this discovery and sense of capacity in themselves so excited them that they wanted to continue playing the parts in life that they learned they could play at Hurricane. It was quite thrilling to me too. I should have remembered what Larry Paquin had told me. Larry was an ex-sea captain who became superintendent of schools in New Haven and whom I met as a newspaper reporter. He had gone into the job with some ambitious ideas. One day I asked how his projects were going. 'Son,' he said, 'he who would change schools must learn to grow trees.' Action Bound was very imperfectly conceived. Still, for all our mistakes it worked well. I learned a major lesson about institutional change: The effort required for an Outward Bound adaptive program of Action Bound's scope is roughly equal to that involved in starting a new Outward Bound school. You need at least ten years to mature. You must learn to grow trees."

Bob Hanson, a staff member of the New Jersey Department of Education wearing two hats—management consultant and program-design specialist—has stopped by to say hello to his old friends at Project USE. Inevitably the talk runs to the old Action Bound days. He says: "Had we not had such a radical turnover in the top staff of the school system, had we had some really supportive people over a long period of time, something much more substantial would have resulted. After all, we left them a fine legacy—a multimillion dollar federal grant, a dedicated staff of twenty-one people, loads of equipment, a lot of achievement. We took youngsters nobody else wanted or could handle, potential dropouts, and helped them through school. We never had a staff member transfer out. And in four years of operating the wilderness program we never had a serious accident.

"I have lots of feelings of failure about my own involvement, that I was thrown into a management role without having been trained for it. But I know now that the experience we had was typical of all Title Three programs, except those that happen to be a favorite of a superintendent or principal, and those cases are not the way change usually happens. Usually the innovation is asked for by a teacher or someone else who is not part of the power structure, and there is always that set of barriers to how you introduce change and how you incorporate the beneficial products of the change. In recent years a lot of thought has been given to the change process by the states and by the federal agencies. Today you can go to the shelves and pick off whole books directed solely to the change process in public schools whereas at the time of Action Bound nobody was even talking about it."

Joe Moore is home from his daily commute, Princeton to Newark, where his work involves him in the long-term implications of the Supreme Court ruling that financing education through local property taxes is unconstitutional. He recalls that first successful year of Action Bound when so many of the students went on to college, his evolving administrative role with its growing interpretive function between staff and students, Action Bound's achievement in skirting racial dissidence. He also articulates, carefully, a dichotomy in his own thinking and feeling about "the transfer," about the difficult question of what the individual does with the self-discovery newly won in the wilderness when he returns to his own environment. "I often think about the transference. I sometimes look back on that experience, 1966 to 1969, with some resentment because of the assumption Outward Bound made in terms of the urban environment and the urban youngster. We could take a kid away on a weekend, and he could have the thrill of his life, and normally did. We could normally provide a positive school experience for him. But often we did not appreciate all the kinds of problems the youngster had. It's naive to think that a kid who can scale one hundred and eighty-foot cliffs can resolve all the problems that urban communities have. The basis of survival was not necessarily that of the wilderness, but of the day-to-day survival in the urban environment. That sometimes, I think, provided some of the misgivings that I personally had about the Outward Bound concept. Not that the experience was not good for the participant. It did stretch the kids, in terms of accomplishing things they thought they could not do. But you had a successful weekend experience and an unsuccessful environment. That was a negative factor—in that some of the youngsters had hoped that Outward Bound would not only change their lives but make a continued success possible, but the urban barriers were too great. I think most of the kids had very successful experiences on an individual level—kids that I still see today, who remember the program in a very, very positive light. There's no question about that. On the one hand we were providing very powerful experiences, but on the other hand we were augmenting frustration."

Farrell's learning to grow trees. Hanson's quest into change theory. Moore's caveat on augmenting frustration. All these and corollary lessons are gained through the Action Bound experience. Although we lacked the wisdom to derive these lessons early on—time, repetitive patterns, and a sharing of thinking about experience are probably imperative parts of this kind of learning process—we did come to recognize them. More and more today Outward Bound in its counseling role and the Outreach programs with their accumulation of own and shared experience are profiting from them.

Action Bound's failure to survive is less significant than the extraordinary degree to which it succeeded—and could have gone on succeeding. It continues to have a hold on many whose lives it touched. Often when Joe Moore visits Trenton he will run into some of the guys: "I can sit with those kids today and have a beer with them and talk about those experiences. 'Hey, Joe, do you remember Jose Gonzales helping us do this, showing us how to do that? Do you remember telling us that story around that campfire?' The level of relationship was probably as intense as you'll ever get in terms of closeness of adults to kids." The Gonzaleses live in the country now, but when the doorbell rings, it is often a former Action Bounder stopping to say Hi, or to discuss a problem. Phil Costello, walking along a Trenton street, bumps into Mrs. Meyers, Bobby Meyers's mother. Bobby was an Action Bound student, and his mother was one of the paraprofessionals who did liaison work for the program among her fellow parents in the black community. The two embrace and there on the sidewalk hold a happy reunion, remembering the good days of the program. Or Costello is visiting in Alexandria, Virginia, and he happens to see in the paper that the local high school principal's name is Susan Halbert. That has to be Sue Halbert, who taught social studies and English in Action Bound and did all the wilderness things. He calls her up, and she says come on over to the school, and the two put in an excited couple of hours of reminiscence.

Freddy Burke? He graduated and was gone, and nothing was heard of him. Four or five years went by, and one day Costello's phone rang, and it was Freddy calling. He was in the Navy, home on leave. He was going to be married next week. Would Phil be his best man? Sure, Phil said, he'd be honored.

North Carolina

≡✕≡✕≡✕≡✕≡✕≡✕≡✕≡✕≡✕≡✕≡✕≡✕≡

*I didn't see why we had to do the things we did, like
getting up at 5:30 a.m., and running and dipping. I
didn't see any sense in going through the ropes course
or standing out in the pouring rain all afternoon. I got
sick of it all really fast, so I left. But, once I left, I just
couldn't face myself. I guess I was just looking for an
easy way out. I've always taken the easy way of things,
and at first Outward Bound was not going to be an exception. After I left, I started thinking about my life
and the way it's been, and I really got sick. I guess I felt
like about the biggest cop-out alive. So, I came back
and I've found that to be the best decision I've made
in my life.*
—From a North Carolina student's course impression

In April 1964 the *Princeton Alumni Weekly* carried an article
about me and Outward Bound. One alumnus who read it with
more than passing interest was Watts Hill Jr. of Durham, North
Carolina, who had been at college a year ahead of me. Hill was
president of the Home Security Life Insurance Company, had
served in the state legislature, and was active in state civic and
cultural affairs. He sent the article with a "this-may-interest-you"
note to George Esser, president of the North Carolina Fund. The
fund was a five-year project set up the previous year by Governor
Terry Sanford to attack problems of poverty in the state through
demonstration programs with monies provided by the Ford
Foundation and two North Carolina foundations. Esser passed

the article along to Jack Mansfield, his director of special projects. Mansfield, a Methodist minister who had left the pulpit for social activism, and his assistant, Marjorie Calloway, a recent honors graduate of the state university at Chapel Hill who had taught elementary school in England and Durham, were both greatly intrigued by Outward Bound and sought more information about it. One of their sources was Tom Hartmann, my old sidekick at the Hun School. This requires a diversion.

In 1958 Hartmann became headmaster of St. Marks School in Dallas. In periodic trips east he visited us in Andover, always keen to know what was happening on the Kurt Hahn front. By the time the Colorado Outward Bound School was founded he had also come to know Chuck Froelicher as a fellow headmaster. He recruited students for Colorado and helped raise money for Outward Bound. When he returned to Princeton in 1963 to shepherd the merger of two Princeton day schools, the Atlantic Foundation elected him to its board. As noted, he was one of the original OBI trustees. Early on he was elected board secretary.

Through Tom I met Paul Ylvisaker, who was then director of the national affairs activities of the Ford Foundation. As the initiator of half a dozen pilot urban programs around the country, Ylvisaker was the conceptual father of the Johnson administration's antipoverty program. One evening in early 1965 Greg Farrell, Hartmann, Joel Sugarman, and I were dinner guests of Ylvisaker, who was interested in Outward Bound's potential as an antipoverty force. Subsequently he hired Hartmann as a consultant to survey innovative antipoverty programs and simultaneously to seek ways Outward Bound might be applied in the antipoverty arena. Tom's survey brought him into contact with Mansfield.

When Mansfield and Calloway learned that the Minnesota School was starting the first course for girls in the United States, Marjorie went up to Ely for a firsthand look. At Homeplace she observed the female students undergo basic training, talked with the instructors and the Piehs, took note of the inner-city kids who were there on scholarship from the Massachusetts Youth Services and Trenton. One evening after supper Jerry Pieh suggested a walk. When they reached the ropes course, he persuaded Marjorie to climb up to the starting platform and then to do the initial traverse. Marjorie remembers: "I had watched the students do the ropes course and hadn't even conceived of attempting it myself. Once I'd started, I wanted to keep going. Down on the ground Jerry talked me through the whole thing. I finished on top of the world!"

As it happened, we were holding an OBI trustee meeting at the Minnesota school at the time. Mansfield came up for that. He talked with Tom and me about the North Carolina Fund's possible interest in starting a school. It was decided that Marjorie should go on to Colorado. There she went on a three-day safari with two instructors and the wife of one, checking students on solo. They carried live chickens, an experiment (not repeated) in solo cuisine that summer. It was hailing and snowing, and Marjorie shared a tent with the chickens. "I found the reality of Outward Bound even more than I expected," she says. "The instructors were a terrific bunch of people. They really inspired me. I came back to Durham sold on Outward Bound as a proposition for the North Carolina Fund."

But when Mansfield drew up a proposal for the fund to found an Outward Bound school, the trustees decided they would be exceeding their charge in sponsoring an organization that would not be exclusively for the poor. At that juncture help came from another quarter. Hartmann, now deputy director of the North Carolina Fund, called me to come down. The occasion for the trip was a dinner at the home of Harold and Sibby Howe in Chapel Hill. Harold "Doc" Howe had taught at Phillips Academy; the year we arrived there he left to be principal of the Punchard High School in Andover, the first of a series of public-school posts he filled with distinction. In 1964 he became head of the Learning Institute of North Carolina (LINC), a private organization acting as a kind of holding company for a series of educational experiments going on in the state.

The Howes' dinner guests were George Esser, Hartmann, and I. We ran the *Tall as the Mountains* film, and I reviewed the organizational story. When I finished, Doc said, "All right, let's outline the steps to start a North Carolina Outward Bound School." Esser was sympathetic. He reiterated that the North Carolina Fund could not sponsor a school but offered to provide staff aid to do missionary work, seeking out citizens who would be willing to come together as a board of trustees. He gave that assignment to the Mansfield–Calloway team, who reported to Hartmann. I have always remembered Doc Howe's *amicus curiae* role that evening as a splendid demonstration of what an understanding, concerned liaison person can do in a situation where catalysis is needed. As events transpired, the timing was critical. Two months later Howe was gone from North Carolina, to be the U.S. Commissioner of Education.

In the fall of 1965 a piece of property in the Blue Ridge mountain region was offered to the North Carolina Fund. Mansfield and Calloway went to look at it as a possible school site, accompanied by Dave Mashburn and Herb Kincey, two Colorado instructors who were advising them. When the location was found not suitable for Outward Bound purposes, Mashburn and Kincey said, "Let's go to Table Rock. We'll show you some real pretty terrain, even though you can't have it because it's U.S. Forestry Service country." Table Rock Mountain rises above the hamlet of Jonas Ridge, near the town of Morganton in the western part of the state; a great tablelike rock gives the mountain its dramatic apex and its name. While well-known at that time to a few rock climbers and the hunters and fishermen who frequented the adjoining spectacular Linville Gorge country, the general public did not impinge on it much, and it was remarkably wild considering its closeness to populated areas. Mansfield and Calloway resolved on the spot to investigate the chances of obtaining a special usage permit from the Forestry Service. Their day peaked when Mashburn and Kincey put them through their first rappel.

The North Carolina board that Mansfield and Calloway recruited was incorporated with Watts Hill as chairman in January 1966. When Mansfield left the fund soon after, Calloway carried on as the board's agent. One of her first assignments was to pursue the Table Rock site. Richard Eriksson, the Forestry Service's deputy regional director, became an enthusiast for the Outward Bound idea and helped immeasurably in guiding her through the red tape. By spring the usage permit was assured, and the lawyers were working out a lease of eighty acres. The North Carolina Outward Bound School was chartered in April, with plans to open the following year and aspirations to become the first year-round school in the United States. Tony Mulvihill, a former Marine officer and youth worker in New York's Harlem ghetto, who had worked for me in the Andover office, was hired as director of development. In June he and Calloway, who was now an employee of the school, moved into an office in Durham provided by Watts Hill's insurance company.

In pursuit of their year-round objective, the board commissioned Vincent Lee, a Hurricane Island instructor who was a graduate student in architecture at Princeton, to design the school. His plans, which earned him his graduate degree, were an exciting concept for a mountain school organized on "dunk 'em and dry 'em" principles. The board's intent to offer courses ten months of the year, on the British year-round model, received an enthusiastic response from educators and youth workers around the state. Events, however, were to prove the idea overly ambitious.

The school site was a short distance below Table Rock itself and a mile off the gravel road that wound its way over the mountain. On a rainy night in October 1966, four young men, three of them under twenty, drove up the mountain and hiked into the site. Their leader was Lance Lee (no relation to Vincent), a New Englander who had had his first Outward Bound instructing experience at Aberdovey and then joined the Hurricane Island staff. On the 200-mile trip from Durham they had picked up tools, lanterns, cooking equipment, and food. They pitched tents in the darkness and driving rain, bunked down, and at 6 A.M. began the first day's work of clearing the site for the new school. They were the first of many rosters of Lance's "woods crew," an ever-changing phenomenon of mostly willing, however unskilled, artisans who would build the school. "I recruited them from every place imaginable," Lance says. "We had dropouts from schools and colleges, from Cuba, from a reform school and a mental institution. I would capture kids from the road, if they looked like they would work on the mountain. We got some of the dregs and fashioned them into quite a good woods crew." The initial group worked into December, closed down for the winter, and resumed in the early spring with the school's opening less than three months off.

The board appointed James "Pop" Hollandsworth as school director. He was dean of students and chairman of the science department at the Asheville School, with a thirty-year background of operating summer wilderness programs. They hired the usual new school complement of two experienced British instructors.

One of them was John Lawrence, an Oxford graduate who had been teaching at New Zealand Outward Bound; the other was Peter Sheehan, a British-born Eurasian from the Moray Sea School. Knut Smith, a Colorado instructor, was engaged to teach rock climbing. Dave Mashburn also transferred from Colorado; later Herb Kincey came.

When George Greene, a Marine sergeant major just retired after twenty-six years in the Corps, hired on as business manager in April, he found the one-mile access road cut in but not yet graveled. A crew was drilling for water, with no luck. The woods crew had completed the clearing work and were building platforms for six-man tents. They had acquired a boss carpenter in the person of Jesse Padrick, retired police chief of Wilmington, North Carolina. For Greene the woods crew's motley quality and long-haired kind of esprit were a sharp shift from the structured, crew-cut environment of the U.S. Marines, but he found the change not unrefreshing: "Lance had all these problem-type kids coming and going, most of them had hardly ever hammered a nail before, and they were building tent platforms under the leadership of an ex-police chief. Maybe working next to the chief would be a Puerto Rican kid on probation out of Spanish Harlem who didn't know anything about sawing a straight line, and didn't saw a straight line, but the old chief tolerated it, and the two would learn a lot from each other."

The only building put up the first year was a secondary structure in the Vince Lee plan; open on all sides, it included the kitchen and eating facilities, and would temporarily provide office and equipment storage space. Everybody pitched in—woods crew, instructors, volunteer alumni of other schools. The lumber was timbers from an old furniture factory recently torn down in Morganton. The great 15-by-12-inch beams were trucked up the mountain and put in place with block and tackle. Since there was no electric power, all sawing, drilling, and other work was by hand.

On July 2, 1967, the school was dedicated by Mrs. Emma Clark, U.S. postmistress at Jonas Ridge. Two days later it opened with forty-seven students divided into four "crews." The summer courses went well, despite a plague of rain in July and a goodly assortment of other start-up difficulties. The lack of electric power and a water system became part of the Outward Bound experience. The summer's students came from twenty-odd states. The desired socioeconomic mix, which was well met, included a number of North Carolina lads, white and black, from poverty environments, and a group of DYS youngsters from Massachusetts.

The North Carolina School did not include an age ceiling in its eligibility rules. An important reason for this was Lawrence Cohen and his Jewel Box Corporation, a chain of jewelry stores operating in the South and Southwest. Larry Cohen was one of the most enthusiastic and dedicated of the school's trustees. He believed in Outward Bound strongly enough to invest a considerable portion of the company's training budget in the program. For several years the Jewel Box organization enrolled some of its store-manager trainees in each course and contributed an equal number of scholarships.

In the fall the plan to operate a year-round school ran into trouble. A September course did not fill, and after that the overall off-season schedule was not adequate to meet expenses. Since there were not enough courses to occupy the instructors, they were used for recruiting. Living conditions on the mountain were less than remarkable for comfort. Eight mobile homes were brought in to provide staff housing, but the task of putting down seven miles of underground electric power and telephone lines to the site was not finished until February.

The school was seriously strapped for funds, with little additional income anticipated before the new summer season. Greene remembers a gloomy rainy-night, lantern-lit meeting in one of the mobile homes, with Willi Unsoeld (who had recently joined us at Andover) and Peter Willauer sitting in, when a trustee group discussed closing down the school for several months. For George this raised the specter that it might not open up again: "I think that night some people would have said, 'Let's give up.' Being an outspoken sergeant major, I let it be known that I thought that would be the worst thing we could do. I offered to work for nothing. Watts Hill said we should keep going, and he carried the day, but it was close. A few months later good things were happening, and we could see we were going to make it."

An aspect of the North Carolina story that gives it special interest is that it brought Murray Durst into U.S. Outward Bound. This was a happening that not only safeguarded the survival of the North Carolina school but in the long run had considerable import for the national organization, and ultimately for the national experiential education movement that Outward Bound was destined to generate.

Murray Durst lived his childhood in Brownsville, Texas, and his early adolescence in New Canaan, Connecticut, before the family moved to his father's native California. In 1950 he was a junior at San Jose State when the Korean War broke out. Rejecting the idea that the fortunate should be exempted from military service for having the advantage of being in higher education, he volunteered. His war experience affected him strongly in two ways. One was that in undergoing the army's training, of which he was critical, he became deeply interested in the processes of training and education. The other was the consequence of President Truman's executive order desegregating the army. "It exposed for us that two-world situation in which we had been living and probably were very comfortable. It really opened my mind to that whole issue and created the consciousness that led me later into concerns for dealing with the disadvantaged minority person. As a college kid who had grown up in the New Canaans of the world, the social interaction with the less-advantaged person that one gets through a citizen army was, I think, very key to the directions I took."

Having done his military service, including a year in the Korean front lines, Durst went back to college and got his degree. Knowing he wanted to be an educator but unwilling to continue in the classroom to gain teacher certification, he took a job with the state of California, working with private industry to encourage training and employee development activity. He steeped himself in the new literature dealing with management as a function. After three years he became director of training for Sacramento County, a densely populated governmental entity with a large, varied employee force. Five years later he was appointed a regional training director of the U.S. Bureau of Reclamation. From that post he was called to Washington to be director of training for the entire bureau.

It was the time when Lyndon Johnson was launching his "war on poverty," which included the Job Corps, a program for helping unemployables in an affluent society to become employable. One of the first proposed Job Corps Conservation Centers was to be at Collbran, Colorado, close to the home of Congressman Wayne Aspinall, whose chairmanship of the House Interior and Insular Affairs Committee gave him great political clout. The Department of the Interior, anxious to have a good operation in Aspinall's backyard, assigned Durst to direct it.

One of Murray's ideas was that the corpsmen should be encouraged to take a large part of the responsibility for operating their center. The implementing of this policy, however, was beset by a problem: "We were bringing kids into that center at the seven-thousand-foot level in the Rocky Mountains, forty miles from civilization up a canyon road, in what to my middle-class eyes was absolutely gorgeous country, but to those urban and southern rural eyes was a fearful place. We had not done the job of looking at the potential in the locations of Job Corps Conservation Centers. We had failed to see that we could use their very environments for learning purposes."

As it happened, Durst was seeking a way to deal with this problem at the same time Joe Nold was looking for ways in which Outward Bound might serve some of the issues involved in the war on poverty. As it also happened, Collbran was a mere forty miles as the crow flies on the other side of a mountain range from Marble. Still another happenstance was that the head of the Office of Economic Opportunity (OEO), of which the Job Corps was an agency, was Sargent Shriver. That simultaneity of interests led to a contract between the Collbran Center and the Colorado School to introduce Outward Bound concepts into the Job Corps training effort as a means of helping the center utilize its own environment for its educational goals.

The collaboration was successful. Nold assigned a staff to assist Durst in achieving his several purposes. The primary goal was to help the corpsmen transform their negative feelings about their environment to positive ones, giving them a confidence-building learning experience in the process. Another was to apply Outward Bound techniques to the training of those who showed promise of leadership capabilities for carrying out Durst's self-government policy. There was yet a third payoff, which Durst recalls gratefully: "We had a big public-relations problem because the general population viewed the centers as places where the U.S. government was bringing real risky people into these rural environments. So another important use of Outward Bound was directly to apply the service notion with which Kurt Hahn was so especially concerned—to train those corpsmen to serve as rescue teams in our mountain area. They made rescues in situations ranging from airplane crashes to floods. Their abilities, trained through the Outward Bound process, brought to that center a great deal of positive response."

Quite apparently the Durst method had merit, for in a time when the Job Corps generally was experiencing a dropout rate of thirty-five percent, the rate at Collbran was only three percent. Subsequently, after being called back to Washington to serve as deputy director of the Interior Department's Job Corps effort, Durst was twice returned to the field on rebuilding missions to troubled centers. In each instance he used the Outward Bound principles that had worked well at Collbran to contribute significantly to the turnarounds he was able to achieve. The second of these rescue tasks was at a large urban center in Grand Rapids, Michigan. Durst was still involved in his mission there when the center fell victim to President Johnson's new policy of cutting back on the war on poverty to help finance the growing American commitment in Vietnam. It was clear that the entire OEO program was beginning to run down. "Knowing what was happening," Murray recalls, "I started wondering about where I might go. My first thought was Outward Bound—I had become so interested in that whole effort. So I called Joe Nold and asked, 'Que pasa?' "

Nold was aware that Hollandsworth was going back to his old school and that the North Carolina trustees were looking for a new director. He called us, and I arranged for Unsoeld to meet with Durst in Chicago. Since I had come to admire the way Murray combined managerial competence with creative insight to Outward Bound as an educational process, I strongly supported Willi's endorsement of his candidacy for the North Carolina post. As it was, Durst sold himself to the trustees, and they to him. Murray's regard for the solid quality of the board's commitment was reenforced when it assumed an obligation that was imperative to the school's survival—a bank loan of $100,000 personally guaranteed by the board members.

Taking over in the spring, Durst made several basic decisions. He closed the Durham office and established an overall headquarters on the mountain, "where the investment was." Marjorie

Calloway had left the Durham operation shortly before; she continues to serve on the board she helped to create and in 1980 became chairman. Tony Mulvihill also left at that time. As the official school history notes, "the long hours, personal dedication, and sacrifice on the part of Hill, Calloway and Mulvihill provided the foundation on which the school was built." Durst also persuaded the board to abandon its ambitious building plans. Subsequently he concluded it did not at that time make sense to aspire to year-round operation.

Murray was a new kind of school director, hired not because he was a highly competent outdoorsman-educator, but because of the managerial abilities that he combined with educational concerns. He had no difficulty in making the transition from the worlds of big government, management theory, and personnel development. "In coming to grips with the whole translation of the Outward Bound learning process into the Job Corps setting," he says, "I had learned the process. I do have an affinity for the out-of-doors, and I understood the Outward Bound concepts—but more importantly, I think, I understood the processes of learning. I have been particularly intrigued with the process of learning out of consciously structured experience, and Outward Bound is nothing if it is not that."

And he did his Kurt Hahn homework: "I read all of Hahn's speeches and addresses I could get hold of. I went directly to the man, to avoid having to interpret interpreters of Kurt Hahn, and tried to interpret directly from him. I looked not for the forms that he espoused to fit initially his work in Germany and subsequently his work in Britain, forms reflecting those two societies, but rather the principles that he was articulating. There was then no difficulty in interpreting those principles into an appropriately comfortable form."

Five schools. As the organization continued to grow, and school enrollment with it, demands on the OBI staff and the scholarship needs of the schools kept increasing—and the perennial quest for funds became more pressing. In 1969 it was estimated that the total funding required to make full use of the school capacities was very close to $2.5 million. We were getting into the big time. Outward Bound never could have succeeded as it has without the generous contributions that individuals, corporations, foundations, and others have given to support its work. In 1969 we were treated to a vivid demonstration of how profoundly human generosity can advance the welfare of an institution.

When the Colorado School was inundated with applications after the appearance of Lydia Ratcliff's *Reader's Digest* article in 1963, I looked up the name of the magazine's publisher on its masthead and wrote Mr. DeWitt Wallace about the extraordinary response the article had generated. I was quite ignorant of the story of how DeWitt and Lila Wallace had conceived and created the world's most successful magazine. Nor was I aware of any of the lore that had grown up around their many benefactions. As the months went by, I wrote Mr. Wallace several times more, telling him of the impact the *Reader's Digest* was continuing to have on Outward Bound and saying I hoped they were as pleased as we.

On a Monday in the fall of 1964 I answered my office telephone, and a man's voice asked for me. When I identified myself, he said, "Mr. Miner, my name is DeWitt Wallace, and I am associated with the *Reader's Digest*." Lights went on and the adrenalin started pumping. I had visions of another article. He continued, "I've been watching the progress of your organization with much interest. Outward Bound's philosophy seems to jibe with my own. When you're in New York, I'd like you to come out to our offices in Pleasantville and talk with me about Outward Bound." I said, "I'm going to be in New York on Thursday." He said, "Thursday seems a long way off." I said, "If that's the case, I could come tomorrow." He said, "You could? How would you get here from Andover?"

I told him I would fly to New York and rent a car. He said, "That seems to be putting you to too much of an inconvenience. I've checked into it, and find our plane could land at North Andover. Would it be an imposition if I sent the plane up for you to come down for lunch with me tomorrow?" The next morning I got on the *Reader's Digest*'s twin-engine, twelve-passenger transport. There were two pilots, a hostess, and me. In forty minutes we landed at the Westchester Airport, and in short order I was seated alone with DeWitt Wallace in the dining room of the *Digest* guest house. He was a tall, vigorous seventy-four-year-old, but appeared much younger. Mentally he was razor-sharp.

We talked about Outward Bound through lunch, and the conversation continued for most of the afternoon. Mr. Wallace kept asking me, "How much would it cost to put a school in every state?" My answer was, "It depends on how fast you want to do it. If you're willing to take twenty years, there's one price, if you want to do it next year, that's another." I knew we did not want a school in every state but I did not want to be anything but enthusiastically responsive to this lovely gentleman.

I left that meeting with a sense of having made a good friend. Not long after, out of the blue, the mail brought a check for $10,000 from DeWitt Wallace. Nothing like that had come out of the blue before. The next thing was that Mr. Wallace called to say he wanted to meet an Outward Bound trustee. He knew Jack Stevens's brother and was inviting Jack and me for lunch at the Pan American Club. The two older men hit it off beautifully. Mr. Wallace asked Mr. Stevens if he was supporting Outward Bound. Mr. Stevens said he was, that it was a worthwhile cause he enjoyed supporting.

Mr. Wallace said, "I have a proposition to make. Why don't we give it some more support, you and I together?" "Wait a minute," Jack said, "I'm not in your league." Then he added, "But I'll be delighted to support Outward Bound with you." They came to an agreement whereby Mr. Wallace would give $50,000 and Mr. Stevens would give $10,000. I listened happily as another unanticipated $60,000 entered the till. As Jack and I left the club together, he said, "That was the most expensive lunch of my life!"

A year or so later the three of us met for another lunch. Mr. Wallace inquired if Mr. Stevens had kept his pledge. Mr. Stevens said he had, and made the same inquiry of Mr. Wallace. When Mr. Wallace said indeed he had, the two men made a second, similar agreement. There were other Wallace contributions as well.

All this happened at a time when we were struggling and trying hard to grow and very much aware of our potential. Mr. Wallace kept asking, "What is it you need most?" Stevens kept saying, "This guy needs money to get this thing rolling. He needs unrestricted funds to support an organization." But Mr. Wallace, it was clear, did not like to give that kind of money. He preferred to give for something tangible. In the spring of 1969 came one of his periodic calls: "I've never met any of the men who actually run the schools. Do you think you could get them all together? I'd like to have a lunch for them at the Pan American Club." I said, "Wally, they'll be delighted!" and he named a date. It was May, and the directors were tooling up for their school openings; it was the worst possible time to take them away from their work. Only with the greatest dragging of feet did they agree to make the journey to New York.

I had butterflies about the meeting. On the night before, I met with the group and went over the ground rules. No laundry lists. We were not going to ask for anything. We were just going to do all we could to give a fine old gentleman a wonderful time at the luncheon he was giving us. Meanwhile, about a week before, Mr. Wallace had called me to say he was nervous about the luncheon; he would like to know more about these fellows so that he could ask intelligent questions. So I had made up a one-page information sheet on each director, with a picture and biographical information and the salient features of his school.

As the directors arrived at the Pan Am Club, Mr. Wallace went up to each new arrival and greeted him by name: "Alan Hale, you don't look as old as your picture!" After he had seated us, he turned to Joe Nold and queried him about his experiences as head of the oldest U.S. school. He went on to Bill Byrd and said, "Bill, you're the fellow who invented the mobile course, tell me about it. What are the good things about the mobile course, and what are its disadvantages?" And so on around the table to Peter Willauer, Murray Durst, and Alan Hale. By then he had the group in the palm of his hand. The entire luncheon became a happy affair. When the dessert and coffee came, Mr. Wallace turned to me and said, "Josh, these boys hardly ever get to New York. It's silly for them to travel all that distance and then go right home. I'd like them to stay in New York for the next two or three days and do anything they want, and I'd like to pay for it." And he slipped an envelope into my pocket.

The lunch over, we said our thanks and good-byes. Going down in the elevator from the top of the building, someone said, "What's in the envelope?" I opened it; inside was a letter and a check. I took a quick look at the check in the subdued light and said, "It's a check for ten thousand dollars!" Somebody said, "Holy smoke!" Bill Byrd, who was looking over my shoulder, said, "You can't read. It's for a hundred thousand!" Joe Nold said, "Let me see it." He took a look, then a closer look, and said, "My God, it's for a million dollars!"

We came out of the Pan Am building six inches above the pavement. We just could not absorb the reality of it. The other five split to fan back across the country. I walked over to the Princeton Club and wrote Mr. Wallace a letter. I was deeply moved. It was not anything as simple as the money, although the levitating effect of a million dollars is extraordinary. It was the marvelous esprit of the man, the verve with which he continued to reach out to life in the eighth decade of a remarkably creative lifetime, and the generous spirit that shone through his acts of disbursing his wealth for socially creative purposes.

Mr. Wallace's letter specified that the money was for an endowment for scholarships, and there was a subsequent letter of instructions. Jim Wallis, one of our trustees, was a vice-president of Guaranty Trust Company, where we had our account, and he would not let me loose until he had that check in his bank. Jack Stevens wrote a hard bargain with the bank. We wanted six percent return on the money and the principal was to be appreciated with the aim that it would always provide the same number of scholarships as $60,000 provided then. The bank moaned and groaned, but Jack had a way of getting what he wanted.

It was not the only million dollars that DeWitt Wallace gave us, nor was the second the last. For almost the entire span of U.S. Outward Bound's existence he has been its greatest benefactor. He has never asked anything in return—other than that we do our job well.

Winter Courses

Winter is a resonant instrument that twangs its own music.

—Henry Thoreau

Ambivalence is when nature is calling, and it's ten below zero, and you know that you're never going back to sleep unless you unzip your bag and risk freezing your bleep.

—Phil Plubell

In the midst of winter I finally learned that there is in me an invincible summer.

—Albert Camus

I

A year after he graduated from Dartmouth, where he captained the 1961 swim team, Alan Hale and his wife Anita were looking to join the Peace Corps. Discovering that the Outward Bound camp at Arecibo had staff positions to fill, they decided instead to cast their lot with the Puerto Rican training mission. When Bill Byrd hired Alan, neither had an inkling that it was a case of one future Outward Bound school director bringing another into the fold. In Washington the Hales found Sargent Shriver and his people concerned about the prevailing six-month staff turnover in Puerto Rico. They made a commitment to stay two years. Their leave-taking in 1964, along with colleagues who had completed their tours, pretty much marked the passing of the Outward Bound era at Arecibo. It pretty much severed, too, the

221

transcultural bonds with the local people that Bill Coffin encouraged initially and that Bill Byrd and others nurtured. When the Hales revisited the island, their old friends in the Arecibo countryside said, "After you people left, we never again saw any Peace Corps volunteers. They never came to our homes for coffee. They never bothered to talk with us." Alan says: "They were learning all their Spanish in a language laboratory when the roads, and the *tiendas* like the ones where we stopped for a beer after rock climbing, were full of people speaking it." *

In 1967 Alan was in business in the farming center of Jefferson, Ohio, when Bob Pieh offered him a place as assistant director of the Minnesota Outward Bound School. Subsequently he succeeded Pieh,† from whom he inherited a soundly grounded program and a first-rate staff. In time, as the Piehs had and as every director does, Hale put the mark of his own personality on the school. Looking ahead after the 1968 season he had two innovations in mind. One was coeducational courses, a development logically sequential to Minnesota's pioneering of courses for young women. The other was winter courses. Both were important developments within the U.S. Outward Bound family—winter courses in particular in that they were a key step toward year-round activity.

It would be hard to find a more testing environment for confronting winter's challenges on starkly implacable terms than the Superior-Quetico country. In winter it is a land of fiercely unyielding cold. Temperatures that seldom get as high as zero Fahrenheit plunge to sixty below in the long nights. Winds tunnel

---

* This becomes the more significant on reading Kevin Lowther and C. Payne Lucas's *Keeping Kennedy's Promise—The Peace Corps: Unmet Hope of the New Frontier* (Westview Press, Boulder, Col., 1978). These two veteran corps administrators, strong adherents of the Peace Corps ideal, write a severe indictment of the corps' ultimate failure to get the volunteers to cope with their own ethnocentrism and to establish creative transcultural relationships in the countries where they served.

† Bob Pieh returned to college teaching, joining the Faculty of Education at Queens University, in Ontario, where he has built a distinctive academic record in the areas of experiential education, adult basic eduation and retraining, and community service. In 1973 he returned to Minnesota Outward Bound as acting director for that summer. Subsequently he was appointed director of the new Canadian Outward Bound Wilderness School in Ontario, combining that post with his university duties for several years.

their deadly chill factors across the open lakes, driving the snow into drifts that make the going even more difficult. The rule of thirties is commonplace: thirty below zero, thirty knots of wind, thirty seconds to freeze bare flesh. The vast white blanket builds, storm after storm without retreat, burying trees and obliterating the lacework of lakes and streams. It is a brooding environment, innately hostile to the human body. The cold that crackles spit in midair threatens to drive the blood inward to the visceral core, exposing the bodily surfaces and extremities to frostbite and the body itself to the insidious toll of hypothermia. Ten seconds with a glove off and the hand goes numb, in instant prelude to frost-bite. One must keep testing the body for signs that some part may have lost sensation. In the first stages of hypothermia, the brain falters, prey to hallucination.

Because there was no U.S. precedent for a course conducted in so severe a winter environment, Hale sought help from the one source of expertise on cold weather operations in worldwide Outward Bound. A letter to the Outward Bound Trust wangled him an invitation to take part in the British Army Outward Bound's winter course in Norway. The reply from London was cordial: even though the manuals made no provision for an American civilian's participation in a training exercise of Her Majesty's soldiers, the military liaison people were disposed to accommodate the American warden.

With Alan scheduled to leave for Norway in January, Jeff Evans, his chief instructor, conceived of a bon voyage present from the staff. Jeff was a highly capable British instructor who a few years hence would become director of the new Canadian Outward Bound Mountain School at Keremeos, British Columbia. He told Hale that at Christmas vacation he would assemble a group of instructors at Ely and lead them on a reconnaissance course to check out the winter terrain and a cold-weather mode of operation. Deeming the proposed expedition overoptimistic, Alan doubtfully gave it his blessing. Christmas came, and Evans and twelve staff members headed north, filled with pioneer zeal. They drove to Lake 1, an end-of-the-road spot in the wilderness east of Ely, about thirty miles short of the Canadian border. Getting there was an initiative test in itself. The original plan had been to head north into the Quetico on a beeline expedition across the frozen lakes, but a warning that the lake ice was thin under several feet of insulating snow had induced cautionary second thoughts. Now the plan was to start from Lake 1 at the west end of the Kekekabic Trail and follow it east for about forty miles of rugged, hilly country to where it intersected Gunflint Trail, which runs north into Canada, then double back.

At the trailhead the participants must have seemed a motley bunch. Nobody quite knew what the best equipment would be or what methods would work. Most were on snowshoes, with limited experience in their use. Although none had been on cross-country skis, three were using them. Individuals were carrying gear in everything from pack frames to rucksacks. Evans had got hold of two Norwegian heavy-duty-aluminum rescue toboggans for carrying supplies, and these had to be towed.

In 1968 the Kekekabic Trail was hardly broken out, difficult enough to follow in summer. In winter, with the snow level above the tree blazes, it was virtually nonexistent. Two hours after the start the expedition was lost. Doug Page, one of the expeditionaries, remembers: "We were off the trail, bushwhacking through this horrible morass of hills, deep snow, and trees—six-, seven-, eight-foot trees with only the tops sticking out. Breaking trail in the deep snow in that up and down country was exhausting. The toboggans were a major problem—they just weren't designed for that kind of overland travel. The skiers had no waxes, so they couldn't help pull them. At times they had to take off their skis to get uphill. Once one of them hit a hole and sank up to his chest with his skis on. Some of the guys on snowshoes were falling. We were all done in in the slow going."

According to the best estimates offered in the many debriefings that have been given on the "Great Minnesota Winter Recon," the expedition covered between one-and-one-half and two miles in nine hours. As darkness closed down the short winter day, bivouac was a fresh challenge. The toboggans held an assortment of two-man and four-man tents. "Ensolite pads for insulation were new then," Page recalls. "We'd heard about them but we didn't have any. Some of us had cut up old pieces of wool. Guys scrounged around, some used pillows, one took a pad from a toboggan. In the night the temperature got down to thirty-five below. In the morning, when someone hit against your tent, hoarfrost that had built up from frozen breath and body moisture cascaded down on you."

After breakfast a retreat was agreed on. The second day was a repeat of the first in the reverse direction, except that everyone was less strong and less gung-ho. One man became ill and had to be carried on a toboggan. It was dark again when the expedition staggered back to its starting point at Lake 1. In two days they had covered between three and four miles. They took another eight hours getting the cars started, using everything from ether to open flame to warm up the motors. In the morning the caravan limped into Homeplace. That was where Hale, who had driven up from Minneapolis to await their return, found them. When he took off for Norway, he carried their bon voyage present with him, in the form of a brief informal report: "You can never have a winter course."

It is a striking coincidence that in the same Christmas week, half a continent to the west, a Northwest School group of three instructors—Steve Wennstrom (later Northwest's program director), Vernon Bush, and Adrian Todd—and six Northwest alumni attempting an experimental six-day "winter trek" on skis were forced to abandon the expedition on the third day. A combination of deep, drifting snows, rising winds, low visibility that necessitated skiing by compass bearing, cold, and heavy packs finally proved too much for the expeditionaries, who well after midnight put in to the hospital at Bend for emergency treatment of frost-bitten fingers and toes. It was, Wennstrom reported, the end of "the most exhausting ordeal most of them had ever endured." Then, less than two weeks later and three thousand miles to the east, as part of the new Dartmouth Outward Bound Center's course for undergraduates bucking to be instructors, a cadre of students and leaders had a comparable experience in a whiteout atop Mount Moosilauke.

Learning through failure is one effective mode of the experiential method. It was a healthy thing for the movement that widely separated, virtually simultaneous early essays into three quite different kinds of winter wilderness taught the same memorable lesson. There is a connection between those lessons and the fact that in the ensuing dozen or so years the Outward Bound schools put thousands of students through cold-weather courses without serious mishap.

Learning through failure is motivational. The motivation made

Alan Hale all the more appreciative of the expert tutelage in winter expedition leadership he got at the Outward Bound School in Norway. This was an auxiliary unit run by the British First Army Corps, with key instructors from the Norwegian military, to give young officers wilderness training. Hale's presence was strictly non-reg. On the roster he was Lance Corporal Hale, First Tank Battalion, Hertford. As the course expedition was ending, he was cautioned to lie low because an inspection party was at the base to which he was returning. Skiing along a mountain trail on the expedition's final day, he was last in line. Suddenly a group of officers in smart uniforms were skiing past him. The colonel in charge of the inspection group ranged up alongside. "Pretty cold last night, son!" the colonel said. Because it was still cold, Hale had his balaclava, a stocking-like knitted headgear, pulled down to cover most of his face. He gave the colonel the briefest possible glance befitting military courtesy, uttered an overclipped "Yessir!" in his best Hertfordshire accent and resumed his head-down poling. Back at the base he was the butt of much kidding. The colonel had come in and spoken directly to the commandant: "There's an American on this course!" The commandant did not bat an eye: "No, sir. You must have met Lance Corporal Hale. Born of British parents and brought up in Brooklyn, New York. Terrible accent, sir!"

The Hales ran Minnesota's first winter course out of their lodge at Homeplace in January 1970, with twelve students, Alan and an assistant instructing. The next winter the school scheduled a full offering, January through March, of twenty-three-day "standard" and shorter skills courses. Budgeted for ninety-six students, it drew one hundred and twenty-seven. Hale's original course closely followed the Norwegian model. The brigade was issued U.S. Army surplus skis, which were solid and sturdy. Each student carried a Bergen pack—a rucksack on a small metal frame—and the brigade pulled a "pulk." This was a homemade version of a Scandinavian-type snow vehicle—half-sled, half-toboggan, with canvas sides that could be tied to form a cover over the load— designed to function as a supply carrier. While the pulk was a burden—its superiority to the rescue toboggans used on the ill-fated reconnaissance expedition was mainly a matter of degree— its greater attribute was that it freed the students from having to carry everything on their backs and made skiing much easier.

Not all the staff, Hale recalls, was happy with the original scheme. "After Jeff Evans left, my new chief instructor and some of the other instructors, most of whose orientation was to the mountains, wanted to shift to a faster way of going. They used aluminum pack-frames, and they thought it would be better not to take the pulk, which literally was a drag, and carry everything on the back. I said, Well, try an experiment for a course or two, and then we'll make a decision. While the experiment didn't go very well, it was defended because people didn't like the pulk. But many of the students skiing with very heavy packs were falling down so much that they were not learning to ski, and they certainly were not enjoying themselves. What worried me most was the risk. If someone sprains an ankle, what do you do with his pack? So they started taking a very small pulk-like vehicle to carry a few extras. That didn't work well either. They tried homemade sledges on ski runners, and those fell apart. Things were getting ridiculous. I said, Let's settle on one method so we can concentrate on process. So the next winter we went back to pulks—this time we imported the genuine article from Norway— and Norwegian ski stretchers. We used medium-weight touring skis, and packs. Having proper equipment, designed for the purpose, made a world of difference. I felt we finally had something we could take pride in calling an Outward Bound course."

II

The Colorado weather in May of 1969 was something to remember. Five feet of snow fell on the mountains and foothills, and the thaw flooded the roads on the Denver plateau. The plan to stage a Manpower Challenge * course in the foothills proved impractical, forcing instructor Rick Medrick to improvise in various parts of the mountains. He and his patrol ended up in the San Juans, a range in the southern Rockies, slogging through

* Manpower Challenge was a course for chronic unemployed persons that was developed by the Colorado School in collaboration with the Adolph Coors Company, the Gates Rubber Company, and the Mountain States Telephone Company, as part of the National Council of Businessmen program to provide jobs for socially disadvantaged people. Company supervisors took the course along with trainees. For the trainees the objective was to break the syndrome of failure; for the supervisors an opportunity to gain new insights into working with the disadvantaged.

the deep, soft snow of Uncompahgre Basin. Until each midmorning the going was good. The crust that had refrozen in the night was strong enough to bear the patrol, climbing on foot. But by 10 A.M. the crust softened, and the climbers were in snow up to their thighs. Struggling, the Manpower Challenge students, some of them newly out of the penitentiary, gave full range to street vocabularies.

Struggling with them, admiring the more creative maledictions his charges were pronouncing on their objective, Medrick gazed at the upward sweep of virgin snow and wished for skis. High above, the summit of 14,309-foot Uncompahgre Peak offered a worthy expedition objective. A year hence, he promised himself, he would return to lead a ski-mountaineering course in this terrain. The Colorado School, mindful of the avalanche dangers, sub-zero temperatures, high winds, and other hazards, did not yet have a winter course in the mountains. The May environment, with its ameliorated above-snowline temperatures, would provide a useful laboratory.

How Rick Medrick came to be at the Colorado School is representative of a good many instructor histories that tell as much about Outward Bound as about the instructor. At Dartmouth, where he followed Alan Hale by one year, Rick was successively president of the Mountaineering and Outing clubs. Winters he spent as much time as he could—even dropping out for a semester —as a ski patrolman at Suicide Six at Woodstock, Vermont, summers as much time as he could climbing in Wyoming's Teton Mountains. Eventually the mountains won; he still lacked graduating credits when at the end of his senior year he left for Jackson Hole to serve as an apprentice Teton guide in Glen Exum's mountaineering school. Subsequently he picked up the credits in the process of moving into a Ph.D. program in philosophy at the University of Colorado in Boulder. He combined his graduate studies with ski instruction and each summer went "home" to the Tetons, moving up in the Exum staff hierarchy.

Somewhere in that time Medrick had his first awareness of Outward Bound, when a fellow guide left to join the staff of the Colorado School. "My impression then," he recalls, "was that this was a militaristic boot-camp type of outfit. In any event, as a professional mountain climber who conceived of the mountains as a sanctuary from society, I couldn't see myself associating with an organization that was using the wilderness for a social process."

Three years into his Ph.D. regimen, he found himself more and more out of tune with a philosophy faculty that had a traditional orientation from which his own intellectual interests increasingly diverged. In that same time he was no longer finding the mountains the haven they had been. "I guess I had grown as disillusioned with the life of a professional mountain guide and professional ski instructor as I had with a future life as a philosophy professor," he says. "My wife, who was a schoolteacher in Boulder, had been making me conscious of political and social issues that I had lost concern for after my undergraduate days. Looking for a way to give my life new direction, we decided to join the Peace Corps."

The Medricks were the first Americans at a remote secondary school in Kenya that had formerly been run by the British. Making themselves active members of the African community, they had a happy experience there. While Rick had some doubts about the value of the American presence in Africa, he had none at all about the value to himself of his volunteer service. Halfway through his two-year commitment, a Peace Corps green-sheet listing of potential jobs for returning volunteers brought the tidings that his old Teton sidekick, Willi Unsoeld, was now an executive of Outward Bound. Medrick remembers: "My orientation had shifted enough that I liked Willi's description of what Outward Bound was involved in. Still, I wasn't going to let him off easy. I wrote him, in effect asking what he was doing in this militaristic summer-boot-camp-for-rich-kids type of organization. Willi wrote me back a letter in which he said he had gone through three stages as a climber. First, as a young buck where you had to climb the hardest thing you could find, make your reputation, and develop your craft. There were the 'second-year winners' who flame out the third year and climb no more; you had to get past that and undergo the process of becoming a mature climber. The second stage was where the climber had to look to making a living through his craft, where the process was simply one of exposing people to a mountain experience, and sending them away better off for what you'd done, with you better off for being able to stay in the mountains on the money you had earned. I understood that; that was the way I had felt. Then, Willi said, there came a further stage when you began to look at the mountain as a means of serving social ends. The way he portrayed that to me was that Outward Bound was an opportunity to use the mountains to share the opportunity they had provided us in developing our philosophies. This was so congruent with my own thinking at the time that it was all I needed. I wrote Joe Nold and applied for a job at Colorado a year before I came back."

Medrick reported for duty at Colorado in March 1969. His first course was a contract course, leading a group of students from Mitchell High School in Colorado Springs, where there had been a student riot. His patrol—three blacks, two Chicanos, and five whites—included the opposing riot leaders as well as one of the school's most popular athletes and a student council leader. It took place in the Baja, the peninsula on Mexico's Pacific Coast formed by the Gulf of California and the Pacific Ocean. Medrick learned what the Outward Bound process was by letting it happen.

"I had read the literature and been well briefed at Denver, and with my guiding and Peace Corps experience I was at ease leading the group. But since I had no experience with the dynamics of the Outward Bound process, I decided I would not try to structure any of it, as I would have later, but would just let things happen. Those students were at each other's throats a lot of the time. Two of the rival riot leaders had a fistfight over who had taken more peanuts. One day I introduced the trust-fall exercise.* It broke the ice in enabling us to explore the feelings in the group. A real neat rapport began to develop, with a grudging appreciation of one another. We had a lot of rap sessions about problems at the school, why the riot had evolved, students' attitudes toward each other. We developed a very close relationship where I could share the benefit of my experience and they theirs. I remember one of the black students saying, 'Man, I just like to sit and listen to you talk.' It all seemed to fit naturally into the experience, and I came out of the course with some real insights as to what Outward Bound was about."

In May came the Manpower Challenge experience and the re-

---

* In this exercise, often used in Outward Bound to promote a better group feeling, each member successively stands on the edge of a platform several feet off the ground and lets himself fall backward, holding himself rigid and trusting the group to catch him.

solve to do something about a winter mountain program. The following winter Medrick planned and promoted a twenty-day ski mountaineering course for the coming May. Eighteen signed up, mostly a mix of high-school and college students and others who had dropped out of college to "ski bum." Two girl students made it one of the first coed courses. Two patrols were organized under instructors Harry Friscman and Mike and Carol Lowe, with Medrick as course director.

As the basis for a winter course, Medrick decided to experiment with skiing into high mountain terrain that otherwise would be unapproachable. The students brought their own equipment—downhill skis with bindings that could be adjusted for touring, laced boots, and climbing skins. For most of them it was a first experience with ski touring, climbing skins, climbing ropes, ice axes, and snow camping. Their initial expedition was a strenuous three-day climb from snowline to a plateau at 12,000 feet. En route they got their first indoctrination in such skills as map reading, knot-tying, avalanche safety, and search and rescue. They slept in tents and cooked on gasoline stoves. On the plateau they dug and lived in snow caves.

The first expedition climaxed with a climb to the summit of Uncompahgre Peak, the students going as high as they could on skis, then roping up to complete the ascent. There was a long downhill run from the plateau back to snowline, on trickily variable snow that sent the skiers pack-over-head-over-skis. Rock climbing and rappelling, another peak excursion, a three-day solo, and a final expedition that included a full-moonlight ascent of 14,048-foot Handies Peak and a bivouac above 13,000 feet. Lessons were learned in such forms as sleeping bags soaked by dripping snow caves, a tent burned in consequence of careless stove use, loosely packed bags that rolled away and had to be retrieved from far below in an exhausting descent and climb. In a key respect the experience echoed that of so many courses before; one student put it, "I didn't expect the total involvement with the people I was with. You had to get tight with them to make it."

Medrick reconnoitered in advance throughout the course, creating it as he went, simultaneously thinking ahead to the deep-winter adjustments that would have to be made the following January. At intervals he rejoined one or the other patrol for a safety check; each fresh snowfall was adding to the avalanche danger. Trekking out to make a resupply rendevous, he brought back fateful tidings. The course coincided with the American invasion of Cambodia and the shootings at Kent State. In contrast to the normal course, which shuts students off from the "real world," this one was deeply affected by events outside it. "A dialogue had been evolving throughout the course," Medrick remembers. "Everything seemed to come together the day before it ended, when we all sat down for an afternoon and tried to get a grasp for what had happened 'outside' and what our own experience had been worth. There was a strong feeling of its being a unique, special time, and of having been 'out of time' for a short period and having felt the idea of, If people can get together like this in this environment, why isn't it possible to carry it back in some way into other communities? For me, anyway, the course became in microcosm the whole concept of using an Outward Bound experience as a means for people exploring values and their commitments to involvement with the processes of society. And on the program side it opened up a new horizon of possibilities for the school."

Colorado offered its first true winter ski-mountaineering course in January 1971. While incorporating the lessons of the previous May, its design had to accommodate the much more severe seasonal elements of a Rocky Mountain midwinter—notably, temperatures of as much as forty to fifty degrees below zero and the corresponding wind-chill factors. It was necessary to set up emergency-stocked cabins that could be heated and serve as a refuge during the high mountain storms. The cabins also came to provide occasional overnight stopping places where a patrol could come together for an evening's rap, furthering the group dynamics that function more slowly in the winter courses. The course was repeated in April. The next year it was offered each month, January through April.

The Northwest School likewise started winter-mountaineering courses in the Cascades in 1971; it now also offers a ski-touring program in the lovely Wallowa Mountain country of northeast Oregon that was once the habitat of Chief Joseph and his Nez Percé Indians. As noted, the Dartmouth Outward Bound Center started cold-weather courses as early as 1969. North Carolina, which actually had pioneered winter operation with a special course for Jewel Box managers in 1968, initiated regular winter courses in 1972. In that winter the Hurricane Island School conducted a special course in north-central Maine for students from Lincoln–Sudbury High School (Massachusetts). A year later Hurricane opened a winter mountaineering program to the public, confirming its new amphibious status. Presently all the schools run ten-day or two-week courses in the winter months; most of them also offer a twenty-one-day "standard" course.

The advent of winter courses was a significant advance in U.S. Outward Bound's growth. On one score it was the beginning of year-round operation. On another, it introduced to the curriculum one of the most formidable of nature's challenges: deep cold. Will Lange spoke to this in his director's report on the Dartmouth Center's first courses: "In conclusion I would say that the cold was essential to the program. It required everyone to think constantly about his physical welfare; it kept everyone under a constant stress and brought human qualities out into sharp focus; and merely surviving, let alone being creative, under these conditions gave all the students a real sense of accomplishment."

But this gets ahead of the Dartmouth story, which is coming up.

The Dartmouth Center

Be not content with the commonplace in character any more than with the commonplace in ambition or intellectual attainment. Do not expect that you will make any lasting or very strong impression on the world through intellectual power without the use of an equal amount of conscience and heart.

—WILLIAM JEWETT TUCKER,
ninth president of Dartmouth College

A faculty colleague at Phillips Academy who became deeply interested in U.S. Outward Bound during the movement's early years was Charles "Doc" Dey, a Dartmouth alumnus of the class of '52. Charley was among the first to conceive that an important learning potential lay in finding ways to integrate the Outward Bound philosophy and method into academic environments. When he left Andover to join the Dartmouth administrative staff, he had in mind the idea of establishing a liaison between Dartmouth and Outward Bound.

In 1966 Dey was appointed dean of the William Jewett Tucker Foundation, an independent endowment within the college charged by the trustees with furthering the moral and spiritual work of the Dartmouth community.* Among its activities were a number of program vehicles, such as off-campus internships, enabling undergraduates to translate their social concerns into constructive action while also learning. Reflecting on new paths

* Dey was made president of the Choate School and Rosemary Hall in 1973.

234

the Tucker Foundation might take under his leadership, Charley perceived Outward Bound as one appropriate vehicle. He came down to Andover for a meeting with Bob Bates and me. At that time Secretary of Defense Robert McNamara's proposal to broaden, so as to include nonmilitary activity, the kinds of service that would qualify for national selective service was getting serious consideration from a presidential advisory committee. Charley's initial idea was for an Outward Bound school under the wing of the Tucker Foundation that would train instructors for service programs. Dey remembers:

"There were a variety of ways in which we were working with Dartmouth students to help them confront some of the tougher issues of life, thereby to reach beyond themselves in service to others. I believe that's an important experience as part of a liberal education. The purpose of a higher education is not simply to take courses and amass information and worry about yourself. Outward Bound seemed to be one vehicle through which a college student, at a highly egocentric point in his career, could be put in a situation where he had to give himself to others." In this aspiration Dey had the support of Dartmouth's then president, John Sloan Dickey, a strong believer in the educational potential of the out-of-doors. For our part at OBI, we saw a means of strengthening our ties to the educational community and implementing both our own internal training needs and our commitment to the service ethic.

As it happened, the nation's deepening involvement in the war in Vietnam precluded any liberalization of the selective service law. It took another two years for Dartmouth, working with the New Hampshire Department of Education, to arrive at a plan giving the college a satisfactory service rationale for a campus-associated Outward Bound activity, and OBI a sound basis for issuing a charter. Under the plan, undergraduates would be offered Outward Bound instructor training with related academic study, followed by an opportunity to conduct a course for New Hampshire secondary-school students. In developing the plan Dey had a staunch faculty ally in Sociology Professor Wentworth Eldredge, a longtime adherent of Hahn's ideas who was one of OBI's original trustees.

The Dartmouth Outward Bound Center was formally chartered as a component of the Tucker Foundation early in 1969. The idea of a chartered "center" as differentiated from a "school" was a concept that evolved in response to a need we saw in the Dartmouth situation and that might well arise again. There was a logical possibility that an educational or other nonprofit institution operating under a trustee governance for its own purposes could simultaneously advance those purposes and the Outward Bound cause by offering sanctioned courses and consulting services. For such a special kind of school within an independent institution or agency, we hit on the center designation.

Thanks to Peter Willauer's interest, the Dartmouth Center was activated *de facto* under the cooperative umbrella of the Hurricane Outward Bound School ahead of the formal chartering, when Will Lange, a Hurricane staff member, came on campus as director in the fall of 1968. A graduate of Wooster College in Ohio, Lange had been a high-school teacher in the Adirondack region of upstate New York. One day in 1964 he happened on a feature article on the Colorado School in a back issue of *Life.**
It was the first he had heard of Outward Bound. He promptly wrote to ask how he could get an instructor's job. I referred him to the school directors, and Willauer hired him. At Hurricane he developed into one of the school's top instructors.

D-1-I (Dartmouth instructors' course number one) began in January 1969 with an enrollment of six Dartmouth undergraduates and one graduate. The students were required to carry two regular academic courses, making special relevance arrangements with their professors. The Outward Bound activities, along with lectures, seminars, and required papers, earned credits as a third course, designated Education 41.† The first week, based at the college-owned lodge on Mount Moosilauke, was given to basic skills training and indoctrination in Outward Bound philosophy and method.

On the third day the group set out on a winter training expedition that proved a remarkable echo of the Minnesota group's debacle on the Kekekabic Trail just a fortnight before. The plan was to climb Moosilauke's eastern slope, spend the night in the summit cabin, descend the western side of the mountain to a

* "Marshmallow Becomes a Man," *Life*, Aug. 7, 1964.
† Dartmouth's academic year then consisted of three three-course terms twelve weeks in length. The college now operates year-round, offering four terms ten weeks in length.

Dartmouth Outing Club cabin on the second day, and circle back to the lodge on the third. Nature had other plans. Lange remembers: "We had not anticipated that breaking trail would be such tough going. The new snow was so deep and light that our snowshoes sank more than a foot with each step. Several times somebody disappeared completely when he stepped on a buried treetop arching over an air pocket. Our climbing rate was half a mile an hour, and we did not reach the summit until four o'clock. Above the tree line fog was creating a virtual whiteout. If you let the nearest person get twenty feet away from you, you could no longer see him. In that white soup we could not find the summit cabin. We were losing our bearings, and it began to get dark and colder. The footing was extremely icy, and we were having the utmost difficulty in keeping the group together.

"We headed back down the summit cone. By the time we reached the tree line it was dark, and we called a bivouac. Using snowshoes for shovels, we dug a two-level shelf about seven by twenty feet, laid our ponchos out over the dug area, and climbed into our sleeping bags. Since the trees and underbrush were coated with ice, there was no fuel for a fire. We started the Svea stove and cooked up a concoction of cocoa, coffee, sugar, dried soup, Coffee-mate, and sour balls. Tinctured as it was with burnt sugar, the mixture was extremely tasty. At least, it took the edge off the chill. We slept well, except for calls of nature. For breakfast we had another portion of the previous evening's menu. We packed and retreated down the mountain by a route made very difficult by the deep snow. Back at the lodge a day ahead of schedule, we licked our wounds and held a highly educational debriefing."

Lange found the experience fortuitous: "In a few hours, early in the course, all the instructors were indelibly impressed with the lesson that somehow and sooner or later they had to learn— of how subtly deadly the winter wilderness environment can be for the unwary or the unprepared. Even Paul Ross, our British-trained rock-climbing specialist and a fine mountaineer with Alpine experience, gained new respect for the New Hampshire mountains."

After ten days in Hanover to get a good leg up on their academic work, the students traveled north to the Dartmouth College Grant, a forest area close to the Canadian border classified by the U.S. Air Force as subarctic, for their second period of wilderness training. Back on campus for another academic period, the students also kept up the morning run, did drownproofing in the college pool each day, compiled an instructors' manual, and prepared for the advent of the high-school students enrolled in D-1, the course they would now instruct under the supervision of the center staff.

The D-1 students, thirty-one youngsters from high schools throughout the state, were put through a twenty-two-day winter course. They seemed a good deal more content after they moved from the Moosilauke lodge training base, with its compromising comforts, to living outdoors at the College Grant in two-man tents or snow caves. They were miserable, they said, but were they not there to discover themselves through hardship? The cold ranged from twenty degrees below zero to thirty-five above, with three to ten feet of snow. Despite the cold, or perhaps because of it, the solo proved a surprisingly positive experience, as it had for the undergraduates who were now their instructors. Any staff concern that the high-school youngsters might not have had an authentic Outward Bound experience was dispelled by a reading of their course impressions. They felt they had been tested as never before, physically, emotionally, and morally. Their enthusiastic endorsement of their experience on returning to their schools helped to recruit students for future courses.

The wilderness phases of D-2-I, the second instructors' course, took place entirely in the still snow-mantled College Grant. In the concluding phase the undergraduates sailed and rowed two pulling boats from Boston to Hurricane Island, where they became assistant instructors in Hurricane's May course.

Starting that summer the Dartmouth Center offered thirty-day courses for teachers that helped to pioneer a three-pronged development in the national movement: teachers' practica, adult courses, and coeducational courses. "In terms of affecting the human condition we were highly successful with the teachers in our summer courses," Lange reflects. "Whether or not they went back to start their own outdoor projects, as some did, almost all reported themselves to be different *people* as teachers—not hiding behind the book or the assignment, relating to their students much more as human beings, having a much greater sense of caring and feeling about their work."

Lange's second-year staff consisted of Perry Gates, another fine instructor who had come with him from Hurricane Island, Mike Stratton, a D-2-I student who had graduated in June, and, unofficially, Will's wife Ida. The center had a strong "pop and mom" aspect in the early days. While primarily a response to low-budget imperatives, this was also thanks to the fact that from the time the Langes first went to Hurricane Island, Ida had responded affirmatively to the Outward Bound environment. That is not always easy for an instructor's wife. Ida's recollection of the family's summers at Hurricane Island points up the problems of women in being married to Outward Bound instructors: "It's a difficult existence, especially for a young woman with two or three children. She does not feel her husband is her husband, he's there but he's not. When he's not off on an expedition, she may see him across the island, but he may run right by her with a bunch of students and not even say, 'Hi!' She may see him in the mess hall with his Outward Bound kids, but she's the one who has to make their three kids behave. And he comes home to their tent and says, 'Hello,' and collapses; when he is there, there's nothing left of him. You both have to face the fact that his first priority is his students. If he comes back at night, and the two of you are having an important talk, and a student comes knocking on the door and says, 'I'm going home,' your husband forsakes you and goes off with the youngster for a heart-to-heart talk. The best way to lick it is somehow to join it, to take on some volunteer helping task that makes you part of the school. If you as a wife lose your identity, it's bad. If you look on it as finding another corner of your identity, and become involved in it, you're O.K."

In its second year the center's undergraduate program was getting marks as a successful experiment. An imprimatur was placed on it when the Dartmouth faculty of arts and sciences accepted a refinement and elaboration called the Outward Bound Term, which became part of the college curriculum in the 1970–1971 year. The term had six segments: a preliminary reading period; a standard three-week Outward Bound course (also open to students from other colleges) with added seminar components; an intensive three-week academic period; the Outward Bound course for secondary-school students under undergraduate leadership; a critique and evaluation period, and the writing of a major paper. Partly because of the highly interdisciplinary character of the academic components, but presumably also due to gingerly handling of the question of credits for the experiential innovations that were a central feature of the term, students successfully completing the requirements received the equivalent of full credit in the form of a three-course reduction in the degree requirement, from thirty-six to thirty-three, in Dartmouth's twelve-term, three-course system.

The term earned the center a significant feedback in the form of recognition by faculty members of the educational value of an Outward Bound experience. For some this was the result of participation, for others of perception of effect on students. English Professor Robert Siegel became aware of Outward Bound when a student turned in a short novel after completing a Dartmouth Center course. "It was a fictional analysis of the self along the lines of Dostoyevsky's *Notes from the Underground*," Professor Siegel reported. "It vividly evoked the intensity of an individual's feeling on facing the cold and the group and then finding himself in relation to the group. The pressure of the experience gave the piece an arresting authenticity. It was clear to me that this man's Outward Bound experience had driven him to a brilliant depth of introspection that I feel sure will have carryover impact on his life and what he does with it."

Professor George Theriault, Lincoln Filene Professor of Human Relations in the sociology department, was among the first to perceive the center's value as an academic resource and to employ it for exposing students in his courses to appropriate experiences. In retirement he remains an enthusiast, saying, "I believe strongly that the most effective way to teach is to combine a student's experience, either through natural or contrived situations, with what he's trying to learn."

In 1970 Lange asked Robert MacArthur, a former curate of his church, to join his staff. A member of Dartmouth's class of '64, Bob had pitched varsity baseball on a championship team, sung in the glee club, been active in the Episcopal student association, belonged to a prestigious fraternity, and been one of a handful in his class elected to Casque and Gauntlet, a senior society. Three years later he graduated *cum laude* from Berkeley Divinity School (now part of Yale Divinity). Having enjoyed a success-oriented youth, he reacted all the more keenly to the career and personal difficulties he encountered after leaving divinity school. He accepted a job offer from the rector of St. Thomas's Church in Hanover, involving work in the hospital, the college, and the parish. The two years he spent there, a time of rising tension in the college community over the war in Vietnam, proved a hard period for him—"although very rich in retrospect"—as Bob recalls: "I became aware of how difficult it can be to reconcile a prophetic ministry—in the sense of the role of the prophets in both Testaments calling people back to the right path—and a pastoral ministry, in which the clergyman stands with people throughout the personal crises of life. In order to stand with people, you can't stand over against them. It's very difficult to balance those two callings, particularly when you're young and just out of the seminary.

"I believed we were wrong to be in Vietnam, conducting the war the way we were, and I felt strongly that part of the Christian witness was to proclaim this. My conflict was symbolized by the commandant of the Navy ROTC unit at the college, who was a parishioner. His daughter was a pillar of the youth group, and his father had recently died, a sadness which brought me quite close to the family. He invited my wife Peggy and me to sit in the reviewing stand at the ROTC commencement. It was a painful dilemma, since I was active with both the student and faculty groups who were trying to protest the war, and they were planning anti-ROTC demonstrations at the exercises. Peg sat with the family to acknowledge our relationship with them while I ended up going to a corner of the field by myself, unable to associate totally with either viewpoint and feeling very frustrated. The incident focused my feeling that at that point in my life I was not prepared to deal with the conflicts and ambiguities of the parochial ministry in relation to the war."

Because he was interested in community life, Bob took a job at a folk school in the mountain country of southwest North Carolina. The school was a three-hundred-and-sixty-acre farm community based on the model of the nineteenth century Danish folk-school movement, with the purpose of revitalizing the Southern mountain population. Bob remembers it as a time of ironic crosscurrents: "You had college people from the East coming back to the land, while the indigenous people were reaching out to the more urbanized life that the college people were rejecting. Unfortunately, from my point of view, the folk-school people were not serving the indigenous population. I became rather critical of the leadership and was fired after eight months."

Aware of Bob's skills with people and learning of his avail-ability, Lange offered to make him his assistant at the center. Bob took the post with little more knowledge of Outward Bound than what he knew from his wife, who as secretary for the Tucker Foundation had been a part-time secretary to the Outward Bound Center: "Peggy used to come home from her work with much amusement and strange tales of this crazy bunch of people who were pursuing the grail in their own way. Outward Bound seemed to bring together my athletic interests and my enjoyment of the outdoors in a new way, and I was intrigued by that. As for its place in the Tucker Foundation, I saw it as another arena for encouraging the capacity of individuals to examine their resources and improve their ability to relate to other people within a compassionate framework."

Realizing that the first thing he had to do was take an Outward Bound course himself, MacArthur signed up for a teachers' practicum at Colorado in the summer of 1970. The experience had a bad start. "I was in a low state of self-esteem, having just been fired, which was my first failure experience of any magnitude. The course director happened to be the skipper on my raft on our trip down the Green River. While we were preparing the rafts, I got into conversation with him. When he found out I was a minister, he told me bluntly that in his mind a minister was the lowest form of male human being. He was chagrined that I would be working with Outward Bound. I'm sure that my performance reenforced his stereotype of me. I'd never been on a river before, and he put a lot of pressure on me when it was my turn to captain the raft. We locked horns repeatedly throughout the course. On one occasion he told me he got bad vibrations from me, which was a big putdown in front of the group. I was then very susceptible to the mystique of the elite Outward Bound instructor—the image he portrayed of the fit, strong, keen, resourceful individual. Because I had no credentials of merit to offer, I had little skill with which to counter his judgmental criticism. I have since learned that he was not a representative course director in the eyes of his peers at Colorado, and I realize now that he had his own insecurities. I can look back on what happened with more humor, but at the time it was a shattering experience. Yet on the whole the course was a positive experience for me. Which says something for Outward Bound. I think there's something organic in those basic activities and in the structure of the course that enables the individual to grow in ways he needs to."

Two years later MacArthur came off a course he had led at North Carolina to learn he had been selected as the new director of the Dartmouth Outward Bound Center. The appointment came at a time of major change for the college, which in turn called for transition within the center. That year Dartmouth went coeducational; simultaneously it initiated the "Dartmouth Plan," a scheme for operating the college year-round. MacArthur's first response to a coeducational student body was to bring Sharon Goodyear, a highly regarded instructor at the North Carolina School, to Hanover as Outward Bound's first female program director.

The Dartmouth Plan presented a major problem, in that it rendered the Outward Bound Term academically unviable. Since the plan reduced the degree requirements for all students from thirty-six to thirty-three credits, it was no longer feasible to employ the negative credit device. A year's modus operandi was afforded by the Education Department's offering of three course credits for a term that linked the Outward Bound phase of the old plan to a high-school teaching-counseling internship. Meanwhile MacArthur, charged by his Tucker Foundation superiors to build more bridges between the center and the academic community, developed two programs that have proved the strong core of his directorship: the Outward Bound Laboratories and the Living–Learning Term.

The laboratory idea is based on the Outward Bound method of involving people in initiative-demanding situations that generate strong learning experiences. MacArthur invited the faculty to use this competence as an experiential resource to assist their teaching. As a consequence of that invitation, groups of Dartmouth students have found themselves in an extraordinary assortment of environments not normally thought of as ancillary to classroom endeavor. The environment may be a strange woods a hundred miles from Hanover. ("You have been dropped behind the enemy lines without food. Do not engage strangers in conversation, use roads, or trespass on private property.") It may be rowing all night in a pulling boat, or bunking down in the cell of a maximum security prison, or using a subway train as a traveling base from which to carry out a scavenger hunt. Individuals who until now have only known each other as fellow students across a classroom aisle may be called on to take up communal residence in a tree for two days and nights. Or a group may be led blindfolded into the pitch blackness of an elaborate World War II bomb shelter and left to organize themselves into a resourceful and cooperative community for the next forty-four hours.

Professor G. Christian Jernstedt of the psychology department is among the faculty members who uses the center extensively. He incorporates an optional series of three Outward Bound weekend laboratories in his highly popular Psychology 22 course on Learning. "Outward Bound and Psychology 22 have a number of critical similarities," Chris Jernstedt tells his students. "Both are concerned with one's understanding of the behavior-change process in oneself, both provide one with experiences that will carry one beyond the limits of the course, both encourage one's personal freedom and responsibility in a directed educational venture, and both involve a period of intensive individual learning."

The Psych 22 laboratories provide a slice-of-life resource that otherwise has to be obtained by secondary means. Since the course requires some kind of real-life situation to which the students can apply the learning principles it elucidates, the normal method is to use a novel, such as Steinbeck's *The Grapes of Wrath* or Wambaugh's *The New Centurions*. Those who sign up for the laboratories can use their Outward Bound experiences instead. "It makes the course more work—they have to give those weekends, as well as lose several days of other classes," Jernstedt points out. "But it's such a rich experience that there is always a considerable number who want to do it. Their papers are better than those that deal with the novel because they're writing of something they feel strongly about."

The scheme is symbiotic. The students examine the philosophy and techniques of learning presented in the course in the light of their laboratory experiences, and examine the individual and group learning that occurs in these experiences in the light of what they learn from their reading assignments and in the classroom. The first two laboratories of the course have typically been an overnight ropes course and rock-climbing experience and a three-and-a-half-day pulling boat expedition out of Hurricane Island. The third varies from year to year, the objective being to place the group in a context different from any they have known up to then and to break up the group patterns formed in the first two experiences. One of the most successful was a weekend so structured that the group was chronically stressed by change. They were divided into two crews who made separate planning decisions based on different information; then half of each crew was switched. Reunited in the bomb shelter and having organized themselves on the assumption they were in for a long stay, they were blindfolded and whisked off. Two hours later in their windowless vans, given fifteen seconds notice to select whatever they wished to take with them, they were deposited in Harvard Square in Cambridge with a new set of instructions. Each time they became set to cope with a new environment and new rules, the environment and rules were shifted.

"They really enjoyed the experience," Jernstedt says. "It opened up a lot of questions for them about what kinds of skills do you bring to new situations, and how can you prepare yourself? About leadership, and how to make decisions. They voted on a lot of things and they didn't like that, it was inefficient. And they were stressed, which was part of the purpose. When they came to write, they had a lot to write about. All sorts of good issues had been created that they could discuss in their papers."

The center has serviced courses in sociology, psychology, geography, government, education, environmental studies, economics, and a graduate-level course at Dartmouth's Tuck School of Business Administration. When Tuck School Professor Roy Lewicki incorporated a long weekend's pulling-boat experience into his sensitivity training Seminar in Interpersonal Behavior, he found it an effective way to enable the class to "dominantly focus on individual and group *behavior*, rather than the *discussion of behavior*." The center also has devised and serviced therapy elements for treating patients at the Dartmouth-Hitchcock Mental Health Center and provided team-building exercises for the Mental Health Center's staff.

A Hurricane Island conversation between Professor Lewicki and MacArthur produced the skeletal idea for the center's Living–Learning Term. This is an experience in community life that integrates wilderness activities, academic endeavor, cooperative living, and community service. Launched in the spring of 1974 and since offered year-round, the Living–Learning Term was conceived in part as a vehicle for bringing to on-campus life some of the values that students derived from Tucker Foundation off-campus internships. In the Tucker model, MacArthur explains, off-campus situations gave rise to an intensity of experience through people working together as a team, with valuable by-products gained from the cooperative activity. In the Living–Learning Term the center has developed an intense on-campus program combining the unity-of-participants, common task, and group living features of an off-campus program with elements of an Outward Bound course, while integrating academic life more fully with residential life.

Each term ten to twelve students—preferably an equal number of men and women—share a residence that they operate cooperatively, including food budgeting and purchase, cooking, and household chores. In addition to the two academic courses they select individually, the students take one course together, as a common intellectual task and to make for interaction with faculty outside the classroom. An Outward Bound instructor lives in the residence as counselor and energizer. The residents hold periodic group sessions for purposes of communication and planning, interpersonal feedback, and self-examination of the ways a group develops and functions. This residential and academic regimen is intertwined with wilderness and service activity.

The Living–Learning Term begins with an Outward Bound wilderness experience in the ten days preceding the opening of the college term. This usually turns out to be a good way for a dozen strangers who are going to be living together for a fairly stressful ten weeks to initiate their family arrangement. "From the start there was a nice attitude of helping those who weren't as strong," instructor Knox Johnstone says about the expedition that had kicked off the winter term for which he was then counselor-in-residence. It had been a ski-and-snowshoe trek that peaked in a final night sleeping in the fire tower atop Mount Cardigan. "With a little bit of luck, when you take people on a nice adventure like that, you give them a real common denominator to build their living experience on." During the term there are two additional wilderness elements, a three-day-and-night solo, and a four-day final expedition that the students plan and carry out on their own. Thus the term is in part an extended Outward Bound course, but in a context much different from the standard experience.

The Term House is one of several campus-living experiments that the Dartmouth administration has observed with interest in its ongoing quest for advantageous alternatives to traditional dormitory living. Peter Bryant, the center's program director and one who has had the residence "duty" a number of times, considers the return on the term's communal living to be a major value: "I am sure that along with the Outward Bound challenges, virtually all of our Living–Learning alumni would award top marks to the term for having given them a sense of place, of living in a family kind of atmosphere that allowed them to express needs they somehow put away when they go into a dormitory. Those who go back to a dormitory talk especially about this."

The service project—normally some form of assistance to children, or elderly or handicapped persons, or adolescents who have been in trouble with the law—is another important element. The students are usually involved in a commitment—building a children's playground, for example—that is part of a community project administered by the Dartmouth–Hitchcock Mental Health Center. In Bryant's view, a significant aspect of the service project is that it gives participants an opportunity, rare for college students, to test their values: "It's easy in a college setting for students to be theoretical about the values they feel they have. When the Living–Learning students go into communities in the Mascoma Valley, which is a federally designated poverty area, and are called on to relate to economically deprived families in an open, understanding way, they have a chance to find out if they are up to doing what until now they've just idealized themselves as doing."

The Outward Bound Center's association with the Dartmouth–Hitchcock Mental Health Center * has grown in a progression of successively more ambitious undertakings. Expansion of their joint activities began in 1975 when Bryant and Robert "Sparky" Millikin of Outward Bound, Kristi Kistler, director of activities therapy at the Mental Health Center, and Dr. Gary Tucker, director of psychiatric residents at the Medical School, undertook a five-week experimental therapeutic project with seven disturbed adolescents and young adults. Not least of the reasons the mental health staff were pleased with the results was that the patients themselves—who had been given to feel the activity was a chance to do something "normal" rather than a form of treatment—felt they had had a successful experience.

Following this encouraging start, a regular weekly schedule of activity with inpatients at the Mental Health Center was established. In 1977 the Van Amerigen Foundation made a grant to underwrite a substantial enlarging of the program, support evaluation and research, and provide a coordinator and research assistant. For the coordinator post the college tapped Tom Stich, director of the Wilderness Program of the Forensic Treatment System in New Mexico Department of Hospitals and Institutions. Stich had originally gone to that post in a consultant capacity when Colorado Outward Bound was engaged to help the New Mexico agency set up a wilderness program for prisoners, including the emotionally disturbed. In his first year at Hanover, in addition to expanding the inpatient activity, Stich initiated a comparable program at the Veterans Administration Hospital in White River Junction, Vermont, where the psychiatric unit is under the auspices of the Dartmouth Medical School's Department of Psychiatry and the staff are members of its faculty.

The Dartmouth Center has recently expanded its public course offerings to virtually a year-round operation. These include two courses in the development of which the center played a pioneering role. One is a cycling version of the standard course. The other is the Adult Leadership Program (ALP), a course the cen-

* The Dartmouth–Hitchcock Mental Health Center is a joint operation of the Dartmouth Medical School and the Mary Hitchcock Memorial Hospital.

ter first conducted in 1975 for adults who are primarily interested in adapting Outward Bound to their schools or agencies. In 1981 Dartmouth is initiating two three-month semester programs, one of them jointly with the Minnesota and the North Carolina Schools.

Hazard and Adventure

Out of this nettle, danger, we pluck this flower, safety.
—HENRY IV, PART II

A powerful Outward Bound tradition of intelligent respect for hazard and the responsibilities it places derives directly from the founder. In his book *Impelled into Experiences*, Jim Hogan, first warden of Aberdovey, the first Outward Bound school, relates how Kurt Hahn constantly insisted it was Hogan's duty to understand all the factors affecting safety. "Certainly," he writes, "the early operations at Aberdovey gave ample material for concern, and there were periods when Hahn telephoned hourly for news of our adventures," and then:

> There is no doubt that the Outward Bound schools could not conceivably have established themselves with their remarkable record of freedom from accidents had it not been for Hahn's almost obsessive concern that there should be no trace of carelessness or recklessness in our affairs.

At the time of our first fatality in U.S. Outward Bound, I wrote Hahn the sad tidings. In reply he urged us to spare no effort in seeking the accident's cause, making good use of impartial experts. He suggested that we share our findings with all kindred institutions in order to pool knowledge and prevent similar tragedies. And he bade us to carry on, keeping in mind that two enemies of Outward Bound are "the safety-firsters and the toughness worshipers."

The morning of July 23, 1978, was clear and warm in the northwest North Carolina mountain country. The twelve members of Number Two crew of NC-118, with instructor Aram Attarian and assistant Virginia "Ginny" Davis, were on the final day of their main expedition, day eleven of the standard twenty-three-day course. They spent the morning bushwhacking up the north side of Bandy Cove Mountain to a roadway, where they stopped for lunch. The weather was changing. Sensing that a storm was brewing, the instructors took the occasion to brief the crew on the lightning hazard.

There are several things that everybody ought to know about lightning. Two of them are cardinal rules—one for avoiding injury, the other for treating injury if it happens. The first is to get away from mountain summits and peaks, as well as from open rock faces and high rock outcroppings wherever they may be. Seek protection on low, flat ground or in shallow declivities. In the woods, don't stand under tall, isolated trees; take shelter instead under thickets of shorter trees. A deep cave or overhang gives excellent protection, but a shallow cave does not, nor do narrow ledges or stream gullies, because of the danger from ground currents generated by nearby lightning strikes. When someone is hit by lightning, the cardinal rule for treatment is not to assume that the victim is dead because no breathing or heartbeat can be detected. Quite commonly the victim suffers from arrest of breathing, and often from heart arrest, as well as burns and involuntary muscle contractions. Breathing can be revived by the swift application of mouth-to-mouth resuscitation. Resumption of heartbeat can sometimes be induced by a sharp blow to the left side of the victim's chest, over the heart; otherwise, external cardiac massage should be employed.

All this was part of the briefing to Number Two crew. Twenty minutes after they resumed their trek a hard rain began, and crew and instructors stopped to put on rain gear. Having donned theirs, Aram and Ginny waited, seated on their packs about thirty feet from the students. By now there were lightning flashes—coming closer, Aram noted. The students too were checking the time between strikes and how long it was taking for the sound of thunder to reach them. They had just counted a strike two seconds (about two-fifths of a mile) away when a ground current * from yet another strike hit the group. Afterward crew members severally reported a blue flash, a bright flash, smoke, a booming sound, and seeing Aram and Ginny thrown to the ground. Four students likewise were knocked down, but not hurt. Another was "jerked and jolted" and a sixth felt a "tingling sensation." The others experienced no sensation from the lightning.

When the students reached Aram and Ginny, neither was breathing, and the latter was unconscious; the hearts of both were beating. Crew members, who had been well coached in first aid by their instructors at the start of the course, immediately started mouth-to-mouth resuscitation. After twenty to thirty ventilations, both instructors began to breathe. The students treated Aram for shock and second degree burns on the lower right leg and foot. Treating Ginny for shock, they monitored her closely.

Help was summoned from the North Carolina School's base camp and the Burke County Rescue Squad, and the injured pair were transported to the hospital at Morganton, where they were treated and admitted. Ginny, still only semiconscious, complained of severe pain in her lower back. Aram was discharged three days later and returned to his crew on July 29, day sixteen of the course. Ginny was discharged three days after Aram and returned to the crew on August 1.

As is the practice in Outward Bound, the accident was written up by program director Mike Fischesser, and the report was circulated to the other schools for their information and guidance. It was noted that a supplement to the instructor field manual dealing more thoroughly with lightning was being distributed to the staff, and that future staff training would amplify coverage of the lightning hazard. Also, because the school and rescue squad

---

* As the North Carolina *Instructor's Field Manual* notes, "The current which flows in a lightning bolt does not dissipate itself at the point of direct hit; it tends to flow along the easiest paths of electric conduction on the surface of the earth. These may include wet, lichen-covered rock, cracks and crevices filled with water, natural fissures and chimneys, wet ropes, cables and the like along the ground, and 'spark gap' areas [when the ground current takes a short straight path through the air, rather than a longer path around through the ground]." Investigators from the North Carolina School found no physical evidence of a direct lightning hit in the accident area. The type of discharge that struck Aram and Ginny remains a mystery.

had lost time in locating the victims due to incorrect information, a telephone report form had been designed to minimize similar confusions in the future. Among Fischesser's comments on the accident and its outcome was this: "It shows that in-depth first aid instruction reduces the odds for serious injury or fatality when taught at the earliest time during a program." To which Director John Huie appends: "Training *works*; preparation *matters*. People acting wisely can make a difference."

This was an accident with a happy ending. Accidents frequently do not have happy endings, and Outward Bound has had its share with truly tragic consequences. We have related this particular incident because it dramatically points up the primary concern for the safety of students and instructors in the conduct of an Outward Bound course. A great deal of instructor training relates to accident prevention and to rescue technique. Instructors are taught that an integral factor in their relationship to the cadre is the setting and maintaining of a tone of concern for safe performance. In the first week, students receive a basic grounding in first aid, and throughout the course they are briefed on how to protect themselves and their fellows.

In U.S. Outward Bound's first nine years of operation the mysterious drowning of Dan Lucas in 1964 was the single student fatality. Even though marred by that still unexplained tragedy, and by two equally tragic instructor deaths,* this record reflected the diligent efforts of the schools to conduct their courses as safely as possible. Then in the summer of 1971, with calamity's brutal suddenness, fatal accidents occurred at two schools. First a male student, Walter Kennedy, drowned at Minnesota, in circumstances as strange in their way as those surrounding the death of the Lucas boy. (Starting on his one-mile swimming test, young Kennedy dove into the lake water and raced away from shore while the accompanying canoe was being launched. Within a short distance he was in serious trouble and disappeared suddenly, just as the canoe caught up with him. If the students in the canoe had not been wearing life preservers, they might have been able to dive for Kennedy in a second or two while he was sinking.)

* In 1965 Lew Covert, a Colorado instructor, was killed on a peak ascent when struck by a falling rock. In 1969 Colin Henderson, a British instructor on the staff of the Colorado School, drowned in the Green River while on instructor training.

A short time later three young women on their final expedition at the Northwest School were caught in severe, prolonged storm and low-temperature conditions. When the group failed to seek adequate protection away from an exposed slope above timberline, two of them, Joyce Howden and Lorene LaRhette, died of hypothermia (exposure).

Altogether, in the nineteen years through 1980, thirteen students have lost their lives in eight fatal occurrences in U.S. Outward Bound schools. It would be a mistake, however, to conclude from the chronology of these occurrences that Outward Bound courses grew more hazardous with time; if anything, the opposite was true. The fact that most of them occurred in the 1971–78 period reflects the great increase in the exposure factor as the number of students grew from a 1962 enrollment of 100 to nearly 3800 in 1970 and around 8000 in 1979. The exposure figures indicate a student to be safer, statistically, on an Outward Bound Course in the wilderness than in a motor vehicle on the public highway. No comfort, however, is to be drawn there. No statistical sophistry can minister to the heartsickness of all whom the tragedy of a lost life touches.

The irony of virtually all adventure-oriented accidents is that they could have been prevented without diminishing the adventure. Safety, in fact, is essential to the adventurous experience; this is apparent enough when a disabling accident puts an end to participation. Reviewing the record of all Outward Bound deaths —ten drownings, three falling-rock mishaps, two cases of hypothermia—what strikes one most forcibly is that most of them either occurred in seemingly low-risk situations, such as an apparently competent swimmer in still water or a group bivouac in the desert on a starlit night, or where people had been lulled into relaxing their guard against such hazard as swift water, loose rock, or the possibility of cloudburst. They reteach the most retaught of safety lessons—that the first rule of safe passage is constant vigilance.*

* However many times it may be retaught by bitter experience, this rule cannot be repeated too often. It is universally true for all hazard. In his penetrating analysis of nuclear-energy risks, nuclear physicist Dr. George L. Weil quotes Dr. Edward Teller: "The real danger occurs when a false sense of security causes a letdown of caution." Dr. Weil also cites the instance of the prelaunch exercise in the Apollo spacecraft in 1967 when three of the original

Earlier we related that from the beginning each school implemented the guiding principles the British Outward Bound Trust provided us by prescribing safe practices designed for its particular environment and courses and supporting these through instructor training and student instruction. In choosing staff, program directors placed increasingly heavy emphasis on maturity, sense of responsibility, experience, and technical competence. It was felt that these attributes, in conjunction with the accident prevention and first-aid and rescue doctrine, staff training, and supervision at the course-director level, would come together in the leadership skills and attitudes that made for a safe program.

There has never been a reason to discard this approach. In time, however, the school directors came to feel that there ought to be a more formal structuring and coordinating of the schools' safety standards and practices than was afforded by the informal coordinating activity that had come about spontaneously during the organization's formative years. In 1971 the OBI safety committee and the directors jointly agreed on the need for the national office to develop a national safety policy to which each school would be committed and for which each school would be subject to a periodic evaluative check.

The main burden of formulating a national safety program and implementing the structure for carrying it out fell on Ralph Puckett, who held the post of national program coordinator in OBI. Ralph consulted with national leaders in the accident-prevention movement, top industrial safety engineers, and experts in various phases of outdoor safety. At the same time, the supervisory staff and instructors of each school contributed to the thinking and the eventual consensus that made an all-school safety policy possible.

---

astronauts lost their lives in an oxygen-fueled flash fire, concerning which a NASA official suggested that "alertness . . . had become dulled" by previous successes in the Mercury and Gemini programs. *The New York Times* editorialized: "It is true that astronauts and others have worked in pure oxygen atmospheres hundreds of thousands of times without incident. But that only means that the probability of accident was small, not—as the designers seem to have assumed—that an accident was virtually impossible." (*Nuclear Energy: Promises, Promises*, by George L. Weil, Washington, D.C., 1973; privately printed.)

As finally adopted, the National Safety Policy was prefaced by the British Trust's policy declaration summarized in an earlier chapter. Bound loose-leaf in anticipation of periodic revision, it defined the national safety organization and its responsibilities, set administrative procedure standards, and detailed safe operating and expedition practices. Achievement of the policy was an organizational milestone. Its success is due in great measure to the fact that the school directors gave it their strong backing and made certain that its intent of dedicated self-discipline by the schools toward safe conduct of their courses was realized. Their implementing of the policy has integrated a continuing concern for the well-being of students and instructors into the day-to-day activity at all administrative and operating levels, to a degree of success not otherwise possible.

Inevitably, the National Safety Policy has evolved. A primary difficulty arose because often there is more than one right way to do things—for example, to tie in for a rock climb. The impracticality of making a central document satisfy all conditions at the local level eventually led to a "local operating procedures" policy permitting greater initiative at the school level. In its present form the National Safety Policy establishes guidelines for emergency procedures, accident reporting and investigating, staff selection and training, student admissions and training, and school safety reviews, and sets forth "standard national operational policies" under such headings as general, fire, first aid, weather, equipment, expeditions, solo, water activities, drugs, run and dip, vehicles, and new programs and environments. Each school then determines its own local operating procedures within the parameters of the national standards.

Each school has its own safety committee, whose responsibilities include approval of local operating procedures, ensuring that they do in fact conform with the National Safety Policy, and an annual on-site safety review of the school. The national safety committee consists of the school committee chairmen, the president of OBI, an OBI staff assistant who is responsible for coordinating the committee's activities with the schools, and an OBI trustee who chairs it.

The duties of the OBI staff member assigned to the national safety committee are so considerable as to make him virtually a full-time safety officer. He is expected to keep familiar with safety practices at all schools, to ensure that the useful experiences of one are communicated to all, and to investigate and respond to safety questions referred to him. He recommends changes in the National Safety Policy in the light of new developments, provides an annual summary of accident reports submitted by the schools to OBI, and monitors and reports to the national safety committee concerning the activities and effectiveness of the school committees. One of his most important duties is to lead a team in a periodic on-site safety review of each school.

When Hank Taft appointed John Rhoades program coordinator at OBI in 1973, John inherited the safety job, including the inspection responsibility. Studying the accident report files, John was struck by the fact that historically there had been no serious accident or near miss attributable to defective equipment. He concluded that the big problem was in the area of human judgment and that inspections should center there. "The problem I set myself," he recalls, "was how to evaluate that human element, recognizing that there were built-in resistances to my coming in to do the evaluation. One of the first things I did was change the name of what we were doing from inspection to safety review. My goal was a consultative model. Not one that was pointing fingers, taking names, and kicking fannies. But one that used a team of people to come in and ask the school administration—the director and the program director and the course directors—what their safety concerns were, what they particularly wanted us to look for, and we would do our job with a view to giving them the most helpful feedback possible as to whether or not what they wanted to be happening was in fact happening."

Rhoades and his review team associates put in as much time as possible in the field. They asked the students questions— "What's in that first-aid kit? What would you do if you got lost right now?"—as one way to obtain feedback for the administration. They worked hard for a rapport with the instructors. "To get that rapport," Rhoades says, "it was absolutely essential to get into a consultative mode, where any one of us could ask, 'You've been instructing here for three years, what do you worry about most? Where do you think the system is soft?' In the normal inspection system that kind of data doesn't appear, because it's to your best interest to cover up, or to answer only those questions that are put to you directly."

The safety review that Rhoades, building on the foundation of Puckett's work, developed and defined over a period of four years, was the model Bob Box inherited when he held the post of program coordinator at OBI from 1978 to 1980. Box came to OBI after five seasons as chief climbing instructor at the North Carolina School. In his instructor training there, he had done an exemplary job of making safety a central concern of the climbing program without diminishing its challenge and had created one of the most competent mountain rescue teams in the East. He took up his new post with an experience-based conviction that, in Outward Bound, adventure and safety belong hand in hand.

"The review as I see it," Box says, "has two functions—control and staff training. On the control side, the school administration gets an outside perspective on how well the school is living up to its safety responsibilities as defined by the National Safety Policy. On the training side, the school is getting feedback on how it might improve its program in any number of areas. Also, the flow goes both ways. The review-team members from other schools take home a tremendous amount of spinoff, knowledge that they put to work in their school. They may see a problem, and a team member may think, I'd better check that out in my own school. Or they may see a creative answer to a problem. For example, at Hurricane Island we discovered that their admission procedure included an outstanding system for screening applicants' medical reports. We said, 'You guys are doing this better than anyone else—let's share it!' With Peter Willauer's permission I sent it around to all the schools. That kind of thing happens a lot; people doing the reviews told me it was a staff-training function for them as well."

The review team normally consists of three persons, led by the OBI staff safety specialist. One of the other two is customarily a program director, or perhaps a school director, from one of the other schools. The third is usually an expert from outside Outward Bound, probably with a special competence in the school's operating environment—mountains, sea, lake, cold weather, etcetera. Depending on its scope, the review normally takes one to two weeks.

Box points out that since it is not possible to draw a line defining where safety concerns stop, the review has a broad reference base. In essence, it is a chance for the program director to be evaluated by his peers, not only on safety but in any number of aspects where the review team has expertise. It starts with the how-can-we-help approach. "The very first question in a safety review is, 'What do you especially want us to look at?' and as often as not the program director says, 'I'd like you to see how well I'm communicating with my staff. Tell me if my expectations are being met in reality.' This won't be in the review report, but the team will give the feedback verbally, and they can do that on any number of requests."

In Box's view, the valuable function of the review team is in looking at systems. They do not often find that the students have their carabiners turned the wrong way or that techniques, equipment, and procedures are incorrect or deficient. They focus on the supervision, the staff training, the follow-up procedures needed to assure the safety program's smooth running. The review customarily starts with a once-over session with the school and program directors and safety committee chairman, to become familiar with the safety scheme of operation, check on the previous review's recommendations, and learn where the school feels its problems lie. The team examines the files with special attention to what feedback the top echelons are getting from course directors and instructors in the field, and to see how effectively headquarters is responding.

In the field the team splits, each member going with a different cadre, observing and talking with instructors and students, then reunites to compare notes. Box explains: "They probably have gone out there with questions that grew out of their interviews, their run-through of the files, and so on. They're making a reality check. Say an instructor has reported the students are not eating properly on winter courses, where calorie intake is important. If the team then goes out in the field and sees students are not eating properly, that's two important observations. One, the procedural one of the need to tighten up, make sure of calorie intake. Second, the school is not listening to its own staff. That could be the larger of the two problems."

Box affirms the importance of time for talking with staff. "Probably the best feedback we'd get in the whole time was the informal conversations with instructors and their course directors. They'd clue us into things we ought to look into. For the most part they are professionals first. They're concerned about safety they've got those ten to twelve kids out there. They have the ability to ask the hard questions rather than just cover their own rear ends to avoid any problems."

A safety review is hard work. "The high energy level is sustained throughout the review," Box says.* "You're running in planes and cars and on the trail, in constant contact with your teammates and school personnel. For me the most debilitating part was the nervous and emotional energy I expended. You deal with real sensitivities. Regardless of how openly the team comes in, and how receptive the school may be, there's always that element of these guys are here to tell us what's wrong, and that makes them nervous. As a team we spent a lot of energy being sensitive to that and counteracting it, to break down those barriers of communication. Sometimes they don't break down, and that's even worse."

After the field review the team huddles to develop the framework of its report, agreeing on the key issues and other observations and suggestions they want to make. They share these orally with the school administration and safety trustee. Much of the report ends there; the observations and less significant suggestions are noted by the school, to be acted on as it may determine. The key issues are set forth in the written report that the OBI representative writes upon return to his office. When the full team is in agreement on the report content, including all recommendations, the report is formally sent through the president of OBI to the school director and safety trustee. The school is required to reply to the recommendations within thirty days. If the school does not wish to comply with a recommendation, it states its reasons. The review team may accept the school's response as valid; if it does not, it restates its case, perhaps revising the recommendation. If an agreement cannot be reached, the issue is re-

* Bob Box left OBI in 1980 to accept the post of program director at the Southwest Outward Bound School. He was replaced by Ted Moores, a former program director of the Minnesota School.

ferred to OBCC, which arbitrates it and makes the final decision.

In recent years the annual school safety reports have become increasingly sophisticated; they inform in greater detail and employ a uniform system of statistical analysis. These reports become a part of the National Safety Committee's annual report, so that each school benefits from the others' experience as well as its own. A good instance of this is the fortuitous consequence of an incident at North Carolina, where a student's severe allergic reaction to a bee sting caused stoppage of breathing and necessitated his hurried evacuation to a hospital. Two years later students suffering similar allergic reactions on North Carolina and Dartmouth courses received an emergency injection of epinephrine from staff in the field, a treatment that prevented severe trauma. The change of procedure over the two years was directly attributable to the shared recommendations in the report on the first incident.

An essential part of the accident reporting system is that covering "near misses." The difference between little or even no injury and serious or even fatal injury may be more "accidental" than the accident itself. It is just as important to have information about serious accidents that almost or might have happened as about those that did. In either case a hazard existed, and the incident has shed light on how to deal with such dangers or on the need for a preventive strategy. The schools follow a policy of circulating full reports on all "safety-related incidents that had the potential for critical injury or fatal results, but resulted in no injury or minor consequence."

In 1978 Outward Bound requested the National Executive Service Corps, a volunteer citizen organization, to conduct an outside, independent review of Outward Bound's safety systems. Following an in-depth review at each school and of the national system, the team of three reviewers * submitted its report in December 1979. The report said in part:

> Taken as a whole we felt that the Outward Bound people are extraordinarily talented and dedicated and are commit-

* The team: Howard W. Blauvelt, retired president and chairman of Conoco, Inc.; Marian S. Heiskell, then president of the Community Service Society of New York; and Charles A. Anderson, retired president of Stanford Research Institute.

262 / OUTWARD BOUND U.S.A.

ted to giving the students a challenging, adventurous and educational experience but with continuous and unremitting attention to safety. In a few instances, we concluded that improvements were very much needed and that they could and should be made. . . .

Following receipt of the report by OBI, the national office and the schools made positive responses to all the team's recommendations.

At this writing, in the nearly three years just past, some 23,000 people have taken a U.S. Outward Bound course without serious accident. The self-education of the schools in better ways to deal with hazard in order to have finer adventure is a continuing response to that discipline placed on Jim Hogan some four decades ago: "Hahn had constantly insisted it was my duty to understand all the factors affecting safety." The founder's iron rule still prevails. In the final passage of *Impelled into Experiences* Hogan reflects on an effect of the growth in popularity of adventurous outdoor pursuits, for which the success of Outward Bound is in considerable measure responsible: "Many of the well-meaning adults who lead young people in such pursuits are insufficiently aware of the dangers involved and the technical training that is essential to safety." The reflection causes him to recall that most memorable of Hahn aphorisms, which had given him the title for his book, that it is culpable neglect not to impel young people into experience. He concludes:

To those who seek to adopt Hahn's precept one would like to stress that behind all his practices there was a passionate concern that youngsters should not merely survive the experiences in which he plunged them but that they should emerge strengthened. If Outward Bound has demonstrated anything, it must surely be that adventure should be used as an ingredient in education only by those who have accepted the restraints and disciplines which are essential to successful practice.

Hogan's commentary on the heart of the founder's philosophy itself becomes a precept for those entrusted with carrying on his work. To it let us add the observation of another British Outward Bound philosopher who likewise acknowledges a grateful allegiance to the founder's wisdom. In 1966 Tom Price, warden of the Eskdale Outward Bound School, addressing the Royal Society of Arts on the meaning of Outward Bound, spoke directly to this point: "If one disregards safety, one in effect holds life cheap, and that is contrary to the whole spirit of a training which devotes so much time to first aid, mountain rescue, lifeboat work, and other forms of service."

The Adjudicated

≡≡×≡≡×≡≡×≡≡×≡≡×≡≡×≡≡×≡≡×≡≡×≡≡×≡

A great part of [the frightening rate of increase in crimes of violence] is not individual violence; it is fed by the gang spirit, which is a degraded form of the comradeship, the platoon-spirit in an army. The gang, the cell, is an immensely strong unit. It may be easier to convert it into a shock-troop for some good purpose than to break it up into individuals. It must be admitted, though, that such "gangs for the good" would lose their strongest cohesive force: the disapproval of society.

—Dennis Gabor

I had been to some of the state and county [training schools] and God, I was repulsed—to think that we were paying something like $10,000 a year just to keep a kid in a cage without any type of rehabilitation. It was just really horrible. And I figured that if I didn't do any other damn thing while I was governor, I was going to [change] that system.
—Former Governor Francis Sargent of Massachusetts

In February 1967 Frank Kelly, who by then had left the Massachusetts Division of Youth Services to teach psychology at Boston College, called me. He had a bulletin on his research project tracking the sixty delinquent youths who had attended Outward Bound schools the preceding summer. After seven months only

264

eight had recidivated—been committed to an institution for a new offense. Since the normal expectation was twenty—one in three—this report was encouraging. But we still had to wait a year for processing of comparative data for both the Outward Bound group and the control group who had been treated in the normal institutional routine.

The project report by Kelly and his Boston College colleague, Professor Daniel Baer, was published in June 1968.* Containing much comparative data for the two groups, the report centered on a recidivism comparison, initially for nine months, subsequently updated for a year. In the first twelve months of parole, thirteen of the Outward Bound group (20%) recidivated, as against twenty-five (42%) of the control group. The Outward Bound group's rate was half that expected for boys of their age committed to DYS, while the control group's was about as expected. The superior record of the Outward Bound group was rated statistically significant.†

In analyzing their data Kelly and Baer noted that in addition to the Outward Bound experience, several "background variables" appeared also to relate to the recidivism. One of their surmises was that Outward Bound might have a greater influence on those whose offenses were against persons or property than on those who were committed as "stubborn or runaway children" ("status offenses" that have no adult counterpart and usually reflect familial conflicts expressed in disobedience, incorrigibility, and running away from home). Even so, although the recidivism rate for the stubborn/runaway category in both groups was high,

---

* Francis J. Kelly and Daniel J. Baer, *Outward Bound Schools as an Alternative to Institutionalization for Adolescent Delinquent Boys* (Boston, Mass.: Fandel Press, Inc., 1968). Includes a Participant Observers' Report by Richard Katz and David Kolb.

† Kelly and Baer have since made a five-year follow-up. While the difference in recidivism rates continued to favor the Outward Bound group (38% vs. 53%), the difference was no longer considered statistically significant. Noting that the increase in recidivism among the Outward Bound group occurred in the second half of the second year, Kelly comments: "This suggests that Outward Bound had an effect on some delinquents sufficient to sustain them in the community for a longer period than traditional treatment, but that the effect eroded before the onslaught of negative environmental pressures." The offenses of the control group tended to be much more serious than those of the Outward Bound group.

it was twice as high in the control (83%) as in the Outward Bound group (40%).

The Kelly-Baer report, along with other papers the two subsequently published, had a considerable impact—on the corrections community at large, on DYS, and on Outward Bound. In my first call on John Coughlan in 1964 I had told him I thought that Outward Bound might be something that could help. Now we had solid empirical support for what had been little more than a gut feeling. Others—people who could put this knowledge to work—were made aware of it. In particular, young social and behavioral scientists who had entered corrections work aspiring to find more productive ways of dealing with young criminals and potential criminals were receptive to the implications of the DYS experiment. Since then we have had amply more indication that Outward Bound has something valuable to offer the juvenile corrections community. In recent years, in fact, corrections professionals have increasingly sought out Outward Bound and Outward Bound–derived agencies for aid in developing programs alternative to incarceration for young offenders.

DYS was sufficiently impressed with the Kelly-Baer findings to continue the Outward Bound liaison, again sending sixty boys in 1967 and 1968. This was expensive—$600 per individual on the average to cover tuition, transportation, and miscellaneous. But since it would cost between $3,000 and $4,000 to maintain each boy in an institution for a year, the alternative was rated a good investment. At the same time the Outward Bound success inevitably raised a question. If the method worked so well with youngsters sent from the institution, why not introduce it directly into the institution? The query was not an easy one. To superimpose the Outward Bound process on a homogeneous delinquent group on what was essentially their own turf would be quite different from integrating several delinquent youths into a standard course in a totally strange environment. Still, it was a challenging idea. In 1968 the Hurricane Island School contracted with DYS to provide a staff and program for one living unit at the Lyman School for Boys. Lyman was the state's largest institution for youthful offenders, with a regimen of remedial education in classrooms and rehabilitative treatment under counselors.

The conventional wisdom is that the story of the Lyman School experiment is one of honorable failure. It deserves a better testimony. Moreover, it supplies a linkage in the evolution of the thorniest of Outreach undertakings—bringing the Outward Bound dynamic to bear in society's attempts to deal with adjudicated youth and their antisocial behavior.

The program ran ten weeks, from the end of January 1968 to early April. Peter Willauer assigned three of his staff—Adrian Middleton, Hurricane's chief instructor, Baha Uddin Abdul-Malik, and Gil Leaf—to staff the Lyman project. Middleton, an Australian who had come to Hurricane Island via Australia Outward Bound and the British school at Aberdovey, was project director. Baha, a music-major graduate of the University of West Virginia, had been one of Malcolm X's chief lieutenants before that Black Muslim leader's assassination. He was from New York and had worked at the Urban League's Harlem Prep, a street academy. Leaf, a Harvard graduate, teacher, and staff assistant to Willauer, had helped to set up the Hurricane Island School and had instructed there and at the Outward Bound schools in Australia and Kenya. Author of Hurricane's report on the first phase of the Lyman experiment and still its oral historian, he reminisces:

"We were the first Outward Bound program to be residentially located in a reform school, and we went in ill-prepared. None of us had training for dealing with a homogeneous delinquent group, although Baha's skills in working with kids from the inner city, both black and white, were fantastic. Nor had we done any kind of pedagogical homework before leaping into this situation. They gave us Oak Cottage, a funny little three-story building almost as old as the school, which was founded in 1846. The school was full of euphemisms like cottages and cottage masters. We had twenty-four kids, mostly sixteen and seventeen years old, about sixty-forty percent white and black. They were a mix ranging from 'stubborn children' in mild trouble to real psychopaths or to kids who would tell you, 'I got a bum rap,' and then you'd learn this was their umpteenth conviction. The mix was disruptive and diminished a good deal of what might have been accomplished. The first day there were a lot of fights as the pecking order got sorted out. We named the project the Overlanders and divided the group Outward Bound–style into two patrols. We had four cottage masters and a counselor assigned to help us. Three of the cottage masters did make a real effort. They didn't know what we were about but they tried to be open-minded. They were dubious because we started breaking all the classic rules of the institution, and they were just waiting for us to fall on our faces, which we did a number of times."

In the standard cottage plan at Lyman the boys kept their personal gear in lockers in the basement and slept in rows of beds on the third floor, surveyed by a watchman. The Overlander staff put the beds in three rooms on the second floor, had each student place his locker by his bed, and gave him some personal wall space to use or decorate. They took the boys out of the uniform-like nightshirts that were obligatory for others at Lyman. Because they wanted mealtime to be an important part of the group experience, they maintained dining quarters at Oak Cottage, two boys fetching each meal from the school cafeteria. Fairly rigid rules for sharing and organization and clean-up were enforced. Many of the boys took kindly to this as a sort of surrogate home atmosphere. Some of them—presumably those who had worked with their mothers—were extraordinarily house proud, zealous in cleaning up. Part of that, Leaf thought, was a way of escaping from threatening interactions with other inmates.

The curriculum consisted of classroom work at eighth- to tenth-grade levels, outdoor pursuits and gymnasium, a ropes course, initiative tests, drownproofing, weekend wilderness expeditions, trips to museums and the like, maintaining and drilling with the school fire engine, operating the big bulldozer that Reverend Bob Brown, the school chaplain, had got hold of, and service projects, with letter and journal writing and recreation in the evening. The basic plan for the daytime schedule was to alternate ninety-minute academic and action-oriented periods. The staff learned early that while the general intelligence level of the boys was higher than expected, their attention span was quite limited. Midway in the course the period lengths were halved, and efforts were made to increase variety and action in the curriculum.

The staff gave the students considerable rein from the outset and soon regretted it. They realized they had made a serious mistake not structuring a transition from the completely regulated Lyman regimen to the responsibility and initiative inherent in their open-cottage pattern. The boys were quick to seize advantage of what they took to be supervisory weakness, and the result was a kind of seesaw balance of power. "These kids had us in their element most of the time," Leaf says. "They could have destroyed the program at will. In many ways our ineptitude and naivete were our strength. When the boys found we were such pigeons, they sort of carried us out of curiosity. We also had the outdoors and the wilderness as our allies; there we had them more in our territory, which made a huge difference."

The counselor assigned to the project gave the staff no help. At the same time the staff found their own efforts at counseling going for naught. "It's a real myth," Leaf says, "that you can work with these kids effectively one on one. You would have a fine talk and think you were really communicating with that boy. You were absolutely kidding yourself because five minutes after you put him back with his peers, his behavior pattern was entirely different. Most of the psychiatric social workers we saw could not work with kids in a group because they were scared of them. Yet the core of what we were trying to do was to get at these kids' problems—deficient sense of delayed gratification, lack of some kind of internal discipline system, need for some kind of values training—within the context of the group of peers."

The staff became aware of a three-way contrast: the standard Lyman disciplinary scheme, the approach that worked effectively with delinquents at Outward Bound schools, and the peculiar conditions creating difficulty for the Outward Bound method in the Lyman environment. The traditional Lyman structuring, as the Overlander staff saw it, was designed to detain in a highly regulated atmosphere, cut off from decision making and responsibility, well-suited to creating a docile and passive attitude. The archaic cottage system was built on the concept of a ratio of thirty, forty, even fifty boys to one cottage master. To make the machinery of the daily schedule work, the cottage master ruled by the clenched fist. "It became quite evident to us," Leaf says, "that most of the cottage masters had a good sense of humor and a general affection for the boys. But the system denied them the opportunity to be much other than guards. As a result the boys, who frequently came from violent backgrounds, had their previous experiences reenforced by an institutional system dependent on physical force."

By contrast, Leaf points out, Outward Bound operates on a different disciplinary basis that in residential courses is effective with delinquents. Since all students are on strange ground and placed in situations of interdependence, group pressure is highly effective. "The predominantly middle-class ethics system is very powerful and supportive to the delinquent kid. In that setting he has to conform to the majority's will. Invariably the positive elements in a twelve-man group outnumber the negative forces. Boys are given great responsibility and respond remarkably to the challenge. There is little or no incidence of bullying, as situations demand total group cooperation. But at Lyman we had a homogeneous delinquent group, albeit of all different gradations. In the all-delinquent community you don't have the kinds of mechanisms you have at an Outward Bound school. The pecking order becomes a far more powerful force."

The most striking fact about the Lyman experiment is that the Overlander staff was able to carry the course to completion. Seriously understaffed to begin with, an expedition injury to Leaf and much less help from the cottage masters than anticipated aggravated the situation close to the breaking point. In the latter part of the course Miles Becker, a Northwest School instructor, was a welcome addition. But the staff had to keep running just to maintain the daily routine, with no break in the stress. In the light of this unrelenting pressure Middleton's fortitude as leader was the more remarkable.

"Adrian was the real heart of the program," Leaf says. "His sense of personal morality, his incredible Christian behavior, was the primary force working for us. Adrian fostered the idea that the Overlanders would be something special within the school. He was just a tower of strength, and delinquent kids reacted to him in a fascinating way. He was the squarest, most out-of-it character you ever want to meet, and the kids loved him for it. So many of the adults they had dealt with seemed to be devious, or exerted their power. Adrian never played the power business with them. It was quite extraordinary."

While the course was a mix of plus and minus values throughout, as it progressed the plus side gained. Performance levels improved, generally as much among the smaller or less aggressive youngsters as among the "tough guys." The boys found rock climbing, which started late due to the weather, scary and thrilling; many exuded a new confidence as a result of their climbing achievements. While most were initially terrified of operating the big bulldozer, they all came to handle it competently. Never before, Reverend Bob Brown remarked, had he seen a group of Lyman boys combine confidence, attention, and skill in such an activity. This and other performances encouraged the staff to believe they had made real progress in building self-esteem. Many of the boys enjoyed keeping a journal, as long as the writing period was established for them, and letter writing was a favorite activity. Surprisingly, some of those who had tested poorly in verbal aptitude seemed to write the best prose—a finding that reenforced the staff's suspicions that motivation, or lack of it, played a large part in the group's test performances.

The Overlanders responded especially well to community service. Trained to use the school fire truck and equipment, they handled emergency calls when the nearby town of Westboro was hit by a flood, pumping out a factory and the basement of a private home. They were extremely proud when an open letter thanking them was published in the Worcester newspaper. With the cottage masters, they put in a three-day service effort for the State Fish and Game Commission, wielding bushhooks, axes, and saws to clear a large picnic area in a state forest. Cottage masters and boys alike returned to Lyman with high morale and new pride. The pleased commission marked the area with a sign that read, "Cleared by Overlanders I, 1968—Rogers and Henson Patrols."

Throughout the ten weeks the wilderness expeditions, growing increasingly difficult, were the program elements where the students experienced the greatest sense of personal achievement. There too the cottage masters were forced to regard the youngsters in a new light. Taken out of their cottage where they had reigned supreme, the masters were now thrown into situations where the boys could hike longer and had learned better how to orienteer, so that the men had to follow them. "For the first time," Leaf says, "the masters saw their charges as kids rather than young bums." The youngsters' behavior on the expeditions and in the periods directly after their return was at its best. On one such morning, a Sunday late in the course, Middleton's log read: "Boys up at 0630, had all beds made etc. 0700 breakfast brought up to staff! All ready for church. Cottage v. clean."

Although youngsters ran away from Lyman all the time, often despite locked doors, no Overlander ever ran, even though they had keys to the cottage and could come and go virtually at will.

By the course's end most boys cared about staff opinion and tended to be upset with themselves when they did not perform up to standard. In the third week from the end there was an incident that had a telling effect on the entire experience. Some member or members of the Overlanders stole a ring and money from a visitor in the gymnasium. It was 9:30 P.M. when Middleton got everybody together and delivered an emotion-charged ultimatum: They would sit there until the stolen items were returned, or the project would be terminated.

The boys were shocked. "They were truly conscious of the personal dedication and affection for them that Adrian had shown throughout," Leaf says, "and his intention to fold the project if compelled to shook them profoundly. He appealed to their sense of honor, and their treatment of visitors. He restated the meaning of the unofficial Overlanders motto: 'Liberty is the right to discipline oneself so as not to be disciplined by others.' For the first time its meaning hit home."

The culprit's identity was not known among the boys. As the night dragged on, they negotiated among themselves and between the two patrols. Emotions ran high as suspicions were voiced and indignantly denied. One boy made a false confession, but this was seen through. Finally, at 4 A.M., the boy who had stolen the ring turned himself in to Baha, and in the follow-up inquiry another who was involved gave himself away. The entire group was sent to bed but roused at the usual 6:30 hour. On rising they were called together for a secret ballot on whether to expel or keep the thieves. By large majorities they voted to dismiss both from the program. "The whole issue of returning the ring, the rightness and wrongness of it, was very effective," Leaf says. "It was not lost on them at all. From that night on they seemed to take a greater pride in their group. They amazed us by self-administered discipline with their swearing."

The final expedition, an eleven-day journey to the Pemigewasset Wilderness in New Hampshire's White Mountain National Forest and on Vermont's Long Trail in the Green Mountains, was a capping success. On their three-day solos without food, only three boys broke. Near the end youngsters who had thought covering five miles a day in deep snow was almost impossible managed to do thirty-four miles in two-and-one-half days. When they returned "home," as they had come to call Oak Cottage, self-regard was obviously strong, and the euphoria was sustained through the final three days. The boys took pains to wear their Overlander shoulder patches everywhere. A peak final occasion was a dance, with guests from a nearby girls' school. The boys conducted themselves as gentlemen, without incident during the pleasant evening.

Thinking back on the experience a decade later, Leaf essays an evaluation: "I think it was a reasonably successful experiment. It was clumsy, but I think the best that could be expected in terms of our lack of training and our lack of logistical support. We were run down because of the emotional climate. Some of the kids were very unstable personalities so that you became very uptight yourself. You had to keep the kids busy all the time, or you were in trouble.

"At the end we didn't know what would be the impact on the kids. That would have had to be measured over a long period of time, and still would have been fuzzy. I think whatever impact we had was second to the impact on the institution—forcing the state to reexamine its process. We certainly messed with the minds of the cottage masters, at whole different levels of trusting kids. A series of things of that nature were, I think, more significant than our rather amateurish performance with the kids. I think we provided a nudge to Jerome Miller toward what he eventually did, closing down the institutions."

Dr. Jerome Miller was the innovative—some would say maverick—individual brought in as commissioner of a new state Department of Youth Services in 1969. In the course of the next several years he closed down all but one of the state institutions for youthful offenders. The fact that the exception was Homeward Bound, an Outward Bound spinoff, indicates that Leaf's surmise is sound. There is in fact a connection between the Outward Bound influence in DYS and Miller's ultimate dramatic actions.

By the time Miller came into office, Hurricane Island had run a second Overlander activity in the 1968–69 winter. Learning about the Kelly-Baer study, the Overlander history, and the department's continuing success with scholarship students, Miller found Outward Bound's accessory participation in the department's work to be one of the few aspects of what the department was doing that he approved. In addition, he discovered that Alan Colette, superintendent of the DYS forestry camp at Brewster, had already started an activity with a potential for becoming the department's own Outward Bound–type treatment.

The Stephen L. French Youth Forestry Camp in the state forest on Cape Cod had been activated in 1960 as a facility to which youngsters committed as first offenders were sent for six to nine months. The rationale was that in the course of working in the woods they would learn silviculture and other forestry skills. But when Colette transferred from the Lyman School staff to become the camp's assistant superintendent in 1965, he found no silviculture or related instruction. The inmates were functioning primarily as maintenance crews in the state park, picking up litter, cleaning the latrines, and the like. While at Lyman, Colette had accompanied DYS scholarship youngsters to Minnesota Outward Bound, where the school's method had impressed him. In 1967 he obtained a scholarship to a teachers' course at Hurricane Island. Considerably overweight and in less than the best of physical shape, he suffered greatly throughout the course. "Nevertheless," he says, "I learned an awful lot." Returning to Brewster, he persuaded the then superintendent that Outward Bound offered a fresh new approach to rehabilitative work with delinquents. His superior agreed to let him set up an adaptive program for the final month of the inmates' stay. The kids dubbed it "Homeward Bound."

Miller, enthusiastic about what he found at the camp, encouraged Colette in his ideas for building up the adventure-experience element and cutting back sharply on the overall length of stay. A series of Hurricane Island instructors—Arthur Conquest, Bill Hughes, John Conant, and others—were brought in to help structure the program. By 1971 only the Outward Bound element remained—eventually its time span was whittled down to one month—and the entire Brewster operation was being called Homeward Bound. Having made up his mind to phase out the other institutions, Miller used Homeward Bound to divert youths who would otherwise have been assigned to the training schools and transferred others there for a final "homeward bound" experience prior to parole.

The shutting of the Massachusetts institutions for young offenders, with the exception of Homeward Bound, was virtually completed in January 1972 when, on Miller's authorization, a caravan of cars manned by University of Massachusetts students carried off the remaining thirty-nine inmates of the Lyman School. Two years later Herb Willman, by then an executive assistant in the department, would say in retrospect, "If you want to close down the institutions, start a Homeward Bound." Nearly a decade later the complex of alternative treatments that Miller initiated to replace the training schools was still operative, Massachusetts remaining unique in its radical dealing with the delinquency problem. A matured Homeward Bound, with the beginnings of a plan for maintaining a follow-up relationship with its students, was going strong.

School in the Southwest

≡✕≡✕≡✕≡✕≡✕≡✕≡✕≡✕≡✕≡✕≡✕≡

I have learned the depths of strength and trust that are present in me and my fellow man. I shall try to remember that any of my neighbors or fellow workers could have belayed the climbing rope for me or given me his hand when I was slipping off a steep slope. I may forget, but I will try to remember.
  —Reporter Allen Hall, writing in the *Dallas Morning News* about his course in the Texas Big Bend.

The year 1970 saw important developments within the organization. Late in 1969 we named Murray Durst national executive director of OBI. In two years as director of the North Carolina School Murray had convincingly demonstrated his managerial competence. We now sought that competence to implement the OBEX (Outward Bound Executive Committee) policy that "the paid president is not responsible for the operation or administration of Outward Bound Inc." Willi Unsoeld had been largely relieving me of those responsibilities, but now the Unsoelds planned to return to their beloved Northwest. At midyear they departed for Olympia, Washington, where Willi had accepted a place on the founding faculty of new, innovative Evergreen State College. Much as I regretted Willi's going, I would have been even more desolate had I realized how few times our paths would cross thereafter. I was among the thousands whom tragedy deprived when he and one of his students were killed by a snow avalanche on Mount Rainier in 1979.

276

In the fall of 1970 Durst and his staff moved to offices in Reston, Virginia. Going with him as director of operations was Lee Maynard, whom I had hired as OBI business manager shortly before Murray joined us. My president's office remained in Andover. Durst's move was dictated by the trustees' sense that with the increasing recognition being accorded Outward Bound as an important educational movement, it was time to relocate the national headquarters closer to "the action." The choice of Reston was based in part on the increasing difficulty of obtaining federal funds for educational purposes in the Nixon administration and the feeling that it would be advantageous for the national office to be in the Washington area.

The increasing scope of Durst's task in response to the growing needs of the schools was one reflection of Outward Bound's growing significance on the national scene. In 1971 the student total leaped from 3800 to 5300. For ten years the annual enrollment increase had been averaging twenty percent, a record few other educational programs of the period could match. OBI was responsible for helping sustain that growth, meeting the scholarship funding quota that grew with it, and satisfying other expanding service requirements of the schools. By 1971 every school was conducting women's courses, coeducational courses, contract courses, and offering a host of educational experiences ranging in duration from five to eighteen days that were broadening the Outward Bound appeal—to teachers, businessmen, adults generally, juniors, and special groups. Each school now had some form of winter program, and with each passing year was approaching closer to the goal of year-round operation. The calls from schools and colleges for help in establishing adaptive programs were mounting. Outward Bound was winning academic acceptance; a growing number of colleges were recognizing Outward Bound as a valid educational experience for credit, all the way up to doctoral programs. In another area of social concern Outward Bound's usefulness as an alternative to incarceration for juvenile delinquents was receiving respectful attention from youth service agencies.

At the same time developments in the management area were building our institutional vigor. OBEX membership was revised to provide for representation of the schools, assuring them a role in the decision-making process on national policy and operation.

Procedures for regular evaluation of school operations were emerging. One of these was a peer review plan initiated by the directors through OBCC, whereby each is periodically evaluated by a group of leaders—usually directors and program directors— from other schools. Cooperative activity between the national trustees' safety committee and OBCC was leading to the school safety review plan.

The organization was also being offered the opportunity for another growth leap. We had a charter application for a new school.

In our earlier years the school directors met regularly in their identity as the Outward Bound Operating Committee (OBOC). There was a period when these meetings were held in cities unconnected to the schools, chosen as likely places for recruiting students and spreading the Outward Bound word. In the winter of 1967 the Colorado School, whose sponsoring turn it was, chose Dallas. The meeting generated considerable interest among a group of Dallas citizens, not just to send young people to Outward Bound but also to initiate some form of permanent activity in the Dallas area. For a time the Colorado School considered setting up a subsidiary operation as a means of seeding a new school in Texas. Subsequently Dick Galland, a Texan who was on the promotional and instructional staffs at Colorado, persuaded the Dallas group to seek a school charter. His father, Richard I. Galland, took the lead in the organizing work. A committed group of prospective trustees incorporated in mid-1970. The board of twenty included twelve from Dallas, two from Fort Worth, and six from Houston. On an evaluating visit Durst was impressed by the quality of the support for the proposed new school. With the senior Galland he worked up a gradualist *modus operandi* for bringing it "on line" and reported an affirmative recommendation to OBEX. In November 1970, OBI's trustees voted a charter for the Texas Outward Bound School.

The Texas development strategy was to proceed slowly, centering first on organization and conduct of Outreach programs on a contract basis. In February 1971 the trustees appointed Dick Galland Jr. executive secretary and set up an operating committee to work closely with him. They provided $10,000 for scholarships, mostly for teachers' practica, at other schools in the

1971 summer. Dick's main tasks, in addition to publicity and fund raising, were to reconnoiter potential areas for conducting courses and promote Texas Outward Bound's availability for contract services among schools and colleges in the state. The course site search revealed the merits of the Big Bend National Park area. Named after the "big bend" of the Rio Grande that forms the dip and rise of the border line between southwest Texas and Mexico, the area is a spectacular combination of desert, mountain, and canyon country. Galland made two reconnaissances there and won permission of the National Park Service and neighboring ranchers to use the area.

Texas Outward Bound's first program was a ten-day orientation course for the freshman class of St. Marks School in Dallas in August 1971, with eighty students and faculty sharing a mountain-river experience. Among nine 1972 contract courses for schools and colleges was a mini-semester for a large coeducational freshman group from Tarrant County Junior College in Fort Worth —the first junior college adaptive program of such scope in the country. The school conducted its first standard courses for the general public in the summer of 1972, with the younger Galland as director. A year later Texas Outward Bound was in full operation.

By then it had become apparent that the entire Southwest was rich in environments ideally suited to Outward Bound programs, and that a school more centrally located could better serve an area with the potential of reaching from Texas to California. In 1974 the name of the Texas School was changed to Southwest Outward Bound. The following year the school moved its headquarters to Santa Fe and enhanced its trustee membership to reflect the new regional realities. Lee Maynard, who after leaving OBI had served as vice chancellor of Prescott College and president of Prescott Institute, was the new director. The school expanded its operating terrain—to the Grand Canyon, the Gila and Pecos Wilderness areas of New Mexico, the Gulf of Mexico, the Sierra Nevada Mountains in California, and even overseas to Nepal. When Maynard stepped down in 1978, the school's enrollment had greatly increased and its program broadened considerably in course offerings as well as geography.

Maynard's successor was Rafe Parker, who came from his post as associate director of the Hurricane Island School. For Parker, the sharp shift from the ocean environment of the Maine coast to the desert and mountain ambiance of the Southwest was a new stage in a multistage life journey that gives insight to international Outward Bound. Born in Sussex, England, Rafe lived most of his youth in Cyprus. On that island in the eastern Mediterranean that once harbored Phoenician ships, he became an ardent sailor, and he won his mountain-climbing spurs in the ranges that form its double spine. He was sixteen when terrorism bred by ethnic tensions among the Cypriots caused his family to return to England. A student at Sandhurst, the royal military academy, he ocean-raced on its sailing team, captained his college rugby team and competed on the college shooting team, taught judo, climbed in the Alps, and won the Queen's Medal in Military History for his thesis on the French–Algerian conflict. Commissioned in the Royal Corps of Signals, he qualified for duty in the Special Air Services, an elite corps comparable to the U.S. Army's Special Services. Along the way he picked up skills in gliding, underwater demolition, and winter warfare and won a bronze medal in the royal military fencing tournament. Taking part in a simulated air invasion in the NATO exercises of 1962, his parachute malfunctioned. Severely injured, he was invalided out of the army and hospitalized for three months. Of the parachute mishap he says, "I packed it myself so I'm entirely to blame."

At twenty-two Rafe had a go at the business world. His enjoyment of the work was diminished by a sense of having little in common with his colleagues. He was in much more congenial company when Freddy Fuller hired him to instruct at the Aberdovey Outward Bound Sea School. After ten courses at Aberdovey he went to East Africa as chief instructor, and subsequently deputy warden, of the Outward Bound school just then opening up in the new Republic of Zambia, formerly Northern Rhodesia. Rafe remembers the Zambian experience as an exciting time: "The first couple of years we had a substantial percentage of white students, but that changed rapidly with the changeover from the colonial pattern to the new black-governed status. The main rationale for the school was to give black Africans from tribes all over the country an experience together. Zambia is a large country with a tremendous diversity of tribes. It is very important for those tribes to nurture a national identity and work out a common understanding toward developing their country. We were putting through seven hundred students a year. We started the first girls' course in African Outward Bound and adult courses for executives. We pushed hard at turning out people qualified to teach rescue and first aid. We organized an alumni association, and developed to a high degree the sponsorship needed to make the school fiscally viable. I felt it was on sound footing when, after three years, I left."

Now married, Parker had decided he wanted to make a career with Outward Bound, but in a new theater. "It was important for me to go to America rather than back to England. From my African perspective I could see American Outward Bound as a much more dynamic, fluid program that allowed a great deal of creativity and imagination to be used by the instructor. I was disappointed by the way the British-oriented schools in Africa had tended to implant the British concept rather than try to mold the process to the African needs of the African students. It was the good old colonial attitude; I had contributed my share in Zambia. Also, Outward Bound was a great deal more accepted by the mainstream of education in the United States than in England. That was important to me because I felt strongly, as I still feel, that the Outward Bound process has a place in education."

Parker came to Hurricane Island, where Adrian Middleton, his old sidekick at Aberdovey, was chief instructor, as a watch officer in 1968. Four years later, when Middleton returned to his native country to become warden of the Australian Outward Bound School, Parker succeeded to the chief instructor post. He was successively promoted to be program director and associate director.

After the Reston move, my office in Andover was primarily a development office. My chief responsibilities were general promotion of Outward Bound, fund raising, building a broader national trustee base and close liaison with school trustees, and liaison with Outward Bound in other countries. "General promotion of Outward Bound" was a broad mission. An evidence of the recognition being accorded the movement was that I found myself on frequent call for TV and radio talk shows. On "What's My Line?" I just about blew it when one of the "imposters," in answering a question, said Outward Bound had no courses for women, and I indignantly cried out, "Oh, yes we do!"

When you are on NBC's "Today" show you have to rise at 5:30 A.M. and get over to the studio early to be made up. On arriving, I was ushered into a room with three barber chairs. Barbara Walters was in one, Hugh Downs in another, with an empty one between. As I entered, Walters looked around and said, "Here comes muscle boy!" I was very nervous and I did not need that at that moment. While I was being made up, a producer came in and said to Downs, "Hugh, here are the Outward Bound film clips. You'd better have a look at them." When the clips were run, my heart sank. They had clipped our new film, which had sequences from each of the schools, taken only the dramatic and sensational scenes, and spliced them together. Downs said, "What do you think?" I did not know what to say; I decided, What the hell, I'll tell him exactly what I think. I said, "I think it's awful. It's like ninety percent of the publicity we get, which just plays up the sensational, makes us look like a toughness program, and misses the whole point."

Downs said, "Well, do you have one word to summarize Outward Bound?" I said, "Yes, I do. It's 'compassion,'" and I quickly told him about Hahn and Hahn's concept of serving those in danger and in need. Downs said, "There's certainly nothing compassionate in those clips, or in the questions I've been given to ask you." Then he said, "Look, we have just seven minutes. Let's sit down and see if we can't figure out the questions you'd like me to ask you."

In seven minutes, plus time during the commercials, we wrote our own script. Downs did such a beautiful job of it, and he showed such compassion himself, that soon afterward we made him a trustee.

Into the Educational Mainstream

≡×≡×≡×≡×≡×≡×≡×≡×≡×≡×≡×≡×≡

I realize that the treatment of me, both at the rock climbing and the rappelling, has several implications for my teaching. First of all, set the goal high enough, so that the person will have to extend himself to reach it. Second, let the person know you consider it to be well within his capabilities. Third, where possible stay with them until they accomplish it. All the while being calm, patient, and giving emotional support. Outward Bound seems to be an attitude, a way of doing things.
—Student in one of the early teachers' practica.

Early in 1967 Arthur Bragg, coordinator of student activities at East Denver High School, attended a dinner where Joe Nold was the speaker. Bragg's excited reaction was that Nold talked the same educational language as Robert Colwell, his principal at East High. When he brought the two together, they struck sparks. Nold told Colwell about Outward Bound. Colwell told him about East High, Denver's oldest high school. Its 2500 students in a forty-year-old building comprised a cross section of the city's economic and social strata. Its enrollment was about fifty percent white, forty percent black, and ten percent Chicano. While the racial situation within the school was better than on the outside, the inherent tensions were there, and Colwell was looking for ways to counter them by breaking down social and communication barriers in the student body. Wanting also to make academics more effective, he liked what he heard about the Outward Bound emphasis on experience as a learning tool. The

283

upshot of the Nold-Colwell dialogue was a grant from the Phipps Foundation of $25,000 a year for three years to the two institutions for an undertaking to try to find, as they expressed it, "the moral equivalent of the mountain in the city."

As a seeding device, a number of East High students and seven teachers were given scholarships to Outward Bound courses that summer. Significantly, two of the initial effects were on Outward Bound rather than on the high school. The first resulted from Colwell's proviso that no East High youngster would be denied a chance to take an Outward Bound course because of race, creed, or sex. Sex was the problem; the courses were for boys only. It was to accommodate East High female students that Colorado offered its first girls' course in 1967. A further difficulty arose from Colwell's persuading seven teachers, men and women, to take part. But there were no courses for adults. Nold dealt with that by giving assistant instructorships in the girls' course to some women and placing the other teachers as "participant-observers" in male or female patrols.

The response of the teachers to this experience led to the high school's second impact on the mountain school. "That following fall," Nold recalls, "I couldn't get Bob Colwell to talk about kids, because he wanted to talk about what had happened to his teachers." Colwell admits that the exaggeration, if any, is mild: "The results I could measure most readily were those with the teachers. One of them was a very sarcastic beginning instructor in science. A few years later he became head of the department, but at that time, because he was so abrasive, I had seriously considered not keeping him. The Outward Bound experience smoothed him out a lot; he came back much more sensitive to the needs of other people. On the opposite end was a Chicano girl, one of our Spanish teachers. She knew her Spanish beautifully, but she was so shy in the classroom that the kids could hardly hear her. When she came back, she was still quiet, but in the classroom she was forceful and driving and became one of our best Spanish teachers. Those were the two extremes, and there were others in between."

To Nold this was revelation: "We thought, if this is what a participant-observer role can do for teachers, how much more we should be able to achieve with a course designed expressly for them!" The following summer (1968) the Colorado School, jointly with Colorado State College at Greeley (now the University of Northern Colorado) offered the first Outward Bound "practicum" for teachers. This was a month-long course starting with an urban experience of several days in a Denver slum and followed by Colorado's standard course. It concluded with a several-day seminar wherein the students considered together how the experience had affected them as individuals and teachers and what, as a result, they might take back in the way of new insights to classroom method and special program. Thirty-six men (Colorado did not essay a coed course until a year later), virtually all classroom teachers, took part. Student and staff evaluation concurred that the practicum filled a valuable educational need.

This success had a considerable impact on U.S. Outward Bound. In 1969 Hurricane Island and the Dartmouth Center joined Colorado in offering teachers' courses; the other schools soon followed suit. Almost as soon as the practica were initiated, they were made coeducational. At the same time, as a departure from the sixteen-and-a-half-to-twenty-three age rule that had largely been observed up to then, they exposed the age ceiling as arbitrary and artificial. The schools began to offer coeducational courses for adults at large and had little or no trouble filling them. The opening up of Outward Bound to adults was a natural evolutionary step, but a decade would pass before we fully realized its import.

In 1969 the Carnegie Corporation accorded solid legitimacy to what was happening in the educational sector with a three-year grant of $110,000 to OBI. The grant provided for our hiring someone to coordinate and service the teachers' course activity and in particular to be a follow-up resource for the teacher-students when they went back to their schools and undertook to introduce adaptive programs. A key stipulation was that the teachers' courses should carry graduate credit from an accredited college or university.

Some of the Carnegie funds were used to obtain an independent evaluation of the 1969 practica by a group of educators at the University of Massachusetts School of Education headed by Professor Glen Hawkes. Using a subjective method of inquiry, the evaluation committee found the practica "a valuable and innovative strategy for teacher education." Teacher comments are interesting for the diverse course values they reflect: gain in understanding and appreciation of other people, boosted self-confidence, discovery of the joy of helping less able course-mates, greater courage to confront others, more willingness to risk failure as against "going the easy and nonparticipatory way." Many went back more empathetic with their students, better able to understand their feelings and see the educative process through their eyes. Others felt much less threatened, if at all, by students, were much more at ease with them, more willing to communicate on a personal level and to reveal weaknesses as well as strengths. There was a new willingness to give students more independence, to encourage student participation and decision making, and much less concern about dress codes, haircuts, and the like. ("More lenient due to more self-confidence," one wrote.) But while many were less concerned about the lesser behavioral matters, they remained strict—or grew stricter—about student achievement. Said one, "Since I faced up to many challenges that I thought I could never accomplish, I have now given my students much more to do. They are much more capable than I ever thought they were."

In the spring of 1969 we were looking for the right individual to carry out the Carnegie Corporation's charge. As luck had it, the person we were seeking was simultaneously looking for us. He was Robert Lentz, a young schoolmaster who had graduated from Brown in 1961, earned a Master of Arts in Teaching degree at the Harvard School of Education, was head of the upper school of a private day school in Ohio, and led canoe trips in the northern Ontario wilderness in the summers.

In Ohio Bob Lentz had become increasingly concerned about what he saw as a dichotomy between the classroom and the world outside. "As a teacher and administrator it troubled me that too often in school we just deal with experience vicariously, through books, that we deny many kids experience outside that classroom, and if they do get it, we can't relate anything within the classroom to what's going on out there. My personal frustrations from that were compounded by the fact that there were several boys whom I saw during the year at school and then saw in the summer canoe tripping. I would be with them on long, eight-week expeditions. I could see that they were growing in a variety of ways up there, and somehow that didn't keep happening when they got back within the conventional school environment."

Bob started a program at the school in which tenth- and eleventh-graders were required to put in two weeks on an outside project, working with an institution. While the program went well, it did not end his frustration: "We got back report after report on these kids about what a lively, alert, intelligent, responsible student this is. And you would visit this student on his project and my God, he *was* alive and alert and responsible. You'd look through his records and ask teachers about him and the answer you'd get was, wasn't alive, was lethargic, wasn't alert, wasn't responsible. A kid would come back in off his project, for a few days he'd be alive and alert, then his old behavior would come back. That simply said to me, We're missing some vital things here. I decided to make a move. One of the people I wrote to was Outward Bound."

We hired him for the post of director of education programs. This was a milestone in implementing Mainstream. For the first time we had a staffed multiplier program on a comprehensive scale, well thought out and adequately financed, tying directly into the educational mainstream, and serviced by a follow-up resource. There were 106 teachers enrolled in the practica in 1969, nearly double that the next year, a still larger number in 1971. Many returned to their schools to start an adaptive program. Others were content to bring Outward Bound into the classroom through new ways of teaching, or simply by virtue of being changed persons. Sometimes, Lentz recalls, it meant that a teacher moved from one school environment to another that would be more supportive.

Lentz left us in 1972 to become director of Project Adventure at the Hamilton–Wenham High School in Hamilton, Massachusetts. At that time he had a unique perspective on our teacher education program: "I see it as perhaps the most important thing that Outward Bound ever got involved with. When you get involved with teacher training, you're relating to the country's on-going educational system, where ninety-eight percent of kids spend a good bit of their time. You have the opportunity to evaluate what the Outward Bound process means beyond just the context of a twenty-six-day course involving four thousand kids a year, which is about the size of one good-sized urban high school. It's good to have that impact on those four thousand kids, but if the process speaks in important ways in the development of young people and of teachers as well, then teacher learning may be the most important thrust." It was an echo of the old Jack Stevens thesis, seven years along in the Mainstream activity launched by his stubbornly held position.

Lentz saw the consequences of the teachers' courses as important in several ways. They had brought us to the realization of an adult constituency, whom we had to address somewhat differently from the youthful one. They had caught up a growing number of educators in the stream of Outward Bound enthusiasm and had begun to open up university affiliations, with a powerful potential for influencing teacher education. They had generated all kinds of growth in the way of adventure programs in high schools and colleges. The development was still fragile, but the involvement with schools that had been so tenuous was now much less so.

Lentz also put his finger on some key Mainstream problems: "School superintendents, state departments of education, federal funding sources, teacher educators, school committees, that whole world that feeds, sustains, and grows upon itself, is hard to crack. Outward Bound is a strange institution in relation to that establishment, as you discover when you try to fill out any form that asks who you are. In a sense that lack of fit gives you a freedom. But it also means you have to deal with frustrations other institutions don't have. It also creates a danger within Outward Bound that you become very insular. You just talk among those people who don't ask you, 'What's Outward Bound?' and you become almost intellectually incestuous. The need is to bridge the two worlds. The teacher program is a crucial first step."

From courses for mixed cadres of men and women teachers, it was an easy and inevitable step to coed courses for adults at large, a major new source of students. It also completed the departure that began with Minnesota's first girls' course in 1966. With both young and grown women comprising a substantial part of the student body, Outward Bound became a fully coeducational institution.

A profound effect of women students was their corollary: the growing presence of female staff. The entry of females into a very male world was bound to create problems—the more so in that at times the males would be slow to perceive that the problems were there. Joe Nold, for one, candidly recalls "the days when Outward Bound was very much a male chauvinist organization." The situation was compounded by the coincident tensions generated by the feminist movement as it surfaced in the late Sixties.

While this story has a happy ending, the resolution of those problems and tensions did not come easily or in the course of a season or two. There was a period of considerable female grievance—that the early girls' courses were made too easy, that the men did not trust the women instructors and treated them as "borderline incompetents," that the women were paid less than the men, were denied promotion to girls' course supervisory positions, and so on. Susan Rogers, who notes that she was "the first female instructor not married to a male instructor," became Colorado's first woman senior instructor in her third season and then was told, "You did a good job, but we are not yet ready for a woman course director." Sue Kinne, who three years later did become Colorado's first woman course director, recalls a preceding period of distaff unhappiness at two schools: "It's difficult now to separate out how much was paranoia, which we intensified by talking and thinking about it a lot, and how much was a function of the male administration not feeling comfortable having us out there. I think both played a part."

Today women course directors and women in upper echelon administrative posts are common throughout the U.S. Outward Bound community. When Bob MacArthur selected Sharon Goodyear for program director of the Dartmouth Center in 1972, it was both a pioneering move and a special case, as Dartmouth was just then starting to admit women. But five years later it caused no great stir when Minnesota School Director Derek Pritchard appointed Andree Stetson to the school's number two spot, or when Director Gary Templin promoted Leslie Emerson to be the Colorado School's program director, giving her top-echelon responsibilities in the country's biggest school. The gratifying fact is that in the outcome Outward Bound successfully met this family "initiative test"—a kind of psychosocio bushwhack through thickets of stubborn mind-sets and strong emotions while holding to the correct compass bearing. The analogy is not as far-fetched as it may sound, for the Outward Bound spirit undoubtedly played a built-in role in working through to the happy ending.

One of the more recent school curricular developments is a particular testimony to the influence of women staff. At a 1974 Conference on Experiential Education jointly sponsored by the Colorado Outward Bound School and the University of Colorado School of Education, one of the workshops was "Experiential Education Planning for Women." The presenter was Dr. Jean Kugler, a clinical psychologist working with college students at the Counseling Center of the Claremont Colleges in California. Jean had already organized an informal outing club at Claremont when she took a teachers' course at the Colorado School. She was thirty-nine—ten years older than the next most senior member of her patrol. Her professional reflexes stimulated, she began to analyze the Outward Bound process: "I see Outward Bound as a process that takes people out of their situations and gives them a meaningful experience around which insights are articulated in such a way that they understand, or feel, or find out what it is to learn and solve their own problems, independent of the process or the group. It puts people into a context of other people where they have to learn things they need to know about their own learning processes. A person learns his or her own learning style, own way to make decisions, and he or she can go back then and do that in the real world." She came out of the course with the bright light of an idea burning in her head. If this coeducational course had been so helpful to her, a woman approaching forty with grown children and pursuing a professional career, would not Outward Bound courses designed specifically for adult women fill an important need? This was the central idea she broached in her conference workshop.

Among Jean's listeners was Ann Ketchin, a veteran Colorado School instructor—one of those who had started as "a female instructor who was married to a male instructor." Ann was just turning thirty. She remembers: "It was a happy circumstance where Jean Kugler's workshop happened to find a number of us from different parts of the Outward Bound community around the country thinking along the same lines. It seemed that a lot of women like me had suddenly realized that not only had Outward Bound been relevant to them in personal growth, but that there was reason to pool our sense of this and create a course that would be relevant to older women generally."

Jean's proposal and the discussion that followed ignited a group conviction that this was the moment of truth for the idea they had been sharing without realizing it. The workshop produced a task force of Outward Bound women who, with some male support, designed and sold to the organization a plan for courses for "women over thirty." OBI appointed Clare Rhoades and Ann Ketchin a two-woman promotion and coordinating team to advance the project. The pioneer courses, with their appeal and challenge to women in "mid-life transition," were successful, in some instances dramatically so. The schools now offer a variety of courses in all seasons, seven to fourteen days in length, for adult women.

The Alternate Semester

≡≡×≡≡×≡≡×≡≡×≡≡×≡≡×≡≡×≡≡×≡≡×≡≡×≡≡×≡≡

I got so I hated riding on that damn yellow bus and listening to the bullshitting that went around like a disease. A lot of times I felt very lonely because I didn't trust a lot of people and because they didn't seem committed to anyone or anything. I was sort of trying to protect myself from having all that rub off on me. It's only now that the realization of leaving Seminar is hitting me. And it's only now that I'm finding out how much it is a part of me and how much I really dug it. I've gotten closer than ever before to people in a learning situation. And I've learned from them even more than I've learned from the sources we sought for information and example. I've learned new depths in feeling people and understanding them since Mexico. I've learned a lot about life and myself. I've found out that it's going to be that way—learning and growing—for the rest of my life . . ."

—Student in the first Senior Seminar, Denver East High

I

When Denver's East High opened in the fall of 1967, after the first groups of students and teachers had been to Marble, the school looked for ways to work Outward Bound into its own scheme of operation. A first step was to start up a mountaineering club, the Aufsteigers, with instructors from the Colorado School. Bob Colwell later thought this was a mistake. The club attracted

292

mostly upper- and middle-class youths who became a kind of elite, feeling superior to their nonmountaineering peers. A more productive train of events followed a Joe Nold talk to the faculty. One of his listeners was Craig Spillman, a young history teacher. "Joe showed us his movie," Spillman remembers, "and asked us, how do we find an educational interpretation of the Outward Bound concept in the school context? I was teaching in the very traditional, necktie, lectern-style approach. I'd never heard of Outward Bound and I'd never been an outdoorsman. But Nold's questions intrigued the hell out of me, and soon I was in a dialogue with him."

Nold asked Spillman to help Arthur Bragg and John Timmons, another teacher, organize a service expedition during Christmas vacation to San Felipe, a Mexican village in Baja California that had suffered a tidal wave. Four faculty members and about forty youngsters wound up painting the village school. "Overall, the expedition was a success," Spillman says. "We learned lots from our mistakes. One was going as a single large group. I was to learn that the most interpersonal growth occurs in a primary group—a dozen kids and one teacher."

Other teachers led other service expeditions and weekend mountaineering trips. English teacher Ellene Franzen Austin took the lead in developing a white-water rafting program. (This was how Colorado Outward Bound's rafting program got its start.) Spillman and another history teacher teamed up to teach a class in which students did volunteer work in the city, and resource people from the city—everybody from the mayor to the head of the Black Panthers—came to the classroom. They organized an expedition to the Navajo reservation in northern Arizona that revealed useful cross-cultural possibilities. During the next Christmas vacation Spillman took a vanload of students to Greenwood, Mississippi, where they did a service project in a black community center. The East High–Outward Bound collaboration was feeling its way in bits and pieces.

It was on a second trip to Mississippi that Spillman's youngsters planted the seed that would bring it all together: "We had just camped overnight on a Civil War battleground. As we drove down the Natchez Trail Parkway every kid in the van crowded into the front seats to talk about how could we create a full-time school environment where students could learn in the field? That started me thinking. I went to Bob Colwell and proposed a full semester where we would do, on an academic basis, the kinds of things we were then doing extracurricularly on weekends and vacations." With Colwell and Nold's encouragement, Spillman, Austin, and several other teachers developed the idea over the summer of 1969. In the fall the school decided, with the support of Assistant School Superintendent Richard Koeppe, to conduct an experimental "Senior Seminar" in the second semester. The seminar would be organized into a series of off-campus educational modules, kicked off by an Outward Bound kind of experience. The seminar was open to about one hundred student applicants, chosen by lot from ethnic categories in ratios matching those in the school population at large. An exception to the lottery procedure was the recruiting of twenty-five dropout and near-dropout students who, while unmotivated, were thought to have a potential for post-high-school academic work.

"An important thing about the way we organized the seminar," Colwell says, "was that there were no criteria for entry in terms of good behavior, or academics, or anything else. In fact, we deliberately tried to make it representative of a cross section of the senior class—racially, sexually, academically. Some of the kids were in advanced placement courses; some we dragged in off the streets. The cadres also represented this cross section. One of the things the kids accepted was that they were not going to choose whom they were going to camp with."

The two-and-a-half-week Outward Bound adventure module that launched the seminar took place, following a marathon bus trip, in western Mexico. Four teachers accompanied the ninety-odd students; adding four graduate-student practice teachers from the University of Colorado provided eight leaders for as many primary-group cadres. Returning to Denver, the students opted alternatively for a module in Politics and Power or Urban Arts—the one a firsthand study of government processes centering at the state capitol, the other an exposure to individuals and groups involved in creative arts. All took part in a module on the Navajo reservation, studying the Navajo pastoral, noncommunity society. Each student lived with an Indian family, many in isolated hogans, helping to herd sheep and goats, shear wool, cook, and share in other chores. Back again at the Denver base, the students chose between Space Technology and Man and Hispanic Culture.

All participated in an Urban Design module in which they collected trash with city sanitation crews, visited urban-renewal construction sites, talked with city planners, and through other leads explored the challenges confronting a city at once aging and growing. The seminar ended with a twelve-day white-water rafting expedition, with the original Outward Bound module cadres reunited on the Green and Yampa Rivers in northwestern Colorado. Seminar staff and park rangers exposed the students to geological, ecological, palaeontological, anthropological, and historical aspects of the Dinosaur National Monument region through which the rivers flow.

Joining the students for two days and nights, Colwell found the tumbled barriers and communication among the students that he had set as a prime objective in the early talks with Nold. "First of all I saw competence. Here were kids who two months before had never slept under the stars who were so comfortable living outdoors that you wouldn't believe it. They were clean. Girls were washing their hair in the river. A white girl was teasing a black girl's afro, and a black girl was braiding a white girl's hair. The second thing I noticed was that the preoccupation with sex that you see at the school had disappeared."

On the second night he circulated among the campfires, from one group of cadres to another. "I asked them, 'What is the primary group like?' and a girl over in the shadows said, 'It's like a family,' and I heard general assent. They had adopted family as the only word that would adequately describe the relationship among those kids and their teachers. Another girl said, 'Yes, we love each other.' The kids picked that up and explained, 'We know who's going to be late getting up in the morning. We know who's going to be short-tempered at night, and who's going to be short-tempered in the morning. We know who the best cook is, who the one is that doesn't care about cooking but doesn't mind cleaning up.' And so on—this whole gamut of things that people who live in a family and understand each other will accept because they love each other. They got into a discussion as to whether they were as adequate without their teachers as with, and they agreed they weren't. I came away from the experience with a great soaring confidence in what kids can do."

A striking consequence of the Senior Seminar's first year was that thirteen black youngsters, most of whom had been in the dropout or near-dropout group, took a special qualifying program at Colorado University that summer and entered the university as freshmen in the fall. In 1973 seven of them were still in college as juniors, some of them making B averages. The seminar won strong support from parents of the participants; one stated to the Board of Education that he could not find words strong enough to urge that it be put into effect in all the city's schools. A story in *Life* won it widespread recognition. It became a model for alternate semesters from Massachusetts to California and was an inspiration for others choosing different formats.

Despite the fame and praise, with the Phipps funding running out there was doubt the program could continue. The 1971 seminar was made possible by supplementary contributions from parents, money earned by students, and a $10,000 gift from Charles Kettering to buy buses. In the third year when Spillman joined the Prescott College staff, fellow teacher Emil Ziegler became seminar director. The Outward Bound module was strengthened by increased emphasis on on-site study of marine biology and desert ecology. A live-in with a Mexican family was added, along with a visit to a remote Seri Indian village. The official evaluation of the 1973 seminar reported: "The Mexico Outward Bound module, because of its strong impact on students and staff, has proven to be a most effective way of starting the Seminar. The experience forces students and teachers to confront and solve personal conflicts, to discover personal strengths and weaknesses, and, probably most important, it provides success for those accustomed to failure."

By then the seminar had achieved a solid status in the East High community, although it had yet to win its battle for permanent status. A strong majority of respondents in all categories—seniors, staff, parents, seminar alumni—believed that it should be "continued, as is" or "expanded." * The alumni, looking back with the perspective of time, reported that it had helped them to understand themselves better (96%), to "understand our society" better (92%), to value education (92%), to continue

---

* In 1977, still under Ziegler, who had continued to build up its academic content and rigor, the seminar was made a permanent course in the East High syllabus. In 1978 it was declared open to students at all Denver high schools, and a year later made operative in both semesters.

their education (83%), to develop useful skills (89%), to make friends (93%).

Colwell, who would be promoted to executive director of the Denver schools' new Department of Alternative Education in 1974, could point to several significant offshoots of the seminar. "For one thing, the desire for field experience has become important to East teachers. For another, I am convinced that doing things with the curriculum that more nearly met the needs of the students is one of the things that kept the school on an even keel in turbulent times.

"What we did not even contemplate when we started the seminar was the affectionate cross-cultural association we developed with the Mexicans, the Chicanos, and the Navajos. The Mexican and Chicano families now send their youngsters to us in an intercultural exchange, and there are many instances of East High youngsters taking their parents to visit their Navajo parents on the reservation. When our kids go to a live-in with a Navajo family, they are not observing a culture, they're living in it, and many healthy things have come out of this. The kids come back from the Navajos with manual skills they never would have got in any other way—many of our girls now can weave a Navajo rug. But more than that a lot of our kids come back with the realization that money isn't what makes a family. One of the things we've lost in our country is the idea of the proud poor. The Navajos have it. Here is a hogan with dirt floor where the love a kid receives from his Indian family is as great as—in many cases greater than—the love he gets from his own family at home.

"Another offshoot that's very interesting is that about twenty-five percent of the parents report that the seminar experiences have noticeably narrowed the generation gap in their homes. When you stop to think about it, this would naturally be the result of the Outward Bound experience—self-realization, understanding yourself. Kids have written about it in their journals: 'I suddenly realized my parents have problems too.'"

II

The most valuable role of the East High–Outward Bound alliance was that for which, in fact, it was chiefly created—to help the school weather the racial crisis of the late Sixties and early Seventies and achieve a relatively happy resolution. Because the school was apparently doing a number of things right, the crisis was slow to develop there. Principal Bob Colwell remembers: "The Black Revolution hit us with the murder of Martin Luther King in April 1968. Until the shooting of King this school, we felt, was well on its way to becoming a truly integrated institution. The idealism of the kids for integration, and their drive to achieve it, were very high. The shot that killed Martin Luther King, I think, will go down in history as being just as important as the shot that killed Lincoln. The day after King's murder was hell around here. Nobody was seriously hurt, although there were several beatings. Some heroic things also happened. About noon two black boys were beating up a white kid in front of my office. A black girl of pretty fair proportions grabbed both the black boys and said, 'Lay off him, he didn't do it!' Black boys took white girls home in their cars to protect them. A mob of black students gathered in the street, and our black teachers went out there and worked to control them—those kids wouldn't look at a white teacher that day. But the main thing was the feeling on the part of both black and white kids that the world was falling in pieces."

Regis Groff was a black teacher at East High whom Craig Spillman recruited for the first Senior Seminar. He was not however, keen on participating in the Outward Bound module. He agreed to drive one of the buses to Mexico with the proviso that he could then fly back home. But at the airport the authorities insisted that since he had entered the country driving a bus, he must leave with it. Regis had no choice but to take part in the Outward Bound experience. "I had absolutely no intention of enjoying any of it," he says. "I had it figured out why I wasn't going to like it, why my background would not let me get excited by that kind of experience. And shoot, I still got shot down. One of those first nights I was lying in my sleeping bag, watching all those stars over my head, and my pillow started getting wet—it wasn't raining either. Something happened, working with the kids and running into some brand spanking-new challenges.

"It was the same at the end of the semester when we went on the river. I had no intention of going through the Warm

Springs Rapids. Then someone said, 'O.K., Regis, you're next,' and I took a paddle and jumped into the boat because I was expected to. We went through those rapids, and it was the kind of experience a person almost has to have. I felt some kind of exhilaration I never felt before, and I've never felt since. I had to splash water on my face so the kids couldn't see all that stuff slipping out of my eyes wasn't river water."

Most meaningful to Groff was the effect of the Outward Bound experience on the students of his own race. "It takes a lot of hate out of you. I think that's what happened to the black kids. I don't know one who went to Mexico and went down the river and came back and said he didn't like it. I don't think they lost their anger, but they lost their hate. They still get uptight, they still have some rage, but the hate is gone. You just can't hate some guys you spend all that time with in the desert or on the mountain or on the river, cooking and drinking out of the same thing and struggling up the same hill, you can't hate him. I came back fifty feet off the ground. Really, not only did my armor get destroyed, but I got pushed way over on the other side, which doesn't happen that much when you've got your mind made up on it."

One of those in the "near-dropout" group who went on to college from the first Senior Seminar was Marshall Chambers. Colwell has a vivid memory of his first meeting with Marshall. Several teachers had stopped the principal in the hallway to alert him that a boy named Chambers had been sent to his office. They added such remarks as, "You'd better get him out of here," and "I don't ever want to see him again." When Bob reached the office, a seventeen-year-old black youth who was sitting on the counter outside greeted him: "I thought they'd get you in here!" Then, poking the principal in the chest, he said, "You and I will get along if we understand one thing. You're a white racist son of a bitch and I'm a black racist son of a bitch. If we understand that, we'll be lucky."

Marshall Chambers transferred to East High from Cheyenne, Wyoming, when, at the age of sixteen, he moved to Denver with his mother and two brothers. East's bigness daunted him. On his first day he stood outside his homeroom, afraid to go in. In junior high in Cheyenne he had been a leading athlete, city wrestling champion in his age group, and a member of a prize-winning drum and bugle corps. Now, in the strange new big-city environment, he eschewed extracurricular activity, did well in his studies. Then came the murder of Martin Luther King. In the months that followed Marshall became, as he puts it, "a very political person." He grew to feel that the black students were being discriminated against in the quality of their academics and that the school community made its judgment on the black students either ignoring or in ignorance of conditions in the black community. His texts became contemporary works like Robert Conot's *Rivers of Blood, Years of Darkness* and Eldridge Cleaver's *Soul on Ice.* He became the leader of the dissident black activists in the school. During Christmas vacation he went to Los Angeles for a conference where he listened to H. Rap Brown and other radical leaders. Back at East the confrontations between him and the school and police grew more intense. "One day in front of the school," he remembers, "a policeman told me I was bound for jail because smart-ass niggers like me just didn't make the scene. He said, 'We're going to get you,' and I said, 'How can you get me, I'm not a thief, and I don't believe in ripping people off. I do believe in speaking out and being strong and believing in what I say.'" Soon after that Marshall was arrested for loitering. The loitering charge didn't stick, but he was fined $32 for having called a policeman a pig.

About that time something happened in his thinking. "I thought everything was going all wrong, and I had to get away from all the hassle and all the people. In February, when my eighteenth birthday was coming up, I went to Wyoming and stayed at a place my mother had that was vacant. I didn't communicate with people for quite a while. I was mentally drained. I couldn't even read a book. I pretty much came to the conclusion that it wasn't worth my effort any more to fight the system, that the system was a massive powerful social force that the social laws had set apart, and they weren't going to change or be flexible to the needs of the people. They were simply going to say, we're going to put you in jail, or we're going to eliminate you altogether. This is the way I felt the system works—you're going to work with it, because you simply cannot work against it."

In the fall of 1969 Marshall persuaded East High to let him back in. He needed ninety hours of credits to graduate; the normal load was sixty. He was taking six courses, missing only one day of school in the entire term, when Craig Spillman prevailed on him to sign up for the Senior Seminar the following semester. The seminar was an educational eye-opener. "We were doing Politics and Power," he says, "and I thought, I've spent all this time studying history, and now they've taken me out of school for one semester, and I've learned more by going down to the capitol than I did the entire time I was in school. I thought, How can it be? I really became involved in the seminar. It was taking me away from all the things I had been involved in. I felt a change in myself. I was still very radical, but I related to people better; I didn't try to maintain that facade that made people reluctant to speak to me because I might tell them to go to hell or drop dead. I enjoyed the river trip. On the last day of the river trip we were sitting around, and I was thinking, Well, what are you going to do now, Marshall?"

He was a while finding out. That summer he took two summer-school courses and a third via television to earn enough credits for his high school diploma. In the fall, junior college was a disappointment. So was the world of employment and a second try at college. In the winter of 1971, through the intercession of Howard Hoffman, an East High teacher and Outward Bound instructor, the Colorado School signed him on as an assistant instructor and recruiter of minority students. The Outward Bound association completed the process of turning Marshall's life around. He helped Hoffman develop a spring vacation orientation course for inner-city youngsters who were slated to take an Outward Bound course in the summer. Two years later, in charge of the program and with a successful third orientation course completed, he had a clear view ahead. His job arrangement enabled him to attend college part-time, and he was looking past his education to ideas he had for becoming a resource person for young adults in the ghetto. His philosophy for beating the system had crystallized: "I think all people should decide what they want to do; once they've done that, they can pretty much achieve the goals they want. Once you have that commitment, there's nothing that can stop you, no barriers that will hold you back. That's one thing that Outward Bound has made me realize, the fact that I can achieve any goals I want."

III

As word of East Denver High's Senior Seminar spread across the country at the end of the 1960's, it coincided with a rising tide of student dissatisfaction with conventional schooling. School people were ready to try alternatives that promised to help repair a widespread failure to motivate many youngsters, both well- and ill-prepared. East High's example led a number of schools—a cluster in Colorado and others as far away as California and Massachusetts—to try a similar alternative term. The Massachusetts alternative is perhaps of special interest, in part for the teacher evaluation of the Outward Bound element and more particularly for the well-defined ambivalence it created among some fine teachers.

In the spring of 1971 a group of students at Lincoln–Sudbury Regional High, a school for some 2000 students living in two Boston suburbs, approached one of their teachers and voiced their discontent with the character of the schooling they were getting. At that time, Lincoln-Sudbury had a first-rate adaptive program, Nimbus, that had been created by the Hurricane Island School and placed under Joseph Kleiser, head of the physical education department. Instead of seeing the new outdoor program as a threat—a not-uncommon athletic department reaction—Joe embraced it, simultaneously articulating Nimbus into his department's program and making it available to the academic side of the school for assisting classroom projects. Nimbus received strong support from Superintendent Willard Ruliffson, a staunch convert to the Outward Bound idea from the time he observed the effects of Hurricane's pilot course on both his students and teachers. So it was not surprising that the teacher who was approached by the unhappy student group turned to Kleiser for counsel.

A consequence was that two classroom teachers and Kleiser journeyed to Denver to observe and be briefed on the Senior Seminar at East High. When they reported back, the excited reaction of the students was that this was what they were seeking. Ruliffson gave the go-ahead for an alternate semester, provided the students did the organizing and fund raising. He made English teacher Dixie Pierson the faculty member in charge.

The student body for Lincoln–Sudbury's Alternate Semester

was quite different from the carefully devised cross section of the student body that comprised East's seminar enrollment. Pierson describes the original seminal group as academically oriented, very bright, with initiative and confidence—and disaffected. While their intent was to have all kinds of students in the seminar, that did not happen the first year. Most of the thirty-five juniors and seniors who signed up were the intellectual elite. What these kids wanted was an experience-oriented alternative to classroom learning. They wanted a decision-making role in their own education; the planning phase of the semester was very important to them. They wanted a sense of community. Many felt lonely, alienated. They were looking to explore new roles with each other and with teachers—they no longer wanted to see teachers as teachers. They also wanted to relate to the larger community through experience.

While Lincoln–Sudbury employed the East module structure, the nature of the modules was different in that the main emphasis was on internship projects. One module, however, was decisively retained; the students strongly supported the precedent of starting with an Outward Bound experience. The module was contracted to Hurricane Island. Land-based in north-central Maine, it was Hurricane's first winter course; once again it was a case of an adaptive program stretching the capability of an Outward Bound school.

"Outward Bound was perhaps the most overwhelmingly successful unit," the faculty evaluating group reported. "It appears in retrospect to be the one which came closest to meeting its goals of establishing group unity, building individual self-confidence, expanding self-awareness, and encouraging appreciation of the wilderness." They reported that after four months of other experiences the students still stressed the impetus the intense opening experience had given the entire semester; many cited ways in which it had influenced them throughout the program and perhaps changed them personally. The staff concurred, noting that it had taught the students to work together, and helped break down barriers between staff and students. They were impressed by the way it had affected individuals:

All seemed touched by it in some way. There were no dramatic changes in character, no instant solutions to deeply-rooted personal problems—it would be naive to expect either —but there were significant changes in attitude . . . Many left feeling better about themselves in some way—and their behavior bore witness to these things throughout the semester. Outward Bound held out certain values which were a continual source of personal and group strength.

While both student and staff evaluations of the overall Alternate Semester were positive, they differed significantly. The students stressed its experiential character, that they were able to do "real work," shape their own education, and explore and nurture relationships in which they came to trust and care for others. The teachers, however, while rating the experiment a success and favoring its being offered again the following year,* had reservations in the form of deep personal concerns. The dilemma of the teacher dedicated to scholarship as the sinew of our culture, who at the same time acknowledges the educational values obtainable outside the classroom, may never have been more poignantly stated than in the staff report signed by teachers Dixie Pierson, Barry Copp, and Karen Sargent:

> Our most profound reservations about the program are philosophical. We watch all the praise pour in. Most employers were enthusiastic; many students claim it was the most important thing that has ever happened to them. But we remain skeptical and cautious. We speculate about what all this adds up to and question by what criteria an experience like this can be understood. As a staff who, although still young, are really the product of another system, we cannot avoid feeling threatened on some level by a program which so basically calls the academic approach into question. We see that this program released incredible amounts of productive energy, that the students exercised more self-discipline, wrote more articulately, and showed greater curiosity than they do in most of our classes. And there is no doubt that for some students this provided a very valid learning experience. But, at the same time, we question very seriously an approach which seems so oriented to the con-

* The Alternate Semester was still in the Lincoln-Sudbury curriculum in 1980–81. However, both Nimbus and the semester's Outward Bound component were casualties of time and other factors.

cerns of the present, so hostile to academic pursuit and so disinterested in intellectual and cultural heritage.

It may be, as Arnold Shore has tentatively suggested in his commentary on the research literature on Outward Bound, that the anti-intellectual bias is overstated and itself indicative of a narrow sense of what constitutes learning. These teachers, however, did perform their responsibilities to the Alternate Semester on a dedicated level, did testify to its impressive results, did support its continuation. They were, as we interpret them, articulating a question more than affirming an answer. It is a valid question, and the answer is not as simple as some on either side would have it. However, much in this book makes clear that there is no inherent contradiction between conventional classroom and experiential approaches to learning, and that in fact the happiest results are obtained where a symbiotic relationship exists. In any event, the final thoughts in the staff's evaluation appear to resolve whatever doubts they shared about the Alternate Semester's value. In part they were influenced by their students' evaluation:

> We also hear the students saying how profoundly Alternate Semester affected them. If in fact this is true, if they do feel significantly better about themselves, if they do feel they have exercised control over their education and assumed responsibility for the direction of their own lives, then we most definitely believe it is worthwhile.

In part, they were persuaded by the experience's influence on their own feelings:

> We also look at ourselves and find that, despite all the difficulties, we have come to understand and care for these young people in a way that never would have been possible in a classroom. We think we have a better comprehension of their needs, a clearer idea of what is important to them, and thus a far sounder justification for our involvement in education.

College Orientation:
The Mobile Term

≡✕≡✕≡✕≡✕≡✕≡✕≡✕≡✕≡✕≡✕≡

I

It is our belief at Prescott College that through the medium of the mountains, the sea, canyons and rivers, the qualities of style, compassion, integrity, responsibility, and leadership can be fostered and encouraged.
—RONALD NAIRN

Prescott College opened its doors in Arizona in 1966 as a new kind of private, four-year, liberal-arts college "unfettered by any tradition that could limit its opportunity to relate itself dynamically to the emerging 21st century." In the light of its ill fate eight years later, the declaration became ironic. Prescott made its mark on higher education, and its influence continued even before its present remarkable revivification. In the generating and shaping of that influence, Outward Bound played a prominent part.

Prescott's first students made do with an informal physical-education program based on the availability of a new combined field house and gym and an athletic field. As Dr. Ronald Nairn, Prescott's founder-president, wrestled with the decisions of shaping a long-term physical education and athletic policy, his thinking was governed by three primary considerations: The college was poor; it lacked funds for a formal athletic program. Geographically it was isolated; competitive athletics with other institutions would require much travel. It was situated in glorious country, close to some of the greatest natural challenges in the continental United States.

Raised on a ranch in wild, back-country New Zealand, Nairn had enjoyed an adventurous youth. A World War II fighter pilot in the RAF at seventeen, he had returned to find the rugged countryside of his boyhood considerably tamed. By then Outward Bound had come to New Zealand. Nairn identified with its purpose to expose young people to the kind of wilderness challenges that had been his natural lot. Later, as an educator in the United States—he obtained his doctorate and taught at Yale—he kept tabs on the spreading U.S. Outward Bound movement. Now he conceived of a physical-education program grounded in Outward Bound kinds of activity. He put the proposal to Charles F. Kettering Jr., a Prescott trustee and a principal benefactor. Kettering, who lived in Denver and had already become interested in what the Colorado School was doing, endorsed the idea. The college engaged Joe Nold as a consultant and on his recommendation hired Roy Smith, a British instructor then working for Colorado, to organize a physical-education program along Outward Bound lines.

Roy met heavy student apathy to Outdoor Action, as he called his program: "I talked to the whole school and said I wanted to get them out into the Southwest, to get them excited about things like backpacking, mountaineering, and rock climbing. It was pretty strange talk to them. These were fairly spoiled middle-class kids. Only a few were academically inclined and even fewer were inclined to my area. I used to walk around the commons at mealtime, and knock on dormitory doors to line up students. My battle cry was, 'Get involved!' "

Gradually Smith's involvement process took hold. "Out of the climbing came mountain rescue. I explained the service idea, had the sheriff come up and tell how mountain rescue would help the community. Now the students were excited. We formed a mountain-rescue team that was deputized for Yavapai County and later in Grand Canyon National Park." He trained ten student assistant instructors for a more ambitious program the next year. The program broadened to include white-water kayaking, sailing, scuba diving, rafting, horsemanship and, for a time, gliding. The water-activity people formed a water-rescue team.

The increasingly ambitious expeditions included winter moun-taineering, Grand Canyon river trips, the first sea-kayak explora-tion of the Golfo de California between Baja (Lower California) and the Mexican mainland.

In the midst of this expanding activity the program that made Prescott famous, its freshman orientation, was conceived. Smith remembers the idea getting its start in a conversation with Nold. "He asked me how things were going, which prompted me to say what these kids needed *before* starting college—not for my purposes but for their own benefit—was an experience to shake them up. I told Joe they had no idea of their potential as people —not as backpackers but as people. They needed to discover what they could do. They needed an Outward Bound experience before they came here."

Starting with the fall of 1968, Prescott began the freshman year with a three-week wilderness-based orientation. It was essen-tially a standard Outward Bound course designed to help prepare students for life at the college—the first time an institution of higher learning tied the Outward Bound experience directly into its curricular scheme. Together with the offbeat physical-education plan, it won Prescott national publicity that brought a flood of applications. In effect, Outward Bound solved the col-lege's recruiting problems. The character of the student body changed remarkably. Smith no longer had to proselyte. Now the students arrived with their rucksacks and climbing boots, gung-ho for what he had to offer.

In his president's office, Ronald Nairn reflected on Outward Bound's impact on the Prescott campus; the time, and the student climate, was 1973: "I think Outward Bound is one of the coun-try's more important movements. In this particular climactic time, young people have virtually no roots—hence they cannot heed the old Chinese aphorism, 'Have roots, yet soar like an eagle.' If one has roots, one can afford, especially in adolescence, to experiment, explore. If one has a perch to come back to, one can soar—but otherwise one is lost out there in space. Outward Bound has a particular quality in that when you deal with a mountain, a river, with cold or heat—these natural issues—you are dealing with total honesty. It's there. It is, if you like, a root. While I don't think that Outward Bound is going to provide a substitute for those intrinsic roots in our society—family, church, school, justice, and so forth—that all seem to leave so much to be desired, it is very important in default of these things. In our freshman orientation those students come back here totally different from any freshmen that I've ever seen in my life, as cohesive, ready-to-get-at-it young adults. The transformation in three weeks is just extraordinary."

Twenty months later, in December 1974, Prescott College closed its doors, a bankrupt victim of a presumed helping agency's fraudulent manipulation of funds. The closing was an educational tragedy. But although the institution's plant and campus were lost, its esprit did not capitulate. Following on the close-down, two-fifths of the students and all but one of the faculty returned for the final semester of the 1974–75 year. They borrowed classrooms where and when they could, made generous use of the out-of-doors, made do with the faculty's personal libraries. Many of them graduated. The following year, with accreditation lost but a stubborn faculty nucleus holding on, student enrollment was down to fifty in the Prescott Center for Alternative Education, a phoenix seeking to rise from the Prescott ashes. The struggle for survival has been led by Jim Stuckey, another who came to the Prescott staff from the Outward Bound community. In 1980, now Prescott Center College, the institution was carrying on under Stuckey's presidency with growing strength. The final step in accreditation appeared to be close at hand. A documentary film about the college was being made for showing on public television. Its title: *The College That Wouldn't Die.*

Even apart from Prescott's survival, education in the United States continues changed from what it would have been had the college never existed. Outdoor Action and the Prescott freshman orientation have proved to be important models for other colleges and secondary schools. Challenge/Discovery, the extension of Outdoor Action that Roy Smith started at Prescott as a summer program for youth from the general public, carries on under Smith's direction at Crested Butte in the Colorado Rockies. A number of Outward Bound adaptive programs that Prescott alumni founded or helped to initiate—among them the Boojum Institute in San Diego and Arizona's Adobe Mountain School for incarcerated youth—are also manifestations of a once presumed dead institution's living spirit.

II

Our classroom covered 6,000 miles of road, 150 miles of trail, and 20 miles of river. In contrast to campus life, academics were not separated from our every day living. There was no distinction between days of the week to give us a routine to follow. Our whole selves were involved, not always by choice—spiritual, emotional, intellectual growth merging together. Intensity and integration were two words of which we gained a fuller understanding.

> —Student report on Southwest Field Studies, Earlham College, 1976

Earlham College is a coeducational, Quaker-affiliated college founded at Richmond, Indiana, in 1847, with a student body of about one thousand. In the late 1960's, four members of the faculty—Geology Professor Charles Martin, Biology Professor Cameron Gifford, Mathematics Professor Richard Rodgers, and History Professor Douglas Steeples—began to talk seriously of ways they could share educationally with students their interest in the outdoors and so give them kinds of experience they were not gaining otherwise. During that time several Earlham students who had received Outward Bound scholarships brought back enthusiastic reports to the campus. The press and the intercollegiate grapevine were spreading word of Prescott's Outward Bound–based freshman orientation. Doug Steeples recalls students periodically prodding the faculty group for activity involving real physical and psychological challenges "to make a little more true the college's rhetoric about educating the whole man." Steeples finally set about providing Earlham's president, Landrum Bolling, with information for a grant proposal.

In April 1970 the Reader's Digest Foundation made a grant of $100,000 to Earlham to fund an "adventure program" in a wilderness environment. That summer a faculty member and a student were sent to Minnesota Outward Bound, another student to the Colorado School, and three of the faculty core group took wilderness skills courses at the National Outdoor Leadership School (NOLS). In addition to his NOLS course, Steeples twice visited Prescott for briefings on its orientation program. We sent Bob Lentz twice from OBI, the second time with Dyke Williams, to offer counsel and encouragement. After considering several alternatives, a faculty-student planning group concurred on the idea of a month-long wilderness expedition as an orientation to the college, with coeducational cadres, to take place prior to the college's formal opening and earn one academic credit. Dick Rodgers was released from his teaching duties to serve as director.

Earlham's first Pre-term, as it is called, took place in August–September 1971 in the High Uinta Primitive Area of northeast Utah. The course design combined the Outward Bound and NOLS models, including Outward Bound's solo, with academic elements and other specifically Earlham content. The patrols were led by student instructors. A faculty member functioning partly as counselor, partly as learning resource, accompanied a pair of patrols, and largely succeeded in cloaking the collegial status that gave him ultimate veto authority.

The program was endorsed by the faculty, who were generally agreed that classroom and other contacts with students bore out the report of Professors Rodgers and Steeples. In their summary of "what worked," these two observed that the Pre-term had expanded the participants' moral sensitivity, nourished their self-confidence and eagerness to meet challenges, and enhanced their awareness of the relationship between mind and body in a balanced life. It had effectively oriented participants to the college. Another important plus, Steeples noted, was that the Pre-term's coeducational policy had done much to break down stereotyped attitudes about the sexes: "In our student debriefing one of the more prominent themes was that for a number of the fellows it was now possible to view girls as something other than sex objects. They had become human beings in their own right."

Earlham was fortunate to have in Landrum Bolling a president who was quick to perceive the value of a wilderness program to the institution. During the planning year, Alan Hale came down from Minnesota to North Carolina Outward Bound to conduct a three-day minicourse for a group of Earlham faculty members and spouses that included Dr. and Mrs. Bolling. "Here we were," Dr. Bolling says, "two middle-aged past-fifty types, climbing up a cliff and hanging by ropes and this sort of thing.

It was an exciting new experience and great fun. It gave me a kind of inner gut feeling that the students must get from learning these skills, and you could see what it would do to help a person. I've had many talks with students who have been through the Pre-term. There are two themes they stress over and over. One is, 'I found myself doing things I never thought I would or could do, and this helped me to have a more confident feeling about myself.' The other is, 'I learned that in a close, tight, stressful situation I could trust and cooperate with other people in ways I had never experienced before.'

"Self-confidence and trustfulness toward others are two things I think our society very much needs. As I see young people today, and the kinds of problems they wrestle with, it does seem that one of the most persistent points of tension and difficulty is low self-esteem. This seems strange, with all the advantages they have, but the fact is, I think, in our modern, industrialized, gadget-ridden society in urban settings, most young people in one sense really grow up to maturity as parasites. They've never had to do anything particularly useful. They're always in a sense parasites on their parents, on the community, on the school, and so on. They're not really contributors, as people who grew up in a farm community would be.

"I think there's a kind of psychological scar that even the most well-adjusted kids carry from growing up in a setting where they don't really count for very much. There's a deep inner hunger in a lot of young people to feel a sense of personal worth and confidence, and I think the Outward Bound experience gives them that sense to a remarkable degree—belief in themselves, a fundamental inside feeling that they can meet a challenge. And I think there is a kind of transfer of this kind of experience in the wilderness to other stressful situations. I think the experience has demonstrated its value and can be fitted into a college curriculum." *

In their memorandum following the first Pre-term, Rodgers and Steeples took particular note of the value of reliance on student instructors, with faculty members filling less obtrusive roles as experts in some fields and model learners in others—which,

* Dr. Bolling subsequently was made president of the Lilly Endowment in Indianapolis, and later became president of the Council on Foundations, the representative organization of private foundations in the United States.

they maintained, is the actual teacher status, however less apparent it may be in a conventional academic setting. "The result," they said, "could be a sense of a genuine community of learners, largely free of the common expert-novice polarity and threat." This prophecy was to prove more apt than its authors realized.

Margaret Lechner, Earlham '72, was one of the two students initially tapped to take an Outward Bound course and join with the faculty group in developing a wilderness program, and one of the original Pre-term instructors. Following graduation as a biology major, she instructed at Minnesota Outward Bound, then in the second Pre-term, after which she returned to the college for a visit. A classmate, Ben Foster, was also back; a geology major, he too had been a Pre-term instructor and now was fresh from a summer's instructing at North Carolina Outward Bound. One evening in a rap session with friends, the two advanced the idea that some kind of a term-length academic program, designed on the mobile field learning pattern of the Pre-term, could provide an educational experience in which the values of that program would be multiplied. "Write it up!" their listeners urged. During and subsequent to a backpack trip in the Sierra Nevada, they put their concept on paper.

"Our basic point," Margaret recalls, "was that Pre-term was fine for its purposes, but we wanted to go beyond people getting acclimatized to the wilderness, being exposed to personal challenge and the interpersonal process, being introduced to a wide variety of subject matter, getting adjusted to college, and that sort of thing. We knew how wilderness experience had helped us academically, and we wanted to extend that kind of opportunity to other students. For example, I was a plant buff who was completely turned off geology until I traveled in the wilderness with Ben. We began to build a plan of what we could do if we had a full academic term to work in."

In December they submitted to the college a proposal for a mobile term in the Southwest embracing three courses—Regional Natural History, Land and Resource Uses, and Outdoor Education. Revised and refined with faculty assistance, the plan was accepted on a trial basis. The program was made available to students at member colleges of the Great Lakes College Association (GLCA) and funded through a joint grant from the Lilly Endowment and the Reader's Digest Foundation. The first "Winter

Wilderness" term, as it was initially called, took place in Earlham's 1974 winter term, with an enrollment of seventeen students. Lechner and Foster were the instructors; Professor Orland Blanchard, a plant botanist, and geologist Charles Martin joined the group part-time in the field.

By the fourth year (1977), now titled Southwest Field Studies, the term had evolved to a two-course curriculum, Regional Natural History and Experiential Outdoor Education, earning three credits. The content was interdisciplinary, embracing biology, geology, and education as the primary areas of study and including aspects of geography, land use, meteorology/climatology, and history. Three major natural areas—the Grand Canyon, the Lower Sonoran Desert on the Arizona-Mexico border, and Big Bend National Park on the Texas-Mexico border—were used as outdoor classrooms. In addition to the two faculty leaders, Lechner and Biology Professor William Buskirk, the students had access to local resource persons. A number of these were embarked on research, education, and land-management projects, in careers of possible interest to the students. Other useful resources were such people as park rangers, ranch managers, a town mayor, a Mexican goatherd.

Still another resource was the students themselves—primarily but not exclusively upperclassmen who had acquired a degree of expertise in their fields of study. While peer teaching and learning had been contemplated from the outset, it got an assist from dynamics that proved to be built into the experiment. "The one big lesson we learned the first year," Lechner recalls, "was that we were putting people into a unique educational situation, a twenty-four-hour, peer-group learning situation, and this produced significant course content. There was a tremendous amount of useful course material generated around questions like, How come this feels so different from school, even though we're dealing with the same subject content? We hadn't planned that. We said, Hey, let's put in educational philosophy as part of the outdoor education course, because it's happening anyway. We consciously made the decision to use what was happening to us within the group as a sociological and psychological resource."

Biology Professor Bill Buskirk's involvement is instructive. His appointment as one of the two 1977 staff leaders was a response to the Curriculum Policy Committee's recommendation, in postponing final action on the experiential term's permanent status, that the natural science component be upgraded so as to "combine the special advantages of field study with a level of academic expectation equal to that typical of classroom instruction." The previous year he had been a part-time faculty participant, leading the group through a two-week comparative vegetation study of the Sonoran and Chihuahuan deserts. (A Buskirk dictum: "When we learn to respect the desert for what it is rather than what it is not, we learn to respect and like it.") Prior to that, his only exposure to the program had been in attending a slide-show report by the students who had taken part in the 1975 term. Thinking back to that occasion a year later, he recalled: "I felt a very high level of group coherence and togetherness in the program. It came off as strongly experiential. As a teacher on campus I felt that maybe I'd never be able to produce a learning experience that had excited people so much and sharpened their thinking so about the educational process. I thought it was commendable that the program had done that. But I also sensed that these people coming back might be very challenging in their attitudes toward education once they were here."

But then he had done his two weeks with the 1976 term and had come to have a quite special feeling about students in his classes who had taken part in Southwest Field Studies. "I'm always glad if any of these people are involved in a group exercise in my course because I feel there's a certain amount of leadership there. The group interaction capabilities are much higher, as is motivation to learn for themselves. On the average I feel much more comfortable with these people than with other students. I feel open to them, and that they're open to both criticism and criticizing. They are more ready to tell me what they like or don't like. But I have never felt it in a way that was threatening to me. I've always recognized that they were genuinely interested in what I was doing and how I was doing it, and how it reflected on them—as opposed to other feedback you sometimes get that's, say, more divisive."

As he spoke in the spring of 1976, he was anticipating with concern his leadership role the following winter: "I'm amazed at what can be done at the level of personal growth and in peer learning in this program. Margaret, this last winter, seemed to be able to generate an atmosphere in which everybody pulls together for their own learning, and shares a lot. In thinking about teaching with it next year, I think there may be a tendency, if a full professor with whom they've had some prior experience in courses shows up, that it's going to become more directional as far as information flow is concerned, and not this more synergistic sort of relationship. I'm very concerned that it not become a strongly academic program alone. Its uniqueness in the past has come from a blend of the two."

The empirical evidence—an enthusiastic student report on the 1977 term—indicates that the experience served to remove the concern. In the spring, the faculty accepted Southwest Field Studies with permanent status in the curriculum.

In pursuing the story of Southwest Field Studies, it may seem that we have become a phase separated from Outward Bound. In a strict sense, it is not an adaptive program. It derives from Outward Bound, contains Outward Bound elements, and employs Outward Bound learning principles. Growth and interpersonal phenomena comparable to those common to Outward Bound experiences occur in it. It is not, however, a stress program, and it is not characterized by severe physical demand. In the beginning Lechner and Foster thought that it would be. But they early came to realize that the time and energy required for full personal and interpersonal challenging had to be conserved for academic endeavor. Nevertheless, Earlham's Southwest Field Studies, along with the rest of its Wilderness Program, is a significant chapter in the story of Outward Bound. For it sheds considerable light on a question that, while not quite a mystery, is nevertheless difficult to explain: How did it eventuate that Outward Bound became a spearhead of the experiential movement in U.S. education? The phenomenon is best elucidated by the case method, and the Earlham story is among the most cogent of the case histories.

There are natural laws, not always understood, governing the development of human organizations. In 1972, U.S. Outward Bound was eleven years old, relative to the date of the Colorado School's incorporation. I had served nine years as president or chairman of Outward Bound Incorporated. It was apparent that the organization was now in a period of dynamic growth, with the kind of problems such growth produces, where it would be well served by a president who was somewhat less of an educational administrator and somewhat more of a practitioner of those managerial skills that are usually gained through experience in the business world. Also, Theodore R. Sizer, dean of the Harvard School of Education, was appointed headmaster of Phillips Academy following John Kemper's untimely death.* Ted offered me a new challenge as Director of Admissions. Less interested in the selection process, he wanted to expand the applicant pool from 1100 to "over 3000." Plans were being made for the Academy's bicentennial; coeducation was on the horizon. So was the largest fund drive in the history of secondary education—fifty million dollars. Ted was determined to refine the emerging "house" or "cluster" structure, and he was dedicated to an increased foreign student constituency. Most importantly, he offered a recommitment to the founder's constitutional mandate that the Academy be "ever open to requisite youth from every quarter." He had dreams of realizing this last objective to an even greater extent than had been the case at any time in the last century.

The challenge was exciting. I returned to Andover in the fall of 1972, where I continued with my Outward Bound responsibilities until the OBI search committee found the man with the elusive combination of attributes they had set for the new president.

The committee's man proved to be Henry W. "Hank" Taft, whom they finally located in the top echelon of the Bristol-Myers Company. Hank had attended the Taft School, which his great-grandfather Horace had founded, Yale, and Harvard Business School. Interlaced with his formal education were two hitches in the U.S. Navy, in World War II and the Korean War. Coming out of the Harvard Business School, he got in and out of the plastics industry fairly rapidly and joined the publishing house of Doubleday and Company, later becoming its treasurer. In 1959, at a time when he was considering a career change, a friend with whom he had just played a game of squash stuck his head out of the shower and said, "Hank, would you like to go to the South Seas?" Hank said, "Yes." His friend's lead was to three California men who were planning a flight from the "rat race" by sailing to Tahiti in a forty-six-foot ketch. Hank joined them.

---

* John Kemper died of cancer in December 1971. He is one of Andover's greats, and no less in the annals of Outward Bound.

The adventure took a year—three months living aboard the ketch in Sausalito while outfitting it; a voyage of a month and a half, with island stops, to Tahiti; three months living on the Tahiti waterfront; a seventy-two-day eastward voyage with only one anchoring before making a landfall in Peru; and the final northward voyage, through the Panama Canal to New York. It was a self-made, super-Outward Bound experience. Hank feels it changed his life for the better in many ways.

He went to work for Bristol-Myers, was made the company treasurer, and later became vice-president for acquisitions. He was executive vice-president of the Products Division when the search committee found him. He was also a trustee of the Taft School and chairman of the board of trustees of the Rye Country Day School, and had been thinking he would like to become directly involved with education. The committee felt it had done well to ferret out a highly able businessman who had a yen for adventure and a deep interest in education. They would be proved right.

Upward Bound
and Outward Bound

≡≍≡≍≡≍≡≍≡≍≡≍≡≍≡≍≡≍≡≍≡

Higher education has usually limited enrollment to those who were already known to be bright and had the background needed to get in. Few higher education institutions have had experience in educating the type of youngster who does not have the conventional talents, conventionally measured. How can we educate some of these young people? I am sure that there are scores of ways of educating people that none of us has ever used. Whatever Upward Bound does, I would hope that it identifies and systematizes many of these ways.
          —Dr. Richard T. Frost,
          National Director, Upward Bound, 1971

The sixty-eight passengers in the bus that took off from Middletown, Connecticut, for Morganton, North Carolina, at the end of May 1969 were an odd mix. Predominantly ninth-grade boys and girls, they also included teachers, staff members of Wesleyan University's Master of Arts in Teaching program, and members of the Harvard Motivation Achievement Development Project. About half the youngsters were black, a number of others Hispanic; the adults too were a racial mix. This was the entire student body of NC-12, a course contracted by the North Carolina Outward Bound School to Wesleyan Upward Bound. As a contract course primarily for disadvantaged youngsters with a co-educational and student-teacher peer-level mix, NC-12 achieved a

319

new level of uniqueness among Outward Bound courses. At its conclusion the experiment was adjudged seriously flawed. Time, however, has proved it the successful start of a significant strand in the Outreach story.

People who do not know what Outward Bound is sometimes confuse it with Upward Bound, and vice versa. Upward Bound, a federal War on Poverty project initiated by the U.S. Office of Education in the 1960's, is a precollege program for high-school students from low-income families, sponsored by colleges and universities as a service to their area. Its task is to identify economically and culturally deprived youngsters about to enter the ninth grade who have college potential but whose attitudes are apathetic or negative, perhaps even hostile, and to motivate them, follow up with development of academic skills, and eventually assist in college placement. It is not surprising that sooner or later Upward Bound and Outward Bound should have found each other.

An Upward Bound program was established at Wesleyan University in 1966. Richard Brown, a recent Dartmouth graduate who had worked under Charley Dey with the A Better Chance program in Hanover, New Hampshire, was director. In 1968 Peter Budryk became his assistant. Budryk, who would succeed to Brown's position two years later, had graduated from Boston College, taught high-school English for seven years, then earned a master's degree in school administration at the Harvard School of Education. He is a self-described poverty-hater: "I grew up in urban poverty amidst all of its concomitant pathologies, which touched me, my family, my friends. My reaction to poverty was, and still is, hatred bordering on revulsion."

Following the 1968 summer of the Wesleyan project, Brown and Budryk were dissatisfied with what had become more or less a standard pattern for most Upward Bound summer phases—a seven-week campus residence with primarily remedial study and recreation. The theory was that living in a campus ambiance would itself prove a motivational experience, turning on underprivileged youngsters to the idea of going to college. Budryk says, "It created a kind of plastic bubble world for kids that was totally unrelated to their home experience. And it created a huge baby-sitting job for the staff. We felt it wasn't working. We wanted something that was really going to hit at the kid's sense of failure, his sense that he couldn't control his own life, and at his failure to read the signals about negative behavior he was picking up from his environment. What would give the kids an opportunity to look at themselves in a different light? We wanted something organic we might do—like a model farm. We researched the possibilities and discovered Outward Bound."

They came to us at Andover seeking ideas. Out of a series of meetings with Bob Lentz and Dyke Williams from OBI and Murray Durst, then director at North Carolina, came a plan for the North Carolina School to conduct a contract course with the primary goal of building self-esteem and self-confidence in the Upward Bound students. The teachers who would have the students in the subsequent academic part of the summer session and in the school year to follow were to participate on a peer level with the students. This would, it was felt, give the teachers a more palpable sense of their Upward Bound mission and increased confidence for their task, and make for a more productive student-teacher rapport. The Harvard representation was a group of black psychologists who had organized to apply motivational methods developed at Harvard by Professor David McClelland in their work with minority children; they were to help develop student and teacher strategies for applying the gains of the outdoor program to the classroom.

"Pretty far out when it's stacked up against other Upward Bound programs," was the comment coming back from Washington. But the timing was fortunate. Both the educational community and Congress were then giving respectful attention to the Coleman Report on equal opportunity in education that the Congress had mandated. Among the Coleman group's key findings was the tenet that a youngster's sense of controlling his own destiny is by far the best predictor of academic excellence. Washington gave its approval for a summer's experiment.

NC-12 got off to a bad start, triggered by the severe culture shock of the overnight shift from Connecticut urban streets to the North Carolina wilderness. The initial unhappiness was aggravated when the articulate youngster who emerged as the leader of the dissidents created a racial issue: "It's not that we want to go home because we're finding it hard. We want to go home because this is a Whitey outfit, it doesn't really fit us kids." The Upward Bound staff had no crisis management plan; in particular they had not built a strong parental support that could have stemmed the dropout tide. Twenty-two of the sixty-eight students, mostly black, opted to return home after the first week, and two went later.

Most of the Outward Bound staff were ill-prepared to work with hostile inner-city youngsters, the more so since these were younger than the students they were accustomed to. "Our kids were spewing epithets at the instructors that had the hair on their chests curling," Budryk says. "The response of some, speaking metaphorically, was to stick fingers in their ears and walk around in circles. When the kids saw this kind of ambivalence, they just drove the wedge in deeper. Then some of the instructors started to lower the course standards, which was the last thing we wanted. Our kids are very perceptive at picking up this kind of thing. There was an implicit but very clear message to a lot of them that you're poor, you're black, you're dumb, we can't expect you to do what the upper-middle-class bright kids can do, so we're going to water down the course. There was a little friction between our staff and theirs about that. On the other hand, there were also a number of instructors like Karl Rohnke, Jed Williamson, and others who were very good at handling the situation."

Williamson was one of the Colorado School instructors who had worked with Durst in the Job Corps project at Collbran three years before. Anticipating the need for perceptive staff work with the NC-12 students, Durst had summoned Jed and his wife Perry from New Hampshire. Jed remembers: "There were very few instructors who were in tune with where those kids were at. The kids were thirteen, fourteen, fifteen, and you just had to change gears completely. Perry and I enjoyed it. It drove Perry a little bit up the wall because she was so oriented to doing what you're supposed to do, and these kids weren't. But one day she was teaching some of them how to string up a shelter out of plastic when suddenly it hit her that these kids didn't have enough self-confidence to believe they could tie a half-hitch. And of course, the urban kid's response, when he doesn't feel he's going to have a success, is to say, 'That's chicken-shit. I ain't going to do that shit.' They're not like nice middle-class kids who say, 'I don't understand how to do that.' Rather than look bad, they come up with all kinds of bravado."

Jed recalls walking into a tent where a dozen or so black

youngsters "on strike" were lying around. "I said, 'Any of you here can read maps yet?' 'Yeah, I can read those mother maps.' So I put a map on the side of the tent and I said, 'O.K., there are two or three here from my crew, and I want to give you a piece of information. This shows you where we'll be at noon today. Not only will we be there, but your lunch will be there.' One kid said, 'We're going to eat in the cafeteria,' which was what they called the mess hall. 'They're not serving lunch in the cafeteria,' I said. 'You see, everybody's leaving the base today. If you want to eat your lunch it will be out here at X.' That's how I got mine back."

Progressively, Outward Bound fashion, the situation righted itself. "The kids who stuck it out were glad they stayed," Williamson says. "They were glad it was over, and so were we, but they felt good about themselves." The Upward Bound staff gained perspective on what had initially seemed a disaster. "Part of the reason we had wanted to change the summer format," Budryk says, "was that we had been having a lot of dropouts. So when we lost all those kids in North Carolina we were traumatized. But then things improved. For those who stayed, and for the staff, the course was a success. Even the boy who led the go-home agitation, but then didn't go, had a good experience and afterward worked with us until he went to college. The Office of Education evaluator gave the course a glowing report despite the negative factors. And even in the matter of the dropouts we were in for pleasant surprises later."

The students who were still in the program continued with four weeks of academic work. "It is no surprise," reported the evaluator, "that the Wesleyan Upward Bound students who ran the whole distance were able to articulate the relationship between scaling a rock face and climbing the walls of ivy." At the same time there were indicators that the dropout episode was not a closed book. A factor that seems to have been an influence was that in the black communities of Middletown and Meriden parents of the youngsters who had stuck it out in North Carolina took a superior attitude toward parents of the dropouts. Whatever the psychology or sociological chemistry at work during that summer, a payoff came when school reopened. One by one the dropouts, seventeen out of twenty-four in all, showed up at the Upward Bound office and asked to be taken back.

To Budryk and his staff, those individuals were a phenomenon. In the past dropouts had simply dropped out of sight. "We didn't make it easy for them to come back in," Budryk says. "We sat down with them, stretching it out over the winter, getting them to think about why they wanted to be in the program and what they wanted to achieve in their futures." He thought it likely that some of the effects of Outward Bound on the others had rubbed off on them. "In any event, the process of re-enrolling that they initiated and we sustained with them seemed to be a very valuable maturing force. They did generally well."

Becoming director at the start of the new college year and convinced that the Outward Bound dynamic offered the motivating energy he and Brown had sought, Budryk researched the university's land holdings. He found they included a fifteen-hundred-acre wilderness preserve called Great Hollow in southwest Connecticut. Work was rushed to make the Great Hollow Wilderness School ready for the summer of 1970. Durst, now at OBI, gave counsel and moral encouragement. Jed Williamson, who had grown up in nearby Quaker Hill, New York, was on-site consultant. Jim Merritt, a Trenton State College and Northwest School alumnus who had instructed in Trenton Action Bound and at North Carolina as well as Outward Bound schools abroad, helped to set up a ropes course and was made chief instructor.

Budryk, not wanting to risk a recurrence of the previous year's dropout debacle, set about enlisting parental backing. Staff members met privately with each set of parents, describing the difficulties, fatigue, loneliness, and pain the students would encounter. "We put it right on the line," Budryk says. "What would you do if your youngster called you from a pay phone at eleven o'clock at night and he was crying and telling you he was miserable, was being starved and overworked, and he wanted to come home? In most cases we were able to convince the parents to trust us, that this was going to be a good experience for their child, and if they gave in to him or her, the child's chance to grow through it would be lost." A second tactic that guarded against dropping out was scheduling the crews so that from day two to day seventeen they were separated from each other, one at the base camp, the others on expedition. They had no opportunity, as had occurred in North Carolina, to get together and reenforce their misgivings. The two tactics, together with a staff prepared for difficult behavior, worked. No students left the Great Hollow course that summer. For Budryk the lesson "confirmed our belief that young boys and girls labeled 'under-motivated' and 'underachieving' can succeed where expectations are clear and consistent."

The 1970 experience established the summer-program pattern to which Wesleyan Upward Bound has since adhered: a twenty-one-day "motivational ignition" course at Great Hollow, followed by four weeks of academic skills development plus enrichment workshops and athletics. Upperclassmen frequently continue their wilderness learning experiences in subsequent years, assisting adult leaders or as assistant counselors in a community camping program.

One of the black staff members in Great Hollow's second summer was Arthur Conquest, a former Hurricane Island instructor. This was the same Arthur Wellington Conquest III who nine years before, freshly separated from high school for truancy, took the C-2 course at Colorado on a New York Boys' Club scholarship. Arthur's self-styled "stern but loving parent" instructing style worked well with the Upward Bound youngsters. At one point on the trail, stricken with food poisoning and vomiting yellow bile, he came close to stopping and sending for a doctor; instead, conscious of his role-model responsibility, he pushed on with his crew. He thinks the kids got the message; none made a move to drop out. The only would-be defector was a teacher. Conquest told him, "Just like the kids, you start this thing, you finish." The teacher stayed. The following year, in 1972, Conquest was made chief instructor.

At sixteen, living with his mother and brothers in New York's East Harlem ghetto, Arthur Conquest was a zealous participant in all activities at the Jefferson Park Boys' Club. He was on the club swimming team and a good all-around athlete for the Monitors in the intraclub competitions. Since the club was located in the Italian section of East Harlem, most of the Monitors were youths of Italian descent. If you were black or Puerto Rican and lived in East Harlem at that time, you were very careful where you walked; east of Second Avenue, where the Italian neighborhood started, was pretty much off limits. Arthur was one of only a handful of blacks who prized membership in the club enough to venture there. "Looking back," he says, "I can see that I was chosen to go to Colorado because I could get along with whites." Only one other of the nine-member Boys' Club contingent was black; the rest were white youngsters of academic promise who were attending prep schools on club scholarships.

Arthur remembers: "I had some problems going through the course, partly because of my inability to understand the long-range goals. But also it was a matter of other people not understanding me and where I was coming from." The utterly strange mountain environment tested him severely. He has vivid recall of his patrol's first practice climb and his inept effort to build a fire for cooking his lunch. "I ate almost raw chicken and raw potatoes. Joe Nold took us up to twelve thousand feet and he said, 'It's five o'clock, we've got an hour and a half to get off this mountain before dark,' and he begins to run off the mountain. Here I am a city kid and never been off a piece of concrete, and Joe Nold's running down the mountain. It was unreal. I was sick from eating the raw food and I was running down this mountain, bumping into trees, stumbling over rocks, and falling into dirt, getting to base camp in the dark and going to the nurse, telling her that I'm half dead, and she said, Take two aspirins. I could have killed her."

He did not find it easy as the only black in his patrol, one of two in the entire course. Defensive, he was not letting anyone forget he was from East Harlem. There was a series of confrontations and other incidents. Once, at 13,000 feet, he had a fight with an older boy after which, he believes, the school considered asking him to leave. "I kept telling myself, I can't wait to get out of this place. But the most important thing, I never said I was going to quit." Gradually things got better. A strong friendship grew between Arthur and his tentmate George, a student at the Thacher School in California. George became Arthur's sturdy advocate when tensions developed in the patrol. On final expedition, Arthur acquitted himself well in his group of four. In the marathon he finished tenth; he remembers Helen Rawalt saying, "I didn't expect you to do so well." Toting his gear down to the bus on the final day, tears welled in his eyes, spilled over. "I kept thinking, I'm going to miss this place."

Young Conquest had no sense then of having forged a lifelong association with Outward Bound. Back home from Colorado he worked at various jobs and went to night school. When he was eighteen, he joined VISTA. Placed in one of Mayor John Lindsay's mini city halls on New York's lower East Side to deal with slum tenant complaints, he discharged his responsibilities with more diligence than his VISTA superiors appreciated. Once he brought a band of tenants whose building the landlord had abandoned to stage a sitdown in the city building commissioner's office. Another time he punched an inspector who refused to order a new window installed and insisted instead that the tenants move to a hotel for welfare families. Eventually Arthur and VISTA agreed to part company. "I was a free spirit," he says.

Not long before, he had attended an Outward Bound alumni reunion at the downtown New York Boys' Club. He went because he was broke and knew there would be food. The club director asked him to show Peter Willauer around the building. As they made the tour, Conquest told Willauer his story. Peter offered him a chance to compete for a staff job at Hurricane Island. Conquest was one of six who won assistant watch-officer jobs for that summer. In his third summer at Hurricane, when he was twenty-one, he was promoted to watch officer. He worked at Hurricane for five years. Following the third summer he was one of the Hurricane group who comprised the second Overlander staff at the Lyman School. A year later he went back to Lyman for a time as a cottage master. In 1970 he was doing work for Jerome Miller at one of the state detention centers when a job offer came from Wesleyan Upward Bound.

Taking over the chief-instructor post at Great Hollow, Conquest made the course more difficult, despite the misgivings of Budryk and Ronald McMullen, Budryk's assistant and himself a member of the Middletown black community. Arthur's confidence when working with disadvantaged youngsters is an act of faith, both in himself and the youngsters. "If I don't know anything else," he says, "I know poor kids and delinquent kids. I believe in them. Because that's where I come from—and if I could do it, they can do it. Believing in the kids is all it boils down to. These kids will take you to great lengths to test if you really believe in them. They make you give second, third, fourth, and fifth effort. I made the course a little tougher, and people didn't think the kids would do it. But they did. Sure, they were leaner, and they had been through a hard experience. But I think in the end, and I don't just mean the end of the course, but when the kids have to deal with life—they'll have whatever it takes to go to the well. That's what an Outward Bound course for these kids is for—when things get tough, you've got to really believe in yourself, persevere, go to that well, and do all the things you're capable of doing. My four years at Great Hollow were good ones. I'm always fascinated by things growing, and Great Hollow was growing."

Now in its second decade, Wesleyan's is one of the longest running and most successful Upward Bound programs in the country. All new staff members at Great Hollow, however well-qualified in outdoor skills or experienced as Outward Bound instructors, are required to take a university-accredited course in the group skills of working with disadvantaged youngsters. The special training is necessary, Budryk maintains: "Our kids need a hell of a lot more support and encouragement and warmth, at the same time that they need high standards and firmness and direction. Due to both their age and cultural condition, they don't have the kind of aggressiveness and social responsibility that middle-class kids bring to the Outward Bound experience. For example, with middle-class kids there's a great deal more sharing of responsibilities. Our kids have what we call a vulture syndrome. While one gathers wood and another cooks dinner, the rest sit around the edges, letting the same kids handle the responsibility each day. When the food's on, they swoop down, get theirs and swoop back to the edges. If they were in a preponderantly middle-class group, they might get the lesson themselves. But with our kids, that kind of negative group behavior is dominant, and there have to be ways of processing it.

"Or the ten-bananas syndrome. If in a typical Outward Bound patrol one of the kids wiped out the banana supply, the other kids might deal with that in a group way. The way it would register with our kids is, he was back to camp first and got the ten bananas. Next time I have to be back to get the ten bananas. It's these kinds of behavior we have to sensitize our staff to handle.

"Also, we have to prepare them for a constant daily high frustration threshold. An easy solution would be to remove the source of the frustration. But the whole charge of our program is not to do that, is to come up with some means of living with it. We have to help give our instructors the ability to reach down into their bag of expertise, training, humanity, and come up with something that's going to make for a positive relation with the kids. We constantly have staff who, even though they are conditioned not to ask outright to get rid of a kid, come to us making noises that clearly say please get rid of this kid. But it's unlikely that we will."

After a dozen years of working with it, Budryk has lost none of his conviction about the value of the Great Hollow adaptation of the Outward Bound dynamic. Each year the objectives manual that he prepares for his academic staff carries his statement of that conviction:

> The completion of our Outdoor Program delivers an almost inestimable boost to our youngsters' sense of achievement and self-esteem. There is nothing "phony" about the challenges they have met, and this discovery hits strong and runs deep. Their confrontations with nature have shown them a new layer of self—a self with more mental, emotional, and physical endurance than they have ever had the opportunity to discover before.
>
> There is no "conning" these youngsters into believing they've had an expanding experience—they feel it in their guts and muscle fiber—their very beings vibrate with this new sense of awareness. We are convinced there is no greater programmatic tool for igniting motivation.

Project Adventure headquarters, Hamilton, Massachusetts, spring of 1977. Karl Rohnke is thinking back eight years to the North Carolina contract course for Wesleyan Upward Bound, when he was the school's chief instructor. "That was NC-12. I don't think you could go through that course and not say it was pivotal in the growth of the North Carolina School. It was the first time we did a course for all disadvantaged kids. It was our first coed course. It was the first time we had teachers in peer relationships to their students. And it was the time we began to make concessions to students. Up to then, everything had been pretty hard-ass—push, macho stuff. Then we got a bunch of kids who weren't going to go along with that type of thing. I remember a black girl, she said, 'There's no way I'm staying here, I'm going home.' Just as a lark—I knew she was a big smoker—I said, 'Will you finish the course if I give you a cigarette?' That was blasphemy. She said yes. I gave her the cigarette, and she finished the course. Some of the instructors thought that was a terrible thing to do—going against the smoking code—but she finished the course and she got the experience. So it started my thinking in a little different vein.

"The course shook up a lot of instructors, particularly dealing with black kids in that number. It was kind of easy on our part, the upper echelon, to sit back and say do this and do that, but the guys who were really in there putting up with it didn't want to put up with it. It wasn't their background, it wasn't their previous Outward Bound experience. They were into having kids do what they wanted them to do. After the course was over, and we looked back on it, there were big discussions about whether we should have that type of student come to Outward Bound. Some said, If they don't want the experience, we don't want them here, if we don't have motivated kids, we're spoiling it for everyone else—that kind of thing. When it became clear that we would continue to have kids like that, I think it made a change in the program from that point on. It wasn't all macho, bust-your-ass type of experience. It was more sensitive to the type of student you had."

Nottingham, New Hampshire, summer of 1979, in Jed and Perry Williamson's house. It's after midnight, and Arthur Conquest is winding up an evening's reminiscence that has reached from his course at Colorado in 1962 to his current graduate studies at the University of New Hampshire. The previous spring he has been awarded a master's degree by the university's School of Education. Now, holding to a bizarre high-energy schedule of work-study, family concerns, and physical fitness, he is pushing toward his doctorate. The way from the days of skipping school in the inner city to his current status of graduate student and family man has been a long poke, and Arthur reflects:

"I wish that more inner city kids, more black kids, more delinquent kids could have an Outward Bound experience and come away like I did with something positive. The kind of experience where you just feel so powerful about yourself, you feel so strong, and it's way down in the gut, just inside your belly button. An Outward Bound experience along with a few other things would be one of the answers I can think of that might be able to change the way inner-city or delinquent kids think about themselves. I've certainly taken what I got from Outward Bound and transferred it to other kids who've been through courses with me—the enthusiasm and the joy and the good feelings. I know what it feels like. I also know what it feels like to be on the street. And I've been close enough to failure to know how it feels, and I see it all the time among my boyhood friends when I go home to East Harlem."

Project Adventure

≡⋕≡⋕≡⋕≡⋕≡⋕≡⋕≡⋕≡⋕≡⋕≡⋕≡⋕≡

*. . . our culture is so urbanized and soft and our school
systems foster so much competition and isolation—we
need healthy counterbalances and alternatives. Project
Adventure proved to be an invaluable beginning.*
—Hamilton-Wenham High parent evaluation.

Jerry Pieh left Andover to be assistant to the dean of the
School of Education at Harvard in 1966 and two years later
entered the school as a doctoral candidate. Studying educational
theory at the graduate level, he found his own philosophy being
shaped as much by what he had learned about teaching and
learning when helping his father run the Minnesota Outward
Bound School as by what he was getting from his books.

"It didn't seem to me," he says, "that the critical things in the
Outward Bound approaches to learning were twenty-six days or
the age of the students or expeditions or anything like that.
There were more fundamental issues involved that were applicable in almost any educational setting: The use of challenges
with kids. The notion that people learn best in situations where
they're stretched, where they have to do more than they think
they can. Where they learn quickly whether or not they've been
successful, and where a failure is a learning experience, not a
negative thing. The openness. The stress on caring, on human
values and the importance of people. The idea that it's healthy
to know your limits, and that it's healthy to expand them. Those
kinds of things were going through my mind as I thought about

the process that took place in what happened to be a twenty-six-day wilderness format.

"It seemed to me that the important teaching principles were to establish a high level of expectation with students, to place them in unfamiliar situations that would confront them with their own limits, and to give them opportunities for experiences that would take them beyond those limits. There is an incredible amount of energy that comes when you break through what you have felt were barriers to your ability and discover a new kind of strength. If that energy could be harnessed into schools and into traditional learning situations, I felt we could accomplish much more than we were. That became the focus I took, the bent I went."

That was Pieh's focus and bent when he was appointed principal of Hamilton-Wenham Regional High School, serving some eight hundred and fifty suburban Boston students, in 1970. He went to his new post with a keen aversion to the concept he had encountered in some of his reading—that of the school as a production system wherein the product is considered to be output in terms of number of students graduating, number of Merit Scholars, number going on to post-secondary education, and the like. He had equally strong convictions about the model he believed in; here again he drew on his Minnesota experiences:

"In an Outward Bound school everybody is conscious that the changes occurring within students is what the school is there for. The instructors organize the experiences that make for the changes in the students, and it's a very important role, but what the students do with the experiences is the actual learning that the school is meant to produce. The instructors place things before kids, but they don't lead them carefully through a problem step by step. They give them a problem to solve and get out of their way. Sometimes they let them fail, if the cost isn't too high, so they can learn from it.

"That relationship of the instructors to the students is very clear. It is not like that of a teacher who dominates a class and conveys information and then asks students to give back that information. There isn't the confusion between learning and teaching that sometimes happens in schools where the most important person is thought to be the teacher."

Thus in the Pieh model, the student—since he is the only one who can apply himself to the learning and changing—is the "first-line worker." The teacher, rather than being the first-line worker as commonly thought, is a first-line supervisor providing a series of resources of vital importance to the change process. The product of the schooling process is *change in students*—in values, knowledge, physical strength, skills, behavior, and so on.*

In his first year at Hamilton-Wenham, Pieh created a vehicle for carrying out his educational ideas that is still producing missionary reverberations in the nation's schools. The vehicle, made possible by a $94,000 Elementary and Secondary Education (ESEA) Title III grant, was a curriculum innovation called Project Adventure. The project had two main phases. Initially, a personal-growth course fashioned on Outward Bound principles was to be developed as the physical education requirement for all sophomores. Secondly, the Project Adventure staff was to serve as a resource, providing students with off-campus experiences to enhance classroom learning and facilitate service to the community. The plan called for subsequently extending the staff's services to other area schools and creating a regional teacher-training and curriculum-development center.

Pieh hired Bob Lentz to direct the project. Much as we regretted losing Bob, we were pleased that his competence was being enlisted by what we saw to be a Mainstream development of major import. His associate director was Mary Smith, a teacher who had been in Laos under the aegis of the International Voluntary Service. Completing the staff were Karl Rohnke, who left his post as program coordinator at North Carolina Outward Bound, and Jim Schoel, a Hurricane Island instructor who had been teaching in a Harlem street academy. In addition, four of the school's physical-education teachers and a biology teacher took Outward Bound teachers' courses in the summer of 1971.

Under Rohnke's direction a ropes course—a decade later it remains one of the finest in the country—was built on the school grounds. The major part of the new sophomore physical-education course, taught in the fall and spring, consisted of progressively challenging ropes-course tests, focusing primarily on each student's sense of personal competence. A second part, taking

* Pieh's model is developed more fully in his doctoral dissertation, which deals with the origins and implementation of Project Adventure and evaluates its first two years.

place mostly outdoors in January and February, included initiative tests and discussion problems, fire building, map and compass instruction, first-aid training for cold weather hazards, and special snowy-day activities; its primary concerns were with small group dynamics.

In carrying out the other phases of their mission—to give students opportunities for experiential learning to reinforce their classroom endeavor—the project staff's method was first to induce a teacher to articulate a need. "We made a couple of decisions early on," Lentz says. "One was that whatever we did with academic subjects should be something that over time those teachers could pick up and do on their own. So the kinds of things we helped initiate had to be things the teachers were interested in doing. Another decision was not to create separate structures—the school-within-a-school kind of thing. We said, Let's see what can be done within the assumption that the school doesn't have to adjust to us in any fundamental way.

"So we began a series of conversations, saying here are some things we can do, some resources we have in terms of time and dollars, and here are some things we're concerned about, like how do kids learn, how to connect up things that are talked about in class with things outside of class, how to make better use of the community. In almost every case there was at least one teacher in a department who said something like, Gee, I'm having a problem with colonial history and there's a lot of it around here, there ought to be a way to put these together; or, I'm very concerned with ecological concepts, and with all the living illustrations in the area we ought to be able to make a connection; or, I have a group of kids who don't like to write and think they have nothing to write about, maybe you could help us there. That would be a start. We wanted at least the germ of the idea to come from the teacher, so it could be teacher and project staff working together."

Projects coming out of these collaborations were as diverse as, on the one hand, a biology class's slog through a swamp in a body-and-hands-on study of everything from wetlands plant and animal life to town history and, on the other, a social studies class's investigative trek to Boston's ethnically mixed and black ghetto neighborhoods in pursuit of concern with urban and minority problems. Students in the colonial-life module of an

American history course divided into small groups to make a series of cemetery researches. An art class in advanced design took a "texture walk" from the school, finding textures in great variety and doing creative things with them. A social-problems class and a media-studies class joined forces to set up and operate a community paper, can, and bottle recycling project. Sixty high-school students signed up to tutor elementary-school and junior-high youngsters. Supporting Pieh's belief that the experiential projects should have a strong service element, the tutoring scheme was to prove among the most durable.

Project Adventure conceived the "action seminar"—a semester-long course scheduled in half-day sessions, with its subject content bridging several disciplines and offering options. In "The Sea as Teacher," for example, study of navigation, weather, salt-marsh ecology, and the design and use of oceanographic equipment provided credits in science; local history, town profiling, interviewing techniques, journal writing, a survey of the crab industry, and a history of the dory tied into social studies and English; boat design and dory building into industrial arts; rowing, rock climbing, hiking, and jogging earned physical-education credits. Students used what they learned—for example, the boat they built. Life skills were learned with academics; carpentry, *Moby Dick,* and oceanography went hand in hand.

No other innovative educational proposal spinning off from Outward Bound has enjoyed a greater success with the educational establishment than Project Adventure. When the state evaluating team made its first on-site evaluation in March, it reported: "The team obtained an extremely favorable impression of the Project, confirming the Title III Supervisor's opinion that this is one of the very best Title III projects that we have." The second year, the school's physical-education staff took over the sophomore course, enabling the project staff to start working with other school systems in the region, thus broadening its base of financial support. In its third year the project was "validated" by the U.S. Office of Education (USOE) as a program "innovative, effective, transferable, and reasonable in cost," and designated a National Demonstration Site. The National Advisory Council of Title III bestowed its Educational Pacesetter Award. The state provided funding for diffusion to schools in the state, and a second office was opened in western Massachusetts.* Simultaneously, USOE made the project nationally available through its National Diffusion Network.

By 1980, Lentz and his associates had conducted workshops for administrators and teachers countrywide, keeping up student ties in their Massachusetts school programs. Lentz noted an ongoing happenstance tying the project to Outward Bound: "One of the things we seem to do that others don't do as precisely is say, for example, you're an English teacher, we'll help you develop something you can do with your English students. So we can help folks who have picked up the Outward Bound idea and like what they hear, but who are still left with that hanging question of what does it mean for me as a teacher in my school. Some of our strong states have been New Mexico, Colorado, Wyoming, Minnesota, South Dakota, Missouri, North Carolina, Maine, and you can recognize there states that either have Outward Bound schools or are regions that have been influenced by the Outward Bound movement."

Visiting Lentz and Co., we drove the few miles from national Project Adventure headquarters to Hamilton-Wenham High where, we discovered, the fount model was alive and well. The tenth-grade physical-education program, still known as "Project Adventure," was solidly entrenched. Biology's mudwalk and urbanology's city expedition had become curricular norms. "Every year we just run the urbanology field trip like clockwork," social studies chairman Richard Aieta told us. The science department's adventure-learning expedition to Acadia National Park or Cape Cod was an annual highlight. The tutoring program, in Principal Isa Zimmerman's view, was getting better every year. Project Adventure people were helping with an annual orientation session for the ninth-graders.

Dick Aieta, who had become chairman of the social studies department the year Jerry Pieh arrived at Hamilton-Wenham, harked back to the project's advent on campus: "They came to us with this idea of 'adventuring' the curriculum—this idea that learning had a more forceful impact and staying power if the students were somehow exposed to a challenge, somehow put to

* The project also moved its headquarters from Hamilton-Wenham High to Wenham.

a personal internal test that wasn't necessarily cognitive. The first thing they did was adventurize our staff. They took them to Boston and had them do the things we would be asking the kids to do. There was a spirit at that time of a renaissance, a new feeling, and it was a nice, positive, alternative way of looking at things. The ideology wasn't new—it was with us when we went to school in the Sixties. The problem was, How do you institutionalize it? In my opinion, the success of Project Adventure is that they do their homework. It's not let's go and swing from the trees and have a good time on a field trip approach. It's very purposeful, deliberate, systematic, carefully thought out and planned."

Aieta was enthusiastic about the new Project Adventure-inspired activity to which his department was keying the economics elements of the Social Studies I course taken by all ninth-graders. Three times each year, one third of the class travels to the nearby city of Gloucester. Working in teams of four, they visit and conduct interviews at some forty-five locations that together reveal a cross section of the economic life of the city, which is largely based on the fishing industry.

Although Aieta's primary concern is for the cognitive uses of the experience, he also values its affective impact. "The adventure of that curriculum is that fourteen-year-olds have great trepidation about approaching an adult and asking him or her anything— particularly something the adult knows more about than they. They learn on their own what to do when they don't know what to do. And don't overlook the environment these kids are coming from. They live in comfortable suburban bedroom towns. They've had virtually no ethnic exposure. The original response of many kids in our community is, 'If it's different, it must be bad.' It's healthy for those kids to meet up with men who are wresting a livelihood from the sea and talk in heavy Italian and Portuguese accents, and with the members of the fishermen's wives organization, who made the government go back to calling their husbands 'fishermen' instead of 'fishers.' Also, this is valuable for me as a teacher. I had a real adventure going into that strange city and setting up those forty-five contacts. I've grown and I've learned a lot."

Sally Woodsom, chairman of the physical-education department, took us to see the ropes course. It lives up to its billing. Even the visitor who has seen a number of impressive courses looks up in awe at some of the tests. "Can fifteen-year-olds do that?" Each youngster, however, decides for himself what challenges he or she will try. "It's not how much you do or how high you go," Sally told us. "It's the attempt that's made, and how sincere that attempt is, that counts most."

A member of the Hamilton-Wenham staff since Pieh's day, she has firm convictions about the value of the tenth-grade phys-ed course. "I think we would be losing a lot if we ever eliminated it. I wouldn't want to be at a school that didn't have a program like this. The kids would suffer. It enhances their growth so greatly, makes them more understanding of each other and of themselves. They get a dramatic sense of accomplishment from doing something they're afraid to do and being successful. The response of some when that happens is phenomenal. It's a superthrill for both me and the students to live through from day to day."

Sally, who was one of the four physical-education teachers given Outward Bound scholarships at the project's start, reminisced about her course at Colorado. "I went out there thinking Outward Bound was almost entirely a physical experience. Even though I was in good physical shape, I was afraid because I thought I wouldn't be up to it. Then I found that, even more than the physical aspect, it was dealing with other people and with oneself that was what it was all about. The solo was a highlight, with all those things I'd never experienced before coming together for me. I had taught here for six years. When I came back, the students talked about how I had changed. I really feel that at that time I became a person rather than a teacher. I was afraid of changing back; I didn't want to go back and be what I was. I know that some of it has gone, but I think most of it hasn't, because I still feel I'm a successful teacher. It was one of the great experiences of my life, and I don't expect to find its equal. That's why I think this is so important for these kids now. It's something that most of them are not going to experience anyplace else. It's something we can give them that's going to make them better people."

Back at Project Adventure headquarters we rapped a bit more with Bob Lentz.* The conversation got onto the shifting fashions

* After nine years with Project Adventure, Lentz resigned in the summer of 1980 to accept appointment as high-school principal in Birmingham, Michigan.

in funding. Lentz reflected on the policy line to which the project had adhered, to stay in the area of its particular competence and not be tempted to change focus by the changing purposes for which public and other monies became available. "We have tried very hard to have some sense of what we were about," he said. "You can really prostitute yourself." But he noted that it was important for the project to find new things to keep a sense of being challenged. "Right now one is 'special needs.' In our definition, special needs are pretty much kids who are in school but have learning disabilities or are behaviorally disordered. We're always looking for that new thing that can be begun here to be put through the network. Because it regenerates us."

Still, he had concerns. "With kids who have special needs getting so much funding and attention, one of our fears has been that if we began to work significantly in those areas, it would breed the idea that adventure, or experiential, or outdoor stuff is just for kids with problems, and all the others would be denied it. It's very easy today to get money for labeled kids, and it's damned hard to get money for kids." He told of a recent case in a nearby city where it had been necessary to cut back on a Project Adventure program. "They said to some of the students, 'We're sorry, you don't have any special needs, so we can't work with you.' *Every* youngster going through adolescence has a whole series of needs that he or she knows are very special. There was that look of pain and misunderstanding on the kids' faces as they were told, 'We're sorry, we know it's been good, but you don't qualify anymore, you don't have any needs.' "

Institution for Tomorrow

A race preserves its vigour so long as it harbours a real contrast between what has been and what may be; and so long as it is nerved by the vigour to adventure beyond the safeties of the past. Without adventure civilization is in full decay.

—ALFRED NORTH WHITEHEAD

But a certain Samaritan, as he journeyed, came where he was: and when he saw him, he had compassion on him . . .

—Luke 10:33

In 1979, U.S. Outward Bound's eighteenth year, the total enrollment of the schools jumped from 7,700 to 8,300. As in all but one year since our start, our enrollment rose over the preceding year—another all-time high. A breakdown of the total figure is informative.

By age:

Under 18	31%
18–21	29%
22–29	23%
30-plus	17%

By sex:

Male	59%
Female	41%

By geographic distribution:

East	32%
South	14%
Central	24%
Southwest	5%
Mountain	6%
Pacific	17%
Foreign	2%

The raw figures sum up a remarkable growth and evolution in an institution that began in 1962 with one hundred male students, most of them youths in their late adolescence, half of them from the state of Colorado. Now two fifths of the students are adults over twenty-one—or, if we define adult as the Constitution defines voting age (eighteen and over), the adult total is more than two thirds. Two fifths of the students are women; each year the percentage inches higher. The student body is drawn from every part of the country and abroad.

The evolution in the course offerings is fully as striking. Where the sole 1962 offering was a "standard" twenty-six-day course, based largely on the British model, today's prospective student has an extraordinary range of choices. The current standard* course varies in duration from twenty-one to twenty-six days, depending on the school and the season. A sampling of standard course titles attests to the variety of activity and emphases offered: Mountaineering, Mountaineering/River Running, Canyonlands, Canoe Wilderness, Sailing, Cycling, Desert/Canyon/River Exploration, Forest/Mountains/Canyons, Ski Mountaineering, Winter Camping/Skiing/Snowshoeing, Winter

---

* The national standard course curriculum provides that the course will be formed and trained as a search-and-rescue unit available for public service. It provides for the first-week fitness training and instruction in: safety; field-food planning and preparation; use of equipment; search, rescue, and emergency evacuation and first-aid procedures; map and compass, and route finding; traveling skills appropriate to the environment; knots, rope handling, and belaying; expedition planning and control; use, care, and protection of the environment. For the curriculum subsequent to the initial training phase, the standard course specifies experiences in training expeditions, rock climbing and rappelling, solo, final expedition, a marathon event, a service project, and periodic readings and discussions to help participants interpret the values underlying the course. Participants are encouraged to keep a journal.

Mountain Wilderness, Winter Tropical Expedition, Practica for Educators and Helping Professionals, Cross-Cultural (with Fox-fire), Leadership Development, Junior, Himalayan Trek. A recent development is full-semester (three-month) courses, some offered jointly by two or more schools.

Short courses ranging in duration from sixteen days down to five-day seminars include virtually all the standard course activities and others as well (e.g., Sailing/Natural History, Grand Canyon/Cross Country, Desert Institute, Special Skills). These are adapted to an open-ended list of special populations, e.g., Junior, 16½ years +, 18 years +, Adult, Male, Female, Coed, Couples, Family, College, Executives, Managers, Executive Team Building, Physically Disabled, Women Thirty and Over, Mid-Life Journey, Life Career Renewal.

If the adult-at-eighteen standard can be applied to institutions, Outward Bound was about to enter a new life phase of youthful maturity in 1979. Some such thought was running through President Hank Taft's mind as he considered the variegated nature of the organization's growth. The time had come, he concluded, for Outward Bound to do some serious stocktaking of its institutional posture, of where it wanted to go, and how it intended to get there. When he proposed that the organization initiate a formal period of long-term planning in 1979–1980, it responded with a strong assent. Some activity was already in place. OBI had an active futures committee, and each school had a comparable trustee group. The consensus was that it made good sense to integrate the futures thinking of the individual schools and the national body.

As I became one of those involved in the futures process, I could not help thinking back to whence, and how far, we had come. A considerable part of that progress, I reflected, had been a response to the energies generated by the very act of our coming into being and finding that we filled a significant need. I could understand Hank's sense of the organization's having attained to a watershed time, where simply growing on the strength of its successes was no longer adequate. In the more mature phase on which Outward Bound was embarking, the institution needed to exercise a greater degree of control over the directions in which its energies could carry it. Too many critical alternatives were at hand; it was imperative to think through the questions governing which of those alternatives would prevail.

My reflecting on the past was more than just the natural reflex of the "early settler" or charter member. It was inevitable also, in seeking to nourish my own thinking about the future of Outward Bound, that my mind should reach back to some of the teachings of the founder. I was, however, recalling him less as founder than as the most talented future watcher I had ever known. Hahn.

In the 1960's Kurt Hahn made periodic trips to this country. His visits to Andover were great occasions—for renewing our friendship, hearing his views about the state of the world, telling him about developments in U.S. Outward Bound, getting his counsel. He took a keen interest in my Outward Bound briefings. In the beginning it pleased him greatly that we had been drafted to set up the final training for the Peace Corps. He was enthusiastic about the American innovation of the solo; in his philosophy, periods of solitude were an essential human need. "You cannot harvest the lessons of your life except in aloneness," he said, "and I go to the length of saying that neither the love of man nor the love of God can take deep root except in aloneness." Sometimes he had concerns. Were the schools giving first aid its place of honor in the timetable? Did this or that school operate so far into the wilderness as to get away from other people and hence from opportunities to give aid or effect rescues? Only once, however, in my time as Outward Bound's president, did he give me a directive: "You will not let the word Christianity creep into Outward Bound. You will simply practice it." * He was captivated by the adaptive program phenomena, so different from what had happened in Britain.

Invariably his counsel enriched us. Usually the advice I sought was on some question of strategy or tactic, and he had a way of elevating the discussion to one of principle. I remember once asking him whom at Phillips Academy he thought I should go to for help in weaving Outward Bound philosophy into the fabric of the school. He said, "There are two people—your doctor and your leading historian. If the doctor is worth his salt, he is con-

---

* Hahn joined the Anglican Church in 1945. He remained deeply attached to his Jewish heritage. Speaking at Hahn's funeral service in 1974, the Right Reverend Lancelot Fleming, Dean of Windsor, said, "Kurt made it very plain that he was proud to be of one hundred percent Jewish origin."

cerned about the physical well-being of young people, and their future well-being as adults. If the historian is worth his salt, he will have detected the symptoms of a decaying culture, and will be sympathetic to what you're trying to do."

He spoke often in aphorisms. On teaching: "Teach as little as possible. When you teach someone, you deprive him of the opportunity to learn." Of a non-admirer: "I don't think he includes me in his prayers." An all-purpose commentary: "Human nature is very prevalent." He contributed his share of merriment, although his jokes did tend to be distinctively Hahnian. One visit came just after we had moved into our new home. The previous owner, who had been a big-game hunter, had mounted his prize specimens in one of the rooms, which now required some remodeling for our less esoteric purposes. I explained this to Hahn as we looked in at the workmen. Smiling, he said, "And here you will mount the heads of the academicians you have shot down!"

He and John Kemper grew to be fast friends. Kemper came to enjoy the lessons in headmastering he received from the older man. One time when some of us on the school staff were trying to decide if a boy should be expelled, Hahn told Kemper, "Never let a committee expel a boy. A committee has no conscience. Use it to investigate and advise, but you must make the decision. That boy will carry his expulsion through life. There must likewise be someone who will always carry the decision on his conscience— someone who can think back and ask himself if the right thing was done." That way, he believed, came wisdom. He told me, "I have expelled boys I was right to expel, and others I should not have. And I have kept boys I should not have, and others I was right to keep, but I feel best about the ones I kept."

For all of Hahn's intense interest in what we were doing in Outward Bound, I was aware that his main concerns were elsewhere. It is a remarkable fact that in his long, intimate association with the Outward Bound movement, he never held an official position. He was an inventor of institutions, and it was a part of his genius that he was content to leave their administering to others. On most of those visits his primary interest was in advancing the Atlantic College (later United World College) movement that he and Sir Lawrance Darvall had generated. For that institution it was seven years from dream to reality. Atlantic College—now United World College of the Atlantic—opened in Llantwit Major, Wales, in

1962. Now there is also a United World College of the Pacific in British Columbia, and a United World College of South-East Asia in Singapore, with others to come. Recognizing that international understanding cannot be treated in the classroom alone, the program of every United World College has a distinctively Hahnian component, referred to as its "humanitarian curriculum"—rescue and community services to those "in danger and in need." The late Earl Mountbatten of Burma, long the movement's international leader,* confirmed a heartfelt Hahn thesis: "It's hard to hate someone when you're both helping to save a life."

That is a variation of Hahn's, "Whoever saves a life will never take a life." No other human being, perhaps, responded as avidly as Hahn to William James's call to seek "the moral equivalent of war." He recognized that Tennyson's "peace of the broken wing"—peace that softens rather than tests moral fiber—was itself a menace to peace. The answer, Hahn was convinced, lay in "the passion of rescue." His moral equivalent of war was "to enthrall and hold the young through active and willing Samaritan service, demanding care and skill, courage and endurance, discipline and initiative." With each new visit I observed the conviction grow more resolute.

Some three dozen members of the Outward Bound community gathered at Lake Geneva, Wisconsin, in the fall of 1979 for a "Mission Conference" that had been organized by Greg Farrell, chairman of OBI's futures committee. The gathering included school directors, school trustee representatives, members of Greg's committee and other OBI trustees, of whom I was privileged to be one, and a scattering of outside resource people. For four days consultant-leader Warren Ziegler took us through a fascinating, intensive process that he called "Futures Invention."

At the outset Ziegler asked the question, "What would you like to see Outward Bound achieving in the year 2005?" Each of us listed what we thought were the critical items that ought to be part of the organization's successful mission twenty-five years hence. Our leader then bade us group ourselves according to like interests; he did not care, he said, whether it turned out to be

* Prior to his assassination in 1979, Lord Mountbatten had relinquished his post as president of the International Council of the United World Colleges to Prince Charles of England.

two or ten groups. It turned out to be seven. Each group was instructed to draw up a joint statement. That negotiation of a
statement that everyone in a group could agree on was really
hard work. At the end of a day and a half, the seven statements
were in hand. Ziegler then said to each group in substance, "Here
are the long-term objectives you have established for Outward
Bound. Now go back, refine them, and ask yourselves, how will
you know you are there? For each objective, prescribe several test
measurements that together will show you have indeed arrived
where you wanted to be. Also, set down what assumptions you
have made about the state of the world—economic, social, political,
whatever—in 2005."

When we all returned with this assignment accomplished, the
conference was halfway into its third day. Then our leader said,
"Now we're going to invent the future." He told us that we were
not going to say, This is 1979, the trends are such and such, how
do we get from here to there? Instead we would say, We are now
in the year 2005, and Outward Bound is just where we wanted it
to be—how did we get there? What were the factors that made for
success, what key events occurred along the way, what important
trends were operative? Who were the people who played an important role? That way, instead of being stuck with all the dross
of today, all the pause that the state of the economy and the political state of the world would have burdened us with, our minds
were much more open to the possibilities. It was inventing the
future as history.

What our seven groups finally produced was written up and
circulated to the schools. The school trustees were encouraged
to put themselves, with their staffs if feasible, through a telescoped
version of the process. The OBI board did likewise. Farrell then
collected all the material that had been generated. From it he
winnowed the principal "themes" under which important policy
questions that had asserted themselves tended to group. There
were seven of these themes: Growth, Performance Audit/Quality
Control, Special Target Groups, Reenforcement and Follow-up,
Leadership, Educational and Other [e.g., Corrections] Models,
Service and Community Responsibility. Farrell wrote and circulated a document summarizing the issues that had been raised in
the seven theme areas and that needed to be resolved in order to
permit planning and implementation to proceed.

The OBI futures committee then initiated an iterative process between itself and the schools to arrive at a new updated mission statement for Outward Bound. After back-and-forth revision and refinement, an official mission statement was adopted in October 1980. It reads:

> Outward Bound's purpose is to develop respect for self, care for others, responsibility to the community, and sensitivity to the environment. The Outward Bound process assumes that learning and understanding take place when people engage in and reflect upon experiences in challenging environments in which they must make choices, take responsible action, acquire new skills, and work with others. Outward Bound implements its educational and social purposes by providing leadership in experience-based programs, offering courses in its schools, conducting demonstration projects, and helping others to apply Outward Bound principles.
>
> Outward Bound seeks to: strengthen its organizational effectiveness; improve the quality of its program; and expand the influence and application of its principles.

The mission statement was a solid achievement. The first part clearly defines, for insider and outsider alike, the endeavor we are in. The second part establishes the three paths for determining priorities and implementing that endeavor. This is the phase on which the organization is now embarked.

In 1968 Hahn made what proved to be his final journey to the United States. Deeply concerned about the worldwide violence generated by youthful rebellion and racial conflict, he was looking for guidance from the American experience. Long before, he had given to Sir Robert Birley, headmaster of Eton, counsel that Birley never forgot: "Whenever you have to deal with a boy who is a rebel, remember that you must get him to face the question: Are you going to be a fighter or a quarreler?" Now he was looking for ways to harness productively the fighting spirit of young people in revolt.

For two months he crossed the continent and back, from Harvard to West Coast campuses, from Harlem to Watts, seeking new knowledge about student and racial tensions, new leads to healing forces. Fred Glimp, who was Dean of Harvard during the student riots there that year, still marvels at Hahn's keen comprehension of the issues and events on the Cambridge campus. Five years after his 1968 visit to the headquarters of the National Urban League's street workers in Harlem, they had vivid recall of the eighty-two-year-old gentleman from England who came up the stairs two at a time. On Hahn's visit there, a boy who had recently returned from a course at Hurricane Island told him, "It gives you a feeling of great power if you breathe life into a dead person." This was one more affirmation of the message he was carrying on his cross-country safari: "The passion of rescue releases the highest dynamic of the human soul." As he made that safari, his sun-induced affliction was heavy upon him. At such places as New York's Horace Mann School, Wayzata, Minnesota, and the Athenian School in Danville, California, people still remember the dim, imposing figure at the front of a darkened, crowded room, tirelessly answering—and asking—questions, offering his ideas ("I am anxious to carry conviction on this") in response to theirs.

He was intent on inventing a new institution. His dauntless mind worked toward a grand plan under which a "Service by Youth Commission" would coordinate forces enabling young people to contribute productive energies that otherwise would be spilled in confrontation or drained by frustration. Central to the plan was the removal by aid-and-rescue agencies of age restrictions preventing service by adolescent volunteers, and an international call to young men and women to help in the fight against unnecessary death and suffering. "Lifesaving," Hahn kept telling his American audiences, "is the job of the layman. The less serious things we can leave to the doctors."

In the Watts section of Los Angeles he listened eagerly for two and a half hours as Ted Watkins, chairman of the Watts Labor Community Action Committee, talked about his work with ghetto youth. Ted told him about the Watts young people painting telephone poles to spruce up the streets, starting a chicken and pet farm, converting derelict lots to "vest-pocket parks." Ted said, "Every youngster should be called on to make a sweat investment. He needs something he can protect." Hahn liked that. He made it a theme of his Service by Youth plan.

As his grueling safari ended, his affliction worsened. I drove him to the Boston airport with blankets blacking out the car windows. He wore the homburg hat with the broad, turned-down brim, an arrangement of green felt lined with lead foil shielding the back of his neck, and two pairs of dark glasses. At the plane's door his hand came up in the familiar farewell gesture. I was wrenchingly aware of that aircraft carrying off one whose comprehending concern for our sick world was irreplaceable.

Back in London and Scotland he worked on the Service by Youth plan. For all the grandiose scale of his thinking, the ideas he set down were cogent, down-to-earth, feasible. In a very real sense, I believe, he foresaw the coming tragedies of student shootings at Kent State and Jackson State and was working to prevent them. But he was not able, as he always before had been, to exert the force of his personal drive in support of that project. Struck by a car on a country road near Gordonstoun, he never fully recovered from the accident. Yet he turned even that misfortune to opportunity. The mishap gave him a new idea. He wrote Prince Philip, urging his support for a plan to reduce road deaths by including first aid in the driving test. The prince did take up that cause, giving it his earnest backing.

In retirement at last in Hermannsburg, Germany, living in an apartment at one of Salem's satellite schools, Kurt Hahn died on December 15, 1974. He was eighty-eight.

The new Outward Bound mission statement adopted in the fall of 1980 was circulated to the schools with three sets of policy questions relating to the three areas of activity indicated in the statement's second part: strengthening organization, improving program quality, and increasing influence in the mainstream of American life. In the winter of 1981 the organization was engaged in a procedure to determine which of those questions it wanted to focus on initially.

For Hank Taft the purposeful advance of the long-term planning process he had sparked was a double satisfaction, in that he had announced his intention to resign the presidency in June 1981. After eight and a half years in office he had, he believed, brought the organization to an "exciting node," poised for a new surge forward; he saw the time as right for the institution's bringing in a new leader. He had done a splendid job of shepherding the organization through a period when the total enrollment, and the total budget for operating Outward Bound in the United States, had nearly doubled. He had earned the sense of a task well carried out and an organization well launched on a new stage of maturity.

Participating in the conference at Lake Geneva, I was inspired by the creative spirit prevailing among that group so representative of Outward Bound leadership, as they solidified their ideas for the institution's future. The spirit was creative in the sense of being nonprovincial, broad of vision where it might well have been narrow, far-looking where it could have been nearsighted, questing for optimum institutional usefulness to society, concerned more for the people the institution can serve than for self-serving by the institution. This spirit is reflected in many of the policy questions that have been circulated with the mission statement. For this Outward Bounder—and, I would assume from the discussions, for many others as well—among the most intriguing of those queries are two that relate to a principle I have always considered central to the Outward Bound mission.

The first is, *"Should we seek greater emphasis on and sharper understanding of the role of service?"* I agree with Joe Nold and others who have expressed the opinion that the service commitment of Outward Bound has not yet been carried out as fully and fruitfully as it should be. While some of what is being done is excellent, the service elements of the Outward Bound curriculum still have an untapped potential. In the matter of "sharper understanding," one suggestion is that we can yet inquire more productively into the potential values that Kurt Hahn foresaw when he spoke of according first aid "the place of honor in the timetable" or employed such seemingly old-fashioned phrases as "passion of rescue" and "aristocracy of service." Hahn, of course, would have fiercely insisted that his ideas be evaluated not on the basis of their having come from the founder but simply on their merits.

The second, related query is, *"Should we seek the development of community service and other programs for alumni?"* In the colloquies at Lake Geneva and later, I could not help being delighted to hear support voiced for this proposal, for it tended to confirm an old hypothesis: that there are self-asserting forces in the Outward Bound dynamic that influence its programs toward increasingly Hahnian kinds of practice. I can best explain this by trying to repair what I believe to be a serious misunderstanding in the areas of "follow-up."

U.S. Outward Bounders frequently do an unconscious disservice by quoting out of context the closing line of Hahn's address at the 1965 Outward Bound Conference at Harrogate, England, where follow-up had been one of the important debated subjects. His concluding words were, "Outward Bound can ignite— that is all—it is for others to keep the flame alive." The line is usually quoted under the impression that Hahn in a sense was negating the follow-up question by relegating the responsibility to a vague, undefined "others." The error in the impression lies, I think, in failure to appreciate (perhaps not even to have seen) what the context was. For in his preceding paragraph Hahn had quite clearly defined whom he meant by "others," and quite clearly stated the form he believed follow-up should take:

> I believe that the challenge of Samaritan Service, if properly presented, rarely fails to capture young people, body and soul, not only in the Western World. I hear encouraging news about the young behind the Iron Curtain—many of them look westward, with distrust but also with hope. They ask a question which makes us blush: "Are you in earnest about the ideals you profess?" Who shall give an answer? Young men and women who render hard and willing service to their fellow men in danger and in need.

A few months later, visiting in Andover, Hahn gave me a photograph of himself. Part of the inscription, in the form of a charge, was an even more explicit restatement of the thought he had left with the conferees at Harrogate:

> To Josh Miner . . . May he remember that the best service he can render to Outward Bound is to recognize its limits: Outward Bound can kindle the flame but it will be extinguished in many cases unless the Outward Bounders, returning to their schools and workshops, are confronted by the challenge and the opportunities to go on active service to help their fellow men in danger and in need. Their resolution to do so will be strengthened if we can build up an aristocracy of service throughout the free world, whose example will create a fashion of conduct.

That "aristocracy of service" was the new institution the eighty-two-year-old Hahn was seeking to invent in the aftermath of his 1968 U.S. safari. The lengthy memorandum he wrote upon his return home and sent to his Outward Bound and other American friends is a kind of testament to all of us who care about the well-being of his institutions. In the memorandum's final paragraph, using the designation *helper* for those performing Samaritan service, he stated the salient, consuming idea one more time:

> One would hope that one day the status of helper would be recognized throughout the Western world—thereby a new and challenging avenue of distinction might be opened. Such development would go far to solve the baffling problem of the "follow up" for Outward Bound and kindred enterprises.

Hahn expressed it as a hope. Can we now hope it will prove to be prophecy?

Afterword

≡✕≡✕≡✕≡✕≡✕≡✕≡✕≡✕≡✕≡✕≡✕≡

It's never over until it's over.
—YOGI BERRA

A lot of the Outward Bound movement that was grist for the book just did not get in. It was always our feeling that the book had to be not just about the OB schools but about the *movement.* While each school is a big story in itself, deserving of its own book, the movement is *the* big story. An adequate understanding of what the schools have achieved can be got only through awareness of how their Outreach endeavors—their sparking, begetting, support, and guidance of the whole gamut of adaptive programs and spin-offs—have greatly multiplied their societal influence.

In these final pages we have a chance to follow through in slight measure on the stories of the individual schools subsequent to their founding—in particular, to present the roster of second- and third-generation school directors who have done and are doing so much to make Outward Bound what it is and what it is becoming— and to amplify some on the dimensions of the movement.

Dan Meyer became the fourth director of the North Carolina School (NCOBS) after Murray Durst went to the national office, and Jed Williamson took his place for a year to give the trustees time for making a permanent appointment. Dan came to the North Carolina School via the U.S. Forestry Service and a demonstrated competence as a fine manager. He had known Murray in the latter's Office of Economic Opportunity days and had come to admire what Outward Bound was doing. He brought to the post a warm, friend-making personality, and an innovative temperament balanced by a high regard for the Hahn tradition. The school grew steadily under his leadership. Table Rock became overcrowded, and he opened a second base at Green Cove in the Smoky Mountains. He was the first director to appoint a female course director (Arlene Ustin). Dan also created the first alumni course, with its "final expedition" a parachute jump.

But Dan's chief prides are none of those things. What he remembers with the greatest satisfaction is that he changed the student assessment system that U.S. Outward Bound had adapted from the British. Because so many OB students in Britain were sent by their employers, the schools there followed the practice of sending an instructor's report on each student to his sponsor, or alternatively, to his parents or perhaps both. In the beginning the U.S. schools took over this practice, reporting on each student to parents and, in the case of those on scholarship, to his sponsor. When Dan found this "report card approach," as he called it, he did not like it. He decided to treat the student, rather than the parent or sponsor, as the client. The student was called on to evaluate his or her own performance in the course impression that is written just before going home. The instructor in turn wrote to his students, evaluating the course without singling out individuals. The other schools largely adopted this practice, at first on a trial basis, and eventually as standard procedure.

Dan's other special pride is that he initiated early on a course for juniors, lowering the age limit to fourteen. This was a response to his observation that youngsters were being exposed to drugs and other deleterious temptations at increasingly younger ages. North Carolina petitioned the OBI trustees to try a junior course, and the experiment was deemed successful. Nothing was changed in the way of course severity, except for keeping a closer check on the final expedition. North Carolina is still offering that course, and other schools have their own junior versions.

Gary Templin, initially Joe Nold's number one man, was director of the Colorado School (COBS) from 1974 to 1980. Gary became director, and Nold moved up to the new post of president of COBS in that watershed time when the Colorado School was reorganized into two parts, the school under Templin, and the newly created "Project Center" for contracting adaptive programs and consulting services under Nold.

Gary is the archetype of the early Outward Bound leaders-to-be who, out of college and feeling their way toward a career path, had their lives influenced profoundly upon encountering OB. In the summer of 1961, just after graduating from Wheaton College (the evangelical Wheaton in Illinois, popularly dubbed "Harvard of the Bible Belt"), Gary worked for Jim Vaus in Jim's Youth Development project in New York's East (Spanish) Harlem. Vaus is a long-ago Wheaton dropout who learned electronics in the military in World War II, ended up in an army brig, and became the "electronics specialist" for Mickey Cohen, the Pacific Coast's top gangster, before experiencing a spiritual conversion through the ministry of Billy Graham. Ever since Jim Vaus has served a splendid ministry to young people in trouble.

Gary's job that summer was to work with a couple of street gangs, young toughs aged eighteen to twenty-five, to help rechannel their energies more productively than through the gang violence that was taking as many as twenty-five young lives in an East Harlem summer. In the fall he had just started to teach and coach at Wheaton Academy when he was called up by the Army's Special Forces. He was in the second group of Green Berets to go to Vietnam. His nearly two years there redirected his ideas about what he wanted to do: "I had had no intention of going back to Harlem. But in Vietnam I decided that was where I would put my marbles." Vaus made him director of a summer camp facility that had just been given to Youth Development. Gary's Montana ranch upbringing had given him no idea of how a summer camp functioned, and he wrote, among others, to OBI for information. We sent a copy of his letter to Joe Nold, who looked Gary up on his next visit to New York and showed him the *Tall as the Mountains* film. Gary went home and told his wife, "If anything ever took me out of Harlem, it would be Outward Bound." The two men kept in touch over the next two years. In 1965 Joe hired Gary for a month as a consultant on the OEO project in Collbran. A month after he returned to New York, Gary got a letter offering him the job of assistant director of the Colorado Outward Bound School. He started in the spring of 1966.

Gary is one of the seminal builders of U.S. Outward Bound and can lay claim to an impressive list of initiatives. He played a major role in changing the solo-experience emphasis from survival to one of contemplation and fasting. He did pioneer work in integrating minority, inner-city, and delinquent youth into the standard course and likewise played a central role in the early adaptive programs that spoke to the needs of disadvantaged populations—Dare to Care, Urban Bound, etc. Gary wrote the first curriculum outline as a means of standardizing the experience students would receive. He made significant innovative contributions to sound management practices in operating an OB school. He developed a strong leadership cadre of men who moved on to top positions in Outward Bound and in other areas of the experiential education community. He formulated the first semester-long leadership development course as a vehicle for producing adaptive program leaders. As chairman of the Outward Bound Coordinating Committee he was the leader in bringing about, through charter and by-law revision, a productive reorganization of U.S. OB's structure and procedural policies.

Since 1974, *Derek Pritchard* has been the third director of the Minnesota School (MOBS). Derek began his association with international Outward Bound as a student at Aberdovey in 1949. After earning a degree in fine art from the Royal Academy of Painting in London, he traced a career path from easel to adventure-based education via the British Army, serving as an officer in its Parachute Regiment and taking part in the army's expedition to Mts. McKinley and Brooks in 1956. He instructed in British Outward Bound, and at training centers in East Africa. He was made director of the Outward Bound Mountain School at Loitokitok, Kenya, in 1963, and served as director of the British school at Devon from 1968 to 1973.

In 1972 Derek spent a summer visiting and instructing at the Colorado, Minnesota, and Hurricane Island schools. He came off his American experience with a sense that the British schools were too tightly structured, the American schools too loosely so, and he headed home with ideas about loosening up Devon. He had no inkling then that a year and a half hence he would come back as the Minnesota School's new director.

Pritchard has been a consistent innovator in his Outward Bound leadership. In Kenya he started a course for the blind that culminated in guiding seven blind climbers to the snow-covered summit of Kilimanjaro. At Devon he initiated mobile courses, coed courses, and courses for school dropouts. At Minnesota he introduced courses for the physically disabled and hearing-impaired, making MOBS a pioneering agency in this important aspect of adventure-based education. Within a few years these courses were included in the school's standard curriculum, with a mixed handicapped and "non-handicapped" enrollment. Among Derek's other early innovations at Minnesota were alumni expeditions into some of the most remote parts of the Canadian wilderness, and an eighty-hour advanced wilderness emergency care workshop for senior staff from all Outward Bound schools.

In 1976 Derek established a Project Centre as an experimental arm of the school, reaching beyond the standard curriculum to innovative courses and consulting services, to make the school available as "an educational model dynamic and flexible enough to respond to changing educational and social needs by developing new uses of Outward Bound for new audiences." Some instances of Project Centre activity are: a life/career renewal course in conjunction with the Human Renewal Association of Minneapolis, designed to assist individuals in making decisions and clarifying values in the context of mid-career change; a contract course for adolescents sponsored by the British Children's Thalidomide Trust for which eleven students traveled to the U.S.—featured on *CBS Evening News* with Walter Cronkite; design of a youth leadership community project for the Fort Peck Indian Reservation, and an experimental program for the Minnesota Mental Health Association in which OB instructors worked with thirty therapists and their clients to strengthen client-therapist relationships for improved therapy goals.

John Huie, director of the North Carolina School (NCOBS) since 1977, was Georgia-born and raised. He graduated in 1960 from Davidson College in North Carolina, where he captained the basketball and track teams. He had done some independent school teaching and coaching and was a graduate student at Emory University when he was interviewed by Bob Pieh for a teaching-coaching job at Anniston Academy in Alabama. Bob offered him the job but with the explanation that he would not be coming back as headmaster. "I asked him where he was going," John remembers. " 'To start an Outward Bound school in Minnesota,' he said. I asked him what an Outward Bound school was. Bob's answer—philosophical, even poetic—was beautiful. I told him Outward Bound sounded like the best thing I'd ever heard of. He said, 'Then why don't you come with me?' And so I did, that summer of 1965, starting at twenty-seven as an assistant instructor, and then full instructor in August, and program director the next two summers. Good years, in which I identified Outward Bound as a magnificent vehicle for stimulating and nurturing personal growth, for really making a difference in human relationships."

When the NCOBS trustees were looking for a successor to Dan Meyer, John was their man. By then a Ph.D. candidate at the University of California at Santa Barbara, he had a lot more teaching and headmastering under his belt. As instructor and dean of students at St. Mark's School in Dallas and as headmaster of Verde Valley School in Sedona, Arizona, he had instituted OB adaptive programs.

"The focus of the North Carolina School in the seventies," John says, "has been strongly on personal growth and human relations. The physical side of the Outward Bound experience is not allowed to dominate the tone of the course but is used to open up the mind, touch the spirit. *If* there is any tension in the OB movement between the Athenians and the Spartans, count us among the Athenians. The key to Outward Bound is how the stress is handled, what resources the instructor has to set a tone of reverence for the world, respect for human differences, compassion for people, desire to serve, and so on."

Huie sees the maintaining of high quality standard courses for young people as the "backbone" of the school, its *raison d'être*. In addition, it has experimented and innovated in a number of ways: winter courses in the Florida Everglades, a cross-cultural course with Foxfire, a "sea-to-mountains" cycling course, a full semester (ninety-eight-day) course extending through North Carolina, Georgia, Tennessee, and Florida, and a variety of contract courses for special populations. Among the hallmarks of his directorship, John takes particular pride in the high degree of staff involvement in the school's planning and decision-making processes, a considerably broadened geographic trustee representation, stepped-up engagement of board members in school activity, and a widening of relationships with educational institutions.

A notable instance of the latter is the school's liaison with Lenoir-Rhyne College. Dr. Albert Anderson, Lenoir-Rhyne's president, has been using funds from an enrichment grant to send many of the college's staff and students through OB courses. He is on the NCOBS board, and Rufus Dalton, longtime NCOBS and OBI chairman, is on Lenoir-Rhyne's faculty. Says Al Anderson: "My personal feeling is that if a liberal arts education is the best intellectual entrée to growth in self-esteem (and that is what I hold), then an Outward Bound experience is its best complement. It probably does more for developing wholeness than any other program we might add to make good on our traditional educational aims."

Huie is a staunch adherent of the service ethic in OB. An advantage of his school's location, he points out, is its close access to institutions—a state mental hospital, a school for the deaf, a prison for youthful offenders, a center for handicapped children—that offer opportunity for service projects. "Our emphasis on service," he says, "is important to us—is, in fact, what Outward Bound should be all about. The philosophical assumption behind that statement is that being fully human means acting on the impulse to serve fellow man, to behave unselfishly."

Victor Walsh, director of the Northwest School (NOBS) since 1977, is another one of those Britishers—there is a remarkable group of them in this country—who at a young age were pushed out into the vocational stream by the English educational system and in due course, having found their way into the U.S. Outward Bound community, have been stimulated to earn master and doctoral degrees from American universities. When the English system spit him out at fourteen, Vic was offered the choice of an apprenticeship as a glassblower or car mechanic. His choice of the latter led to a factory toolmaker apprenticeship. He escaped that uncongenial learning track by enlisting in the Royal Air Force, where they made him a photographer. Eventually his proficiency as a mountain climber got him into the Air Force's mountain rescue unit, with which he trained all over Europe, taking part in some three hundred rescues.

Out of the military, Vic emigrated to New Zealand, where he made a living as a photoengraver and did a lot more climbing, including a number of difficult first ascents. His prowess won him a place in a mountaineering expedition to South America that rolled up an impressive record of many more first ascents. Vic stayed on in South America to go down the Amazon and other major rivers. At one juncture he enjoyed a sojourn with the headhunter Jivaro Indians of Ecuador. Back in England, working for a Fleet Street press photography agency, Vic joined a group of climbers from the London School of Economics who were planning an expedition to the only unclimbed 6,000-meter peak in South America, which had turned back some of the world's top mountaineers. The British group climbed it.

Again back in England—this was about 1962—Walsh became an instructor at the Eskdale Outward Bound School under Tom Price, a leader whose educational philosophy has profoundly influenced him. In 1964 Vic was one of the British instructors who helped the Minnesota School get started. The next summer he was at the Colorado School, then with the Moray Sea School in Scotland and German Outward Bound at Baad. He came back to Colorado in 1966 to work with Joe Nold, Jed Williamson, and others in Murray Durst's OEO operation at Collbran. Subsequently he ran, with considerable success, a "Second Chance" camp ancillary to the juvenile reformatory at Golden, Colorado. In the years that followed Walsh combined a brilliant OB staff record with studies that got him an A.B. degree at Fort Lewis College in Durango and a Master of Education degree at the University of Colorado. Also in that time he joined with Jerry Golins in writing "The Exploration of the Outward Bound Process," a seminal paper that is the most successful effort to date to put on paper an analysis of the OB dynamic and trace how the process works.

Enrollment in the NOBS year-round schedule of mountaineering, ski mountaineering, and river-running courses, conducted in six areas in Oregon, Washington, and Idaho, was up 80 percent in Vic's first three years as director. Growth was aided by the headquarters move to Portland, the opening of a Seattle branch office, and a broadening of trustee representation. The most significant aspect of the enrollment increase was that a relatively small part of it was in the standard summer program. This reflects a considerable development of year-round operation and a substantial increase in special programs and contract courses.

The NOBS clientele for contract courses include University of Washington residence hall directors, the American Stock Exchange staff, juveniles in corrections residences, a migrant workers' high school equivalency class at the University of Oregon, the Seattle Girls Club, members of a West Coast human potential development program, hearing-impaired persons, as well as physically and mentally handicapped young adults. "We are committed to the philosophy that Outward Bound experiences should be made available, with adaptations, to populations with special needs," Walsh says. In 1979 he appointed a full-time "special program" chief instructor, whose responsibilities include a continuing effort to refine the school's special program capability.

Walsh's directorship is marked by heavy emphasis on staff training opportunities. In addition to general staff orientation, the school has provided workshops and training experiences in communications, emergency medical care and technical rescue, backcountry medicine, prevention and handling of water accidents, avalanche safety, and skills training in climbing and mountaineering, white water river running, ski touring, ice climbing, and glacier travel. A strong service program centers on such environmental projects as trail construction and maintenance, erosion control and backcountry cleanup. Winter course students normally come indoors to do service in a local nursing home.

In 1980 *Gerald Golins* became the successor to Gary Templin as the director of the Colorado Outward Bound School. A Californian, Jerry graduated from Claremont Men's College in 1968. Two years later, following an uneasy year of teaching social studies in a suburban high school—uneasy because of his feeling that the school, and he, were not addressing the central concerns of many of the youngsters—he took a teachers' practicum at COBS. "I found a vehicle that made sense to me," he says. "It addressed the issues an adolescent needs to face. Who he is, how he gets along with his peers, his relationship to an adult role model. The connection between risk and safety. The meaning of compassion. I was enthralled. I said to myself, 'This is where the action is.' The following June I quit teaching."

Jerry enrolled at the University of Colorado's School of Education in a master's degree program with emphasis on outdoor education. In the dormitories at Boulder the university supported a student peer program. Discovering that the counselors felt inferior to their jobs, Golins undertook to do something about it as a graduate study project. With several others he organized a course for the counselors along OB lines. One of those favorably impressed was Joe Nold, who was intrigued by Jerry's analytical approach to course design for a special population.

After receiving his master's degree, Jerry instructed through the summer at COBS, but there were no permanent staff openings. By the spring of 1973 his situation was desperate. He was broke, unemployed, subsisting largely on OB tinned-food rejects. On a day when he was suffering from a severe cold and had no money to buy medicine, Nold called him in. Handing Golins a check, Joe informed him that he was being sent on a survey trip to find out all he could about Outward Bound and corrections.

Jerry ran with the ball. With that survey as a basis, he became COBS's corrections specialist. Soon he was involved as a negotiator in the strange world of state corrections bureaucracies, government service contracts, and federal grantsmanship. He negotiated a three-year contract with the state of Michigan, whereby COBS would set up and service a Michigan-based adaptive program called "Michigan Expeditions" for selected juvenile delinquents as an alternative to institutionalization and other lengthy placements. A similar contract followed for a program dubbed "Osage Expeditions" at the Missouri Intermediate Reformatory in Jefferson City.

Jerry read intensively and experimented with courses for delinquents. "The Michigan people were testing us," he recalls. "We did a course for a homogenous group of assaultive delinquent kids from some of the worst sections of Detroit that turned out pretty well and taught us a lot. We did another for delinquents from Lansing. When they went back, their social workers were so amazed at the positive changes that they asked how come. So we went to Lansing and put the social workers through a course that was a revelation to them. We did a pre-release course for Colorado adult offenders that had some really extraordinarily good results."

Golins feels the most significant thing about those courses was the adapting of elements of the standard course to the needs and capabilities of the delinquent student. "There is no standard format for delinquents. We said, let's not approach this course from the standpoint of activities, but in terms of process. If it makes sense, say, for delinquents to have a three-day solo, fine; if it doesn't, we won't run one."

In addition to the growing volume of corrections contract work, Jerry instructed teachers' practica and assisted Nold with other projects. He wrote "The Exploration of the Outward Bound Process" with Vic Walsh. When Nold resigned his COBS presidency in 1977, Golins handled much of the Project Center activity Joe had administered. In 1979 he won appointment as a Kennedy Fellow for a year of graduate study at Harvard. In the spring of that college year he learned that he was to be the new Colorado School director.

In 1971 Appalachian State University at Boone, North Carolina, began to give its summer-session students credit for taking an Outward Bound course at the North Carolina School—a first. Professor Keener Smathers, who had administrative charge, participated in a course himself and became a powerful convert. When a stream of inquiries generated by national publicity about the liaison between the university and NCOBS made him aware of a strong current of interest in outdoor adventure at the college level, he conceived of organizing a conference. In the fall of 1973 he wrote Hank Taft to solicit OBI's cooperation. Hank sent John Rhoades, program coordinator of OBI, to Boone, where he and Smathers worked up a plan for a "National Conference on Outdoor Pursuits in Higher Education." Rhoades undertook to line up the speakers and workshop leaders while Smathers assumed the on-site responsibilities of conference director. OBI also put its promotional machinery to work and, through the generosity of the Ingersoll-Rand Company, obtained funds to help defray costs. The conference took place at Boone in February 1974. Despite the short time that had been available for spreading the word, more than 200 attended, coming from as far away as Utah, Ontario, and Maine. For the most part they were a highly informal group, with the collective aspect of a mammoth backpack expedition. Not everyone could afford a room and bath in the university's handsome new $3 million Center for Continuing

Education. A considerable number of young college staffers and students crashed on floor space made available by their more fortunate peers.

Hank Taft gave the keynote address. The conference was a success; the zeal evidenced there left no doubt that Smathers' hunch had probed a movement waiting to spring into existence. Before the year was out a follow-up conference was held at Estes Park, Colorado, under the joint sponsorship of COBS and the University of Colorado's School of Education, with the former's Bob Godfrey as chief organizer. Billed as a "National Conference on Experiential Education," it had a considerably broadened participant appeal that included educators at all levels and representatives of youth and other social agencies. After the Estes Park meeting, Outward Bound continued to provide seed money, personnel, energy, and promotion for organizing subsequent conferences, but also sought to keep an ever-lower profile in anticipation of the annual ad hoc gathering eventually taking on an organizational life of its own. The 1975 conference was held at Minnesota's Mankato State College (now University). The head organizer was Alan Hale, who by then had joined the staff of Mankato's Center for Experiential and Alternative Education.

In 1976 Bob Pieh and his wife, Margueritta Kluensch, had the organizing responsibility for the "Fourth National Conference on Experiential Education" held at Queens University in Kingston, Ontario. It was through machinery set up at Kingston that there finally came a formal organization—the Association for Experiential Education. When the newly identified AEE convened at Asilomar, California, in 1977, it no longer thought of itself as a loose confederation of individuals and agencies mainly but not exclusively oriented to experiential education in the wilderness adventure-based mode. It was now avowedly an association of individuals, schools, and other agencies sharing comparable interests and similar visions in support of a variety of experience-based teaching and learning methodologies. With each new conference there was a diminution in the careless employment, understandably annoying to non-Outward Bounders, of "Outward Bound" as the generic term for the experiential. However, OB people continue to play important roles in the leadership. Dartmouth's Bob MacArthur is the current AEE president.

York: 'Brown? This is Hahn. I want to see you.' He made the Founding Day address the first year of the school." *

In 1969 Athenian contracted with the Northwest School to conduct a compulsory three-week course for the junior class before the regular school opening in the fall. About the compulsory feature Brown says, "There were few things at the school that we were that rigid about, but I felt strongly that the very people who needed it most were those who, if it were optional, would drop out." In time the school developed its own staff to conduct the course. Subsequently it introduced an optional enriched version running an entire six-week term and earning credits in science and humanities. This was just one of a number of steps taken at Athenian to provide field experience in support of classroom learning. Athenian was among the first to discover that an on-campus OB-type facility tends to become a valued experiential learning vehicle.

In 1970–71 Joe Schulze researched, and OBI published, his exploratory (and optimistic) monograph, "An Analysis of the Impact of Outward Bound on Twelve High Schools." At that time there were not so many more than twelve from which to choose. A few years later we were confident in boasting of at least three hundred adaptive programs spread across the country. Now the total is so large and ever-growing as to be uncountable. What once was a trickle of OB influence in the educational mainstream has swollen to a strong, steady current. Howard Greene, a leading educational consultant, has been a fascinated observer of the phenomenon.

"The manner in which the Outward Bound movement—labeled and unlabeled—has impacted the schools in recent years is simply extraordinary," Greene says. "Whereas even a half dozen years ago Outward Bound adaptive programs were more the exception than the rule, today it would be difficult to put together a list of schools that have not instituted some form of outdoor pursuit

---

* In 1966, on Hahn's eightieth birthday, eight European schools that have close ties to him and his educational ideas formed the "Round Square Conference," named after the distinctive building of that name at Gordonstoun, and invited the Athenian School to join. The Conference meets annually to share the member schools' successes and problems and to help keep alive the educational-humanitarian spirit of Gordonstoun's founder. Subsequently the Colorado Rocky Mountain School became the second American member.

activity as a highly acceptable, positive educational force. It's happening in both the independent and the public schools, and increasingly it's spreading downward from the senior to the junior high and the elementary levels. It is quite clear that Outward Bound is directly responsible for much of this, and that it is a principal catalyst in a movement that has considerable significance for education in the future."

How Jack Stevens would thrill to these observations of his vision come alive!

As Greene indicates, there have been enough OB adaptions at the elementary and junior high levels to assure that the idea also works for kids in those age brackets. What probably was the first of these—it remains a model for integrating classroom study with adventure-based learning—was Rafe Parker's Pioneers Program for seventh and eighth graders at the Fenn School in Concord, Massachusetts. Rafe was fresh from England and Africa in 1968, at the end of his first instructing season at Hurricane Island, when Peter Willauer and Fenn's headmaster David Edgar asked him to set up an OB adaption at the school.

Parker discovered that a wild tract near the school, known as the Estabrook Woods after one of Concord's earliest settlers, offered an ideal outdoor classroom. The area, which is rich in Concord history and has reverted to wilderness, is much alluded to in Thoreau's journal. ("Shall we call it the Estabrook Country? It would make a princely estate in Europe. Yet it is owned by farmers who live by the labor of their hands and do not esteem it much.") In addition to regular OB-type activities on school days, the students explored the Estabrook Woods on weekend overnights, as part of a classroom-related project that Rafe worked out with their English, math, history, and science teachers. He took the students to the Overlanders program at the Lyman School, to be instructed in rescue techniques by their incarcerated peers. ("Went to Lyman," Andy Cutler wrote in his journal. "The boys there taught us artificial respiration. They were nice guys. I expected them to be hoods, but they were nice guys.") Rafe involved them with the Fernald Institute, where they spent two afternoons a week helping retarded children. "This was perhaps the most significant thing we did," Rafe says, "because our students were used to a very set, very insular, very comfortable way of life. Being confronted with a kid of their own age who wasn't even toilet trained, didn't know how to tie his shoes or button up his coat, made them adjust. The experience pulled a tremendous amount out of them."

Parker ran the program for three years. A decade later he looked back: "I enjoyed every minute of it, would love to do it again. It was difficult. The hardest thing was selling the faculty. It's not that people were against it. If you're in an enlightened sort of setting with a good faculty, most of them will be enthusiastic about it. But the teachers are so strapped by the heavy requirements laid on them. The pressure is on them to railroad their students through to meet the various formal measurements; at the secondary level it climaxes with their SAT's and getting into a good college. The Pioneers kind of achievement doesn't get points in that league. They don't give points for meaningful experience and they don't give points for character growth."

They don't give points for the kind of education seventh grader Charles Denault summed up in his course impression: "I liked this course because it helps a person know himself and others. I also learned an awful lot on research and how to do it. I really enjoyed this course because I learned so much in an interesting way. I hated this course because of all the mistakes I made, for when snow got into my boots it melted to water and froze me or when I went skiing through the woods I got giant blisters, but those were all in the fun."

Bounders is a modified Outward Bound program for dyslexic youngsters at the Carroll School in Lincoln, Massachusetts. It was established in 1971 under the guidance of the Hurricane Island School (HIOBS), with instructor Mike "Strats" Stratton in charge. Headmaster Bill Adams * had observed the Stowe School's adaptive OB program while on the faculty there and saw OB as fitting eminently into the confidence-building structure that is one key to Carroll's success in helping students overcome their learning disabilities. A Bounder course runs for four weeks, after school plus weekend expeditions. Rocks I is rappelling off the school's third-story fire escape. The expeditions go as far afield as Hurricane Island, Dartmouth, and New Hampshire's Mt. Moosilauke.

We went with the Bounders from the school down through the woods, our feet growing cold in the inch carpeting of mid-November snow, to Sandy Pond. On this pond rather than on

* Now headmaster of Rutgers Preparatory School.

Walden, a Bounder informed us, Thoreau wanted to build his cabin but deemed it too far from Concord. The youngsters, ages nine to twelve, sat on rocks at the water's edge while Strats spoke briefly on the afternoon's topic, which was survival. He told them what Mike Jeneid said in his book, that in a survival situation you have to know how to take care of yourself first— otherwise you can't take care of anyone else. Then came the daily minutes of quiet, the silence broken only by bird cries from across the pond. Afterward they did the electric fence initiative test, and Strats took them off in the Bounders van for the afternoon's adventure.

There are Junior Bounders, Regular Bounders, Advanced Bounders, and Brossbounders (helpers). Their motto is, "Bounders —it can be wicked hard but wicked fun to bust your ass!" (One Bounder-made poster version reads, "Bounders can be wiked heard but wiked fun to bust your ssa!") "If," Bill Adams says, "you can float with your hands tied, climb to the top of the cliff, withstand the cold wind and water, keep rowing with blisters, rappel off Crow Hill, cook a meal in the rain, then you *can* better cope at home or in your classroom, where you *can* learn to read."

In 1973 Rick Medrick produced for COBS a survey of OB and the colleges.* "Pithy and to the point," critiqued Arnold Shore. "The logic of this little pamphlet is tight and its worth high." And so it is. Like Schulze in his study at the secondary school level, Rick did not then have a plethora of college programs to draw conclusions from. He selected seven—Prescott, Dartmouth, Colorado College, Wheaton, Boston University, Evergreen, and the University of North Carolina at Charlotte—for the variety of OB designs or services they utilized.

Colorado College, in conjunction with COBS, was employing Outward Bound courses for counselors in freshman dormitories, as a catalyst contributing to self-knowledge and decision-making ability, and prompting acquisition of new skills. Wheaton's Vanguard School was a pre-college course seeking to prepare freshmen for campus life, emphasizing personal development and enhancement of the ability to work with others in a Christian setting. A product of Gary Templin's influence on his alma

---

* "Outward Bound and Higher Education, A Rationale and Outline for College Development" by Frederick W. Medrick. Colorado Outward Bound School, Denver, Col., 1973.

mater and such of the college's broad-visioned physical educators as department head Harvey "Coach" Chrouse and Bud Williams, Vanguard remains among the finest of the college adaptions. BU's S.U.R.G.E. (Survival. Urgency. Recreation. Growth. Enthusiasm.) was a highly individualist college version of OB training created by Michael Jeneid, an Australian who had taught for ten years in OB schools around the world. The campus brochure for "Surge" courses promised students: ". . . What we will do is challenge you and take you far beyond your present understanding of how much you can take. In this way we may encourage you also to an understanding of how much you want out of life."

The program at new Evergreen State College in Olympia, Washington, reflected the strong influence of faculty member Willi Unsoeld. In the institution's first year, five of the ten academic programs experimented with outdoor programs as part of their course designs. Subsequently Willi shepherded a student-designed course in "Wilderness and Consciousness." He continued each year, until his tragic death, to encourage students to conceive a wilderness-oriented course with OB elements, to design the curriculum, and to participate. Evergreen also developed a fine outdoor pursuit activity under Pete Steilberg. The Venture Program of the University of North Carolina at Charlotte sought to establish an outdoor education program modeled after Outward Bound that could ultimately be run by staff within the college community.

The success of the 1974 conference on Outdoor Pursuits in Higher Education at Boone, wellspring of the Association of Experiential Education, was the tip-off that many college outdoor programs were primed to coalesce into a movement with experiential education ties. While OB was in considerable measure a catalyst for that coalescence, the college level developments essentially represent a merging of OB influences with others that had also generated outdoor pursuit activity in higher education, some of it long established. In 1976 a second higher education conference met at Ithaca, New York, with some thirty institutions represented. These and a number of others became the nucleus of the Higher Education SIG (special interest group) of the AEE.

Some of the ways in which OB has influenced college outdoor pursuit activity have been documented in the Prescott, Earlham, Dartmouth, and Wesleyan stories. Were there space, the documentation could be usefully expanded with other case histories. Examples include:

- Keene State College's Operation LIVE (Learning in Vigorous Environments) at Keene, New Hampshire. Under the dynamic directorship of Keith King, alumnus and instructor of Dartmouth Center (DOBC) courses, this program offers the student body a highly varied week-to-week program of OB-type activities, as well as a summer school curriculum in experiential learning. LIVE also sponsors a Living-Learning Term that includes an outdoor phase modeled on the standard OB course.
- Bob Pieh and Margueritta Kluensch's comprehensive offering of courses in outdoor, affective, and experiential education, Open Country Workshops, etc., as members of the Faculty of Education, Queens University, at Kingston, Ontario, much of it rooted in Bob's OB associations.
- Murray State University's Project Apollo in the western Kentucky TVA country that, under commission by the U.S. Office of Education and shepherded by Professor Bill Holt, has provided more than 2500 Upward Bound students and their teachers from schools in forty-two states and Puerto Rico with an OB-type course.
- Marin Adventures at Kentfield, California, established by the College of Marin. This community college, serving the Marin County area, offers a dazzling choice of activity-based environmental education activities for adults and families. Conceived and created by Dan Campbell in his COBS-sponsored Master of Experiential Education internship at the University of Colorado, and subsequently expanded in the five years or so that he acted as its coordinator, Marin Adventures is a splendid model for a year-round community recreational/educational curriculum, for people of all ages, utilizing nature and the outdoors in an extraordinary variety of ways. It serves more than three thousand people annually, operating "on the theory that direct experience is the best teacher and nature the best text," and in close coordination with the college's natural and physical sciences, social science, and physical education departments.
- The St. Louis story, where Project STREAM (St. Louis Regional Experiential Adventure Movement), that city's re-

markable Outward Bound spin-off servicing a metropolis-wide experiential education network on a multi-faceted, multi-level basis, integrates with a number of higher education institutions. These include St. Louis University, Webster College, Washington University, Augustana College, Florissant Valley Community College, and the University of Missouri at St. Louis. Tying into this network is the College School, an elementary school formerly a unit of Webster College, now independent, where director Peter Wilson and teacher Jan Phillips have developed a highly creative adventure-based curriculum that has its roots in their exposure to Outward Bound. Dr. Wilson and Ms. Phillips are in turn adjunct professors of experiential education in Webster College's graduate level teachers' program.

Bob Vander Wilt was dean of students at Mankato College (now University) in Minnesota when Ronald Barnes came there under commission to develop the educational plan for the proposed Minnesota Experimental City. Barnes's coming was an event for Vander Wilt because not many years before, when Bob was an undergraduate and varsity basketball player at Iowa State University, Barnes had been his associate dean of students and had deeply influenced the broadening of his horizons far beyond the perspectives of the basketball court and the athletic scholarship that had brought Vander Wilt to the campus. Barnes meanwhile had served a period as vice president of Prescott College and had come away with enthusiasm for its OB-derived outdoor program and its freshman orientation, in which he had participated.

"I had heard Ron on the subject several times," Vander Wilt remembers, "when one day I thought, how come we aren't doing anything with Outward Bound when we have a school right here in the state with headquarters an hour and a half up the road." He put in a call to the Minnesota School and made contact with Dyke Williams. The first fruit of that telephone encounter, with strong encouragement from MOBS director Alan Hale, was an experimental three-week orientation course run by MOBS at the start of the 1970–71 year for twenty students, two faculty members, and two residential advisers involved in Mankato's Experimental Studies program. That experiment was rated a success. The critical happening was its influence on Dr. Charles Lofy, who headed up Experimental Studies.

Chuck Lofy, a former Jesuit priest, says that his awareness of the potent role played by experience in the education and motivation of St. Ignatius Loyola, founder of the Society of Jesus, predisposed his response to Outward Bound. At the end of the orientation course, while the students were on solo, Lofy and five members of his staff went up to Homeplace, the base camp of Minnesota Outward Bound, for a three-day mini-course led by Dyke and his wife Kathy. Lofy calls it one of the peak experiences of his life. "Our staff got to know each other better in those three days than in my judgment we would have in two years. We had as much as a two-hour debriefing for every experience. Roles fell away."

Visiting with the Williamses on one of the evenings at Homeplace, Chuck was excited by what Dyke told him about Kurt Hahn and the philosophical roots of OB. "Dyke helped me to comprehend a process involving a lot more than the outdoor skills. What I got was the concept of a group subjected to stress, real stress, existential stress, wherein the roles begin to fall away. People's personalities emerge, their strengths and their weaknesses. Then you debrief them, and in the process you develop a training of the will. I thought, holy cow, that's the neatest thing I've heard in education as long as I've been in education!"

Out of Lofy and Vander Wilt's enthusiasm came a proposal for a graduate program offering a master of science degree in "Studies in Experiential Education." OBI was sufficiently persuaded by the proposal, and by Hale's advocacy, to make a grant of $10,000 from the DeWitt Wallace Fund, a trust newly created by a second million-dollar gift from Mr. Wallace, the income designated for new programs of national significance.

Launched in 1971, Mankato's Experiential Studies, the first graduate program of its kind, has proved a valuable source of leadership for the experiential education movement. In addition to its master's program, Mankato operates a training center for outdoor educators at Bemidji State University's Bald Eagle Center.

In a paper entitled "Growth and Crisis in a Developing Organization: Outward Bound" that he published in 1976, Joe Nold presented a model for the organizational development of an OB-type undertaking. Explaining why he believed such a model was needed, Joe pointed out that of nine OB adaptive programs launched with promise and enthusiasm in the late 1960's, only two had survived—despite having been run by dedicated, energetic, and competent people, and even though they had been effective. Most of the failures, he observed, had resulted not from poor programs but rather from poor management.

Nold realized that "we simply had not come to grips with the whole infrastructure of rooting an adaptive program. What was lacking were people with organization and administrative and political skills and a commitment to stabilize and institutionalize essentially sound programs." OB itself had a vacuum in middle-management areas that made it difficult, for example, to fill a program director post. Nold had asked himself if there was a way to develop "a group of people with leadership ability who had not only the philosophic, emotional, educational commitments that we all identify with so very deeply and fully and readily in Outward Bound, but also could make a commitment to go beyond that —to deal with the hard nuts-and-bolts issues that are really essential to the success of any of these programs over any but the shortest of time frames." This had been Joe's motivation for the Master of Education in the Experiential Education Degree program jointly established by COBS and the School of Education at the University of Colorado at Boulder in 1973.

The program was launched with a grant from the General Services Foundation in St. Paul, to develop a leadership cadre "in the new professional area of education we have come to call experiential education," with focus primarily on those who would translate and transfer the ideas and concepts of Outward Bound into other institutional settings. Enrollment was limited to twelve candidates. Each year there were more than fifty applicants, making this the most sought after of the School of Education's graduate programs. Richard "Rocky" Kimball, who got his M.E. by this route and who continued to monitor the program as a doctoral candidate, wrote in 1977: "Each year the experiential ed group at C.U. is the most interesting, diverse, and exciting in the School of Education."

As it ultimately evolved, the Colorado M.E. curriculum started with an outdoor-based summer that included an OB-instructing internship and a mountain expedition seminar. In the fall the candidates combined an urban intercultural experience, "The City as Classroom," with formal on-campus studies, including Nold's core course in organization and planning. For the spring semester candidates were given the option of a field internship or an academic inquiry. Both as interns and graduates, the M.E. members initiated successful OB-adaptive projects in colleges, secondary schools, state and community programs for disadvantaged and delinquent youth, residential treatment centers for young offenders, and adventure-centered schools. Others took upper-management positions in such national experiential education organizations as IDEAS and Earthwatch. A number continued graduate study at the doctoral level.

The success of the M.E. program was persuasive to several members of the School of Education faculty who were associated with it and took an increasing interest in experiential education as a challenging subject area for graduate study. Aware that many well-qualified applicants were being turned down each year due only to the strict enrollment limit, the group initiated a School of Education version separate from the Outward Bound label and co-sponsorship, starting with the 1977–78 year. For a year the two versions co-existed and in some measure cross-fertilized each other.

Only the university program is now extant. With the phasing out of his successful experiment, Nold could look back with a satisfied sense of achievement: "We've given people deeper insights into the philosophic and sociological underpinnings of Outward Bound. We arrived at a fairly systematic way of how the adaptive art can be applied within institutions that were not initially set up to run programs of an Outward Bound nature. I think we've legitimized management as a worthy profession in Outward Bound—and that's been a problem in that we're highly adventurous and action-oriented and see being at a desk as an inferior way to fulfill one's life commitment. I think we broke through that syndrome."

The foregoing once-over-lightly documentation gives some sense of how palpably Outward Bound is making its influence felt in the educational mainstream, from the elementary grades to the Ph.D. levels of our graduate schools. But the Outreach story reaches well beyond the educational community, as the list of the Association for Experiential Education's special interest groups attests.

In a 1978 survey article in *Corrections Magazine* * staff writer Kevin Krajick reported that "rugged two or three week wilderness

* "Working Our Way Home" by Kevin Krajick, *Corrections Magazine*, June 1978, p. 33.

trips have been added to the battery of correctional programs in more than twenty states in the past few years." It was estimated there were one hundred and fifty to two hundred such programs for juvenile offenders in the country, up from ten or fifteen five years before. "Virtually all of the wilderness courses for juvenile offenders," Krajick noted, "are run by or modeled to some extent on those offered by Outward Bound."

When Jerry Golins first talked with the Michigan Department of Social Services about the idea of an OB-type program for young delinquents in the state—the seed of what was to become Michigan Expeditions—he told them, "If you really want this to work, what you have to do is do it yourself and do it here. We'll help you. I guarantee you will get as good results as you do with traditional methods, and there will be tremendous cost savings." That remains a good conservative selling pitch for the wilderness expedition idea. The picture has changed, however, since 1973. It may no longer be necessary to sell the idea at all; corrections officials now frequently seek out persons able to provide them with this kind of program or to help their agencies set up an internal competence. A key reason for this is that the short-term, OB-type treatment has, with fair consistency, shown a superiority to traditional treatments in terms of recidivism.

A representative case is that of Project STEP (Short Term Elective Program), a modified OB program funded by the state of Florida and operated by the Hurricane Island School since 1975. Continued funding is dependent on a 60 percent success rate—that is, 60 percent of the youths who complete the course must remain free of conviction for six months. Over a five and one-half year period since its inception, with the exception of one six-month period, STEP has enjoyed a better than 70 percent success rate, compared to 60 to 65 percent for youths who go the traditional, and longer, training-school route. In a special twelve-month study the success rate was 72 percent. While the reliability of recidivism figures as a measure of effectiveness is often questioned by those who conduct wilderness programs for corrective treatment purposes, recidivism is of significance to the corrections official. In simple monetary terms the recidivist is a costly failure, since the youth returns to expensive commitment programs.

Arnold Shore, in his 1977 review of research relative to Outward Bound, was critical of much of it that dealt with corrections. He did, however, find the recidivism data generally reliable:

Study results on the effect of Outward Bound on recidivism seem generally consistent. That is, Outward Bound has been shown to reduce the rate of recidivism among youthful offenders. Even after making allowances for methodological flaws, Outward Bound seems worthy of the label "strong stimulus," to employ a term used among methodologists. Whether or not this strength generalizes to other desired outcomes may be problematic; however, concerning the effects of Outward Bound on recidivism, positive evidence seems to be mounting, though it is by no means conclusive.*

There is much in this highly difficult sector of the Outward Bound movement that remains problematic. The need for follow-up (not all practitioners will grant the need) and for ways and means to help the street returnee to hold on to and benefit from the values he has gained from his course is an ever-recurring concern. (Some programs are doing follow-up, and some are doing it better than others.) Sound instructor training in the special skills needed for work with delinquents, and maintaining a quality instructor cadre in the face of low pay, the "burn-out syndrome," and the tendency of many instructors to move elsewhere are likewise common problems. So are the needs for valid means of measuring course effectiveness and for solid research to plumb a host of unknowns. All these needs are well-recognized concerns within AEE's "Adventure Activities in Corrections, Mental Health, and Special Education" community. In the light of this recognition, and of how fast the community has grown and how far it has come in so short a time, it is not unrealistic to anticipate substantial progress in the decade ahead.

Such hopes apply equally to those members of the community whose areas of interest are mental health and special education, just as they apply to those committed to handicapped programming. These areas of concern are likewise important sectors of the Outward Bound movement. There may be special significance in the fact that Outward Bound is becoming increasingly concerned with the well-being of persons who have been visited with misfortunes that the more fortunate among us have escaped. This appears to confirm something that Kurt Hahn seems always to have known: that there is a force inherent in the Outward Bound dynamic that generates compassion.

* *Outward Bound: A Reference Volume*, compiled by Arnold Shore, February 1977, p. 53.

Acknowledgments

Many good people had a part in the writing of this book. A lot of them contributed invaluably by sharing their reminiscences of, experience in, knowledge of, and reflection on the Outward Bound movement. We are greatly indebted to them, for without their collaboration our story of the movement could not be as full, as accurate, as rich in substance as we have tried to make it.

Phillips Academy has been very much a part of this project from the beginning in encouraging the pursuit of Kurt Hahn's ideas at Andover and in granting leaves of absence for six years while U.S. Outward Bound was getting under way.

Thanks to Phebe Miner's powers of recall and her willingness to share personal letters, the Gordonstoun experiences were relatively easy to remember and verify.

Gwen Goodwin was most patient with the added time and energy that research took from her already overloaded schedule.

We are most grateful to the Exxon Foundation and to the Lilly Endowment for generous grants that underwrote costs of travel and research and writing time, and to *Reader's Digest* for its generous financial assistance supporting latter stages of the writing task.

382 / OUTWARD BOUND U.S.A.

In the course of two research trips across the country, many persons provided hospitality, kindness, and assistance that remain the stuff of grateful memory.

Deborah Boldt made an invaluable contribution in reading and commenting on the manuscript as it developed. Her comments and counsel were a consistent source of leavening good sense and sturdy encouragement. Special thanks are also due Marie and Bob Perry, Gussie and Art Graham, Elinor Ehrman, Elsie Anjiras, and Lois Porro.

Nor have we yet called the full roll. In this project about which so many have cared, thanks are owed to a marvelous multitude of family, colleagues, and friends.

J. L. M. and J. B.

Index

Mr Tompkins in Paperback

by

G. GAMOW, 1904-

Illustrated by the author and

John Hookham

CAMBRIDGE

AT THE UNIVERSITY PRESS

1967

PUBLISHED BY
THE SYNDICS OF THE CAMBRIDGE UNIVERSITY PRESS

Bentley House, 200 Euston Road, London, N.W. 1
American Branch: 32 East 57th Street, New York, N.Y. 10022
West African Office: P.O. Box 33, Ibadan, Nigeria

Mr Tompkins in Wonderland
First published 1940
Mr Tompkins explores the Atom
First published 1945

This Edition
©

CAMBRIDGE UNIVERSITY PRESS
1965

Reprinted, with corrections 1967

Printed in the United States of America

*Library of Congress Catalogue
Card Number: 65-20791*

To my friend and editor
RONALD MANSBRIDGE

Preface

In the winter of 1938 I wrote a short, scientifically fantastic story (not a science fiction story) in which I tried to explain to the layman the basic ideas of the theory of curvature of space and the expanding universe. I decided to do this by exaggerating the actually existing relativistic phenomena to such an extent that they could easily be observed by the hero of the story, C. G. H.* Tompkins, a bank clerk interested in modern science.

I sent the manuscript to *Harper's Magazine* and, like all beginning authors, got it back with a rejection slip. The other half-a-dozen magazines which I tried followed suit. So I put the manuscript in a drawer of my desk and forgot about it. During the summer of the same year, I attended the International Conference of Theoretical Physics, organized by the League of Nations in Warsaw. I was chatting over a glass of excellent Polish miod with my old friend Sir Charles Darwin, the grandson of Charles (*The Origin of Species*) Darwin, and the conversation turned to the popularization of science. I told Darwin about the bad luck I had had along this line, and he said: 'Look, Gamow, when you get back to the United States dig up your manuscript and send it to Dr C. P. Snow, who is the editor of a popular scientific magazine *Discovery* published by the Cambridge University Press.'

So I did just this, and a week later came a telegram from Snow saying: 'Your article will be published in the next issue. Please send more.' Thus a number of stories on Mr Tompkins, which popularized the theory of relativity and the quantum theory,

* The initials of Mr Tompkins originated from three fundamental physical constants: the velocity of light c; the gravitational constant G; and the quantum constant h, which have to be changed by immensely large factors in order to make their effect easily noticeable by the man on the street.

appeared in subsequent issues of *Discovery*. Soon thereafter I received a letter from the Cambridge University Press, suggesting that these articles, with a few additional stories to increase the number of pages, should be published in book form. The book, called *Mr Tompkins in Wonderland*, was published by Cambridge University Press in 1940 and since that time has been reprinted sixteen times. This book was followed by the sequel, *Mr Tompkins Explores the Atom*, published in 1944 and by now reprinted nine times. In addition, both books have been translated into practically all European languages (except Russian), and also into Chinese and Hindi.

Recently the Cambridge University Press decided to unite the two original volumes into a single paperback edition, asking me to update the old material and add some more stories treating the advances in physics and related fields which took place after these books were originally published. Thus I had to add the stories on fission and fusion, the steady state universe, and exciting problems concerning elementary particles. This material forms the present book.

A few words must be said about the illustrations. The original articles in *Discovery* and the first original volume were illustrated by Mr John Hookham, who created the facial features of Mr Tompkins. When I wrote the second volume, Mr Hookham had retired from work as an illustrator, and I decided to illustrate the book myself, faithfully following Hookham's style. The new illustrations in the present volume are also mine. The verses and songs appearing in this volume are written by my wife Barbara.

G. GAMOW

University of Colorado,
Boulder, Colorado, U.S.A.

pp. 1-94 "Mr. Tompkins in Wonderland"

Contents

Acknowledgements

Thanks are due to the following for permission to reproduce copyright material: to Edward B. Marks Music Corporation for the settings of *O come, all ye Faithful* ('O Atome prreemorrdial', p. 57) and *Rule, Britannia* ('The Universe, by heavn's decree', p. 60) from *Time to Sing*; and to the Macmillan Company for figure A on p. 144 from *The Crystalline State*, by Sir W. H. Bragg and W. L. Bragg.

Introduction

From early childhood onwards we grow accustomed to the surrounding world as we perceive it through our five senses; in this
stage of mental development the fundamental notions of space,
time and motion are formed. Our mind soon becomes so accustomed to these notions that later on we are inclined to believe that
our concept of the outside world based on them is the only possible
one, and any idea of changing them seems paradoxical to us. However, the development of exact physical methods of observation
and the profounder analysis of observed relations have brought
modern science to the definite conclusion that this 'classical'
foundation fails completely when used for the detailed description of phenomena ordinarily inaccessible to our everyday observation, and that, for the correct and consistent description of our
new refined experience, some change in the fundamental concepts
of space, time, and motion is absolutely necessary.

The deviations between the common notions and those introduced by modern physics are, however, negligibly small so far as
the experience of ordinary life is concerned. If, however, we
imagine other worlds, with the same physical laws as those of our
own world, but with different numerical values for the physical
constants determining the limits of applicability of the old concepts, the new and correct concepts of space, time and motion, at
which modern science arrives only after very long and elaborate
investigations, would become a matter of common knowledge.
We may say that even a primitive savage in such a world would be
acquainted with the principles of relativity and quantum theory,
and would use them for his hunting purposes and everyday needs.

The hero of the present stories is transferred, in his dreams,
into several worlds of this type, where the phenomena, usually

inaccessible to our ordinary senses, are so strongly exaggerated that they could easily be observed as the events of ordinary life. He was helped in his fantastic but scientifically correct dream by an old professor of physics (whose daughter, Maud, he eventually married) who explained to him in simple language the unusual events which he observed in the world of relativity, cosmology, quantum, atomic and nuclear structure, elementary particles, etc.

It is hoped that the unusual experiences of Mr Tompkins will help the interested reader to form a clearer picture of the actual physical world in which we are living.

I

City Speed Limit

It was a bank holiday, and Mr Tompkins, the little clerk of a big city bank, slept late and had a leisurely breakfast. Trying to plan his day, he first thought about going to some afternoon movie and, opening the morning paper, turned to the entertainment page. But none of the films looked attractive to him. He detested all this Hollywood stuff, with infinite romances between popular stars.

All this Hollywood stuff!

If only there were at least one film with some real adventure, with something unusual and maybe even fantastic about it. But there was none. Unexpectedly, his eye fell on a little notice in the corner of the page. The local university was announcing a series of lectures on the problems of modern physics, and this after-noon's lecture was to be about EINSTEIN's Theory of Relativity. Well, that might be something! He had often heard the statement that only a dozen people in the world really understood Einstein's theory. Maybe he could become the thirteenth! Surely he would go to the lecture; it might be just what he needed.

He arrived at the big university auditorium after the lecture had begun. The room was full of students, mostly young, listening with keen attention to the tall, white-bearded man near the blackboard who was trying to explain to his audience the basic ideas of the Theory of Relativity. But Mr Tompkins got only as far as understanding that the whole point of Einstein's theory is that there is a maximum velocity, the velocity of light, which cannot be surpassed by any moving material body, and that this fact leads to very strange and unusual consequences. The professor stated, however, that as the velocity of light is 186,000 miles per second, the relativity effects could hardly be observed for events of ordinary life. But the nature of these unusual effects was really much more difficult to understand, and it seemed to Mr Tompkins that all this was contradictory to common sense. He was trying to imagine the contraction of measuring rods and the odd behaviour of clocks—effects which should be expected if they move with a velocity close to that of light—when his head slowly dropped on his shoulder.

When he opened his eyes again, he found himself sitting not on a lecture room bench but on one of the benches installed by the city for the convenience of passengers waiting for a bus. It was a beautiful old city with medieval college buildings lining the street. He suspected that he must be dreaming but to his surprise there was nothing unusual happening around him; even a policeman standing on the opposite corner looked as policemen usually do. The hands of the big clock on the tower down the street were pointing to five o'clock and the streets were nearly empty. A single cyclist was coming slowly down the street and, as he approached, Mr Tompkins's eyes opened wide with astonishment. For the bicycle and the young man on it were unbelievably shortened in the direction of the motion, as if seen through a cylindrical lens. The clock on the tower struck five, and the cyclist, evidently in a hurry, stepped harder on the pedals. Mr Tompkins did not notice that he gained much in speed, but, as

Unbelievably shortened

the result of his effort, he shortened still more and went down the street looking exactly like a picture cut out of cardboard. Then Mr Tompkins felt very proud because he could understand what was happening to the cyclist—it was simply the contraction of moving bodies, about which he had just heard. 'Evidently nature's

3

speed limit is lower here,' he concluded, 'that is why the bobby on the corner looks so lazy, he need not watch for speeders.' In fact, a taxi moving along the street at the moment and making all the noise in the world could not do much better than the cyclist, and was just crawling along. Mr Tompkins decided to overtake the cyclist, who looked a good sort of fellow, and ask him all about it. Making sure that the policeman was looking the other way, he borrowed somebody's bicycle standing near the kerb and sped

The city blocks became still shorter

down the street. He expected that he would be immediately shortened, and was very happy about it as his increasing figure had lately caused him some anxiety. To his great surprise, however, nothing happened to him or to his cycle. On the other hand, the picture around him completely changed. The streets grew shorter, the windows of the shops began to look like narrow slits, and the policeman on the corner became the thinnest man he had ever seen.

'By Jove!' exclaimed Mr Tompkins excitedly, 'I see the trick now. This is where the word *relativity* comes in. Everything that

4

moves relative to me looks shorter for me, whoever works the pedals!' He was a good cyclist and was doing his best to overtake the young man. But he found that it was not at all easy to get up speed on this bicycle. Although he was working on the pedals as hard as he possibly could, the increase in speed was almost negligible. His legs already began to ache, but still he could not manage to pass a lamp-post on the corner much faster than when he had just started. It looked as if all his efforts to move faster were leading to no result. He understood now very well why the cyclist and the cab he had just met could not do any better, and he remembered the words of the professor about the impossibility of surpassing the limiting velocity of light. He noticed, however, that the city blocks became still shorter and the cyclist riding ahead of him did not now look so far away. He overtook the cyclist at the second turning, and when they had been riding side by side for a moment, was surprised to see the cyclist was actually quite a normal, sporting-looking young man. 'Oh, that must be because we do not move relative to each other,' he concluded; and he addressed the young man.

'Excuse me, sir!' he said, 'Don't you find it inconvenient to live in a city with such a slow speed limit?'

'Speed limit?' returned the other in surprise, 'we don't have any speed limit here. I can get anywhere as fast as I wish, or at least I could if I had a motor-cycle instead of this nothing-to-be-done-with old bike!'

'But you were moving very slowly when you passed me a moment ago,' said Mr Tompkins. 'I noticed you particularly.'

'Oh you did, did you?' said the young man, evidently offended. 'I suppose you haven't noticed that since you first addressed me we have passed five blocks. Isn't that fast enough for you?'

'But the streets became so short,' argued Mr Tompkins.

'What difference does it make anyway, whether we move faster or whether the street becomes shorter? I have to go ten blocks to get to the post office, and if I step harder on the pedals the blocks become shorter and I get there quicker. In fact, here we are,' said the young man getting off his bike.

Mr Tompkins looked at the post office clock, which showed half-past five. 'Well!' he remarked triumphantly, 'it took you half an hour to go this ten blocks, anyhow—when I saw you first it was exactly five!'

'And did you *notice* this half hour?' asked his companion. Mr Tompkins had to agree that it had really seemed to him only a few minutes. Moreover, looking at his wrist watch he saw it was showing only five minutes past five. 'Oh!' he said, 'is the post office clock fast?' 'Of course it is, or your watch is too slow, just because you have been going too fast. What's the matter with you, anyway? Did you fall down from the moon?' and the young man went into the post office.

After this conversation, Mr Tompkins realized how unfortunate it was that the old professor was not at hand to explain all these strange events to him. The young man was evidently a native, and had been accustomed to this state of things even before he had learned to walk. So Mr Tompkins was forced to explore this strange world by himself. He put his watch right by the post office clock, and to make sure that it went all right waited for ten minutes. His watch did not lose. Continuing his journey down the street he finally saw the railway station and decided to check his watch again. To his surprise it was again quite a bit slow. 'Well, this must be some relativity effect, too,' concluded Mr Tompkins; and decided to ask about it from somebody more intelligent than the young cyclist.

The opportunity came very soon. A gentleman obviously in his forties got out of the train and began to move towards the exit. He was met by a very old lady, who, to Mr Tompkins's great surprise, addressed him as 'dear Grandfather'. This was too much for Mr Tompkins. Under the excuse of helping with the luggage, he started a conversation.

'Excuse me, if I am intruding into your family affairs,' said he, 'but are you really the grandfather of this nice old lady? You see, I am a stranger here, and I never. . . .' 'Oh, I see,' said the gentleman, smiling with his moustache. 'I suppose you are taking me for the Wandering Jew or something. But the thing is really quite simple. My business requires me to travel quite a lot, and, as I spend most of my life in the train, I naturally grow old much more slowly than my relatives living in the city. I am so glad that I came back in time to see my dear little grand-daughter still alive! But excuse me, please, I have to attend to her in the taxi,' and he hurried away leaving Mr Tompkins alone again with his problems. A couple of sandwiches from the station buffet somewhat strengthened his mental ability, and he even went so far as to claim that he had found the contradiction in the famous principle of relativity.

'Yes, of course,' thought he, sipping his coffee, 'if all were relative, the traveller would appear to his relatives as a very old man, and they would appear very old to him, although both sides might in fact be fairly young. But what I am saying now is definitely nonsense: One could not have relative grey hair!' So he decided to make a last attempt to find out how things really are, and turned to a solitary man in railway uniform sitting in the buffet.

'Will you be so kind, sir,' he began, 'will you be good enough to tell me who is responsible for the fact that the passengers in the train grow old so much more slowly than the people staying at one place?'

'I am responsible for it,' said the man, very simply.

'Oh!' exclaimed Mr Tompkins. 'So you have solved the problem of the Philosopher's Stone of the ancient alchemists. You should be quite a famous man in the medical world. Do you occupy the chair of medicine here?'

'No,' answered the man, being quite taken aback by this, 'I am just a brakeman on this railway.'

'Brakeman! You mean a brakeman...,' exclaimed Mr Tompkins, losing all the ground under him. 'You mean you—just put the brakes on when the train comes to the station?'

'Yes, that's what I do: and every time the train gets slowed down, the passengers gain in their age relative to other people. Of course,' he added modestly, 'the engine driver who accelerates the train also does his part in the job.'

'But what has it to do with staying young?' asked Mr Tompkins in great surprise.

'Well, I don't know exactly,' said the brakeman, 'but it is so. When I asked a university professor travelling in my train once, how it comes about, he started a very long and incomprehensible speech about it, and finally said that it is something similar to 'gravitation redshift—I think he called it—on the sun. Have you heard anything about such things as redshifts?'

'No-o,' said Mr Tompkins, a little doubtfully; and the brakeman went away shaking his head.

Suddenly a heavy hand shook his shoulder, and Mr Tompkins found himself sitting not in the station café but in the chair of the auditorium in which he had been listening to the professor's lecture. The lights were dimmed and the room was empty. The janitor who wakened him said: 'We are closing up, Sir; if you want to sleep, better go home.' Mr Tompkins got to his feet and started toward the exit.

2

The Professor's Lecture on Relativity which caused Mr Tompkins's dream

Ladies and Gentlemen:

In a very primitive stage of development the human mind formed definite notions of space and time as the frame in which different events take place. These notions, without essential changes, have been carried forward from generation to generation, and, since the development of exact sciences, have been built into the foundations of the mathematical description of the universe. The great NEWTON perhaps gave the first clear-cut formulation of the classical notions of space and time, writing in his *Principia*:

'Absolute space, in its own nature, without relation to anything external, remains always similar and immovable;' and 'Absolute, true and mathematical time, of itself, and from its own nature, flows equably without relation to anything external.'

So strong was the belief in the absolute correctness of these classical ideas about space and time that they have often been held by philosophers as given *a priori*, and no scientist even thought about the possibility of doubting them.

However, just at the start of the present century it became clear that a number of results, obtained by most refined methods of experimental physics, led to clear contradictions if interpreted in the classical frame of space and time. This fact brought to one of the greatest contemporary physicists, ALBERT EINSTEIN, the revolutionary idea that there are hardly any reasons, except those of tradition, for considering the classical notions concerning space and time as absolutely true, and that they could and should be changed to fit our new and more refined experience. In fact, since the classical notions of space and time were formulated on the basis of human experience in ordinary life, we need not be surprised that the refined methods of observation of today, based on highly developed experimental technique, indicate that these old notions are too rough and inexact, and could have been used in ordinary life and in the earlier stages of development of physics only because their deviations from the correct notions were sufficiently small. Nor need we be surprised that the broadening of the field of exploration of modern science should bring us to regions where these deviations become so very large that the classical notions could not be used at all.

The most important experimental result which led to the fundamental criticism of our classical notions was *the discovery of the fact that the velocity of light in a vacuum represents the upper limit for all possible physical velocities.* This important and unexpected conclusion resulted mainly from the experiments of the American physicist, MICHELSON, who, at the end of last century, tried to observe the effect of the motion of the earth on the velocity of propagation of light and, to his great surprise and the surprise of all the scientific world, found that no such effect exists and that the velocity of light in a vacuum comes out always exactly the same independent of the system from which it is measured or the motion of the source from which it is emitted. There is no need to explain that such a result is extremely unusual and contradicts our most fundamental concepts concerning motion. In fact, if something is moving fast through space and you yourself move so as to meet it, the moving object will strike you with greater relative velocity, equal to the sum of velocity of the object and the observer. On the other hand, if you run away from it, it will hit you from behind with smaller velocity, equal to the difference of the two velocities.

Also, if you move, say in a car, to meet the sound propagating through the air, the velocity of the sound as measured in the car will be larger by the amount of your driving speed, or it will be correspondingly small if the sound is overtaking you. We call it the *theorem of addition of velocities* and it was always held to be self-evident.

However, the most careful experiments have shown that, in the case of light, it is no longer true, the velocity of light in a vacuum remaining always the same and equal to 300,000 km per second (we usually denote it by the symbol c), independent of how fast the observer himself is moving.

'Yes,' you will say, 'but is it not possible to construct a super-light velocity by adding several smaller velocities which can be physically attained?'

For example, we could consider a very fast-moving train, say, with three quarters the velocity of light and a tramp running along the roofs of the carriages also with three-quarters of the velocity of light.

According to the theorem of addition the total velocity should be one and a half times that of light, and the running tramp should be able to overtake the beam of light from a signal lamp. The truth, however, is that, since the constancy of the velocity of light is an experimental fact, the resulting velocity in our case must be smaller than we expect—it cannot surpass the critical value c; and thus we come to the conclusion that, for smaller velocities also, the classical theorem of addition must be wrong.

The mathematical treatment of the problem, into which I do not want to enter here, leads to a very simple new formula for the calculation of the resulting velocity of two superimposed motions.

If v_1 and v_2 are the two velocities to be added, the resulting velocity comes out to be

$$V = \frac{v_1 \pm v_2}{1 \pm \dfrac{v_1 v_2}{c^2}}. \tag{1}$$

You see from this formula that if both original velocities were small, I mean small as compared with the velocity of light, the second term in the denominator of (1) can be neglected as compared with unity and you have the classical theorem of addition of velocities. If, however, v_1 and v_2 are not small the result will be always somewhat smaller than the arithmetical sum. For instance, in the example of our tramp running along a train, $v_1 = \frac{3}{4}c$ and $v_2 = \frac{3}{4}c$, and our formula gives for the resulting velocity $V = \frac{24}{25}c$, which is still smaller than the velocity of light.

In a particular case, when one of the original velocities is c, formula (1) gives c for the resulting velocity independent of what the second velocity may be. Thus, by overlapping any number of velocities, we can never surpass the velocity of light.

You might also be interested to know that this formula has been proved experimentally and it was really found that the resultant of two velocities is always somewhat smaller than their arithmetical sum.

Recognizing the existence of the upper-limit velocity we can start on the criticism of the classical ideas of space and time, directing our first blow against the notion of *simultaneousness* based upon them.

When you say, 'The explosion in the mines near Capetown happened at exactly the same moment as the ham and eggs were being served in your London apartment,' you think you know what you mean. I am going to show you, however, that you do not, and that, strictly speaking, this statement has no exact meaning. In fact, what method would you use to check whether two events in two different places are simultaneous or not? You would say that the clock at both places would show the same time; but then the question arises how to set the distant clocks so that they would show the same time simultaneously, and we are back at the original question.

Since the independence of the velocity of light in a vacuum on the motion of its source or the system in which it is measured is one of the most exactly established experimental facts, the following method of measuring the distances and setting the clock correctly on different observational stations should be recognized as the most rational and, as you will agree after thinking more about it, the only reasonable method.

A light signal is sent from the station A, and as soon as it is received at the station B it is returned back to A. One-half of the time, as read at station A, between the sending and the return of the signal, multiplied by the constant velocity of light, will be defined as the distance between A and B.

The clocks on stations A and B are said to be set correctly if at the moment of arrival of the signal at B the local clock were showing just the average of two times recorded at A at the moments of sending and receiving the signal. Using this method

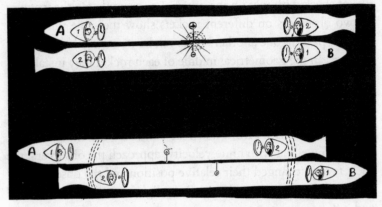

Two long platforms moving in opposite directions

between different observational stations established on a rigid body we arrive finally at the desired frame of reference, and can answer questions concerning the simultaneousness or time interval between two events in different places.

But will these results be recognized by observers on the other systems? To answer this question, let us suppose that such frames of reference have been established on two different rigid bodies, say on two long space rockets moving with a constant speed in opposite directions, and let us now see how these two frames will check with one another. Suppose four observers are located on the front- and the rear-ends of each rocket and want first of all to set their clocks correctly. Each pair of observers can use on their rockets the modification of the above-mentioned method by sending a light signal from the middle of the rocket (as measured by measuring-stick) and setting zero point on their watches when the signal, coming from the middle of the rocket, arrives at each end of it. Thus, each pair of our observers has established, according to previous definition, the criterion of simultaneousness in their own system and have set their watches 'correctly' from their point of view, of course.

Now they decide to see whether the time readings on their rocket check with that on the other. For example, do the watches of two observers on different rockets show the same time when they are passing one another? This can be tested by the following method: In the geometrical middle of each rocket they install two electrically charged conductors, in such a way that, when the rockets pass each other, a spark jumps between the conductors, and light signals start simultaneously from the centre of each platform towards its front and rear ends. By the time the light signals, travelling with finite velocity, approach the observers, the rockets have changed their relative position and the observers $2A$ and $2B$ will be closer to the source of light than the observers $1A$ and $1B$.

It is clear that when the light signal reaches the observer $2A$, the observer $1B$ will be farther behind, so that the signal will take some additional time to reach him. Thus, if the watch of $1B$ is set in such a way as to show zero time at the arrival of the signal, the observer $2A$ will insist that it is behind the correct time.

In the same way another observer, $1A$, will come to the conclusion that the watch of $2B$, who met the signal before him, is ahead of time. Since, according to their definition of simultaneousness, their own watches are set correctly, the observers on rocket A will agree that there is a difference between the watches of the observers on rocket B. We should not, however, forget that the observers on rocket B, for exactly the same reasons, will consider their own watches as set correctly but will claim that a difference of setting exists between the watches on rocket *A*.

Since both rockets are quite equivalent, this quarrel between the two groups of observers can be settled only by saying that both groups are correct from their own point of view, but that the question who is correct 'absolutely' has no physical sense.

I am afraid I have made you quite tired by these long considerations, but if you follow them carefully it will be clear to you that, as soon as our method of space–time measurement is adopted, *the notion of absolute simultaneousness vanishes, and two events in different places considered as simultaneous from one system of reference will be separated by a definite time interval from the point of view of another system.*

This proposition sounds at first extremely unusual, but does it look unusual to you if I say that, having your dinner on a train, you eat your soup and your dessert in the same point of the dining car, but in widely separated points of the railway track? However, this statement about your dinner in the train can be formulated by saying that *two events happening at different times at the same point of one system of reference will be separated by a definite space interval from the point of view of another system.*

If you compare this 'trivial' proposition with the previous 'paradoxical' one, you will see that they are absolutely symmetrical and can be transformed into one another simply by exchanging the words 'time' and 'space'.

Here is the whole point of Einstein's view: whereas in classical physics time was considered as something quite independent of space and motion 'flowing equably without relation to anything external' (Newton), in the new physics space and time are closely connected and represent just two different cross-sections of one homogeneous 'space–time continuum', in which all observable events take place. The splitting of this four-dimensional continuum into three-dimensional space and one-dimensional time is purely arbitrary, and depends on the system from which the observations are made.

Two events, separated in space by the distance l and in time by the interval t as observed in one system, will be separated by another distance l' and another time interval t' as seen from another system, so that, in a certain sense one can speak about the transformation of space into time and vice versa. It is also not difficult to see why the transformation of time into space, as in the example of the dinner in a train, is quite a common notion for us, whereas the transformation of space into time, resulting in the relativity of simultaneousness, seems very unusual. The point is that if we measure distances, say, in 'centimetres', the corresponding unit of time should be not the conventional 'second' but a 'rational unit of time', represented by the interval of time necessary for a light signal to cover a distance of one centimetre, i.e. 0·000,000,000,03 second.

Therefore, in the sphere of our ordinary experience the transformation of space intervals into time intervals leads to results practically unobservable, which seems to support the classical view that time is something absolutely independent and unchangeable.

However, when investigating motions with very high velocities, as, for example, the motion of electrons thrown out from radioactive bodies or the motion of electrons inside an atom, where the distances covered in a certain interval of time are of the same order of magnitude as the time expressed in rational units, one necessarily meets with both of the effects discussed above and the theory of relativity becomes of great importance. Even in the region of comparatively small velocities, as, for example, the motion of planets in our solar system, relativistic effects can be observed owing to the extreme precision of astronomical measurements; such observation of relativistic effects requires, however, measurements of the changes of planetary motion amounting to a fraction of an angular second per year.

As I have tried to explain to you, the criticism of the notions of space and time leads to the conclusion that space intervals can be partially converted into time intervals and the other way round; which means that the numerical value of a given distance or period of time will be different as measured from different moving systems.

A comparatively simple mathematical analysis of this problem, into which I do not, however, want to enter in these lectures, leads to a definite formula for the change of these values. It works out that any object of length l, moving relative to the observer with velocity v, will be shortened by an amount depending on its velocity, and its measured length will be

$$l' = l \sqrt{1 - \frac{v^2}{c^2}}. \tag{2}$$

Analogously, any process taking time t will be observed from the relatively moving system as taking a longer time t', given by

$$t' = \frac{t}{\sqrt{1 - \frac{v^2}{c^2}}}. \tag{3}$$

This is the famous 'shortening of space' and 'expanding of time' in the theory of relativity.

Ordinarily, when v is very much less than c the effects are very small, but, for sufficiently large velocities, the lengths as observed from a moving system may be made arbitrarily small and time intervals arbitrarily long.

I do not want you to forget that both these effects are absolutely symmetrical systems, and, whereas the passengers on a fast-moving train will wonder why the people on the standing train are so lean and move so slowly, the passengers on the standing train will think the same about the people on the moving one.

Another important consequence of the existence of the maximum possible velocity pertains to the *mass* of moving bodies.

According to the general foundation of mechanics, the mass of a body determines the difficulty of setting it into motion or accelerating the motion already existing; the larger the mass, the more difficult it is to increase the velocity by a given amount.

The fact that no body under any circumstances can exceed the velocity of light leads us directly to the conclusion that its resistance to further acceleration or, in other words, its mass, must increase without limit when its velocity approaches the velocity of light. Mathematical analysis leads to a formula for this dependence, which is analogous to the formulae (2) and (3). If m_0 is the mass for very small velocities, the mass m at the velocity v is given by

$$m = \frac{m_0}{\sqrt{1 - \dfrac{v^2}{c^2}}} \tag{4}$$

and the resistance to further acceleration becomes infinite when v approaches c.

This effect of the relativistic change of mass can be easily observed experimentally on very fast-moving particles. For example, the mass of electrons emitted by radioactive bodies (with a velocity of 99% of that of light) is several times larger than in a state of rest and the masses of electrons forming so-called cosmic rays and moving often with 99·98% of the velocity of light are 1000 times larger. For such velocities the classical mechanics becomes absolutely inapplicable and we enter into the domain of the pure theory of relativity.

3

Mr Tompkins takes a holiday

Mr Tompkins was very amused about his adventures in the relativistic city, but was sorry that the professor had not been with him to give any explanation of the strange things he had observed: the mystery of how the railway brakeman had been able to prevent the passengers from getting old worried him especially. Many a night he went to bed with the hope that he would see this interesting city again, but the dreams were rare and mostly unpleasant; last time it was the manager of the bank who was firing him for the uncertainty he introduced into the bank accounts... so now he decided that he had better take a holiday, and go for a week somewhere to the sea. Thus he found himself sitting in a compartment of a train and watching through the window the grey roofs of the city suburb gradually giving place to the green meadows of the countryside. He picked up a newspaper and tried to interest himself in the Vietnam conflict. But it all seemed to be so dull, and the railway carriage rocked him pleasantly....

When he lowered the paper and looked out of the window again the landscape had changed considerably. The telegraph poles were so close to each other that they looked like a hedge, and the trees had extremely narrow crowns and were like Italian cypresses. Opposite to him sat his old friend the professor, looking through the window with great interest. He had probably got in while Mr Tompkins was busy with his newspaper.

'We are in the land of relativity,' said Mr Tompkins, 'aren't we?'

'Oh!' exclaimed the professor, 'you know so much already! Where did you learn it from?'

'I have already been here once, but did not have the pleasure of your company then.'

'So you are probably going to be my guide this time,' the old man said.

'I should say not,' retorted Mr Tompkins. 'I saw a lot of unusual things, but the local people to whom I spoke could not understand what my trouble was at all.'

'Naturally enough,' said the professor. 'They are born in this world and consider all the phenomena happening around them as self-evident. But I imagine they would be quite surprised if they happened to get into the world in which you used to live. It would look so remarkable to them.'

'May I ask you a question?' said Mr Tompkins. 'Last time I was here, I met a brakeman from the railway who insisted that owing to the fact that the train stops and starts again the passengers grow old less quickly than the people in the city. Is this magic, or is it also consistent with modern science?'

'There is never any excuse for putting forward magic as an explanation,' said the professor. 'This follows directly from the laws of physics. It was shown by Einstein, on the basis of his analysis of new (or should I say as-old-as-the-world but newly discovered) notions of space and time, that all physical processes slow down when the system in which they are taking place is changing its velocity. In our world the effects are almost un-observably small, but here, owing to the small velocity of light, they are usually very obvious. If, for example, you tried to boil an egg here, and instead of letting the saucepan stand quietly on the stove moved it to and fro, constantly changing its velocity, it would take you not five but perhaps six minutes to boil it properly. Also in the human body all processes slow down, if the person is sitting (for example) in a rocking chair or in a train which changes its speed; we live more slowly under such conditions. As, how-ever, all processes slow down to the same extent, physicists prefer to say that *in a non-uniformly moving system time flows more slowly*.'

'But do scientists actually observe such phenomena in our world at home?'

'They do, but it requires considerable skill. It is technically very difficult to get the necessary accelerations, but the conditions existing in a non-uniformly moving system are analogous, or should I say identical, to the result of the action of a very large force of gravity. You may have noticed that when you are in an elevator which is rapidly accelerated upwards it seems to you that you have grown heavier; on the contrary, if the elevator starts downward (you realize it best when the rope breaks) you feel as though you were losing weight. The explanation is that the gravitational field created by acceleration is added to or subtracted from the gravity of the earth. Well, the potential of gravity on the sun is much larger than on the surface of the earth and all processes there should be therefore slightly slowed down. Astronomers do observe this.'

'But they cannot go to the sun to observe it?'

'They do not need to go there. They observe the light coming to us from the sun. This light is emitted by the vibration of different atoms in the solar atmosphere. If all processes go slower there, the speed of atomic vibrations also decreases, and by comparing the light emitted by solar and terrestrial sources one can see the difference. Do you know, by the way'—the professor interrupted himself—'what the name of this little station is that we are now passing?'

The train was rolling along the platform of a little countryside station which was quite empty except for the station master and a young porter sitting on a luggage trolley and reading a newspaper. Suddenly the station master threw his hands into the air and fell down on his face. Mr Tompkins did not hear the sound of shooting, which was probably lost in the noise of the train, but the pool of blood forming round the body of the station master left no doubt. The professor immediately pulled the emergency cord and the train stopped with a jerk. When they got out of the carriage the young porter was running towards the body, and a country policeman was approaching.

'Shot through the heart,' said the policeman after inspecting the body, and, putting a heavy hand on the porter's shoulder, he went on: 'I am arresting you for the murder of the station master.'

'I didn't kill him,' exclaimed the unfortunate porter. 'I was reading a newspaper when I heard the shot. These gentlemen from the train have probably seen all and can testify that I am innocent.'

'Yes,' said Mr Tompkins, 'I saw with my own eyes that this man was reading his paper when the station master was shot. I can swear it on the Bible.'

'But you were in the moving train,' said the policeman, taking an authoritative tone, 'and what you saw is therefore no evidence at all. As seen from the platform the man could have been shooting at the very same moment. Don't you know that simultaneousness depends on the system from which you observe it? Come along quietly,' he said, turning to the porter.

'Excuse me, constable,' interrupted the professor, 'but you are absolutely wrong, and I do not think that at headquarters they will like your ignorance. It is true, of course, that the notion of simultaneousness is highly relative in your country. It is also true that two events in different places could be simultaneous or not, depending on the motion of the observer. But, even in your country, no observer could see the consequence before the cause. You have never received a telegram before it was sent, have you? or got drunk before opening the bottle? As I understand you, you suppose that owing to the motion of the train the shooting would have been seen by us much *later* than its effect and, as we got out of the train immediately we saw the station master fall, we still had not seen the shooting itself. I know that in the police force you are taught to believe only what is written in your instructions, but look into them and probably you will find something about it.'

The professor's tone made quite an impression on the policeman and, pulling out his pocket book of instructions, he started to read it slowly through. Soon a smile of embarrassment spread out across his big, red face.

'Here it is,' said he, 'section 37, subsection 12, paragraph *e*: "As a perfect alibi should be recognized any authoritative proof, from any moving system whatsoever, that at the moment of the crime or within a time interval $\pm cd$ (*c* being natural speed limit and *d* the distance from the place of the crime) the suspect was seen in another place."'

'You are free, my good man,' he said to the porter, and then, turning to the professor: 'Thank you very much, Sir, for saving me from trouble with headquarters. I am new to the force and not yet accustomed to all these rules. But I must report the murder anyway,' and he went to the telephone box. A minute later he was shouting across the platform. 'All is in order now! They caught the real murderer when he was running away from the station. Thank you once more!'

'I may be very stupid,' said Mr Tompkins, when the train started again, 'but what is all this business about simultaneousness? Has it really no meaning in this country?'

'It has,' was the answer, 'but only to a certain extent; otherwise I should not have been able to help the porter at all. You see, the existence of a natural speed limit for the motion of any body or the propagation of any signal, makes simultaneousness in our ordinary sense of the word lose its meaning. You probably will see it more easily this way. Suppose you have a friend living in a far-away town, with whom you correspond by letter, mail train being the fastest means of communication. Suppose now that something happens to you on Sunday and you learn that the same thing is going to happen to your friend. It is clear that you cannot let him know about it before Wednesday. On the other hand, if he knew in advance about the thing that was going to happen to you, the last date to let you know about it would have been the previous Thursday. Thus for six days, from Thursday to next Wednesday, your friend was not able either to influence your fate on Sunday or to learn about it. From the point of view of causality he was, so to speak, excommunicated from you for six days.'

'What about a telegram?' suggested Mr Tompkins.

'Well, I accepted that the velocity of the mail train was the maximum possible velocity, which is about correct in this country. At home the velocity of light is the maximum velocity and you cannot send a signal faster than by radio.'

'But still,' said Mr Tompkins, 'even if the velocity of the mail train could not be surpassed, what has it to do with simultaneousness? My friend and myself would still have our Sunday dinners simultaneously, wouldn't we?'

'No, that statement would not have any sense then; one observer would agree to it, but there would be others, making their observations from different trains, who would insist that you eat your Sunday dinner at the same time as your friend has his Friday breakfast or Tuesday lunch. But in no way could anybody observe you and your friend simultaneously having meals more than three days apart.'

'But how can all this happen?' exclaimed Mr Tompkins unbelievingly.

'In a very simple way, as you might have noticed from my lectures. The upper limit of velocity must remain the same as observed from different moving systems. If we accept this we should conclude that....'

But their conversation was interrupted by the train arriving at the station at which Mr Tompkins had to get out.

When Mr Tompkins came down to have his breakfast in the long glass verandah of the hotel, the morning after his arrival at the seaside, a great surprise awaited him. At the table in the opposite corner sat the old professor and a pretty girl who was cheerfully relating something to the old man, and glancing often in the direction of the table where Mr Tompkins was sitting.

'I suppose I did look very stupid, sleeping in that train,' thought Mr Tompkins, getting more and more angry with himself. 'And the professor probably still remembers the stupid question I asked him about getting younger. But this at least will give me an opportunity to become better acquainted with him now and ask about the things I still do not understand.' He did not want to admit even to himself that it was not only conversation with the professor he was thinking about.

'Oh, yes, yes, I think I do remember seeing you at my lectures,' said the professor when they were leaving the dining room. 'This is my daughter, Maud. She is studying painting.'

'Very happy to meet you, Miss Maud,' said Mr Tompkins, and thought that this was the most beautiful name he had ever heard. 'I expect these surroundings must give you wonderful material for your sketches.'

'She will show them to you some time,' said the professor, 'but tell me, did you gather much from listening to my lecture?'

'Oh yes, I did, quite a lot—and in fact I myself experienced all these relativistic contractions of material objects and the crazy behaviour of clocks when I visited a city where the velocity of light was only about ten miles per hour.'

'Then it is a pity,' said the professor, 'that you missed my following lecture about the curvature of space and its relation to the forces of Newtonian gravity. But here on the beach we will have time, so that I will be able to explain all that to you. Do you, for example, understand the difference between the positive and negative curvature of space?'

'Daddy,' said Miss Maud, pouting her lips, 'if you are talking physics again, I think I will go and do some work.'

'All right, girlie, you run along,' said the professor, plunging himself into an easy chair. 'I see you did not study mathematics much, young man; but I think I can explain it to you very simply, taking, for simplicity, the example of a surface. Imagine that Mr Shell—you know, the man who owns the petrol stations— decides to see whether his stations are distributed uniformly throughout some country, say America. To do this, he gives orders to his office, somewhere in the middle of the country

(Kansas City is, I believe, considered as the heart of America), to count the number of stations within one hundred, two hundred, three hundred and so on miles from the city. He remembers from his school days that the area of a circle is proportional to the square of its radius, and expects that in the case of uniform distribution the number of stations thus counted should increase like the sequence of numbers 1; 4; 9; 16 and so on. When the report

Filling stations in the United States

comes in, he will be very much surprised to see that the actual number of stations is increasing much more slowly, going, let us say, 1; 3·8; 8·5; 15·0; and so on. "What a mess," he would exclaim; "my managers in America do not know their job. What is the great idea of concentrating the stations near Kansas City?" But is he right in this conclusion?'

'Is he?' repeated Mr Tompkins, who was thinking about something else.

'He is not,' said the professor gravely. 'He has forgotten that the earth's surface is not a plane but a sphere. And on a sphere the area within a given radius grows more slowly with the radius than on a plane. Can't you really see it? Well, take a globe and try to see it for yourself. If, for example, you are on the north pole, the circle with the radius equal to a half meridian is the equator, and the area included is the northern hemisphere. Increase the radius twice and you will get in all the earth's surface; the area will increase only twice instead of four times as it would on a plane. Isn't it clear to you now?'

'It is,' said Mr Tompkins, making an effort to be attentive. 'And is this a positive or a negative curvature?'

'It is called positive curvature, and, as you see from the example of the globe, it corresponds to a finite surface having definite area. An example of a surface with negative curvature is given by a saddle.'

'By a saddle?' repeated Mr Tompkins.

'Yes, by a saddle, or, on the surface of the earth, by a saddle pass between two mountains. Suppose a botanist lives in a mountain hut situated on such a saddle pass and is interested in the density of growth of pines around the hut. If he counts the number of pines growing within one hundred, two hundred, and so on feet from the hut, he will find that the number of pines increases faster than the square of the distance, the point being that on a saddle surface the area included within a given radius is larger than on a plane. Such surfaces are said to possess a negative curvature. If you try to spread a saddle surface on a plane you will have to make folds in it, whereas doing the same with a spherical surface you will probably tear it if it is not elastic.'

'I see,' said Mr Tompkins. 'And you mean to say that a saddle surface is infinite although curved.'

'Exactly so,' approved the professor. 'A saddle surface extends to infinity in all directions and never closes on itself. Of course, in my example of a saddle pass the surface ceases to possess negative curvature as soon as you walk out of the mountains and go over into the positively curved surface of the earth. But of course you can imagine a surface which preserves its negative curvature everywhere.'

'But how does it apply to a curved three-dimensional space?'

'In exactly the same way. Suppose you have objects distributed uniformly through space, I mean in such a way that the distance between two neighbouring objects is always the same, and suppose you count their number within different distances from you. If this number grows as the square of the distance, the space is flat; if the growth is slower or faster, the space possesses a positive or a negative curvature.'

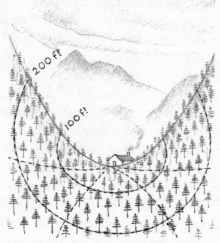

A mountain hut in a saddle pass

'Thus in the case of positive curvature the space has less volume within a given distance, and in the case of negative curvature more volume?' said Mr Tompkins with surprise.

'Just so,' smiled the professor. 'Now I see you understood me correctly. To investigate the sign of the curvature of the great universe in which we live, one just has to do such counts of the number of distant objects. The great nebulae, about which you have probably heard, are scattered uniformly through space and can be seen up to the distance of several thousand million light years; they represent very convenient objects for such investigations of the curvature of the world.'

'And so it comes out that our universe is finite and closed in itself?'

'Well,' said the professor, 'the problem is actually still unsolved. In his original papers on cosmology, Einstein stated that the universe is finite in size, closed in on itself, and unchangeable in time. Later the work of a Russian mathematician, A. A. FRIED-MANN, showed that Einstein's basic equations permit the possibility that the universe expands or contracts as it grows older. This mathematical conclusion was confirmed by an American astronomer E. HUBBLE who, using the 100-inch telescope of Mt Wilson Observatory, found that the galaxies fly apart from one another, i.e. that our universe is expanding. But there is still the problem of whether this expansion will continue indefinitely or will reach the maximum value and turn into contraction in some distant future. This question can be answered only by more detailed astronomical observations.'

While the professor was talking, very unusual changes seemed to be taking place around them: one end of the lobby became extremely small, squeezing all the furniture in it, whereas the other end was growing so large that, as it seemed to Mr Tompkins, the whole universe could find room in it. A terrible thought pierced his mind: what if a piece of space on the beach, where Miss Maud was painting, were torn away from the rest of the universe. He would never be able to see her again! When he rushed to the door he heard the professor's voice shouting behind him. 'Careful! the quantum constant is getting crazy too!' When he reached the beach it seemed to him at first very crowded. Thousands of girls were rushing in disorder in all possible directions. 'How on earth am I going to find my Maud in this crowd?' he thought. But then he noticed that they all looked exactly like the professor's daughter, and he realized that this was just the joke of the uncertainty principle. The next moment the wave of anomalously large quantum constant had passed, and Miss Maud was standing on the beach with a frightened look in her eyes.

'Oh, it is you!' she murmured with relief. 'I thought a big crowd was rushing on me. It is probably the effect of this hot sun on my head. Wait a minute until I run to the hotel and bring my sun hat.'

'Oh, no, we should not leave each other now,' protested Mr Tompkins. 'I have an impression that the velocity of light is changing too; when you return from the hotel you might find me an old man!'

'Nonsense,' said the girl, but still slipped her hand into the hand of Mr Tompkins. But half-way to the hotel another wave of uncertainty overtook them, and both Mr Tompkins and the girl spread all over the shore. At the same time a large fold of space began spreading from the hills close by, curving surrounding rocks and fishermen's houses into very funny shapes. The rays of the sun, deflected by an immense gravitational field, completely disappeared from the horizon and Mr Tompkins was plunged into complete darkness.

A century passed before a voice so dear to him brought him back to his senses.

'Oh,' the girl was saying, 'I see my father sent you to sleep by his conversation about physics. Wouldn't you like to come and have a swim with me, the water is so nice today?'

Mr Tompkins jumped from the easy chair as if on springs. 'So it was a dream after all,' he thought, as they descended towards the beach. 'Or is the dream just beginning now?'

4

The Professor's Lecture on Curved Space, Gravity and the Universe

Ladies and Gentlemen:

Today I am going to discuss the problem of curved space and its relation to the phenomena of gravitation. I have no doubt that any one of you can easily imagine a curved line or a curved surface, but at the mention of a curved, three-dimensional space your faces grow longer and you are inclined to think that it is something very unusual and almost supernatural. What is the reason for this common 'horror' for a curved space, and is this notion really more difficult than the notion of a curved surface? Many of you, if you will think a little about it, will probably say that you find it difficult to imagine a curved space because you cannot look on it 'from outside' as you look on a curved surface of a globe, or, to take another example, on the rather peculiarly curved surface of a saddle. However, those who say this convict themselves of not knowing the strict mathematical meaning of curvature, which is in fact rather different from the common use of the word. We mathematicians call a surface curved if the properties of geometrical figures drawn on it are different from those on a plane, and we measure the curvature by the deviation from the classical rules of Euclid. If you draw a triangle on a flat piece of paper the sum of its angles, as you know from elementary geometry, is equal to two right angles. You can bend this piece of paper to give to it a cylindrical, a conical, or even still more complicated shape, but the sum of the angles in the triangle drawn upon it will always remain equal to two right angles.

The geometry of the surface does not change with these deformations and, from the point of view of the 'internal' curvature, the surfaces obtained (curved in common notation) are just as flat as a plane. But you cannot fit a piece of paper, without stretching it, on to the surface of a sphere or a saddle, and, if you try to draw a triangle on a globe (i.e. a spherical triangle) the simple theorems of Euclidean geometry will not hold any more. In fact, a triangle formed, for example, by the northern halves of two meridians and a piece of the equator between them will have two right angles at its base and an arbitrary angle at the top.

On the saddle surface you will be surprised to find that, on the contrary, the sum of the angles of a triangle will always be smaller than two right angles.

Thus *to determine the curvature of a surface it is necessary to study the geometry on this surface,* whereas looking from outside will often be misleading. Just by looking you would probably place the surface of a cylinder in the same class as the surface of a ring, whereas the first is actually flat and the second is incurably curved. As soon as you get accustomed to this new strict notion of curvature you will not have any more difficulty in understanding what the physicist means in discussing whether the space in which we live is curved or not. The problem is only to find out whether the geometrical figures constructed in physical space are or are not subject to the common laws of Euclidean geometry.

Since, however, we are speaking about actual physical space we must first of all give the *physical definition of the terms used in geometry* and, in particular, state what we understand by the notion of straight lines from which our figures are to be constructed.

I suppose that all of you know that a straight line is most generally defined as the shortest distance between two points; it can be obtained either by stretching a string between two points or by an equivalent but elaborate process, of finding by trial a line between two given points along which the minimum number of measuring-sticks of given length can be placed.

In order to show that the results of such a method of finding a straight line will depend on physical conditions, let us imagine a large round platform uniformly rotating around its axis, and an experimenter (I) trying to find the shortest distance between two points on the periphery of this platform. He has a box with a large number of sticks, 5 inches each, and tries to line them up between two points so as to use the minimum total number of them. If the

The scientists were measuring something on a rotating platform*

platform were not rotating, he would place them along a line which is indicated in our figure by the dotted line. But due to the rotation of the platform his measuring-sticks will suffer a relativistic contraction, as discussed in my previous lecture, and those of them which are closer to the periphery of the platform (and therefore possess larger linear velocities) will be contracted more than those located nearer to the centre. It is thus clear that, in order to

* The name Hookham's Circus refers to Mr John Hookham, who worked as illustrator for the Cambridge University Press and, before his retirement, produced many of the drawings adorning the present volume.

get most distance covered by each stick, one should place them as close to the centre as possible. But, since both ends of the line are fixed on the periphery, it is also disadvantageous to move the sticks from the middle of the line too close to the centre.

Thus the result will be reached by a compromise between two conditions, *the shortest distance being finally represented by a curve slightly convex towards the centre.*

If, instead of using separate sticks, our experimenter will just stretch a string between the two points in question, the result will evidently be the same, because each part of the string will suffer the same relativistic contraction as the separate sticks. I want here to stress the point that this deformation of the stretched string which takes place when the platform begins to rotate has nothing to do with the usual effects of centrifugal force; in fact this deformation will not change however strongly the string is stretched, not to mention that the ordinary centrifugal force will act in the opposite direction.

If, now, the observer on the platform decides to check his results by comparing the 'straight line' he thus obtained with the ray of light, he will find that the light is really propagated along the line he has constructed. Of course, to the observers standing near the platform, the ray of light will not seem curved at all; they will interpret the results of the moving observer by the overlapping of the rotation of the platform and the rectilinear propagation of light, and will tell you that, if you make a scratch on a rotating gramophone record by moving your hand along in a straight line, the scratch on the record will also, of course, be curved.

However, as far as the observer on the rotating platform is concerned, the name of 'straight line' for the curve obtained by him is perfectly sound: it *is* the shortest distance and it *does* coincide with the ray of light in his system of reference. Suppose he now chooses three points on the periphery and connects them with straight lines, thus forming a triangle. *The sum of angles in this case will be smaller than two right angles* and he will conclude, and rightly, that the space around him is curved.

To take another example, let us suppose that two other observers on the platform (2 and 3) decide to estimate the number π by measuring the circumference of the platform and its diameter. The measuring-stick of 2 will not be affected by the rotation because its motion is always perpendicular to its length. On the other hand the stick of 3 will be always contracted and he will get for length of the periphery a value larger than for a non-rotating platform. Dividing the result of 3 by the result of 2 one will thus get *a larger value than the value of* π usually given in the text-books, which is again a result of the curvature of the space.

Not only length measurements will be affected by the rotation. A watch located on the periphery will have a large velocity and, according to the considerations of the previous lecture, will go slower than the watch standing in the centre of the platform.

If two experimenters (4 and 5) check their watches in the centre of the platform, and, after this, 5 brings his watch for some time to the periphery he will find on coming back to the centre that his watch is too slow as compared with the watch remaining all the time in the centre. He will thus conclude that in different places of the platform all physical processes go at different rates.

Suppose now our experimenters stop and think a little about the cause of the unusual results they have just obtained in their geometrical measurements. Suppose also that their platform is closed, forming a rotating room without windows, so that they could not see their motion relative to the surroundings. Could they explain all the observed results as due purely to the physical conditions on their platform without referring to its rotation relative to the 'solid ground' on which the platform is installed?

Looking for differences between the physical conditions on their platform and on the 'solid ground' by which the observed changes in the geometry could be explained, they will at once notice that there is some new force present which tends to pull all bodies from the centre of the platform towards the periphery. Naturally enough, they will ascribe the observed effects to the action of this force saying, for example, that of the two watches, the one will move slower which is further from the centre in the direction of action of this new force.

But is this force really a *new* force, not observable on the 'solid ground'? Do we not always observe that all bodies are pulled towards the centre of the earth by what is called the force of gravity? Of course, in one case we have the attraction towards the periphery of the disc, in another the attraction to the centre of the earth, but this means only a difference in the distribution of the force. It is, however, not difficult to give another example in which the 'new' forces produced by non-uniform motion of the system of reference looks exactly like the force of gravity in this lecture room.

Suppose a rocket-ship, designed for interstellar travel, floats freely somewhere in space so far from different stars that there is no force of gravity inside it. All objects inside such a rocket-ship, and the experimenter travelling in it, will thus have no weight and will float freely in the air in much the same way as Michel Ardent and his fellow-travellers to the moon in the famous story of Jules Verne.

Now the engines are being switched on, and our rocket-ship starts moving, gradually gaining velocity. What will happen inside it? It is easy to see that, as long as the ship is accelerated, all the objects in its interior will show a tendency to move towards the floor, or, to say the same thing in another way, the floor will be moving towards these objects. If, for example, our experimenter holds an apple in his hand and then lets it go, the apple will continue to move (relative to the surrounding stars) with a constant velocity—the velocity with which the rocket-ship was moving at the moment when the apple was released. But the rocket-ship itself is accelerated; consequently the floor of the cabin, moving all the time faster and faster, will finally overtake the apple and hit it; from this moment on the apple will remain permanently in contact with the floor, being pressed to it by steady acceleration.

For the experimenter inside, however, this will look as if the apple 'falls down' with a certain acceleration, and after hitting the floor remains pressed to it by its own weight. Dropping different objects, he will notice furthermore that all of them fall with exactly equal accelerations (if he neglects the friction of the air) and will remember that this is exactly the rule of the free fall discovered by GALILEO GALILEI. *In fact he will not be able to notice the slightest difference between the phenomena in his accelerated cabin and the ordinary phenomena of gravity*. He can use the clock with the pendulum, put books on a shelf without any danger of their flying away, and hang on a nail the portrait of Albert Einstein, who first indicated the equivalence of acceleration of the system of reference and the field of gravity, and developed, on this basis, the so-called general theory of relativity.

But here, just as in the first example of a rotating platform, we shall notice phenomena unknown to Galileo and Newton in their study of gravity. The light ray sent across the cabin will get curved and will illuminate a screen hanging on the opposite wall at different places, depending on the acceleration of the rocket-ship. By an outside observer, this will be interpreted, of course, as due to the overlapping of a uniform rectilinear motion of light and the accelerated motion of the observational cabin. The geometry will also go wrong; the sum of angles of a triangle formed by three light rays will be larger than two right angles, and the ratio of the periphery of a circle to its diameter will be larger than the number π. We have considered here two of the simplest examples of accelerated systems, but the equivalence stated above will hold for any given motion of a rigid or a deformable system of reference.

We come now to the question of greatest importance. We have just seen that in an accelerated system of reference a number of phenomena could be observed that were unknown for the ordinary

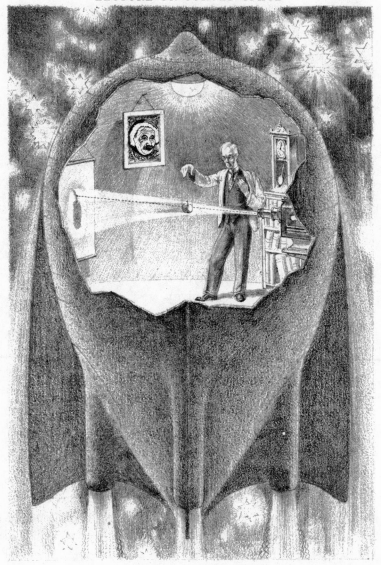

The floor . . . will finally overtake the apple and hit it

field of gravitation. Do these new phenomena, such as the curving of a light ray or slowing down of a clock, also exist in gravitational fields produced by ponderable masses? Or, in other words, are the effects of acceleration and the effects of gravity not only very similar, but identical?

It is clear, of course, that although from the heuristic point of view it is very tempting to accept complete identity of these two kinds of effects, the final answer can be given only by direct experiments. And, to the great satisfaction of our human mind, which demands simplicity and internal consistency of the laws of the universe, experiments do prove the existence of these new phenomena also in the ordinary field of gravity. Of course, the effects predicted by the hypothesis of the equivalence of accelerative and gravitational fields are very small: that is why they have been discovered only after scientists started looking specially for them.

Using the example of accelerated systems discussed above, we can easily estimate the order of magnitude of the two most important relativistic gravitational phenomena: the change of the clock rate and the curvature of a light ray.

Let us first take the example of the rotating platform. It is known from elementary mechanics that the centrifugal force acting on a particle of mass unity located at the distance r from the centre is given by the formula

$$F = r\omega^2, \tag{1}$$

where ω is the constant angular velocity of rotation of our platform. The total work done by this force during the motion of the particle from the centre to the periphery is then

$$W = \tfrac{1}{2}R^2\omega^2, \tag{2}$$

where R is the radius of the platform.

According to the above-stated equivalence principle, we have to identify F with the force of gravity on the platform, and W

with the difference of gravitational potential between the centre and the periphery.

Now, we must remember that, as we have seen in the previous lecture, the slowing down of the clock moving with the velocity v is given by the factor

$$\sqrt{1 - \left(\frac{v}{c}\right)^2} = 1 - \frac{1}{2}\left(\frac{v}{c}\right)^2 + \dots \qquad (3)$$

If v is small as compared with c we can neglect other terms. According to the definition of the angular velocity we have $v = R\omega$ and the 'slowing-down factor' becomes

$$1 - \frac{1}{2}\left(\frac{R\omega}{c}\right)^2 = 1 - \frac{W}{c^2}, \qquad (4)$$

giving the change of rate of the clock in terms of the difference of gravitational potentials at the places of their location.

If we place one clock at the basement and another on the top of the Eiffel tower (1000 feet high) the difference of potential between them will be so small that the clock at the basement will go slower only by a factor 0·999,999,999,999,97.

On the other hand, the difference of gravitational potential between the surface of the earth and the surface of the sun is much larger, giving the slowing down by a factor 0·999,999,5, which can be noticed by very exact measurements. Of course, nobody was going to place an ordinary clock on the surface of the sun and watch it go! The physicists have much better means. By means of the spectroscope we can observe the periods of vibration of different atoms on the surface of the sun and compare them with the periods of the atoms of the same elements put into the flame of a Bunsen-burner in the laboratory. The vibrations of atoms on the surface of the sun should be slowed down by the factor given by the formula (4) and the light emitted by them should be somewhat more reddish than in the case of terrestrial sources. This 'red-shift' was actually observed in the spectra of the sun and several other stars, for which the spectra could be exactly measured, and the result agrees with the value given by our theoretical formula.

Thus the existence of the red-shift proved that the processes on the sun really take place somewhat more slowly owing to higher gravitational potential on its surface.

In order to get a measure for the curvature of a light ray in the field of gravity it is more convenient to use the example of the rocket-ship as given on page 36. If l is the distance across the cabin, the time t taken by light to cross it is given by

$$t = \frac{l}{c}. \tag{5}$$

During this time the ship, moving with the acceleration g, will cover the distance L given by the following formula of elementary mechanics:

$$L = \tfrac{1}{2}gt^2 = \tfrac{1}{2}g\frac{l^2}{c^2}. \tag{6}$$

Thus the angle representing the change of the direction of the light ray is of the order of magnitude

$$\phi = \frac{L}{l} = \frac{1}{2}\frac{gl}{c^2} \text{ radians}, \tag{7}$$

and is larger, the larger the distance l which the light has travelled in the gravitational field. Here the acceleration g of the rocket-ship has, of course, to be interpreted as the acceleration of gravity. If I send a beam of light across this lecture room, I can take roughly $l = 1000$ cm. The acceleration of gravity g on the surface of the earth is 981 cm/sec² and with $c = 3 \cdot 10^{10}$ cm/sec we get

$$\phi = \frac{100 \times 981}{2 \times (3 \cdot 10^{10})^2} = 5 \cdot 10^{-16} \text{ radians} = 10^{-10} \text{ sec of arc.} \tag{8}$$

Thus you can see that the curvature of light can definitely not be observed under such conditions. However, near the surface of the sun g is 27,000 and the total path travelled in the gravitational field of the sun is very large. The exact calculations show that the value for the deviation of a light ray passing near the solar surface should be $1.75''$, and this is just exactly the value observed by astronomers for the displacement of the apparent position of stars seen near the solar limb during a total eclipse. You see that here, too, the observations have shown a complete identity of the effects of acceleration and those of gravitation.

Now we can return again to our problem about the curvature of space. You remember that, using the most rational definition of a straight line, we came to the conclusion that the geometry obtained in ununiformly moving systems of reference is different from that of Euclid and that such spaces should be considered as curved spaces. Since any gravitational field is equivalent to some acceleration of the system of reference, this means also that any space in which the gravitational field is present is a curved space. Or, going still a step farther, that *a gravitational field is just a physical manifestation of the curvature of space*. Thus the curvature of space at each point should be determined by the distribution of masses, and near heavy bodies the curvature of space should reach its maximum value. I cannot enter into a rather complicated mathematical system describing the properties of curved space and their dependence on the distribution of masses. I should mention only that this curvature is in general determined not by one, but by ten different numbers which are usually known as the components gravitational potential $g_{\mu\nu}$ and represent a generalization of the gravitational potential of classical physics which I have previously called W. Correspondingly, the curvature at each point is described by ten different radii of curvature usually denoted by $R_{\mu\nu}$. Those radii of curvature are connected with distribution of masses by the fundamental equation of Einstein:

$$R_{\mu\nu} - \tfrac{1}{2}g_{\mu\nu}R = -\kappa T_{\mu\nu}, \tag{9}$$

where $T_{\mu\nu}$ depends on densities, velocities and other properties of the gravitational field produced by ponderable masses.

Coming to the end of this lecture, I should like, however, to indicate one of the most interesting consequences of equation (9). If we consider a space uniformly filled with masses, as, for example, our space is filled with stars and stellar systems, we shall come to the conclusion that, apart from occasionally large curvatures near separate stars, the space should possess *a regular tendency to curve uniformly on large distances*. Mathematically there are several different solutions, some of them corresponding to the *space finally closing on itself and thus possessing a finite volume*, the others representing *the infinite space analogous to a saddle surface* which I mentioned at the beginning of this lecture. The second important consequence of equation (9) is that such curved spaces should be in a state of steady expansion or contraction, which physically means that the particles filling the space should be flying away from each other, or, on the contrary, approaching each other. Further, it can be shown that for the closed spaces with finite volume the expansion and contraction periodically follow each other—these are so-called pulsating worlds. On the other hand, infinite 'saddle-like' spaces are permanently in a state of contraction or of expansion.

The question which of all these different mathematical possibilities corresponds to the space in which we are living should be answered not by physics but by astronomy and I am not going to discuss it here. I will mention only that so far astronomical evidence has definitely shown that our space is expanding, although the question whether this expansion will ever turn into a contraction, and whether the space is finite or infinite in size is not yet definitely settled.

5

The Pulsating Universe

After dinner on their first evening in the Beach Hotel with the old professor talking about cosmology, and his daughter chatting about art, Mr Tompkins finally got to his room, collapsed on to the bed, and pulled the blanket over his head. Botticelli and Bondi, Salvador Dali and Fred Hoyle, Lemaître and La Fontaine got all mixed up in his tired brain, and finally he fell into a deep sleep. . . .

Sometime in the middle of the night he woke up with a strange feeling that instead of lying on a comfortable spring mattress he was lying on something hard. He opened his eyes and found himself prostrated on what he first thought to be a big rock on the seashore. Later he discovered that it was actually a very big rock, about 30 feet in diameter, suspended in space without any visible support. The rock was covered with some green moss, and in a few places little bushes were growing from cracks in the stone. The space around the rock was illuminated by some glimmering light and was very dusty. In fact, there was more dust in the air than he had ever seen, even in the films representing dust storms in the middle west. He tied his handkerchief round his nose and felt, after this, considerably relieved. But there were more dangerous things than the dust in the surrounding space. Very often stones of the size of his head and larger were swirling through the space near his rock, occasionally hitting it with a strange dull sound of impact. He noticed also one or two rocks of approximately the same size as his own, floating through space at some distance away. All this time, inspecting his surroundings, he was clinging hard to some protruding edges of his rock in constant fear of falling off and being lost in the dusty depths below. Soon, however, he became bolder, and made an attempt to crawl to the edge of his rock and to see whether there was really nothing underneath, supporting it. As he was crawling in this way, he noticed, to his great surprise, that he did not fall off, but that his weight was constantly pressing him to the surface of the rock, although he had covered already more than a quarter of its circumference. Looking from behind a ridge of loose stones on the spot just underneath the place where he originally found himself, he discovered nothing to support the rock in space. To his great surprise, however, the glimmering light revealed the tall figure of his friend the old professor standing apparently with his head down and making some notes in his pocket-book.

Now Mr Tompkins began slowly to understand. He remembered that he was taught in his schooldays that the earth is a big round rock moving freely in space around the sun. He also remembered the picture of two antipodes standing on the opposite sides of the earth. Yes, his rock was just a very small stellar body attracting everything to its surface, and he and the old professor were the only population of this little planet. This consoled him a little; there was at least no danger of falling off!

'Good morning,' said Mr Tompkins, to divert the old man's attention from his calculations.

The professor raised his eyes from his note-book. 'There are no mornings here,' he said, 'there is no sun and not a single luminous star in this universe. It is lucky that the bodies here show some chemical process on their surface, otherwise I should not be able to observe the expansion of this space', and he returned again to his note-book.

Mr Tompkins felt quite unhappy; to meet the only living person in the whole universe, and to find him so unsociable! Unexpectedly, one of the little meteorites came to his help; with a crashing sound the stone hit the book in the hands of the professor and threw it, travelling fast through space, away from their little planet. 'Now you will never see it again,' said Mr Tompkins, as the book got smaller and smaller, flying through space.

'On the contrary,' replied the professor. 'You see, the space in which we now are is not infinite in its extension. Oh yes, yes, I know that you have been taught in school that space is infinite, and that two parallel lines never meet. This, however, is not true either for the space in which the rest of humanity lives, or for the space in which we are now. The first one is of course very large indeed; the scientists estimated its present dimensions to be about 10,000,000,000,000,000,000,000,000 miles, which, for an ordinary

There are no mornings here

mind, is fairly infinite. If I had lost my book there, it would take an incredibly long time to come back. Here, however, the situation is rather different. Just before the note-book was torn out of my hands, I had figured out that this space is only about five miles in diameter, though it is rapidly expanding. I expect the book back in not more than half an hour.'

'But,' ventured Mr Tompkins, 'do you mean that your book is going to behave like the boomerang of an Australian native, and, by moving along a curved trajectory, fall down at your feet?'

'Nothing of the sort,' answered the professor. 'If you want to understand what really happens, think about an ancient Greek who did not know that the earth was a sphere. Suppose he has given somebody instructions to go always straight northwards. Imagine his astonishment when his runner finally returns to him from the south. Our ancient Greek did not have a notion about travelling round the world (round the earth, I mean in this case), and he would be sure that his runner had lost his way and had taken a curved route which brought him back. In reality his man was going all the time along the straightest line one can draw on the surface of the earth, but he travelled round the world and thus came back from the opposite direction. The same thing is going to happen to my book, unless it is hit on its way by some other stone and thus deflected from the straight track. Here, take these binoculars, and see if you can still see it.'

Mr Tompkins put the binoculars to his eyes, and, through the dust which somewhat obscured the whole picture, he managed to see the professor's note-book travelling through space far far away. He was somewhat surprised by the pink colouring of all the objects, including the book, at that distance.

'But,' he exclaimed after a while, 'your book is returning, I see it growing larger.'

'No,' said the professor, 'it is still going away. The fact that you see it growing in size, as if it were coming back, is due to a peculiar focusing effect of the closed spherical space on the rays of light. Let us return to our ancient Greek. If the rays of light could be kept going all the time along the curved surface of the earth, let us say by refraction of the atmosphere, he would be able, using powerful binoculars, to see his runner all the time during the journey. If you look on the globe, you will see that the straightest lines on its surface, the meridians, first diverge from one pole, but, after passing the equator, begin to converge towards the opposite pole. If the rays of light travelled along the meridians, you, located, for example, at one pole, would see the person going away from you growing smaller and smaller only until he crossed the equator. After this point you would see him growing larger and it would seem to you that he was returning, going, however, backwards. After he had reached the opposite pole, you would see him as large as if he were standing right by your side. You would not be able, however, to touch him, just as you cannot touch the image in a spherical mirror. On this basis of two-dimensional analogy, you can imagine what happens to the light rays in the strangely curved three-dimensional space. Here, I think the image of the book is quite close now.' In fact, dropping the binoculars, Mr Tompkins could see that the book was only a few yards away. It looked, however, very strange indeed! The contours were not sharp, but rather washed out, the formulae written by the professor on its pages could be hardly recognized, and the whole book looked like a photograph taken out of focus and underdeveloped.

'You see now,' said the professor, 'that this is only the image of the book, badly distorted by light travelling across one half of the universe. If you want to be quite sure of it, just notice how the stones behind the book can be seen through its pages.'

Mr Tompkins tried to reach the book, but his hand passed through the image without any resistance.

'The book itself,' said the professor, 'is now very close to the opposite pole of the universe, and what you see here are just two images of it. The second image is just behind you and when both images coincide, the real book will be exactly at the opposite pole.' Mr Tompkins didn't hear; he was too deeply absorbed in his thoughts, trying to remember how the images of objects are formed in elementary optics by concave mirrors and lenses. When he finally gave it up, the two images were again receding in opposite directions.

'But what makes the space curved and produce all these funny effects?' he asked the professor.

'The presence of ponderable matter,' was the answer. 'When

Newton discovered the law of gravity, he thought that gravity was just an ordinary force, the same type of force as, for example, is produced by an elastic string stretched between two bodies. There always remains, however, the mysterious fact that all bodies, independent of their weight and size, have the same acceleration and move the same way under the action of gravity, provided you eliminate the friction of air and that sort of thing, of course. It was Einstein who first made it clear that the primary action of ponderable matter is to produce the curvature of space and that the trajectories of all bodies moving in the field of gravity are curved just because space itself is curved. But I think it is too hard for you to understand, without knowing sufficient mathematics.'

'It is,' said Mr Tompkins. 'But tell me, if there were no matter, would we have the kind of geometry I was taught at school, and would parallel lines never meet?'

'They would not,' answered the professor, 'but neither would there be any material creature to check it.'

'Well, perhaps Euclid never existed, and therefore could construct the geometry of absolutely empty space?'

But the professor apparently did not like to enter into this metaphysical discussion.

In the meantime the image of the book went off again far away in the original direction, and started coming back for the second time. Now it was still more damaged than before, and could hardly be recognized at all, which, according to the professor, was due to the fact that the light rays had travelled this time round the whole universe.

'If you turn your head once more,' he said to Mr Tompkins, 'you will see my book finally coming back after completing its journey round the world.' He stretched his hand, caught the book, and pushed it into his pocket. 'You see,' he said, 'there is so much dust and stone in this universe that it makes it almost impossible to see round the world. These shapeless shadows which you might notice around us are most probably the images of ourselves, and surrounding objects. They are, however, so much distorted by dust and irregularities of the curvature of space that I cannot even tell which is which.'

'Does the same effect occur in the big universe in which we used to live before?' asked Mr Tompkins.

'Oh yes,' was the answer, 'but that universe is so big that it takes the light milliards of years to go round. You could have seen the hair cut on the back of your head without any mirror, but only milliards of years after you had been to the barber. Besides, most probably the interstellar dust would completely obscure the picture. By the way, one English astronomer even supposed once, mostly as a joke, that some of the stars which can be seen in the sky at present are only the images of stars which existed long ago.'

Tired of the efforts to understand all these explanations, Mr Tompkins looked around and noticed, to his great surprise, that the picture of the sky had considerably changed. There seemed to be less dust about, and he took off the handkerchief which was still tied round his face. The small stones were passing much less frequently and hitting the surface of their rock with much less energy. Finally, a few big rocks like their own, which he had noticed in the very beginning, had gone much farther away and could hardly be seen at this distance.

'Well, life is certainly becoming more comfortable,' thought Mr Tompkins. 'I was always so scared that one of those travelling stones would hit me. Can you explain the change in our sur- roundings?' he said, turning to the professor.

'Very easily; our little universe is rapidly expanding and since we have been here its dimensions have increased from *five to about a hundred miles*. As soon as I found myself here, I noticed this expansion from the reddening of the distant objects.'

'Well, I also see that everything is getting pink, at great dis- tances,' said Mr Tompkins, 'but why does it signify expansion?'

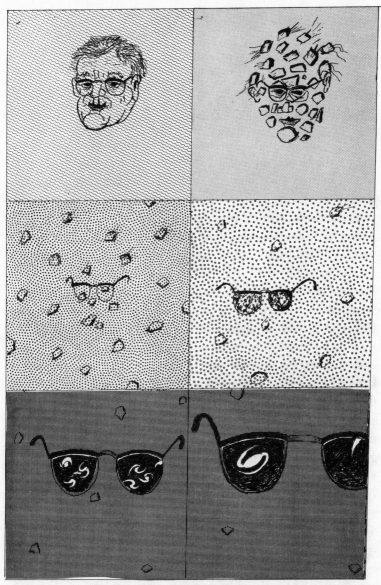

The universe was expanding and cooling beyond any limit. (Adapted from a cartoon in *The Sydney Daily Telegraph*, 16 January 1960)

'Have you ever noticed,' said the professor, 'that the whistle of an approaching train sounds very high, but after the train passes you, the tone is considerably lower? This is the so-called Doppler Effect: the dependence of the pitch on the velocity of the source. When the whole space is expanding, every object located in it moves away with a velocity proportional to its distance from the observer. Therefore the light emitted by such objects is getting redder, which in optics corresponds to a lower pitch. The more distant the object is, the faster it moves and the redder it seems to us. In our good old universe, which is also expanding, this reddening, or the red-shift as we call it, permits astronomers to estimate the distances of the very remote clouds of stars. For example, one of the nearest clouds, the so-called Andromeda nebula, shows 0·05 % of reddening, which corresponds to the distance which can be covered by light in eight hundred thousand years. But there are also nebulae just on the limit of present telescopic power, which show a reddening of about 15 % corresponding to distances of several hundred millions of light years. Presumably, these nebulae are located almost on the half-way point of the equator of the big universe, and the total volume of space which is known to terrestrial astronomers represents a considerable part of the total volume of that universe. The present rate of expansion is about 0·000,000,01 % per year, so that each second the radius of the universe increases by *ten million* miles. Our little universe grows comparatively much faster, gaining in its dimensions about 1 % per minute.'

'Will this expansion never stop?' asked Mr Tompkins.

'Of course it will,' said the professor. 'And then the contraction will start. Each universe pulsates between a very small and a very large radius. For the big universe the period is rather large, something like several thousand million years, but our little one has a period of only about two hours. I think we are now observing the state of largest expansion. Do you notice how cold it is?'

In fact, the thermal radiation filling up the universe, and now distributed over a very large volume, was giving only very little heat to their little planet, and the temperature was at about freezing-point.

'It is lucky for us,' said the professor, 'that there was originally enough radiation to give some heat even at this stage of expansion. Otherwise it might become so cold that the air around our rock would condense into liquid and we would freeze to death. But the contraction has already begun, and it will soon be warm again.'

Looking at the sky, Mr Tompkins noticed that all distant objects changed their colour from pink to violet which, according to the professor, was due to the fact that all the stellar bodies had started moving towards them. He also remembered the analogy given by the professor of the high pitch of the whistle of an approaching train, and shuddered from fear.

'If everything is contracting now, shouldn't we expect that soon all the big rocks filling the universe will come together and that we shall be crushed between them?' he asked the professor anxiously.

'Exactly so,' answered the professor calmly, 'but I think that even before this the temperature will rise so high that we shall both be dissociated into separate atoms. This is a miniature picture of the end of the big universe—everything will be mixed up into a uniform hot gas sphere, and only with a new expansion will new life begin again.'

'Oh my!' muttered Mr Tompkins—'In the big universe we have, as you mentioned, milliards of years before the end, but here it is going too fast for me! I feel hot already, even in my pyjamas.'

'Better not take them off,' said the professor, 'it will not help. Just lie down and observe as long as you can.'

Mr Tompkins did not answer; the hot air was unbearable. The dust, which became very dense now, was accumulating around him, and he felt as if he were being rolled up in a soft warm blanket. He made a motion to free himself, and his hand came out into cool air.

'Did I make a hole in that inhospitable universe?' was his first thought. He wanted to ask the professor about it, but could not

find him anywhere. Instead, in the dim light of the morning, he recognized the contours of the familiar bedroom furniture. He was lying in his bed tightly rolled up in a woollen blanket, and had just managed to free one hand from it.

'New life begins with expansion,' he thought, remembering the words of the old professor. 'Thank God we are still expanding!' And he went to take his morning bath.

6

Cosmic Opera

When, that morning at breakfast, Mr Tompkins told the professor about his dream the previous night, the old man listened rather sceptically.

'The collapse of the universe,' said he, 'would of course be a very dramatic ending, but I think that the velocities of mutual recession of galaxies are so high that present expansion will never turn into a collapse, and that the universe will continue to expand beyond any limit with the distribution of galaxies in space becoming more and more diluted. When all the stars forming the galaxies burn out because of the exhaustion of nuclear fuel, the universe will become a collection of cold and dark celestial aggregations dispersing into infinity.'

'There are, however, some astronomers who think otherwise. They suggest the so-called steady state cosmology, according to which the universe remains unchanging in time: it has existed in about the same state as we see it today from infinity in the past, and will continue so to exist to infinity in the future. Of course it is in accordance with the good old principle of the British empire to preserve the status quo in the world, but I am not inclined to believe that this steady state theory is true. By the way, one of the originators of this new theory, a professor of theoretical astronomy at Cambridge University, wrote an opera on the subject which will have its premiere in Covent Garden next week. Why don't you reserve tickets for Maud and yourself and go to hear it? It may be quite amusing.'

A few days after returning from the beach, which like most channel beaches becomes cool and rainy, Mr Tompkins and Maud were resting comfortably in the red velvet chairs of the opera house, waiting for the curtain to rise. The prelude began *precipite-*

volissimevolmente, and the orchestra leader had to change the collar of his dress suit twice before it was over. When finally the curtain was jerked up, everybody in the audience had to shade his eyes with the palms of his hands, so brilliant was the illumination of the stage. The intense beams of light emanating from the stage

Mr Tompkins saw a man in a black cassock and a clerical collar

soon filled the entire hall, and the ground floor as well as the balcony became one brilliant ocean of light. Gradually the general brilliance faded out, and Mr Tompkins found himself apparently floating in darkened space, illuminated by a multitude of rapidly rotating flaming torches resembling the firewheels used at night festivals. The music of the invisible orchestra now began to sound like organ music and Mr Tompkins saw near him a man in a black cassock and a clerical collar. According to the libretto, it was Abbé Georges Lemaître from Belgium who was the first to propose the theory of the expanding universe, which one often calls the 'big bang' theory.

Mr Tompkins still remembers the first stanzas of his aria:

Majestically

O, Atome preemorrdiale!
All-containeeng Atome!
Deessolved eento frragments exceedeengly small.
   Galaxies forrmeeng,
    Each wiz prrimal enerrgy!
O, rradioactif Atome!
O, all-containeeng Atome!
O, Univairrsale Atome—
   Worrk of z' Lorrd!

Z' long evolution
Tells of mighty firreworrks
Zat ended een ashes and smouldairreeng weesps.
We stand on z' ceendairres
Fadeeng suns confrronteeng us,
Attempteeng to rremembairre
Z' splendeur of z' origine.
O, Univairrsale Atome—
Worrk of Z' Lorrd!

After Father Lemaître finished his aria, there appeared a tall fellow who (according to the libretto again) was a Russian physicist, George Gamow, who had been taking his vacation in the United States for the last three decades. This is what he sang:

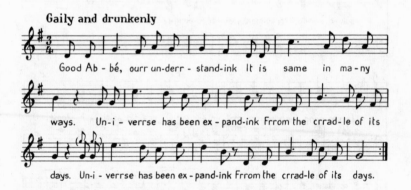

Gaily and drunkenly

Good Ab - bé, ourr un-derr - stand-ink It is   same   in   ma-ny

ways.   Un-i - verrse has been ex - pand-ink Frrom the   crrad-le of its

days.   Un-i - verrse has been ex - pand-ink Frrom the   crrad-le of its   days.

Good Abbé, ourr underrstandink
It is same in many ways.
Univerrse has been expandink
Frrom the crradle of its days.
Univerrse has been expandink
Frrom the crradle of its days.

You have told it gains in motion.
I rregrret to disagrree,
And we differr in ourr notion
As to how it came to be.
And we differr in ourr notion
As to how it came to be.

It was neutrron fluid—neverr
  Prrimal Atom, as you told.
It is infinite, as everr
  It was infinite of old.
      It is infinite, as everr
      It was infinite of old.

On a limitless pavilion
  In collapse, gas met its fate,
Yearrs ago (some thousand million)
  Having come to densest state.
      Yearrs ago (some thousand million)
      Having come to densest state.

All the Space was then rresplendent
  At that crrucial point in time.
Light to matterr was trranscendent
  Much as meterr is, to rrhyme.
      Light to matterr was trranscendent
      Much as meterr is, to rrhyme.

Forr each ton of rradiation
  Then of matterr was an ounce,
Till the impulse t'warrd inflation
  In that grreat prrimeval bounce.
      Till the impulse t'warrd inflation
      In that grreat prrimeval bounce.

Light by then was slowly palink.
  Hundrred million yearrs go by...
Matterr, over light prrevailink,
  Is in plentiful supply.
      Matterr, over light prrevailink,
      Is in plentiful supply.

Matterr then began condensink
  (Such are Jeans' hypotheses).
Giant, gaseous clouds dispensink
  Known as prrotogalaxies.
      Giant, gaseous clouds dispensink
      Known as prrotogalaxies.

Prrotogalaxies were shatterred,
  Flying outward thrrough the night.

Starrs werre forrmed frrom them, and scattered
And the Space was filled with light.
Starrs werre forrmed frrom them, and scatterred
And the Space was filled with light.

Galaxies arre everr spinnink,
Starrs will burrn to final sparrk,
Till ourr univerrse is thinnink
And is lifeless, cold and darrk.
Till ourr univerrse is thinnink
And is lifeless, cold and darrk.

The third aria which Mr Tompkins remembers was delivered by the author of the opera himself, who suddenly materialized from nothing in the space between the brightly shining galaxies. He was pulling a newborn galaxy from his pocket and singing:

Majestically

mf

The un-i-verse, by Hea-ven's de-cree, Was ne—ver formed in time gone by, Was ne-ver formed in time gone by, in time gone by But is, has been, has

been, shall ev-er be For so say Bon — di, Gold and I.

Refrain

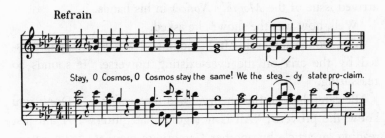

Stay, O Cosmos, O Cosmos stay the same! We the stea — dy state pro-claim.

The universe, by Heaven's decree,
 Was never formed in time gone by,
But is, has been, shall ever be—
 For so say Bondi, Gold and I.
  Stay, O Cosmos, O Cosmos, stay the same!
  We the Steady State proclaim!

The aging galaxies disperse,
 Burn out, and exit from the scene.
But all the while, the universe
 Is, was, shall ever be, has been.
  Stay, O Cosmos, O Cosmos, stay the same!
  We the Steady State proclaim!

And still new galaxies condense
 From nothing, as they did before.
(Lemaître and Gamow, no offence!)
 All was, will be for evermore.
  Stay, O Cosmos, O Cosmos, stay the same!
  We the Steady State proclaim!

But in spite of these inspiring words all the galaxies in the surrounding space were gradually fading out, and finally the velvet curtain was lowered and the candelabra in the large opera hall took their place.

'Oh, Cyril,' he heard Maud say, 'I know you are apt to fall asleep in any place at any time, but you shouldn't in Covent Garden! You slept through the entire performance!'

When Mr Tompkins brought Maud back to her father's house the professor was sitting in his comfortable chair with the newly arrived issue of the *Monthly Notices* in his hands.

'Well, how was the show?' he asked.

'Oh, wonderful!' said Mr Tompkins, 'I was especially impressed by the aria on the ever-existing universe. It sounds so reassuring.'

'Be careful about this theory,' said the professor. 'Don't you know the proverb: "All is not gold that glitters"? I am just reading an article by another Cambridge man, MARTIN RYLE, who built a giant radio-telescope which can locate galaxies at distances several times greater than the range of the Mount Palomar 200-inch optical telescope. His observations show that these very distant galaxies are located much closer to each other than are those in our neighbourhood.'

'Do you mean,' asked Mr Tompkins, 'that our region of the universe has a rather rare population of galaxies, and that this population density increases when we go further and further away?'

'Not at all,' said the professor, 'you must remember that, due to the finite velocity of light, when you look far out into space you look also far back into time. For example, since light takes eight minutes to come here from the Sun, a flare on the Sun's surface is observed by terrestrial astronomers with an eight-minute delay. The photographs of our nearest space neighbour, a spiral galaxy in the constellation of Andromeda—which you must have seen in books on astronomy and which is located about

62

one million light-years away—show how it actually looked one million years ago. Thus, what Ryle sees, or should I rather say hears, through his radio-telescope, corresponds to the situation which existed in that distant part of the universe many thousand millions of years ago. If the universe were really in a steady state, the picture should be unchanged in time, and very distant galaxies as observed from here now should be seen distributed in space neither more densely nor rarely than the galaxies at shorter distances. Thus Ryle's observations showing that distant galaxies seem to be more closely packed together in space is equivalent to the statement that the galaxies everywhere were packed more closely together in the distant past of thousands of millions of years ago. This contradicts the steady state theory, and supports the original view that the galaxies are dispersing and that their population density is going down. But of course we must be careful and wait for further confirmation of Ryle's results.'

'By the way,' continued the professor, extracting a folded piece of paper from his pocket, 'here is a verse which one of my poetically inclined colleagues wrote recently on this subject.' And he read:

'Your years of toil,'
Said Ryle to Hoyle,
  'Are wasted years, believe me.
The steady state
Is out of date.
  Unless my eyes deceive me,

My telescope
Has dashed your hope;
  Your tenets are refuted.
Let me be terse:
Our universe
  Grows daily more diluted!'

Said Hoyle, 'You quote
Lemaître, I note,
  And Gamow. Well, forget them!
That errant gang
And their Big Bang—
  Why aid them and abet them?

63

You see, my friend,
It has no end
    And there was no beginning,
As Bondi, Gold,
And I will hold
    Until our hair is thinning!'

'Not so!' cried Ryle
With rising bile
    And straining at the tether;
'*Far galaxies*
Are, as one sees,
    More tightly packed together!'

'You make me boil!'
Exploded Hoyle,
    His statement rearranging;
'*New matter's born*
Each night and morn.
    The picture is unchanging!'

'Come off it, Hoyle!
I aim to foil
    You yet' (The fun commences)
'And in a while,'
Continued Ryle,
    'I'll bring you to your senses!' *

'Well,' said Mr Tompkins, 'it will be exciting to see what will be the outcome of this dispute,' and giving Maud a kiss on the cheek he wished them both goodnight.

---

*A fortnight before the publication date of the first printing of this book there appeared an article by F. Hoyle entitled: "Recent Developments in Cosmology" (*Nature*, Oct. 9, 1965, p. 111). Hoyle writes: "Ryle and his associates have counted radio sources . . . The indication of that radio count is that the Universe was more dense in the past than it is today." The author has decided, however, not to change the lines of the arias of "Cosmic Opera" since, once written, operas become classic. In fact, even today Desdemona sings a beautiful aria before she dies, after being strangled by Othello.

7

Quantum Billiards

One day Mr Tompkins was going home, feeling very tired after the long day's work in the bank, which was doing a land office business. He was passing a pub and decided to drop in for a glass of ale. One glass followed the other, and soon Mr Tompkins began to feel rather dizzy. In the back of the pub was a billiard room filled with men in shirt sleeves playing billiards on the central table. He vaguely remembered being here before, when one of his fellow clerks took him along to teach him billiards. He approached the table and started to watch the game. Something very queer about it! A player put a ball on the table and hit it with the cue. Watching the rolling ball, Mr Tompkins noticed to his great surprise that the ball began to 'spread out'. This was the only expression he could find for the strange behaviour of the ball which, moving across the green field, seemed to become more and more washed out, losing its sharp contours. It looked as if not one ball was rolling across the table but a great number of balls, all partially penetrating into each other. Mr Tompkins had often observed analogous phenomena before, but today he had not taken a single drop of whisky and he could not understand why it was happening now. 'Well,' he thought, 'let us see how this gruel of a ball is going to hit another one.'

The player who hit the ball was evidently an expert and the rolling ball hit another one head-on just as it was meant to. There was a loud sound of impact and both the resting and the incident balls (Mr Tompkins could not positively say which was which) rushed 'in all different directions'. Yes, it was very strange; there were no longer two balls looking only somewhat gruelly, but instead it seemed that innumerable balls, all of them *very* vague and gruelly, were rushing about within an angle of 180° round the

65

direction of the original impact. It resembled rather a peculiar wave spreading from the point of collision.

Mr Tompkins noticed, however, that there was a maximum flow of balls in the direction of the original impact.

'Scattering of S-wave,' said a familiar voice behind him, and Mr Tompkins recognized the professor. 'Now,' exclaimed

The white ball went in all directions

Mr Tompkins, 'is there something curved again here? The table seems to me perfectly flat.'

'That is quite correct,' answered the professor; 'space here is quite flat and what you observe is actually a quantum-mechanical phenomenon.'

'Oh, the matrix!' ventured Mr Tompkins sarcastically.

'Or, rather, the uncertainty of motion,' said the professor.

'The owner of the billiard room has collected here several objects which suffer, if I may so express myself, from "quantum-elephantism". Actually all bodies in nature are subject to quantum laws, but the so-called quantum constant which governs these phenomena is very, very small; in fact, its numerical value has twenty-seven zeros after the decimal point. For these balls here, however, this constant is much larger—about unity—and you may easily see with your own eyes phenomena which science succeeded in discovering only by using very sensitive and sophisticated methods of observation.' Here the professor became thoughtful for a moment.

'I do not mean to criticize,' he continued, 'but I *would* like to know where the man got these balls from. Strictly speaking, they could not exist in our world, as, for all bodies in our world, the quantum constant has the same small value.'

'Maybe he imported them from some other world,' proposed Mr Tompkins; but the professor was not satisfied and remained suspicious. 'You have noticed,' he continued, 'that the balls "spread out". This means that their position on the table is not quite definite. You cannot actually indicate the position of a ball exactly; the best you can say is that the ball is "mostly here" and "partially somewhere else".'

'This is very unusual,' murmured Mr Tompkins.

'On the contrary,' insisted the professor, 'it is absolutely usual, in the sense that it is always happening to any material body. Only, owing to the small value of the quantum constant and to the roughness of the ordinary methods of observation, people do not notice this indeterminacy. They arrive at the erroneous conclusion that position or velocity are always definite quantities. Actually both are always indefinite to some extent, and the better one is defined the more the other is spread out. The quantum constant just governs the relation between these two uncertainties. Look here, I am going to put definite limits on the position of this ball by putting it inside a wooden triangle.'

As soon as the ball was placed in the enclosure the whole inside of the triangle became filled up with the glittering of ivory.

'You see!' said the professor, 'I defined the position of the ball to the extent of the dimensions of the triangle, i.e. several inches. This results in considerable uncertainty in the velocity, and the ball is moving rapidly inside the boundary.'

'Can't you stop it?' asked Mr Tompkins.

'No—it is physically impossible. Any body in an enclosed space possesses a certain motion—we physicists call it zero-point motion. Such as, for example, the motion of electrons in any atom.'

While Mr Tompkins was watching the ball dashing to and fro in its enclosure like a tiger in a cage, something very unusual happened. The ball just 'leaked out' through the wall of the triangle and next moment was rolling towards a distant corner of the table. The strange thing was that it really did not jump over the wooden wall, but just passed through it, not rising from the table.

'Well, there you are,' said Mr Tompkins, 'your "zero-motion" has run away. Is that according to the rules?'

'Of course it is,' said the professor, 'in fact this is one of the most interesting consequences of quantum theory. It is impossible to hold anything inside an enclosure provided there is enough energy for running away after crossing the wall. Sooner or later the object will just "leak through" and get away.' 'Then I will never go to the Zoo again,' said Mr Tompkins decisively, and his vivid imagination immediately drew a frightful picture of lions and tigers 'leaking through' the walls of their cages. Then his thoughts took a somewhat different direction: he thought about a car locked safely in a garage leaking out, just like a good old ghost of the middle ages, through the wall of the garage.

'How long have I to wait,' he asked the professor, 'until a car, not made from this kind of stuff here, but just made of ordinary steel, will "leak out" through the wall of, let us say, a brick garage? I would very much like to see that!'

Just like a good old ghost of the middle ages

After making some rapid calculations in his head, the professor was ready with the answer: 'It will take about 1,000,000,000... 000,000 years.'

Even though he was accustomed to large numbers in the bank accounts, Mr Tompkins lost the number of noughts mentioned by the professor—it was, however, long enough for him not to worry about his car running away.

'Suppose I believe all you say. I cannot see, however, how such things could be observed—provided we do not have these balls here.'

'A reasonable objection,' said the professor. 'Of course I do not mean that the quantum phenomena could be observed with such big bodies as those with which you are usually dealing. But the point is that the effects of the quantum laws become much more noticeable in their application to very small masses such as atoms or electrons. For these particles, the quantum effects are so large that ordinary mechanics become quite inapplicable. The collision between two atoms looks exactly like the collision between two balls which you have just observed, and the motion of electrons within an atom resembles very closely the "zero-point motion" of the billiard ball I put inside the wooden triangle.'

'And do the atoms run out of the garage very often?' asked Mr Tompkins.

'Oh yes, they do. You have heard, of course, about radioactive bodies, the atoms of which spontaneously disintegrate, emitting very fast particles. Such an atom, or rather its central part called the atomic nucleus, is quite analogous to a garage in which the cars, i.e. the other particles, are stored. And they do escape by leaking through the walls of this nucleus—sometimes they will not stay inside for a second. In these nuclei, the quantum phenomena become quite usual!'

Mr Tompkins felt very tired after this long conversation and was looking round distractedly. His attention was drawn to a large grandfather clock standing in the corner of the room. The long old-fashioned pendulum was slowly swinging to and fro.

'I see you are interested in this clock,' said the professor. 'This is also a mechanism which is not quite usual—but at present it is out of date. The clock just represents the way people used first to think about quantum phenomena. Its pendulum·is arranged in such a way that its amplitude can increase only by finite steps. Now, however, all clockmakers prefer to use the patent spreading-out-pendulums.'

'Oh, I wish I could understand all these complicated things!' exclaimed Mr Tompkins.

'Very well,' retorted the professor, 'I dropped into this pub on the way to my lecture about the quantum theory because I saw you through the window. Now is just the time for me to go, in order not to be late for my lecture. Do you care to come along?'

'Oh yes, I do!' said Mr Tompkins.

As usual the large auditorium was packed with students, and Mr Tompkins was happy even to get a seat on the steps.

Ladies and Gentlemen—began the professor—

In my two previous lectures I tried to show you how the discovery of the upper limit for all physical velocities and the analysis of the notion of a straight line brought us to a complete reconstruction of the classical ideas about space and time.

This development of the critical analysis of the foundations of physics did not, however, stop at this stage, and still more striking discoveries and conclusions have been in store. I am referring to the branch of physics known as quantum theory which is not so much concerned with the properties of space and time themselves as with the mutual interactions and motions of material objects in space and time. In classical physics it was always accepted as self-evident that the interaction between any two physical bodies could be made as small as is required by the conditions of the experiment, and practically reduced to zero whenever necessary. For example, if in investigating the heat developed in certain processes one was afraid that the introduction of a thermometer would take away a certain amount of heat and thus introduce a disturbance in the normal course of the process observed, the experimenter was always certain that by using a smaller thermometer, or a very tiny thermocouple, this disturbance could be reduced to a point below the limits of needed accuracy.

The conviction that any physical process can, in principle, be observed with any required degree of accuracy, without disturbing it by the observation, was so strong that nobody troubled to formulate such a proposition explicitly, and all problems of this kind have always been treated as purely technical difficulties. However, new empirical facts accumulated since the beginning of the present century were steadily bringing physicists to the conclusion that the situation is really much more complicated and that *there exists in nature a certain lower limit of interaction which can never be surpassed*. This natural limit of accuracy is negligibly small for all kinds of processes with which we are familiar in ordinary life, but it becomes quite important when we are handling the interactions taking place in such tiny mechanical systems as atoms and molecules.

In the year 1900 the German physicist MAX PLANCK, while investigating theoretically the conditions of equilibrium between matter and radiation, came to the surprising conclusion that no such equilibrium is possible unless we suppose that *the interaction between the matter and radiation takes place not continuously, as we always supposed, but in a sequence of separate 'shocks'*, a definite amount of energy being transferred from matter to radiation or vice versa in each of these elementary acts of interaction. In order to get the desired equilibrium, and to achieve agreement with the experimental facts, it was necessary to introduce a simple mathematical relation of proportionality between the amount of energy transferred in each shock and the frequency (inverse period) of the process leading to the transfer of energy.

Thus, denoting the coefficient of proportionality by a symbol 'h' Planck was forced to accept that the minimal portion, or quantum, of energy transferred must be given by the expression

$$E = h\nu, \tag{1}$$

where ν stands for frequency. The constant h has the numerical value $6 \cdot 547 \times 10^{-27}$ ergs $\times$ second and is usually called Planck's constant or the quantum constant. Its small numerical value is responsible for the fact that quantum phenomena are usually not observed in our everyday life.

The further development of Planck's ideas is due to Einstein who, a few years later, came to the conclusion that *not only is the radiation emitted in definite discrete portions, but that it always exists in this way, consisting of a number of discrete 'packages of energy' which he called light quanta.*

In so far as light quanta are moving they should possess, apart from their energy $h\nu$, a certain mechanical momentum also, which, according to relativistic mechanics, should be equal to their energy divided by the velocity of light c. Remembering that the frequency of light is related to its wave length λ by the relation $\nu = c/\lambda$, we can write for the mechanical momentum of a light quantum:

$$p = \frac{h\nu}{c} = \frac{h}{\lambda}. \tag{2}$$

Since the mechanical action produced by the impact of a moving object is given by its momentum we must conclude that the action of light quanta increases with their decreasing wave length.

One of the best experimental proofs of the correctness of the idea of light quanta, and the energy and momentum ascribed to them, was given by the investigation of the American physicist ARTHUR COMPTON who, studying the collisions between light quanta and electrons, arrived at the result that electrons set into motion by the action of a ray of light behaved exactly as if they had been struck by a particle with the energy and momentum given by the previously given formulae. The light quanta themselves, after the collision with electrons, were also shown to suffer certain changes (in their frequency), in excellent agreement with the prediction of the theory.

We can say at present that, as far as the interaction with matter is concerned, the quantum property of radiation is a well established experimental fact.

The further development of the quantum ideas is due to the

famous Danish physicist NIELS BOHR who, in 1913, was first to express the idea that *the internal motion of any mechanical system may possess only a discrete set of possible energy values and the motion can change its state only by finite steps,* a definite amount of energy being radiated in each of such transitions. The mathematical rules defining the possible states of mechanical systems are more complicated than in the case of radiation and we will not enter here into their formulation. We shall only indicate that, just as, in the case of light quanta, the momentum is defined through the wave length of light, so in the mechanical system the momentum of any moving particle is connected with the geometrical dimensions of the region of space in which it is moving, its order of magnitude being given by the expression

$$p_{\text{particle}} \cong \frac{h}{l}, \tag{3}$$

l being here linear dimensions of the region of motion. Due to the extremely small value of the quantum constant quantum phenomena could be of importance only for motions taking place in such small regions as the inside of atoms and molecules, and they play a very important part in our knowledge of the internal structure of matter.

One of the most direct proofs of the existence of the sequence of discrete states of these tiny mechanical systems was given by the experiments of JAMES FRANCK and GUSTAV HERTZ who, bombarding atoms by electrons of varying energy, noticed that definite changes in the state of the atom took place only when the energy of the bombarding electrons reached certain discrete values. If the energy of electrons was brought below a certain limit no effect whatsoever was observed in the atoms because the amount of energy carried by each electron was not enough to raise the atom from the first quantum state into the second.

Thus at the end of this first preliminary stage of the development of quantum theory the situation could be described, not as the modification of fundamental notions and principles of classical physics, but as its more or less artificial restriction by rather mysterious quantum conditions picking out from the continuous variety of classical possible motions only a discrete set of 'permitted' ones. If, however, we look deeper into the connexion between the laws of classical mechanics and these quantum conditions required by our extended experience, we shall discover that the system obtained by their unification suffers from logical inconsistency, and that the empirical quantum restrictions make senseless the fundamental notions on which classical mechanics is based. In fact, the fundamental concept concerning motion in classical theory is that any moving particle occupies at any given moment a certain position in space and possesses a definite velocity characterizing the time changes of its position on the trajectory.

These fundamental notions of position, velocity, and trajectory, on which are based all the elaborated building of classical mechanics, are formed (as are all our other notions) on observation of the phenomena around us, and, like the classical notions of space and time, might be subject to far reaching modifications as soon as our experience extends into new, previously unexplored, regions.

If I ask somebody why he believes that any moving particle occupies at any given moment a certain position describing in the course of time a definite line called the trajectory, he will most probably answer: 'Because I see it this way, when I observe the motion.' Let us analyse this method of forming the classical notion of the trajectory and see if it really will lead to a definite result. For this purpose we imagine a physicist supplied with any kind of the most sensitive apparatus, trying to pursue the motion of a little material body thrown from the wall of his laboratory. He decides to make his observation by 'seeing' how the body moves and for this purpose he uses a small but very precise theodolite. Of course to see the moving body he must illuminate it and, knowing that light in general produces a pressure on the body and might disturb its motion, he decides to use short flash illumination only at the moments when he makes the observation. For his first trial he wants to observe only ten points on the trajectory and thus he chooses his flashlight source so weak that

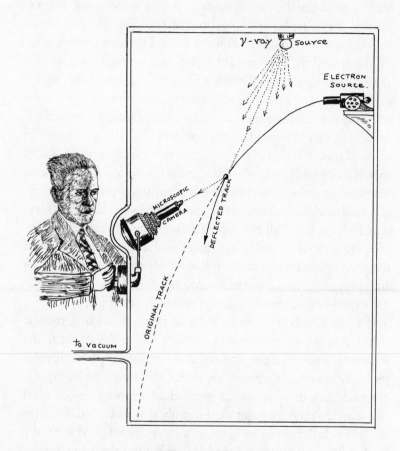

Heisenberg's γ-ray microscope

the integral effect of light pressure during ten successive illuminations should be within the accuracy he needs. Thus, flashing his light ten times during the fall of the body, he obtains, with the desired accuracy, ten points on the trajectory.

Now he wants to repeat the experiment and to get one hundred points. He knows that a hundred successive illuminations will disturb the motion too much and therefore, preparing for the second set of observations, chooses his flashlight ten times less intense. For the third set of observations, desiring to have one thousand points, he makes the flashlight a hundred times fainter than originally.

Proceeding in this way, and constantly decreasing the intensity of his illumination, he can obtain as many points on the trajectory as he wants to, without increasing the possible error above the limit he had chosen at the beginning. This highly idealized, but in principle quite possible, procedure represents the strictly logical way to construct the motion of a trajectory by 'looking at the moving body' and you see that, in the frame of classical physics, it is quite possible.

But now let us see what happens if we introduce the quantum limitations and take into account the fact that the action of any radiation can be transferred only in the form of light quanta. We have seen that our observer was constantly reducing the amount of light illuminating the moving body and we must now expect that he will find it impossible to continue to do so as soon as he comes down to one quantum. Either all or none of the total light quantum will be reflected from the moving body, and in the latter case the observation cannot be made. Of course we have seen that the effect of collision with a light quantum decreases with increasing wave length, and our observer, knowing it too, will certainly try to use for his observations light of increasing wave length to compensate for the number of observations. But here he will meet with another difficulty.

It is well known that when using light of certain wave lengths one cannot see details smaller than the wave length used; in fact one cannot paint a Persian miniature using a house-painter's brush! Thus, by using longer and longer waves, he will spoil the estimate of each single point and soon will come to the stage where each estimate will be uncertain by an amount comparable to the size of all his laboratory and more. Thus he will be forced finally to a compromise between the large number of observed points and uncertainty of each estimate and will never be able to arrive at an

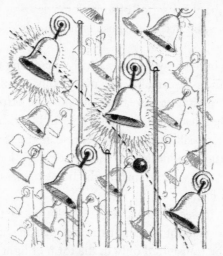

Little bells on springs

exact trajectory as a mathematical line such as that obtained by his classical colleagues. His best result will be a rather broad washed-out band, and if he bases his notion of the trajectory on the result of his experience, it will be rather different from a classical one.

The method discussed here is an optical method, and we can now try another possibility, using a mechanical method. For this purpose our experimenter can devise some tiny mechanical apparatus, say little bells on springs, which would register the passage of material bodies if such a body passes close to them. He can spread a large number of such 'bells' through the space through which the moving body is expected to pass and after the passage the 'ringing of bells' will indicate its track. In classical physics one can make the 'bells' as small and sensitive as one likes and, in the limiting case of an infinite number of infinitely small bells, the notion of a trajectory can be again formed with any desired accuracy. However, the quantum limitations for mechanical systems will spoil the situation again. If the 'bells' are too small, the amount of momentum which they will take from the moving body will be, according to formula (3), too large and the motion will be largely disturbed even after only one bell has been hit. If the bells are large the uncertainty of each position will be very large. The final trajectory deduced will again be a spread-out band!

I am afraid that all these considerations about an experimenter trying to observe the trajectory may make a somewhat too technical impression, and you will be inclined to think that, even if our observer cannot estimate the trajectory by the means he is using, some other more complicated device will give the desired result. I must remind you, however, that we have here been discussing not any particular experiment done in some physical laboratory, but an idealization of the most general question of physical measurement. As far as any actions existing in our world can be classified either as due to radiative field or as purely mechanical, any elaborated scheme of measurement will be necessarily reduced to the elements described in these two methods and will finally lead to the same result. As far as our ideal 'measuring apparatus' can involve all the physical world we should come ultimately to the conclusion that such things as exact position and a trajectory of precise shape have no place in a world subject to quantum laws.

Let us now return to our experimenter and try to get the mathematical form for the limitations imposed by quantum conditions. We have already seen that in both methods used there is always a conflict between the estimate of position and the disturbance of the velocity of the moving object. In the optical method, the collision with a light quantum will, because of the mechanical law of conservation of momentum, introduce an uncertainty in the momentum of the particle comparable with the momentum of the light quantum used. Thus, using formula (2), we can write for the uncertainty of momentum of the particle

$$\Delta p_{\text{particle}} \cong \frac{h}{\lambda}, \tag{4}$$

and remembering that the uncertainty of position of the particle is given by the wave length ($\Delta q \cong \lambda$) we deduce:

$$\Delta p_{\text{particle}} \times \Delta q_{\text{particle}} \cong h. \tag{5}$$

In the mechanical method the momentum of the moving particle will be made uncertain by the amount taken by the 'bells'. Using our formula (3) and remembering that in this case the uncertainty of position is given by the size of the bell ($\Delta q \cong l$), we come again to the same finite formula as in the previous case. Thus the relation (5), first formulated by the German physicist WERNER HEISENBERG, represents the fundamental uncertainty—relation of quantum theory—*the better one defines the position, the more indefinite the momentum becomes, and vice versa.*

Remembering that momentum is the product of the mass of the moving particle and its velocity, we can write

$$\Delta v_{\text{particle}} \times \Delta q_{\text{particle}} \cong \frac{h}{m_{\text{particle}}}. \tag{6}$$

For bodies which we usually handle this is ridiculously small. For a lighter particle of dust with the mass 0·000,000,1 gm both position and velocity can be measured with an accuracy of 0·000,000,01 %! However, for an electron (with the mass 10^{-29} gm) the product $\Delta v \Delta q$ should be of the order 100. Inside an atom the velocity of an electron should be defined at least within $\pm\, 10^{10}$ cm/sec otherwise it will escape from the atom. This gives for the uncertainty of position 10^{-8} cm, i.e. the total dimensions of an atom. Thus 'the orbit' of an electron in an atom is spread out by such extent that 'the thickness' of the trajectory becomes equal to its 'radius'. *Thus the electron appears simultaneously all around the nucleus.*

During the last twenty minutes I have tried to show you a picture of the disastrous results of our criticism of classical ideas of motion. The elegant and sharply defined classical notions are broken to pieces and give place to what I would call a shapeless gruel. You may naturally ask me how on earth the physicists are going to describe any phenomena in view of this ocean of uncertainty. The answer is that we have so far destroyed classical notions, but we have not yet arrived at an exact formulation of new ones.

We shall proceed with it now. It is clear that, if we cannot in general define the position of a material particle by a mathematical point and the trajectory of its motion by a mathematical line because the things had spread out, we should use other methods of description giving, so to speak, 'the density of the gruel' at different points of space. Mathematically it means the use of continuous functions (such as are used in hydrodynamics) and physically this requires us to be used to the expressions like 'this object is mostly here, but partially there and even yonder', or 'this coin is 75 % in my pocket and 25 % in yours'. I know that such sentences will terrify you, but, due to the small value of the quantum constant, you will never need them in everyday life. However, if you are going to study atomic physics, I would strongly advise you to get accustomed to such expressions first.

I must warn you here against the erroneous idea that the function describing the 'density of presence' has a physical reality in our ordinary three-dimensional space. In fact, if we describe the behaviour of, say, two particles, we must answer the question concerning the presence of our first particle in one place and the simultaneous presence of our second particle in some other place; to do this we have to use a function of six variables (coordinates of two particles) which cannot be 'localized' in three-dimensional space. For more complex systems functions of still larger numbers of variables must be used. In this sense, the 'quantum mechanical function' is analogous to the 'potential function' of a system of particles in classical mechanics or to the 'entropy' of a system in statistical mechanics. It only *describes* the motion and helps us to predict the result of any particular motion under given conditions. The physical reality stays with the particles the motion of which we are describing.

The function which describes to what extent the particle or system of particles is present in different places requires some mathematical notation and, according to the Austrian physicist ERWIN SCHRÖDINGER, who first wrote the equation defining the behaviour of this function, it is denoted by the symbol '$\psi\bar\psi$'.

I am not going to enter here into the mathematical proof of his fundamental equation, but I will draw your attention to the requirements which lead to its derivation. The most important of these requirements is a very unusual one: *The equation must be written in such a way that the function which describes the motion of material particles should show all the characteristics of a wave.*

The necessity of ascribing wave properties to the motion of material particles was first indicated by the French physicist LOUIS DE BROGLIE, on the basis of his theoretical studies of the structure of an atom. In the following years the wave properties of the motion of material particles were firmly established by numerous experiments, showing such phenomena as the *diffraction* of a beam of electrons passing through a small opening and *interference phenomena* taking place even for such comparatively large and complex particles as molecules.

The observed wave properties of material particles were absolutely incomprehensible from the point of view of classical conceptions of motion, and de Broglie himself was forced to a rather unnatural point of view: that the particles are 'accompanied' by certain waves which, so to speak, 'direct' their motion.

However, as soon as the classical notions are destroyed and we come to the description of motion by continuous functions, the requirement of wave character becomes much more understandable. It just says that the propagation of our '$\psi\bar\psi$' function is not analogous to (let us say) propagation of heat through a wall heated on one side but rather to the propagation of mechanical deformation (sound) through the same wall. Mathematically it requires a definite rather restricted form of the equation we are looking for. This fundamental condition, together with the additional requirement that our equations should go over into the equations of classical mechanics when applied to particles of large mass for which quantum effect should become negligible, practically reduces the problem of finding the equation to a purely mathematical exercise.

If you are interested in how the equation looks in its final form, I can write it here for you. Here it is:

$$\nabla^2 \psi + \frac{4\pi m i}{h} \dot{\psi} - \frac{8\pi^2 m}{h} U\psi = 0. \tag{7}$$

In this equation the function U represents the potential of forces acting on our particles (with the mass m), and it gives a definite solution of the problem of motion for any given distribution of force. The application of this 'Schrödinger's wave equation' has allowed physicists, during the forty years of its existence, to develop the most complete and logically consistent picture of all phenomena taking place in the world of atoms.

Some of you may have been wondering that until now I have not used the word 'matrix', often heard in connexion with the quantum theory. I must confess that personally I rather dislike these matrices and prefer to do without them. But, in order not to leave you absolutely ignorant about this mathematical implement of the quantum theory, I shall say a word or two about it. The motion of a particle or of a complex mechanical system is always described, as you have seen, by certain continuous wave functions. These functions are often rather complicated and can be represented as being composed of a number of simpler oscillations, the so-called 'proper functions', much in the way that a complicated sound can be made up from a number of simple harmonic notes.

One can describe the whole complex motion by giving the amplitudes of its different components. Since the number of components (overtones) is infinite we must write infinite tables of amplitudes in a form:

$$
\begin{array}{cccc}
q_{11} & q_{12} & q_{13} & \cdots \\
q_{21} & q_{22} & q_{23} & \cdots \\
q_{31} & q_{32} & q_{33} & \cdots \\
\multicolumn{4}{c}{\cdots\cdots\cdots\cdots\cdots\cdots}
\end{array}
\tag{8}
$$

Such a table, which is subject to comparatively simple rules of mathematical operations, is called a 'matrix' corresponding to a given motion, and some theoretical physicists prefer to operate with matrices instead of dealing with the wave functions themselves. Thus the 'matrix mechanics' as they sometimes call it is just a mathematical modification of the ordinary 'wave mechanics'; and in these lectures, devoted mainly to the principal questions, we do not need to enter more deeply into these problems.

I am very sorry that time does not permit me to describe to you the further progress of quantum theory in its relation to the theory of relativity. This development, due mainly to the work of the British physicist PAUL ADRIEN MAURICE DIRAC, brings in a number of very interesting points and has also led to some extremely important experimental discoveries. I may be able to return at some other time to these problems, but here at present I must stop, and express the hope that this series of lectures has helped you to get a clearer picture of the present conception of the physical world and has excited in you an interest for further studies.

8

Quantum Jungles

Next morning Mr Tompkins was dozing in bed, when he became aware of somebody's presence in the room. Looking round, he discovered that his old friend the professor was sitting in the arm-chair, absorbed in the study of a map spread on his knee.

'Are you coming along?' asked the professor, lifting his head.

'Coming where?' said Mr Tompkins, still wondering how the professor had got into his room.

'To see the elephants, of course, and the rest of the animals of the quantum jungle. The owner of the billiard room we visited recently told me his secret about the place where the ivory for his billiard-balls came from. You see this region which I've marked with red pencil on the map? It seems that everything within it is subject to quantum laws with a very large quantum constant. The natives think that all this part of the country is populated by devils, and I am afraid it will hardly be possible for us to find a guide. But if you want to come along, you had better hurry up. The boat is sailing in an hour's time and we still have to pick up Sir Richard on our way.'

'Who is Sir Richard?' asked Mr Tompkins.

'Haven't you ever heard about him?' The professor was evidently surprised. 'He is a famous tiger-hunter, and decided to go with us, when I promised him some interesting shooting.'

They came to the docks just in time to see the loading of a number of long boxes containing Sir Richard's rifles and the special bullets made from lead which the professor had obtained from the lead mines near the quantum jungle. While Mr Tompkins was arranging his baggage in the cabin, the steady vibrations of the boat told him that they were off. The sea journey was nothing remarkable, and Mr Tompkins scarcely noticed the time until they came ashore in a fascinating oriental city, the nearest populated place to the mysterious quantum regions.

'Now,' said the professor, 'we have to buy an elephant for our journey inland. As I do not think any of the natives will agree to go with us, we shall have to drive the elephant ourselves, and you, my dear Tompkins, will have to learn the job. I shall be too busy with my scientific observations and Sir Richard will have to handle the firearms.'

Mr Tompkins was rather unhappy when, coming to the elephant market on the outskirts of the city, he saw the huge animals, one of which he would have to handle. Sir Richard, who knew a lot about elephants, picked out a nice big animal and asked the owner what price it was.

'Hrup hanweck 'o hobot hum. Hagori ho, haraham oh Hohohohi,' said the native, showing his shining teeth.

'He wants quite a lot of money for it,' translated Sir Richard, 'but says that this is an elephant from the quantum jungle and it is therefore more expensive. Shall we take it?'

'By all means,' explained the professor. 'I heard on the boat that sometimes elephants come from the quantum lands and are caught by the natives. They are much better than the elephants from other regions, and in our case we shall have quite an advantage because this animal will feel at home in the jungle.'

Mr Tompkins inspected the elephant from all sides; it was a very beautiful, large animal, but there was no marked difference in its behaviour from the elephants he had seen in the Zoo. He turned to the professor—'You said that this was a quantum elephant, but it looks just like an ordinary elephant to me, and does not behave in a funny way, like the billiard-balls made from the tusks of some of its relatives. Why doesn't it spread out in all directions?'

'You show a peculiar slowness of comprehension,' said the professor. 'It is because of its very large mass. I told you some time ago that all the uncertainty in position and velocity depends on the mass; the larger the mass, the smaller the uncertainty. That is why the quantum laws have not been observed in the ordinary world even for such light bodies as particles of dust, but become quite important for electrons, which are billions of billions of times lighter. Now, in the quantum jungle, the quantum constant is rather large, but still not large enough to produce striking effects in the behaviour of such a heavy animal as an elephant. The uncertainty of the position of a quantum elephant can be noticed only by close inspection of its contours. You may have noticed that the surface of its skin is not quite definite and seems to be slightly fuzzy. In course of time this uncertainty increases very slowly, and I think this is the origin of the native legend that very old elephants from the quantum jungle possess long fur. But I expect that all smaller animals will show very remarkable quantum effects.'

'Isn't it nice,' thought Mr Tompkins, 'that we are not doing this expedition on horseback? If that were the case, I should probably never know whether my horse was between my knees or in the next valley.'

After the professor and Sir Richard with his rifles had climbed into the basket fastened on to the elephant's back, and Mr Tompkins, in his new capacity of mahout, had taken his position on the elephant's neck, clutching the goad in one hand, they started towards the mysterious jungle.

The people in the city told them that it would take about an hour to get there, and Mr Tompkins, trying to keep his balance between the elephant's ears, decided to make use of the time by learning more about quantum phenomena from the professor.

'Can you tell me, please,' he asked, turning to the professor, '*why* do bodies with small mass behave so peculiarly, and what is the commonsense meaning of this quantum constant that you are always talking about?'

'Oh, it is not so difficult to understand,' said the professor. 'The funny behaviour of all objects you observe in the quantum world is just due to the fact that you are looking at them.'

'Are they so shy?' smiled Mr Tompkins.

'"Shy" is an unsuitable word,' said the professor bleakly. 'The point is, however, that in making any observation of the motion you will necessarily disturb this motion. In fact, if you learn something about the motion of a body, this means that the moving body delivered some action on your senses or the apparatus you are using. Owing to the equality of action and reaction we must conclude that your measuring apparatus also acted on the body and, so to speak, "spoiled" its motion, introducing an uncertainty in its position and velocity.'

'Well,' said Mr Tompkins, 'if I had touched that ball in the billiard room with my finger I should certainly have disturbed its motion. But I was just looking at it; does that disturb it?'

'Of course it does. You cannot see the ball in darkness, but if you put on the light, the light-rays reflected from the ball and making it visible will act on the ball—light-pressure we call it—and "spoil" its motion.'

'But suppose I used very fine and sensitive instruments, can't I make the action of my instruments on the moving body so small as to be negligible?'

'That is just what we thought in classical physics, before the *quantum of action* was discovered. At the beginning of this century it became clear that the *action* on any object cannot be brought below a certain limit which is called the quantum constant and usually denoted by the symbol "h". In the ordinary world the quantum of action is very small; in customary units it is expressed by a number with twenty-seven zeros after the decimal point, and is of importance only for such light particles as electrons which, owing to their very small mass, will be influenced by very small actions. In the quantum jungle we are now approaching, the quantum of action is very big. This is a rough world where no gentle action is possible. If a person in such a world tried to pet a kitten, it would either not feel anything at all, or its neck would be broken by the first quantum of caress.'

'This is all very well,' said Mr Tompkins thoughtfully, 'but when nobody is looking, do the bodies behave properly, I mean, in the way we are accustomed to think?'

'When nobody is looking,' said the professor, 'nobody can know how they do behave, and thus your question has no physical sense.'

'Well, well,' exclaimed Mr Tompkins, 'it certainly looks like philosophy to me!'

'You can call it philosophy if you like'—the professor was evidently offended—'but as a matter of fact, this is the fundamental principle of modern physics—*never to speak about the things you cannot know*. All modern physical theory is based on this principle, whereas the philosophers usually overlook it. For example, the famous German philosopher KANT spent quite a lot of time reflecting about the properties of bodies not as they "appear to us", but as they "are in themselves". For the modern physicist only the so-called "observables" (i.e. principally, observable properties) have any significance, and all modern physics is based on their mutual relation. The things which cannot be observed are good only for idle thinking—you have no restrictions in inventing them, and no possibility of checking their existence, or of making any use of them. I should say....'

At this moment a terrible roar filled the air and their elephant jerked so violently that Mr Tompkins almost fell off. A large pack of tigers was attacking their elephant, jumping simultaneously from all sides. Sir Richard grabbed his rifle and pulled the trigger, aiming right between the eyes of the tiger nearest to him. The next moment Mr Tompkins heard him mutter a strong expression common among hunters; he shot right through the tiger's head without causing any damage to the animal.

'Shoot more!' shouted the professor. 'Scatter your fire all round and don't mind about precise aiming! There is only one tiger, but it is spread around our elephant and our only hope is to raise the Hamiltonian.'

The professor grabbed another rifle and the cannonade of shooting became mixed up with the roar of the quantum tiger. An eternity passed, so it seemed to Mr Tompkins, before all was over. One of the bullets 'hit the spot' and, to his great surprise, the tiger, which became suddenly one, was vigorously hurled away, its dead body describing an arc in the air, and landing somewhere behind the distant palm grove.

'Who is this Hamiltonian?' asked Mr Tompkins after things had quietened down. 'Is he some famous hunter you wanted to raise from the grave to help us?'

'Oh!' said the professor, 'I am so sorry. In the excitement of battle I started to use scientific language—which you cannot understand! Hamiltonian is a mathematical expression describing the quantum interaction between two bodies. It is named after an Irish mathematician, HAMILTON, who first used this mathematical form. I just wanted to say that by shooting more quantum bullets we increase the probability of the interaction between the bullet and the body of the tiger. In the quantum world, you see, one cannot aim precisely and be sure of a hit. Owing to the spreading out of the bullet, and of the aim itself, there is always only a finite chance of hitting, never a certainty. In our case we fired at least thirty bullets before we actually hit the tiger; and then the action of the bullet on the tiger was so violent that it hurled its body far away. The same things are happening in our world at home but on a much smaller scale. As I have already mentioned, in the ordinary world one has to investigate the behaviour of such small particles as electrons in order to notice anything. You may have heard that each atom consists of a comparatively heavy nucleus and a number of electrons rotating round it. One used to think, at first, that the motion of electrons round the nucleus is quite analogous to the motion of planets round the sun, but deeper analysis has shown that ordinary notions concerning the motion are too rough for such a miniature system as that of the atom. The actions which play an important role inside an atom are of the same order of

A large pack of fuzzy-looking tigers was attacking their elephant

magnitude as the elementary quantum of action and thus the whole picture is largely spread out. The motion of the electron round the atomic nucleus is in many respects analogous to the motion of our tiger, which seemed to be all round the elephant.'

'And does somebody shoot at the electron as we did the tiger?' asked Mr Tompkins.

'Oh yes, of course, the nucleus itself sometimes emits very energetic light quanta or elementary action-units of light. You can also shoot at the electron from outside the atom, by illuminating it with a beam of light. And it all happens there just as with our tiger here: many light quanta pass through the location of the electron without affecting it, until presently one of them acts on the electron and throws it out of the atom. The quantum system cannot be affected slightly; it is either not affected at all, or else changed a lot.'

'Just as with the poor kitten which cannot be petted in the quantum world without being killed,' concluded Mr Tompkins.

'Look! gazelles, and lots of them!' exclaimed Sir Richard, raising his rifle. In fact a big herd of gazelles was emerging from the bamboo grove.

'Trained gazelles,' thought Mr Tompkins. 'They run in as regular formation as soldiers on parade. I wonder if this is also some quantum effect.'

The group of gazelles which was approaching their elephant was moving rapidly and Sir Richard was ready to shoot, when the professor stopped him.

'Do not waste your cartridges,' he said, 'there is very little chance of hitting an animal when it is moving in a diffraction pattern.'

'What do you mean by "*an*" animal?' exclaimed Sir Richard. 'There are at least several dozens of them!'

'Oh no! There is only one little gazelle which, because it is scared of something, is running through the bamboo grove. Now, the "spread-out" of all bodies possesses a property analogous to that of ordinary light; and, passing through a regular sequence of

Sir Richard was ready to shoot, when the professor stopped him

openings, for instance between the separate bamboo trunks in the grove, it shows the phenomena of diffraction about which you might have heard at school. We speak therefore about the wave-character of matter.'

But neither Sir Richard nor Mr Tompkins could think at all what this mysterious word 'diffraction' might mean, and the conversation stopped at this point.

Passing farther through the quantum land our travellers met quite a lot of other interesting phenomena, such as quantum mosquitoes, which could scarcely be located at all, owing to their small mass, and some very amusing quantum monkeys. Now they were approaching something which looked very much like a native village.

'I did not know,' said the professor, 'that there was a human population in these regions. Judging by the noise, I suppose they are having some sort of festival. Listen to this incessant noise of bells.'

It was very difficult to distinguish the separate figures of natives who were evidently dancing a wild dance round the big fire. Brown hands with bells of all sizes were constantly rising from among the crowd. As they approached still closer, everything, including the huts and surrounding big trees, began to spread out, and the ringing of the bells became unbearable to Mr Tompkins's ears. He stretched his hand out, grabbed something, and then threw it away. The alarm clock hit the glass of water standing on his night-table and the cold stream of water brought him to his senses. He jumped up, and started to dress rapidly. In half an hour he must be at the bank.

9

Maxwell's Demon

During many months of unusual adventures, in the course of which the professor tried to introduce Mr Tompkins to the secrets of physics, Mr Tompkins became more and more enchanted by Maud and finally, and rather sheepishly, made a proposal of marriage. This was readily accepted, and they became man and wife. In his new role of father-in-law, the professor considered it his duty to enlarge the knowledge of his daughter's husband in the field of physics and of its most recent progress.

One Sunday afternoon Mr and Mrs Tompkins were resting in armchairs in their comfortable flat, she being engulfed in the latest issue of *Vogue*, he reading an article in *Esquire*.*

'Oh,' Mr Tompkins exclaimed suddenly, 'here is a chance game system which really works!'

'Do you really think, Cyril, that it will?' asked Maud, raising her eyes reluctantly from the pages of the fashion magazine. 'Father has always said that there can't be such a thing as a sure-fire gambling system.'

'But look here, Maud,' answered Mr Tompkins, showing her the article he had been studying for the last half hour. 'I don't know about other systems, but this one is based on pure and simple mathematics, and I really don't see how it could possibly go wrong. All you have to do is to write down three figures

1, 2, 3

on a piece of paper, and follow a few simple rules given here.'

'Well, let's try it out,' suggested Maud, beginning to be interested. 'What are the rules?'

'Suppose you follow the example given in the article. That's

---

* January 1940.

'But you *must* win this time!'

probably the best way to learn them. As illustration, they have
used a roulette game in which you place your money on red or
black, which is the same as betting heads or tails on the flip of a
coin. I write down

I, 2, 3

and the rule is that my bet must always be the sum of the outside
figures in the series. So I take one plus three, which is four, chips

and put them, let's say, on red. If I win, I cross out the figures 1 and 3 and my next bet will be the remaining figure 2. If I lose, I add the amount lost to the end of the series and apply the same rule to find my next bet. Well, suppose the ball stops on black and the croupier rakes in my four chips. Then my new series will be

$$1, 2, 3, 4$$

and my next bet one plus four, which is five. Suppose I lose a second time. The article says I must keep on in the same way, adding the figure 5 at the end of the series and putting six chips on the table.'

'But you *must* win this time!' cried Maud, getting quite excited. 'You can't keep on losing.'

'Not necessarily,' said Mr Tompkins. 'When I was a boy I used to flip pennies with my friends, and believe it or not, I once saw heads come up ten times in a row. But let's suppose, as this article does, that I win this time. Then I collect twelve chips, but I am still out three chips compared with my original stake. Following the rules, I must cross out the figures 1 and 5, and my series now reads

$$\cancel{1}, 2, 3, 4, \cancel{5}$$

My next bet must be two plus four, or six chips again.'

'It says here you have lost again,' sighed Maud, reading over her husband's shoulder. 'That means you have to add six to the series and bet eight chips next time. Isn't that so?'

'Yes, that's right, but I lose again. My series is now

$$\cancel{1}, 2, 3, 4, \cancel{5}, 6, 8$$

and I have to bet ten this time. It wins. I cross out the figures 2 and 8 and my next bet is three plus six which is nine. But I lose again.'

'It's a bad example,' said Maud, pouting. 'So far, you've lost three times and only won once. It's not fair!'

'Never mind, never mind,' said Mr Tompkins with the quiet confidence of a magician. 'We'll win all right at the end of the cycle. I lost nine chips on the last spin, so I'll add this figure to the series to make it

$$\cancel{1}, \cancel{2}, 3, 4, \cancel{5}, 6, \cancel{8}, 9$$

and bet twelve chips. I win this time, so I cross out the figures 3 and 9 and bet the sum of the remaining two, or ten chips. The second successive win completes the cycle as all the figures are now crossed out. And I am six chips up, in spite of the fact that I won only four times and lost five!'

'Are you sure you are six chips up?' asked Maud doubtfully.

'Quite sure. You see the system is arranged in such a way that, whenever the cycle is complete, you are always six chips up. You can prove it by simple arithmetic, and that's why I say this system is mathematical and can't fail. If you don't believe it, take a piece of paper and check it yourself.'

'All right. I'll take your word for it that that's the way it works out,' said Maud thoughtfully, 'but, of course, six chips aren't very much to win.'

'Yes they are, if you are sure of winning them at the end of each cycle. You can repeat the procedure over and over again, beginning each time with 1, 2, 3, and making as much money as you want. Isn't it *grand*?'

'Wonderful!' exclaimed Maud. 'Then you can drop your work at the bank, we can move into a better house, and I saw a darling mink coat in a shop window today. It cost only....'

'Of course we'll buy it, but first we had better get to Monte Carlo quickly. A lot of other people must have read this article, and it would be too bad to get there only to find some other fellow had beaten us to it and put the Casino into bankruptcy.'

'I'll ring up the air line,' suggested Maud, 'and find out when the next plane leaves.'

'What's all the hurry about?' said a familiar voice in the hall. Maud's father came into the room and looked at the excited pair in surprise.

'We're leaving for Monte Carlo on the first plane and we're

going to come home very rich,' said Mr Tompkins, rising to greet the professor.

'Oh, I see,' smiled the latter, making himself comfortable in an old-fashioned armchair near the fireplace. 'You have a new gambling system?'

'But this time it's a real one, Father!' protested Maud, her hand still on the phone.

'Yes,' added Mr Tompkins, handing the professor the magazine. 'This one can't miss.'

'Can't it?' said the professor with a smile. 'Well, let's see.' After a short inspection of the article, he went on, 'The distinguishing feature of this system is that the rule governing the amount of your bets calls for you to raise your bet after each loss and, on the other hand, to lower your bet after each win. So, if you should win and lose alternately and with complete regularity, your capital would oscillate up and down, each increase being, however, slightly larger than the previous decrease. In such a case you would, of course, become a millionaire in no time. But as you no doubt understand, such regularity usually does not occur. As a matter of fact, the probability of such a regularly alternating series is just as small as the probability of an equal number of straight wins. So we must see what happens if you have a sequence of several successive wins or losses. If you get what gamblers call a streak of luck, the rule forces you to lower, or at least not to raise, your bet after each win, so your total winnings will not be very high. On the other hand, as you must raise your bet after each loss, a streak of bad luck will be more catastrophic and may throw you out of the game. You can now see that the curve representing the variations in your capital will consist of several slowly rising portions interrupted by very sharp drops. At the beginning of the game, it is likely that you will get on to the long, slowly rising part of the curve and will enjoy for a while the pleasant feeling of watching your money slowly but surely increasing. However, if you go on long enough, in the hope of larger and larger profit, you will come unexpectedly to the sharp drop which might be deep enough to make you bet and lose your last penny. One can show, in a quite general way, that with this or any other system the probability that the curve will reach the double mark is equal to that of reaching zero. In other words, the chances of finally winning are exactly the same as if you put all your money on red or black and double your capital or lose everything on just one spin of the wheel. All that such a system can do is to prolong the game and give you more fun for the money. But if that is all you want to do, you don't have to make it so complicated. There are thirty-six numbers on a roulette wheel, you know, and there is nothing to keep you from covering every number but one. Then the chances are thirty-five out of thirty-six that you will win and that the bank will pay you one chip more than the thirty-five you bet. However, about once in thirty-six spins the ball will stop on the particular number you chose not to cover with a chip, and you will lose all thirty-five. Play this way long enough and the curve of your fluctuating capital will look exactly like the curve you will get by following this magazine's system.

'Of course I have been assuming right along that the bank is taking no cut. As a matter of fact, every roulette wheel I have seen has a zero, and often a double zero as well, which raises the odds against the player. Regardless of the system he uses, therefore, the gambler's money gradually leaks from his pocket to the proprietor's.'

'You mean to say,' said Mr Tompkins dejectedly, 'that there is no such thing as a good gambling system, and that there is no possible way of winning money without risking the slightly higher probability of losing it?'

'That is precisely what I mean,' said the professor. 'What is more, what I have said applies not only to such comparatively unimportant problems as games of chance, but to have great variety of physical phenomena which, at first sight, seem to have nothing to do with the laws of probability. For that matter, if you could devise a system for beating the laws of chance, there are much more exciting things than winning money one could do with it. One could build cars that ran without gasoline, factories that could be operated without coal and plenty of other fantastic things.'

'I've read something somewhere about such hypothetical machines—perpetual motion machines, I believe they are called,' said Mr Tompkins. 'If I remember correctly, machines planned to run without fuel are considered impossible because one cannot manufacture energy out of nothing. Anyway, such machines have no connection with gambling.'

'You are quite right, my boy,' agreed the professor, pleased that his son-in-law knew something at least about physics. 'This kind of perpetual motion, "perpetual motion machines of the first type" as they are called, cannot exist because they would be contrary to the law of the Conservation of Energy. However the fuel-less machines I have in mind are of a rather different type and are usually known as "perpetual motion machines of the second type". They are not designed to create energy out of nothing, but to extract energy from surrounding heat reservoirs in the earth, sea or air. For instance, you can imagine a steamship in whose boilers steam was gotten up, not by burning coal but by extracting heat from the surrounding water. In fact, if it were possible to force heat to flow away from cold toward greater heat, instead of the other way round, one could construct a system for pumping in sea-water, depriving it of its heat content, and disposing of the residue blocks of ice overboard. When a gallon of cold water freezes into ice, it gives off enough heat to raise another gallon of cold water almost to the boiling point. By pumping through several gallons of sea-water per minute, one could easily collect enough heat to run a good-sized engine. For all practical purposes, such a perpetual motion machine of the second type would be just as good as the kind designed to create energy out of nothing. With engines like this to do the work, everyone in the world could live as carefree an existence as a man with an unbeatable roulette system. Unfortunately they are equally impossible as they both violate the laws of probability in the same way.'

'I admit that trying to extract heat out of sea-water to raise steam in a ship's boilers is a crazy idea,' said Mr Tompkins. 'However, I fail to see any connexion between that problem and the laws of chance. Surely, you are not suggesting that dice and roulette wheels should be used as moving parts in these fuel-less machines. Or are you?'

'Of course not!' laughed the professor. 'At least I don't believe even the craziest perpetual motion inventor has made that suggestion yet. The point is that heat processes themselves are very similar in their nature to games of dice, and to hope that heat will flow from the colder body into the hotter one is like hoping that money will flow from the casino's bank into your pocket.'

'You mean that the bank is cold and my pocket hot?' asked Mr Tompkins, by now completely befuddled.

'In a way, yes,' answered the professor. 'If you hadn't missed my lecture last week, you would know that heat is nothing but the rapid irregular movement of innumerable particles, known as atoms and molecules, of which all material bodies are constituted. The more violent this molecular motion is, the warmer the body appears to us. As this molecular motion is quite irregular, it is subject to the laws of chance, and it is easy to show that the most probable state of a system made up of a large number of particles will correspond to a more or less uniform distribution among all of them of the total available energy. If one part of the material body is heated, that is if the molecules in this region begin to move faster, one would expect that, through a large number of accidental collisions, this excess energy would soon be distributed evenly among all the remaining particles. However, as the collisions are purely accidental, there is also the possibility that, merely by chance, a certain group of particles may collect the larger part of the available energy at the expense of the others. This spontaneous concentration of thermal energy in one particular part of the body would correspond to the flow of heat against the temperature gradient, and is not excluded in principle. However, if one tries to calculate the relative probability of such a spontaneous heat concentration occurring, one gets such small numerical values that the phenomenon can be labelled as practically impossible.'

'Oh, I see it now,' said Mr Tompkins. 'You mean that these perpetual motion machines of the second kind might work once in a while but that the chances of that happening are as slight as they are of throwing a seven a hundred times in a row in a dice game.'

'The odds are much smaller than that,' said the professor. 'In fact, the probabilities of gambling successfully against nature are so slight that it is difficult to find words to describe them. For instance, I can work out the chances of all the air in this room collecting spontaneously under the table, leaving an absolute vacuum everywhere else. The number of dice you would throw at one time would be equivalent to the number of air molecules in the room, so I must know how many there are. One cubic centimetre of air at atmospheric pressure, I remember, contains a number of molecules described by a figure of twenty digits, so the air molecules in the whole room must total a number with some twenty-seven digits. The space under the table is about one per cent of the volume of the room, and the chances of any given molecule being under the table and not somewhere else are, therefore, one in a hundred. So, to work out the chances of all of them being under the table at once, I must multiply one hundredth by one hundredth and so on, for each molecule in the room. My result will be a decimal beginning with fifty-four noughts.'

'Phew...!' sighed Mr Tompkins, 'I certainly wouldn't bet on those odds! But doesn't all this mean that deviations from equipartition are simply impossible?'

'Yes,' agreed the professor. 'You can take it as a fact that we won't suffocate because all the air is under the table, and for that matter that the liquid won't start boiling by itself in your high-ball glass. But if you consider much smaller areas, containing much smaller numbers of our dice-molecules, deviations from statistical distribution become much more probable. In this very room, for instance, air molecules habitually group themselves somewhat more densely at certain points, giving rise to minute inhomcgeneities, called statistical fluctuations of density. When the sun's light passes through terrestrial atmosphere, such inhomogeneities cause the scattering of the blue rays of spectrum, and give to the sky its familiar colour. Were these fluctuations of density not present, the sky would always be quite black, and the stars would be clearly visible in full daylight. Also the slightly opalescent light liquids get when they are raised close to the boiling point is explained by these same fluctuations of density produced by the irregularity of molecular motion. But, on a large scale, such fluctuations are so extremely improbable that we would watch for billions of years without seeing one.'

'But there is still a chance of the unusual happening right now in this very room,' insisted Mr Tompkins. 'Isn't there?'

'Yes, of course there is, and it would be unreasonable to insist that a bowl of soup couldn't spill itself all over the table cloth because half of its molecules had accidentally received thermal velocities in the same direction.'

'Why that very thing happened only yesterday,' chimed in Maud, taking an interest now she had finished her magazine. 'The soup spilled and the maid said she hadn't even touched the table.'

The professor chuckled. 'In this particular case,' he said, 'I suspect the maid, rather than Maxwell's Demon, was to blame.'

'Maxwell's Demon?' repeated Mr Tompkins, surprised. 'I should think scientists would be the last people to get notions about demons and such.'

'Well, we don't take him very seriously,' said the professor. 'CLERK MAXWELL, the famous physicist, was responsible for introducing the notion of such a statistical demon simply as a figure of speech. He used this notion to illustrate discussions on the phenomena of heat. Maxwell's Demon is supposed to be rather a fast fellow, and capable of changing the direction of every single molecule in any way you prescribe. If there really were such a demon, heat could be made to flow against temperature, and the fundamental law of thermodynamics, the *principle of increasing entropy*, wouldn't be worth a nickel.'

'Entropy?' repeated Mr Tompkins. 'I've heard that word before. One of my colleagues once gave a party, and after a few drinks, some chemistry students he'd invited started singing—

> '*In*creases, *de*creases
> *De*creases, *in*creases
> What the hell do we care
> What entropy does?'

to the tune of "Ach du lieber Augustine". What is entropy anyway?'

'It's not difficult to explain. "Entropy" is simply a term used to describe the degree of disorder of molecular motion in any given physical body or system of bodies. The numerous irregular collisions between the molecules tend always to increase the entropy, as an absolute disorder is the most probable state of any statistical ensemble. However, if Maxwell's Demon could be put to work, he would soon put some order into the movement of the molecules the way a good sheep dog rounds up and steers a flock of sheep, and the entropy would begin to decrease. I should also tell you that according to the so-called H-theorem Ludwig Boltzmann introduced to science. . . .'

Apparently forgetting he was talking to a man who knew practically nothing about physics and not to a class of advanced students, the professor rambled on, using such monstrous terms as 'generalized parameters' and 'quasi-ergodic systems', thinking he was making the fundamental laws of thermodynamics and their relation to Gibbs' form of statistical mechanics crystal clear. Mr Tompkins was used to his father-in-law talking over his head, so he sipped his Scotch and soda philosophically and tried to look intelligent. But all these highlights of statistical physics were definitely too much for Maud, curled up in her chair and struggling to keep her eyes open. To throw off her drowsiness she decided to go and see how dinner was getting along.

'Does madam desire something?' inquired a tall, elegantly dressed butler, bowing as she came into the dining room.

'No, just go on with your work,' she said, wondering why on earth he was there. It seemed particularly odd as they had never had a butler and certainly could not afford one. The man was tall and lean with an olive skin, long, pointed nose, and greenish eyes which seemed to burn with a strange, intense glow. Shivers ran up and down Maud's spine when she noticed the two symmetrical lumps half hidden by the black hair above his forehead.

'Either I'm dreaming,' she thought, 'or this is Mephistopheles himself, straight out of grand opera.'

'Did my husband hire you?' she asked aloud, just for something to say.

'Not exactly,' answered the strange butler, giving a last artistic touch to the dinner table. 'As a matter of fact, I came here of my own accord to show your distinguished father I am not the myth he believes me to be. Allow me to introduce myself. I am Maxwell's Demon.'

'Oh!' breathed Maud with relief, 'Then you probably aren't wicked, like other demons, and have no intention of hurting anybody.'

'Of course not,' said the Demon with a broad smile, 'but I like to play practical jokes and I'm about to play one on your father.'

'What are you going to do?' asked Maud, still not quite reassured.

'Just show him that, if I choose, the law of increasing entropy can be broken. And to convince you it can be done, I would appreciate the honour of your company. It is not at all dangerous, I assure you.'

At these words, Maud felt the strong grip of the Demon's hand on her elbow, and everything around her suddenly went crazy. All the familiar objects in her dining room began to grow with

'Is this what hell looks like?'

terrific speed, and she got a last glimpse of the back of a chair covering the whole horizon. When things finally quieted down, she found herself floating in the air supported by her companion. Foggy-looking spheres, about the size of tennis balls, were whizzing by in all directions, but Maxwell's Demon cleverly kept them from colliding with any of the dangerous looking things. Looking down, Maud saw what looked like a fishing boat, heaped to the gunwales with quivering, glistening fish. They were not fish, however, but a countless number of foggy balls, very like those flying past them in the air. The Demon led her closer until she seemed surrounded by a sea of coarse gruel which was moving and working in a patternless way. Balls were boiling to the surface and others seemed to be sucked down. Occasionally one would come to the surface with such speed it would tear off into space, or one of the balls flying through the air would dive into the gruel and disappear under thousands of other balls. Looking at the gruel more closely, Maud discovered that the balls were really of two different kinds. If most looked like tennis balls, the larger and more elongated ones were shaped more like American footballs. All of them were semi-transparent and seemed to have a complicated internal structure which Maud could not make out.

'Where are we?' gasped Maud. 'Is this what hell looks like?'

'No,' smiled the Demon, 'Nothing as fantastic as that. We are simply taking a close look at a very small portion of the liquid surface of the highball which is succeeding in keeping your husband awake while your father expounds quasi-ergodic systems. All these balls are molecules. The smaller round ones are water molecules and the larger, longer ones are molecules of alcohol. If you care to work out the proportion between their number, you can find out just how strong a drink your husband poured himself.'

'*Very* interesting,' said Maud, as sternly as she dared. 'But what are those things over there that look like a couple of whales playing in the water. They couldn't be atomic whales, or could they?'

The demon looked where Maud pointed. 'No, they are hardly whales,' he said. 'As a matter of fact, they are a couple of very fine fragments of burned barley, the ingredient which gives whisky its particular flavour and colour. Each fragment is made up of millions and millions of complex organic molecules and is comparatively large and heavy. You see them bouncing around because of the action of impacts they receive from the water and alcohol molecules animated by thermal motion. It was the study of such intermediate-sized particles, small enough to be influenced by molecular motion but still large enough to be seen through a strong microscope, which gave scientists their first direct proof of the kinetic theory of heat. By measuring the intensity of the

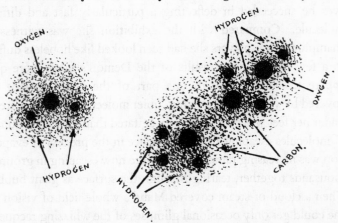

tarantella-like dance executed by such minute particles suspended in liquids, their Brownian motion as it is usually called, physicists were able to get direct information on the energy of molecular motion.'

Again the Demon guided her through the air until they came to an enormous wall made of numberless water molecules fitted neatly and closely together like bricks.

'How very impressive!' cried Maud. 'That's just the background I've been looking for for a portrait I'm painting. What is this beautiful building, anyway?'

'Why, this is part of an ice crystal, one of many in the ice cube in your husband's glass,' said the Demon. 'And now, if you will excuse me, it is time for me to start my practical joke on the old, self-assured professor.'

So saying, Maxwell's Demon left Maud perched on the edge of the ice crystal, like an unhappy mountain climber, and set about his work. Armed with an instrument like a tennis racquet, he was swatting the molecules around him. Darting here and there, he was always in time to swat any stubborn molecule which persisted in going in the wrong direction. In spite of the apparent danger of her position, Maud could not help admiring his wonderful speed and accuracy, and found herself cheering with excitement whenever he succeeded in deflecting a particularly fast and difficult molecule. Compared with the exhibition she was witnessing, champion tennis players she had seen looked like hopeless duffers. In a few minutes, the results of the Demon's work were quite apparent. Now, although one part of the liquid surface was covered by very slowly moving, quiet molecules, the part directly under her feet was more furiously agitated than ever. The number of molecules escaping from the surface in the process of evaporation was increasing rapidly. They were now escaping in groups of thousands together, tearing through the surface as giant bubbles. Then a cloud of steam covered Maud's whole field of vision and she could get only occasional glimpses of the whizzing racquet or the tail of the Demon's dress suit among the masses of maddened molecules. Finally the molecules in her ice crystal perch gave way and she fell into the heavy clouds of vapour beneath....

When the clouds cleared, Maud found herself sitting in the same chair she was sitting in before she went into the dining room.

'Holy entropy!' her father shouted, staring bewildered at Mr Tompkins' highball. 'It's boiling!'

The liquid in the glass was covered with violently bursting bubbles, and a thin cloud of steam was rising slowly toward the ceiling. It was particularly odd, however, that the drink was boiling only in a comparatively small area around the ice cube. The rest of the drink was still quite cold.

'Think of it!' went on the professor in an awed, trembling voice. 'Here I was telling you about statistical fluctuations in the law of entropy when we actually see one! By some incredible chance, possibly for the first time since the earth began, the faster molecules have all grouped themselves accidentally on one part of the surface of the water and the water has begun to boil by itself!

'Holy entropy! It's boiling!'

In the billions of years to come, we will still, probably, be the only people who ever had the chance to observe this extraordinary phenomenon.' He watched the drink, which was now slowly cooling down. 'What a stroke of luck!' he breathed happily.

Maud smiled but said nothing. She did not care to argue with her father, but this time she felt sure she knew better than he.

10

The Gay Tribe of Electrons

A few days later, while finishing his dinner, Mr Tompkins remembered that it was the night of the professor's lecture on the structure of the atom, which he had promised to attend. But he was so fed up with his father-in-law's interminable expositions that he decided to forget the lecture and spend a comfortable evening at home. However, just as he was getting settled with his book, Maud cut off this avenue of escape by looking at the clock and remarking, gently but firmly, that it was almost time for him to leave. So, half an hour later, he found himself on a hard wooden bench in the university auditorium together with a crowd of eager young students.

'Ladies and gentlemen,' began the professor, looking at them gravely over his spectacles, 'In my last lecture I promised to give you more details concerning the internal structure of the atom, and to explain how the peculiar features of this structure account for its physical and chemical properties. You know, of course, that atoms are no longer considered as elementary indivisible constituent parts of matter, and that this role has passed now to much smaller particles such as electrons, protons, etc.

'The idea of elementary constituent particles of matter, representing the last possible step in divisibility of material bodies, dates back to the ancient Greek philosopher DEMOCRITUS who lived in the fourth century B.C. Meditating about the hidden nature of things, Democritus came to the problem of the structure of matter and was faced with the question whether or not it can exist in infinitely small portions. Since it was not customary at this epoch to solve any problem by any other method than that of pure thinking, and since, in any case, the question was at that time beyond any possible attack by experimental methods,

Democritus searched for the correct answer in the depths of his own mind. On the basis of some obscure philosophical considerations he finally came to the conclusion that it is "unthinkable" that matter could be divided into smaller and smaller parts without any limit, and that one must assume the existence of "the smallest particles which cannot be divided any more". He called such particles "atoms", which, as you probably know, means "indivisibles" in Greek.

'I do not want to minimize the great contribution of Democritus to the progress of natural science, but it is worth keeping in mind that besides Democritus and his followers, there was un-doubtedly another school of Greek philosophy the adherents of which maintained that the process of divisibility of matter *could* be carried beyond any limit. Thus, independent of the character of the answer which had to be given in the future by exact science, the philosophy of ancient Greece was well secured with an honourable place in the history of physics. At the time of Democritus, and for centuries later, the existence of such indivisible portions of matter represented a purely philosophical hypothesis, and it was only in the nineteenth century that scientists decided that they had finally found these indivisible building-stones of matter which were foretold by the old Greek philosopher more than two thousand years ago.

'In fact, in the year 1808 an English chemist, JOHN DALTON, showed that the relative proportions. . . .'

Almost from the beginning of the lecture Mr Tompkins had felt an irresistible urge to close his eyes and doze through the rest of the lecture, and it was only the academic hardness of the bench that kept him from doing so. However, Dalton's ideas concern-ing the law of 'relative proportions' proved the last straw, and the hushed auditorium was soon permeated by a gentle wheeze coming from the corner where Mr Tompkins was sitting.

When Mr Tompkins dropped off to sleep, the discomfort of the uncompromising bench seemed to melt into the pleasant sensation of floating on air, and opening his eyes he was surprised to find himself dashing through space at what he considered a pretty reckless speed. Looking around he saw that he was not alone on this fantastic trip. Near him a number of vague, misty forms were swooping around a large heavy-looking object in the middle of the crowd. These strange beings were travelling in pairs, gaily

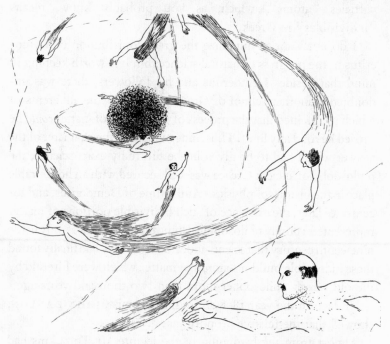

chasing each other along circular and elliptic tracks. Suddenly Mr Tompkins felt very lonely because he realized that he was the only one of the whole group who had no playmate.

'Why didn't I bring Maud along with me?' Mr Tompkins wondered gloomily. 'We could have had a wonderful time with this happy-go-lucky crowd.' The track he was moving along was outside all the others, and while he wanted very much to join the party, the uncomfortable feeling of being odd man out kept him from doing so. However, when one of the electrons (for by now

Mr Tompkins realized he had miraculously joined the electronic community of an atom) was passing close by on its elongated track, he decided to complain about the situation.

'Why haven't *I* got anyone to play with?' he shouted across.

'Because this is an odd atom, and you are the valency electr-o-o-on...,' called the electron as it turned and plunged back into the dancing crowd.

'Valency electrons live alone or find companions in other atoms,' squeaked the high pitched soprano of another electron rushing past him.

'If you want a partner fair,
Jump into chlorine and find one there,'

chanted another mockingly.

'I see you are quite new here, my son, and very lonely,' said a friendly voice above him, and raising his eyes Mr Tompkins saw the stout figure of a monk clothed in a brown tunic.

'I am Father Paulini,' went on the monk, moving along the track with Mr Tompkins, 'and it is my mission in life to keep watch over the morals and social life of electrons in atoms and elsewhere. It is my duty to keep these playful electrons properly distributed among the different quantum cells of the beautiful atomic structures erected by our great architect Niels Bohr. To keep order and to preserve the proprieties, I never permit more than two electrons to follow the same track; a *ménage à trois* always gives a lot of trouble, you know. Thus electrons are always grouped in pairs of opposite "spin" and no intruder is permitted if the cell is already occupied by a couple. It is a good rule, and I may add that not a single electron has yet broken my commandment.'

'Maybe it *is* a good rule,' objected Mr Tompkins, 'but it is rather inconvenient for me at the moment.'

'I see it is,' smiled the monk, 'but it is just your bad luck, being a valency electron in an odd atom. The sodium atom to which you belong is entitled by the electric charge of its nucleus (that big dark mass you see in the centre) to hold eleven electrons together.

Well, unfortunately, for you eleven is an odd number, hardly an unusual circumstance when you consider that exactly one half of all numbers are odd, and only the other half even. Thus, as the latecomer you will have to be alone for a while at least.'

'You mean there is a chance that I can get in later?' asked Mr Tompkins eagerly. 'Kicking one of the oldtimers out, for example?'

'It isn't exactly done,' said the monk wagging a plump finger at him, 'but, of course, there is always a chance that some of the inner circle members will be thrown out by an external disturbance, leaving an empty place. However, I wouldn't count on it much, if I were you.'

'They told me I'd be better off if I moved into chlorine,' said Mr Tompkins, discouraged by Father Paulini's words. 'Can you tell me how to do that?'

'Young man, young man!' exclaimed the monk sorrowfully, 'why are you so insistent on finding company? Why can't you appreciate solitude and this Heaven-sent opportunity to contemplate your soul in peace? Why must even electrons lean always to the worldly life? However, if you insist on companionship, I will help you to get your wish. If you look where I'm pointing, you will see a chlorine atom approaching us, and even at this distance you can see an unoccupied spot where you would most certainly be welcomed. The empty spot is in the outer group of electrons, the so-called "M-shell", which is supposed to be made up of eight electrons grouped in four pairs. But, as you see, there are four electrons spinning in one direction and only three in the other, with one place vacant. The inner shells, known as "K" and "L", are completely filled up, and the atom will be glad to get you and have its outer shell complete. When the two atoms get close together, just jump over, as valency electrons usually do. And may peace be with you, my son!' With these words the impressive figure of the electron priest suddenly faded into thin air.

Feeling considerably more cheerful, Mr Tompkins gathered his strength for a neckbreaking jump into the orbit of the passing chlorine atom. To his surprise he leapt over with an easy grace and found himself in the congenial surroundings of the members of the chlorine M-shell.

'It was delightful of you to join us!' called his new partner of opposite spin, gliding gracefully along the track. 'Now no one can say that our community is not complete. Now we shall all have fun together!'

Mr Tompkins agreed that it really was fun—lots of fun—but

one little worry kept stealing into his mind. 'How am I going to explain this to Maud when I see her again?' he thought rather guiltily, but not for long. 'Surely she won't mind,' he decided. 'After all, these are only electrons.'

'Why doesn't that atom you've left go away now?' asked his companion with a pout. 'Does it still hope to get you back?'

And, as a matter of fact, the sodium atom, with its valency electron gone, *was* sticking closely to the chlorine one as if in the hope that Mr Tompkins would change his mind and jump back to his lonely track.

'Well how do you like that!' said Mr Tompkins angrily, frowning at the atom which had first received him so coldly. 'There's a dog in the manger for you!'

'Oh, they always do that,' said a more experienced member of the M-shell. 'I understand it is not so much the electronic community of the sodium atom which wants you back as the sodium nucleus itself. There is almost always some disagreement between the central nucleus and its electronic escort: the nucleus wants as many electrons around it as it can possibly hold with its electric charge, whereas the electrons themselves prefer to be only enough in number to make the shells complete. There are only a few atomic species, the so-called *rare gases*, or *noble gases* as the German chemists call them, in which the desire of the ruling nucleus and the subordinate electrons are in full harmony. Such atoms as helium, neon and argon, for example, are quite satisfied with themselves and neither expel their number nor invite new ones. They are chemically inert, and keep away from all other atoms. But in all other atoms electronic communities are always ready to change their membership. In the sodium atom, which was your former home, the nucleus is entitled by its electric charge to one more electron than is necessary for harmony in the shells. On the other hand, in our atom the normal contingent of electrons is not enough for complete harmony, and thus we welcome your arrival, in spite of the fact that your presence overloads our nucleus. But as long as you stay here, our atom is not neutral any more, and has an extra electric charge. Thus the sodium atom which you left stands by, held by the force of electric attraction. I once heard our great priest, Father Paulini, say that such atomic communities, with extra electrons or electrons missing, are called negative and positive "ions". He also uses the word "molecule" for groups of two or more atoms bound together by electric force. This particular combination of sodium and chlorine atoms he calls a molecule of "table salt", whatever that may be.'

'Do you mean to tell me you don't know what table salt is?' said Mr Tompkins, forgetting to whom he was talking. 'Why that's what you put on your scrambled eggs at breakfast.'

'What are "scram bulldeggs" and what is "break-fust"?' asked the intrigued electron. Mr Tompkins sputtered and then realized the futility of trying to explain to his companions even the simplest details of the lives of human beings. 'That's why I don't get more out of their talk about valency and complete shells,' he told himself, deciding to enjoy his visit to this fantastic world without worrying about understanding it. But it was not so easy to get away from the talkative electron, who evidently had a great desire to pass on all the knowledge collected during a long electronic life.

'You must not think,' he continued, 'that the binding of atoms into molecules is always accomplished by one valency electron alone. There are atoms, like oxygen for example, which need two more electrons to complete their shells, and there are also atoms which need three electrons and even more. On the other hand, in some atoms the nucleus holds two or more extra—or valency— electrons. When such atoms meet, there is quite a lot of jumping over and binding to do, as a result of which quite complex molecules, often consisting of thousands of atoms, are formed. There are also the so-called "homopolar" molecules, that is molecules made up of two identical atoms, but that is a very unpleasant situation.'

'Unpleasant, why?' asked Mr Tompkins, getting interested again.

'Too much work,' commented the electron, 'to keep them together. Some time ago I happened to get that job and I didn't have a moment to myself all the while I stayed there. Why, it isn't at all the way it is here where the valency electron just enjoys himself and lets the electrically hungry and deserted atom stand by. No sir! In order to keep the two identical atoms together, he has to jump to and fro, from one to the other and back again. My word! One feels like a ping pong ball.'

Mr Tompkins was rather surprised to hear the electron, which did not know what scrambled eggs were, speak so glibly of ping pong, but he let it pass.

'I'll never take on that job again!' grumbled the lazy electron, overwhelmed by a wave of unpleasant memories. 'I am quite comfortable where I am now.'

'Wait!' he exclaimed suddenly. 'I think I see a still better place for me to go. So lo-o-o-ong!' And with a giant leap he rushed toward the interior of the atom.

Looking in the direction in which his interlocutor had gone, Mr Tompkins understood what had happened. It seems that one of the electrons of the inner circle was thrown clear of the atom by some foreign high-speed electron which had unexpectedly penetrated into their system, and a cosy place in the 'K' shell was now wide open. Chiding himself for missing this opportunity to join the inner circle, Mr Tompkins now watched with great interest the course of the electron he had just been talking to. Deeper and deeper into the atomic interior this happy electron sped, and bright rays of light accompanied his triumphant flight. Only when it finally reached the internal orbit did this almost unbearable radiation finally stop.

'What was that?' asked Mr Tompkins, his eyes aching from the sight of this unexpected phenomenon. 'Why all this brilliance?'

'Oh that's just the X-ray emission connected with the transition,' explained his orbit companion, smiling at his embarrassment. 'Whenever one of us succeeds in getting deeper into the interior of the atom, the surplus energy must be emitted in the form of radiation. This lucky fellow made quite a big jump and let loose a lot of energy. More often we have to be satisfied with smaller jumps, here in the atomic suburbs, and then our radiation is called "visible light"—at least that is what Father Paulini calls it.'

'But this X-light, or whatever you call it, is also visible,' protested Mr Tompkins. 'I should call your terminology rather misleading.'

'Well, we are electrons and are susceptible to any kind of radiation. But Father Paulini tells us that there exist gigantic creatures, "Human Beings", he calls them, who can see light only when it falls within a narrow energy-interval, or wave length-interval as he puts it. He told us once that it took a great man, Roentgen I think his name was, to discover these X-rays and that now they are largely used in something called "medicine".'

'Oh yes. I know quite a lot about that,' said Mr Tompkins, feeling proud that now *he* could show off his knowledge. 'Want me to tell you more about it?'

'No thanks,' said the electron yawning. 'I really don't care. Can't you be happy without talking? Try to catch me!'

For a long time Mr Tompkins went on enjoying the pleasant sensation of diving through space with the other electrons in a kind of glorified trapeze act. Then, all of a sudden, he felt his hair stand on end, an experience he had felt once before during a thunder storm in the mountains. It was clear that a strong electric disturbance was approaching their atom, breaking the harmony of the electronic motion, and forcing the electrons to deviate seriously from their normal tracks. From the point of view of a human physicist, it was only a wave of ultraviolet light passing through the spot where this particular atom happened to be, but to the tiny electrons it was a terrific electric storm.

'Hold on tight!' yelled one of his companions, 'or you will be thrown out by photo-effect forces!' But it was already too late. Mr Tompkins was snatched away from his companions and hurled into space at a terrifying speed, as neatly as if he had been seized by a pair of powerful fingers. Breathlessly he hurtled further and further through space, tearing past all kinds of different atoms so fast he could hardly distinguish the separate electrons. Suddenly a large atom loomed up right in front of him and he knew that a collision was unavoidable.

'Pardon me, but I am photo-effected and cannot...,' began Mr Tompkins politely, but the rest of the sentence was lost in an ear-splitting crash as he ran head on into one of the outer electrons. The two of them tumbled head over heels off into space. However, Mr Tompkins had lost most of his speed in the collision and was now able to study his new surroundings somewhat more closely. The atoms which towered around him were much larger than any he had seen before, and he could count as many as twenty-nine electrons in each of them. If he had known his physics better he would have recognized them as atoms of copper, but at these close quarters the group as a whole did not look like copper at all. Also they were spaced rather close to one another forming a regular pattern which extended as far as he could see. But what surprised Mr Tompkins most was the fact that these atoms did not seem to be very particular about holding on to their quota of electrons, particularly their outer electrons. In fact the outer orbits were mostly empty, and crowds of unattached electrons were drifting lazily through space, stopping from time to time but never for very long, on the outskirts of one atom or another. Rather tired after his breakneck flight through space, Mr Tompkins tried at first to get a little rest on a steady orbit of one of the copper atoms. However he was soon infected with the prevailing vagabondish feeling of the crowd, and he joined the rest of the electrons in their nowhere-in-particular motion.

'Things are not very well organized here,' he commented to

himself, 'and there are too many electrons not tending to their business. I think Father Paulini should do something about it.'

'Why should I?' said the familiar voice of the monk who had suddenly materialized from nowhere. 'These electrons are not disobeying my commandments, and besides they are doing a very useful job indeed. You may be interested to know that if all atoms cared as much about holding their electrons as some of them do, there would be no such thing as electric conductivity. Why you wouldn't even be able to have an electric bell in your house, to say nothing of a light or a telephone.'

'Oh, you mean these electrons carry electric current?' asked Mr Tompkins, grasping at the hope that the conversation was turning to a subject more or less familiar to him. 'But I don't see that they are moving in any particular direction.'

'First of all, my lad,' said the monk severely, 'do not use the word "they", use "we". You seem to forget that you are an electron yourself and that the moment someone presses the button to which this copper wire is attached, electric tension will cause you, as well as all the other conductivity electrons, to rush along to call the maid or do whatever else is needed.'

'But I don't want to!' said Mr Tompkins firmly, a note of temper in his voice. 'As a matter of fact I am quite tired of being an electron and I don't think it's so much fun any more. What a life, to have to carry out all these electronic duties for ever and ever!'

'Not necessarily forever,' countered Father Paulini, who definitely did not like back-talk on the part of plain electrons. 'There is always the chance that you will be annihilated and cease to exist.'

'B-b-be annihilated?' repeated Mr Tompkins feeling cold shivers running up and down his spine. 'But I always thought electrons were eternal.'

'That is what physicists used to believe until comparatively recent times,' agreed Father Paulini, amused at the effect produced by his words, 'but it isn't exactly correct. Electrons can be born, and die, as well as human beings. There isn't, of course, such a thing as dying of old age; death comes only through collisions.'

'Well, I had a collision only a short while ago, and a pretty bad one too,' said Mr Tompkins recovering a little confidence. 'And if that one didn't put me out of action, I can't imagine one that would.'

'It isn't a question of how forcibly you collide,' Father Paulini corrected him, 'but of who the other fellow is. In your recent collision you probably ran into another negative electron, very similar to yourself, and there is not the slightest danger in such an encounter. In fact, you could butt into each other like a couple of rams for years and no harm could be done. But there is another breed of electron, the positive ones, which have been discovered only comparatively recently by the physicists. These positive electrons, or positrons, look exactly the way you do, the only difference being that their electric charge is positive instead of negative. When you see such a fellow approaching, you think it is just another innocent member of your tribe and go ahead to greet him. But then you suddenly find that, instead of pushing you away slightly to avoid a collision, as any normal electron would, he pulls you right in. And then it is too late to do anything.'

'How terrible!' exclaimed Mr Tompkins. 'And how many poor ordinary electrons can one positron eat up?'

'Fortunately only one, since in destroying a negative electron the positron also destroys itself. One could describe them as members of a suicide club, looking for partners in mutual annihiltion. They do not harm one another, but as soon as a negative electron comes their way, it hasn't much chance of surviving.'

'Lucky I haven't run into one of these monsters yet,' said Mr Tompkins much impressed by this description. 'I hope they are not very numerous. Are they?'

'No, they're not. And for the simple reason that they are always looking for trouble and so vanish very soon after they are born. If you wait a minute, I shall probably be able to show you one.'

'Yes, here we are,' continued Father Paulini after a short silence. 'If you look carefully at that heavy nucleus over there, you will see one of these positrons being born.'

The atom at which the monk was pointing was evidently undergoing a strong electromagnetic disturbance owing to some vigorous radiation falling on it from outside. It was a much more violent disturbance than the one which threw Mr Tompkins out of his chlorine atom, and the family of atomic electrons surrounding the nucleus was being dispersed and blown away like dry leaves in a hurricane.

'Look closely at the nucleus,' said Father Paulini, and concentrating his attention Mr Tompkins saw a most unusual phenomenon taking place in the depths of the destroyed atom. Very close to the nucleus, inside the inner electronic shell, two vague shadows were gradually taking shape, and a second later Mr Tompkins saw two glittering brand new electrons rushing at great speed away from their birthplace.

'But I see two of them,' said Mr Tompkins, fascinated by the sight.

'That is right,' agreed Father Paulini. 'Electrons are always born in pairs, otherwise it would contradict the law of conservation of electric charge. One of these two particles, born under the action of a strong gamma ray on the nucleus, is an ordinary negative electron, whereas the other is a positron—the murderer. He is off now to find a victim.'

'Well, if the birth of each positron destined to destroy an electron is accompanied by the birth of still another plain electron, then things aren't so bad,' commented Mr Tompkins thoughtfully. 'At least it doesn't lead to the extinction of the electronic tribe, and I....'

'Look out!' interrupted the monk shoving him aside while the newborn positron whistled by, just an inch away. 'You can never be too careful when these murderous particles are around. But I think I'm spending too much time talking to you and I have other business to attend to. I must look for my pet "neutrino"....' And the monk disappeared without letting Mr Tompkins know what this 'neutrino' was and whether or not it was also to be feared. Thus deserted, Mr Tompkins felt even more lonely than before and, when one or another fellow electron approached him on his journey through space, he even nursed a secret desperate hope that under each innocent exterior might be

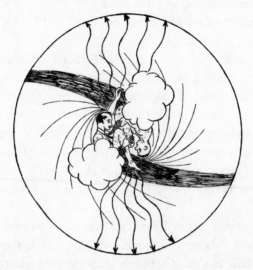

hidden the heart of a murderer. For a long time, centuries it seemed to him, his fears and hopes were not justified, and he unwillingly bore the dull duties of a conductivity electron.

Then suddenly it happened, and at a moment when he expected it least. Feeling a strong need to talk to somebody, even to a stupid conductivity electron, he approached a particle which was slowly moving by and was evidently a newcomer to this bit of copper wire. Even at a distance, however, he noticed that he had made a bad choice and that an irresistible force of attraction was pulling him along, permitting no retreat. For a second he tried to struggle and tear himself away, but the distance between them was rapidly getting smaller and smaller and it seemed to Mr Tompkins that he saw a fiendish grin on the face of his captor.

'Let me go! Let me go!' shouted Mr Tompkins at the top of his voice, struggling with his arms and kicking his legs. 'I don't want to be annihilated; I'll conduct electric current for the rest of eternity!' But it was all in vain, and the surrounding space was suddenly illuminated by a blinding flash of intensive radiation.

'Well, I am no more,' thought Mr Tompkins, 'but how is it I can still think? Has my body only been annihilated, and my soul gone to a quantum heaven?' Then he felt a new force, more gentle this time, shaking him firmly and resolutely, and opening his eyes he recognized the university janitor.

'I'm sorry, Sir,' he said, 'but the lecture was over some time ago and we gotta close the hall up now.' Mr Tompkins stifled a yawn and looked sheepish.

'Good night, Sir,' said the janitor with a sympathetic smile.

A Part of the Previous Lecture which Mr Tompkins slept through

In fact, in the year 1808, an English chemist JOHN DALTON showed that the relative proportions of various chemical elements which are needed to form more complicated chemical compounds can always be expressed by the ratio of integral numbers, and he interpreted this empirical law as due to the fact that all compound substances are built up from a varying number of particles representing simple chemical elements. The failure of medieval alchemy to turn one chemical element into another supplied a proof of apparent indivisibility of these particles, and without much hesitation they were christened by the old Greek name: 'atoms'. Once given, the name stuck, and although we know now that these 'Dalton's atoms' are not at all indivisible, and are, in fact, formed by a large number of still smaller particles, we close our eyes to the philological inconsistency of their name.

Thus the entities called 'atoms' by modern physics are not at all the elementary and indivisible constituent units of matter imagined by Democritus, and the term 'atom' would actually be more correct if it were applied to such much smaller particles as electrons and protons, from which 'Dalton's atoms' are built. But such a change of names would cause too much confusion, and nobody in physics cares much about philological consistency anyway! Thus we retain the old name of 'atoms' in Dalton's sense, and refer to electrons, protons, etc. as 'elementary particles'.

This name indicates, of course, that we believe at present that these smaller particles are *really* elementary and indivisible in Democritus' sense of the word, and you may ask me whether history will not repeat itself, and whether in the further progress of science, the elementary particles of modern physics will not be proved to be quite complex. My answer is that, although there is no absolute guarantee that this will not happen, there are very good reasons to believe that this time we are completely right. In fact, there are ninety-two different kinds of atoms (corresponding to ninety-two different chemical elements) and each kind of atom possesses rather complicated characteristic properties; a situation which in itself invites some simplification along the line of reducing such a complicated picture to a more elementary one. On the other hand, physics of today recognizes only a few different kinds of elementary particles: *electrons* (positive and negative light particles), *nucleons* (charged or neutral heavy particles, also known as *protons and neutrons*), and possibly the so-called *neutrinos* the nature of which has not been completely clarified.

The properties of these elementary particles are extremely simple, and very little simplification could be gained by further reduction; besides, as you will understand, you must always have several elementary notions to play with if you want to build up something more complicated, and two or three elementary notions are not too many. Thus, in my opinion, it is quite safe to bet your last dollar that the elementary particles of modern physics will live up to their name.

Now we can turn to the question concerning the way in which Dalton's atoms are built up from the elementary particles. The first correct answer to this question was given in 1911 by the celebrated British physicist ERNEST RUTHERFORD (later Lord Rutherford of Nelson) who was studying atomic structure by bombarding various atoms with fast-moving minute projectiles, known as *alpha-particles*, which are emitted in the process of disintegration of radioactive elements. Observing the deflection (scattering) of these projectiles after passage through a piece of matter, Rutherford came to the conclusion that all atoms must possess a very dense positively charged central core (atomic nucleus) surrounded by a rather rarefied cloud of negative electric charge (atomic atmosphere). We know today that the atomic nucleus is made up of a certain number of *protons* and *neutrons*, known under the collective name of '*nucleons*', held tightly together by strong cohesive forces, and that atomic atmosphere consists of varying numbers of negative electrons swarming around under the action of electrostatic attraction of the nuclear positive charge. The number of electrons forming the atomic atmosphere determines all the physical and chemical properties of a given atom, and varies along the natural sequence of chemical elements from one (for hydrogen) up to ninety-two (for the heaviest known element: Uranium).

In spite of the apparent simplicity of Rutherford's atomic model, its detailed understanding turned out to be anything but simple. In fact, according to the best belief of classical physics, negatively charged electrons rotating around an atomic nucleus are bound to lose their energy of motion through the process of radiation (light-emission), and it has been calculated that, owing to these steady energy losses, all electrons forming atomic atmosphere should collapse on the nucleus within a negligible fraction of a second. This seemingly sound conclusion of classical theory stands, however, in sharp contradiction with the empirical fact that atomic atmospheres are, on the contrary, quite stable, and that, instead of collapsing on the nucleus, atomic electrons continue their swarming motion around the central body for an indefinite period of time. Thus we see that a very deep-rooted conflict arises between the basic ideas of classical mechanics, and the empirical data pertaining to the mechanical behaviour of a tiny constituent part in the world of atoms. This fact brought the famous Danish physicist Niels Bohr to the realization that classical mechanics, which claimed for centuries a privileged and secure position in the system of natural sciences, should be from now on considered as a restricted theory, applicable to the macroscopic world of our everyday experience, but failing badly in its application to the much more delicate types of motion taking place within various atoms. As the tentative foundation for the new generalized mechanics which would be applicable also to the motion of the tiny moving parts of atomic mechanism, Bohr proposed to assume that *from all the infinite variety of types of motion considered in classical theory, only a few specially selected types can actually take place in nature.* These permitted types of motion, or trajectories, are to be selected according to certain mathematical conditions, known as the *quantum conditions* of the Bohr theory. I am not going to enter here into a detailed discussion of these quantum conditions, but will mention only that they have been chosen in such a way, that all the restrictions imposed by them become of no practical importance in all cases where the mass of the moving particles is much larger than the masses we encounter in atomic structure. Thus, being applied to macroscopic bodies, the new *micro-mechanics* gives exactly the same results as the old classical theory (*principle of correspondence*) and it is only in the case of tiny atomic mechanisms that the disagreement between the two theories becomes of essential value. Without going deeper into the details, I will satisfy your curiosity concerning the structure of the atom from the point of view of Bohr's theory, by showing the diagram of Bohr's quantum orbits in an atom. (First plate, please!) You see here [p. 132], on a largely magnified scale of course, the system of circular and elliptical orbits, which represent the only types of motion 'permitted' for the electrons forming atomic atmosphere by Bohr's quantum conditions. Whereas classical mechanics would allow the electron to move at *any* distance from the nucleus and puts *no restriction* on the eccentricity (i.e. elongation) of its orbit, the selected orbits of Bohr's theory form a discrete set with all their characteristic dimensions sharply defined. Numbers and letters standing near each orbit indicate the name of any given orbit in the general classifications; you may notice, for example, that larger numbers correspond to the orbits of larger diameters.

Although Bohr's theory of atomic structure turned out to be

extremely fruitful in the explanation of various properties of atoms and molecules, the fundamental notion of discrete quantum orbits remained rather unclear, and the deeper we tried to go into the analysis of this unusual restriction of classical theory, the less clear was the entire picture.

Thus we obtain the original Bohr–Sommerfeld scheme for the permitted quantum orbits of an electron in a hydrogen atom

It finally became clear that the disadvantage of Bohr's theory lay in the fact that, *instead of changing* classical mechanics in some fundamental way, it *was simply restricting* the results of this system by additional conditions which were in principle foreign to the whole structure of classical theory. The correct solution of the entire problem came only thirteen years later, in the form of so-called 'wave-mechanics', which has modified the entire basis of classical mechanics in accordance with the new quantum-principle. And, in spite of the fact that at first sight the system of wave-mechanics may seem still crazier than Bohr's old theory, this new micro-mechanics represents one of the most consistent and accepted parts of the theoretical physics of today. Since the fundamental principle of the new mechanics, and in particular the notions of 'indeterminacy' and 'spreading out trajectories', have been already discussed by me in one of my previous lectures, I will refer you to your memory or your notes, and will return to

the problem of atomic structure. In the diagram which I project now (second plate, please!) you see the way in which the motion of atomic electrons is visualized by wave-mechanical theory from the point of view of 'spreading out trajectories'. This picture represents the same types of motion as those represented classically in the previous diagram (apart from the fact that for technical reasons each type of motion is now drawn separately), but instead of the sharp-lined trajectories of Bohr's theory, we have now diffuse patterns consistent with the fundamental *uncertainty principle*. The notations of different states of motion is the same as on the previous diagram, and, comparing the two, you will notice, if you will stretch your imagination slightly, that our cloudy form repeats rather faithfully the general features of the old Bohr's orbits.

These diagrams show you quite clearly what happens to the good old-fashioned trajectories of classical mechanics when the quantum is at play, and although a layman might think it a fantastic dream, scientists working in the microcosmos of atoms do not experience any difficulties in accepting this picture.

After this short survey of the possible states of motion in the electronic atmosphere of an atom, we now come to an important problem concerning the distribution of various atomic electrons among various possible states of motion. Here again we encounter a new principle, a principle quite unfamiliar in the macroscopic world. This principle was first formulated by my young friend WOLFGANG PAULI, and states that *in the community of electrons of a given atom no two particles may simultaneously possess the same type of motion.* This restriction would be of no great importance if, as it is in classical mechanics, there were an infinity of possible motions. Since, however, the numbers of 'permitted' states of motion is drastically reduced by the quantum laws, the Pauli-principle plays a very important role in the atomic world: it secures a more or less uniform distribution of electrons around the atomic nucleus and prevents them from crowding in one particular spot.

You must not conclude, however, from the above formulation of the new principle that each of the diffuse quantum-states of motion represented on my diagram may be 'occupied' by one electron only. In fact, quite apart from the motion along its orbit, each electron is also spinning around its own axis, and it will not distress Dr Pauli at all if two electrons move along the same orbit, provided they spin in different directions. Now the study of electron spin indicates that the velocity of their rotation around their own axis is always the same, and that the direction of this axis must always be perpendicular to the plane of the orbit. This leaves only two different possibilities of spinning, which can be characterized as 'clockwise' and 'counter-clockwise'.

Thus the Pauli principle as applied to the quantum states in an atom can be reformulated in the following way: *each quantum state of motion can be 'occupied' by not more than two electrons, in which case the spins of these two particles must be in opposite directions.* Thus, as we proceed along the natural sequence of elements towards the atoms with a larger and larger number of electrons, we find different quantum states of motion being gradually filled with the electrons, and the diameter of the atom steadily increases. It must also be mentioned in this connexion that, from the point of view of the strength of their binding, different quantum states of atomic electrons can be united in separate groups (or shells) of states with approximately equal binding. When we proceed along the natural sequence of elements, one group is filled after another, and, as a consequence of their subsequent filling of electronic shells, the properties of the atoms also change periodically. This is the explanation of the well-known periodic-properties of elements, discovered empirically by the Russian chemist DIMITRIJ MENDELEÉFF.

12

Inside the Nucleus

The next lecture which Mr Tompkins attended was devoted to the interior of the nuclei which make the pivot point for the revolution of atomic electrons.

Ladies and Gentlemen—said the professor—

Digging deeper and deeper into the structure of matter, we will now try to penetrate with our mental eye into the interior of the atomic nucleus, the mysterious region occupying only one thousand billionth part of the total volume of the atom itself. Yet, in spite of the almost incredibly small dimensions of our new field of investigation we shall find it full of very animated activity. In fact, the nucleus is after all the heart of the atom, and, in spite of its relatively small size, contains about 99·97% of total atomic mass.

Entering the nuclear region from the thinly populated electronic atmosphere of the atom, we shall be surprised at once by the extremely overcrowded state of the local population. Whereas electrons of atomic atmosphere move, on the average, distances exceeding by a factor of several hundred thousand their own diameters, the particles living inside the nucleus would literally be rubbing elbows with one another, if only they had elbows. In this sense the picture represented by the nuclear interior is very similar to that of an ordinary liquid, except that instead of molecules we encounter here much smaller and also much more elementary particles known as *protons* and *neutrons*. It may be noticed here that, in spite of having different names, protons and neutrons are now considered simply as two different electric states of the same elementary heavy particle known as the 'nucleon'. Proton is a positively charged nucleon, neutron is an electrically neutral nucleon, and the possibility is not excluded that there are also negative nucleons, although as yet they have never been observed. As far as their geometrical dimensions are concerned, nucleons are not very different from electrons, possessing a diameter of about 0·000,000,000,000,1 cm. But they are much heavier, and a proton or neutron would tip the scales against 1840 electrons. As I have said, the particles forming the atomic nucleus are packed very close together, and this is due to the action of certain special *nuclear cohesive forces*, similar to those acting between the molecules in a liquid. And, just as in liquids, those forces, while preventing the particles from being completely separated, do not hinder their displacement relative to one another. Thus nuclear matter possesses a certain degree of fluidity and, not being disturbed by any external forces, assumes the shape of a spherical drop, just like an ordinary drop of water. In the schematic diagram which I am going to draw for you now, you see different types of nuclei built from protons and neutrons. The simplest is the nucleus of hydrogen which consists of just one proton, whereas the most complicated uranium nucleus consists of 92 protons and 142 neutrons. Of course, you must consider these pictures only as a highly schematic presentation of the actual situation, since, owing to the fundamental uncertainty principle of the quantum theory, the position of each nucleon is actually 'spread out' over the entire nuclear region.

As I have said, particles forming an atomic nucleus are held together by strong cohesive forces, but apart from these attractive forces there are also forces of another kind acting in the opposite direction. In fact, protons, which form about one half of the total nuclear population, carry a positive electric charge, and are consequently repelled from one another by the Coulomb electrostatic forces. For the light nuclei, where the electric charge is comparatively small, this Coulomb repulsion is of no consequence, but in the case of heavier, highly charged nuclei Coulomb forces begin to offer serious competition in the attractive cohesive forces.

When this happens, the nucleus is no longer stable, and is apt to eject some of its constituent parts. That is exactly what happens to a number of elements located at the very end of the periodic system, known as 'radioactive elements'.

From the above considerations you might conclude that these heavy unstable nuclei should emit protons, since neutrons do not carry any electric charge and are therefore not subject to the

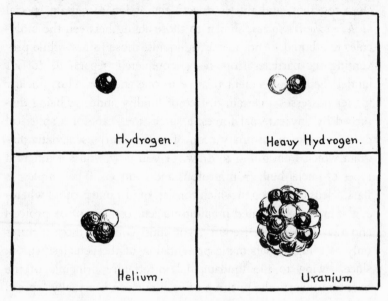

Hydrogen.

Heavy Hydrogen.

Helium.

Uranium

Coulomb repulsive forces. Experiments show us, however, that the particles actually emitted are the so-called *alpha-particles* (helium-nuclei), i.e. complex particles built of two protons and two neutrons each. The explanation of this fact lies in the specific grouping of nuclear constituent parts. It appears that the combination of two protons and two neutrons, forming an alpha-particle, is especially stable, and it is therefore much easier to throw the whole group out at once than to break it into separate protons and neutrons.

As you probably know, the phenomenon of radioactive decay

was first discovered by the French physicist HENRI BECQUEREL, and its interpretation as the result of spontaneous disintegration of atomic nuclei was given by the famous British physicist Lord Rutherford, whose name I have already mentioned before in other connexions, and to whom science owes so great a debt for important discoveries in the physics of the atomic nucleus.

One of the most peculiar features of the process of alpha-decay consists in the sometimes extremely long periods of time needed by alpha-particles in order to make their 'getaway' from the nucleus. For *uranium* and *thorium* this period is measured by billions of years; for *radium* it is about sixteen centuries, and although there are some elements in which decay takes place in a fraction of a second, their life-span can also be considered very long as compared with the rapidity of intra-nuclear motion.

What is it that forces an alpha-particle to stay sometimes for many billions of years inside the nucleus? And if it has already stayed so long why does it finally get out?

To answer this question we must first learn a little more about the comparative strength of the cohesive forces of attraction, and the electrostatic forces of repulsion acting on the particle on its way out of the nucleus. A careful experimental study of these forces was made by Rutherford, who used the so-called 'atomic bombardment' method. In his famous experiments at the Cavendish Laboratory, Rutherford directed a beam of fast moving alpha-particles, emitted by some radioactive substance, and observed the deviations (scattering) of these atomic projectiles resulting from their collisions with the nuclei of the bombarded substance. These experiments confirmed the fact that, while at great distances from the nucleus the projectiles are strongly repelled by electric forces of nuclear charge, this repulsion changes into a strong attraction if the projectile manages to come very close to the outer limits of the nuclear region. You can say that the nucleus is somewhat analogous to a fortress surrounded on all sides by a high, steep bulwark, preventing the particles from getting in as well as from getting out. But the most striking result of Rutherford's experiments consists in the fact that *the alpha-particles getting out of the nucleus in the process of radioactive decay, as well as the projectiles which penetrate into the nucleus from outside, possess actually less energy than would correspond to the top of the bulwark, or the 'potential barrier' as we usually call it.* This was the fact which stood in complete contradiction to all the fundamental ideas of classical mechanics. Indeed, how can you expect a ball to roll over a hill if you have thrown it with far less energy than is necessary to get to the top of the hill? Classical physics could only open its eyes very wide, and suggest that there must have been some mistake in Rutherford's experiments.

But, as a matter of fact, there was no mistake, and if someone was in error it was not Lord Rutherford but classical mechanics itself. The situation was clarified simultaneously by my good friend DR GEORGE GAMOW and by DRS RONALD GURNEY and E. U. CONDON, who pointed out that there is no difficulty whatsoever if one looks at the problem from the point of view of modern quantum theory. In fact, we know that quantum physics today rejects the well defined linear trajectories of classical theory, and replaces them with diffuse ghostly trails. And, just as a good old-fashioned ghost could pass without difficulty through the thick masonry walls of an old castle, these ghostly trajectories can penetrate through potential barriers which seem to be quite impenetrable from the classical point of view.

And please do not think I am joking: the penetrability of potential barriers for particles with insufficient energy comes as a direct mathematical consequence of the fundamental equations of the new quantum mechanics, and represents one of the most important differences between the new and old ideas about motion. But, although the new mechanics permits such unusual effects, it does so only with strong restrictions: in most cases the chances of crossing the barrier are extremely small, and the imprisoned particle must throw itself against the wall an almost incredible number of times before its attempt finally succeeds. The quantum theory gives us exact rules concerning the calculation of the probability of such an escape, and it has been shown that the observed periods of alpha-decay are in complete agreement with the expectation of the theory. Also in the case of projectiles which are shot into the nucleus from the outside, the results of quantum-mechanical calculations are in very close agreement with the experiment.

Before going any further, I want to show you some photographs representing the process of disintegration of various nuclei which were hit by high energy atomic projectiles. (Plate, please!)

In this plate [see p. 142] you see two different disintegration processes photographed in the cloud-chamber which I have described to you in a previous lecture. The picture on the left shows a nitrogen nucleus struck by a fast alpha-particle, and is the first picture of artificial transmutation of elements ever taken. It was made by PATRICK BLACKETT, a pupil of Lord Rutherford. You see a large number of alpha tracks radiating from a powerful alpha-ray source which is now shown in the picture. Most of these particles are passing through the field of vision without a single serious collision, but one of them has just succeeded in hitting a nitrogen nucleus. The track of the alpha-particle stops right there, and you can see two other tracks coming out from the collision point. The long thin track belongs to a proton kicked out from the nitrogen nucleus, whereas the short heavy one represents the recoil of the nucleus itself. This isn't, however, a nitrogen nucleus any more, since by losing a proton and absorbing the incidental alpha-particle it has been transformed into a nucleus of oxygen. Thus we have here an alchemic transformation of nitrogen into oxygen with hydrogen as a by-product.

The second photograph corresponds to nuclear disintegration by the impact of an artificially accelerated proton. A fast beam of protons is being produced in a special high-tension machine, known to the general public as an 'atom-smasher', and enters the

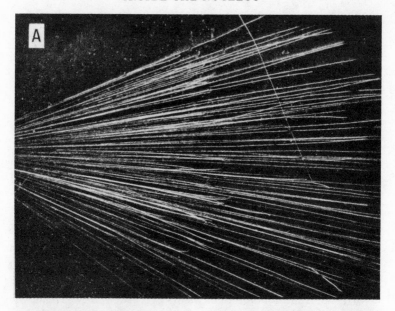

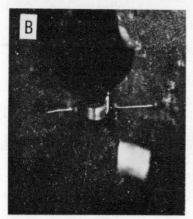

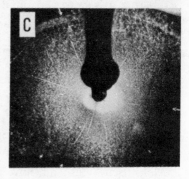

(a) Nitrogen hit by helium turns into heavy oxygen and hydrogen
$$_7N^{14} + _2He^4 \rightarrow _8O^{17} + _1H^1$$
(b) Lithium hit by hydrogen turns into two heliums
$$_3Li^7 + _1H^1 \rightarrow 2_2He^4$$
(c) Boran hit by hydrogen turns into three heliums
$$_5B^{11} + _1H^1 \rightarrow 3_2H^4$$

chamber through a long tube, the end of which is seen in the photograph. The target, in this case a thin layer of boron, is placed at the lower opening of the tube so that nuclear fragments produced in the collision must pass through the air in the chamber, producing cloudy tracks. As you see from the picture, the nucleus of boron, being hit by a proton, breaks into three parts and, counting the balance of the electric charges, we come to the conclusion that each of these fragments is an alpha-particle, i.e. a helium-nucleus. The two transformations shown in the photographs represent rather typical examples of several hundred other nuclear transformations studied in experimental physics today. In all transformations of this kind, known as 'substitutional nuclear reactions', the incidental particle (proton, neutron or alpha-particle), penetrates into the nucleus, kicks some other particle out, and remains itself in its place. We have the substitution of a proton by an alpha-particle, of alpha-particle by proton, proton by neutron, etc. In all such transformations the new element formed in the reaction represents a close neighbour of the bombarded element in the periodic system.

But only comparatively recently, in fact just before the second world war, two German chemists O. HAHN and F. STRASSMANN discovered an entirely new type of nuclear transformation, in which *a heavy nucleus breaks in two equal parts with the liberation of a tremendous amount of energy*. In my next slide (slide please!) [see p. 144] you see on the right a photograph of two uranium fragments flying into the opposite direction from a thin uranium filament. This phenomenon, known as 'nuclear fission', was noticed first in the case of uranium bombarded by a beam of neutrons, but it was soon found that other elements also located near the end of the periodic system possess similar properties. It seems, indeed, that these heavy nuclei are already at the limit of their stability, and that the smallest provocation, caused by a collision with a neutron, is enough to make them break into two, like an oversized drop of mercury. The fact of such instability of heavy nuclei throws light

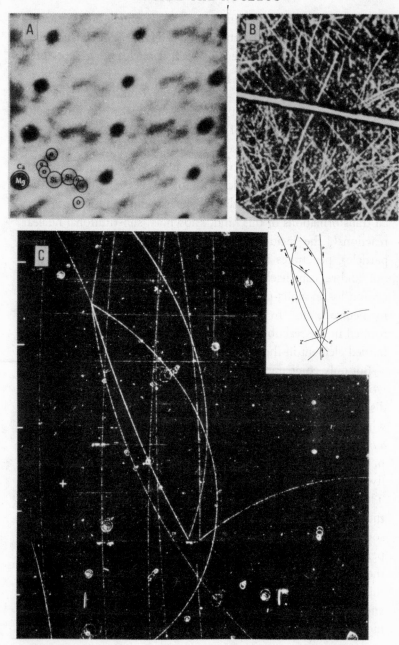

For legend see opposite page

on the question as to why there are only 92 elements in nature; in fact any nucleus heavier than uranium could not exist for any period of time and would immediately break into much smaller fragments. The phenomenon of 'nuclear fission' is also interesting from the practical point of view, since it opens up certain possibilities for the utilization of nuclear energy. The point is that, breaking in half, heavy nuclei also eject a number of neutrons which may cause the fission of neighbouring nuclei. This may lead to an explosive reaction in which all the energy stored inside the nuclei will be set free in a fraction of a second. And, if you remember that the nuclear energy contained in one pound of uranium is equivalent to the energy content of ten tons of coal, you will understand that the possibility of liberating this energy would produce very important changes in our economy.

However, all these nuclear reactions can be obtained only on a very small scale and, although they give us a wealth of information about the internal structure of the nucleus, until comparatively recently there seemed no hope for the release of a vast amount of nuclear energy. It was only in 1939 that the German chemists, O. Hahn and P. Strassmann, discovered an entirely new type of nuclear transformation. In this a heavy nucleus of uranium, hit by a single neutron, breaks into two approximately equal parts, liberating a tremendous amount of energy along with two or three neutrons which, in their turn, may hit other uranium nuclei and break each of them in two also, liberating more energy and more neutrons. This branching fission process may lead to tremendous explosions or, if controlled, supply almost inexhaustible amounts of energy. We are very fortunate that DR TALLERKIN,

(a) Bragg's photograph of atoms in a diopside crystal. The circles in the corner identify individual atoms of calcium, magnesium, silicon and oxygen. Magnification about 100,000,000

(b) Two fission fragments flying in opposite directions from uranium hit by a neutron

(c) Production and decay of neutral lambda and anti-lambda hyperons

who worked on the atomic bomb and who is also known as the 'father of the hydrogen bomb', agreed to come here in spite of his many commitments and give a short talk on the subject of nuclear bombs. He is due here any minute now.

As the professor said these words the door opened and in came an impressive-looking man with burning eyes and overhanging dark bushy eyebrows. Shaking the professor's hand he turned to the audience.

'*Hölgyeim és Uraim*,' he began. '*Mondta Ö röviden kell beszélnem, mert nagyon sok a dolgom. Ma reggel több megbeszélésem volt a Pentagon-ba és a Fehér Ház-ba. Délutan*...Oh, sorry!' he exclaimed, 'sometimes I mix my languages. Let me begin again. Ladies and Gentlemen! I must be short because I am very busy. This morning I attended several conferences in The Pentagon and The White House; this afternoon I have to be present at the underground test explosion at French Flats in Nevada, and in the evening I have to deliver a speech at a banquet at the Vandenberg Air Force Base in California.

'The main point is that atomic nuclei are balanced by two kinds of forces: nuclear attractive forces which tend to hold the nucleus in one piece; and the electric repulsive forces between the protons. In heavy nuclei like those of uranium or plutonium, the latter forces prevail and the nucleus is ready to crack, breaking into two fission products at the slightest provocation. Such a provocation can be provided by a single neutron which hits the nucleus.'

Turning to the blackboard, he continued: 'Here you see a fissionable nucleus and a neutron hitting it. Two fission fragments fly apart, carrying about one million electron volts of energy each and several fresh fission neutrons are also shot out—about two of them, in the case of the light uranium isotope, and about three for plutonium. Then crack! crack! goes the reaction as I have drawn it here on the blackboard. If the piece of fissionable material is small, most of the fission neutrons cross the surface before they have a chance to hit another fissionable nucleus and the chain reaction never starts. But when the piece is larger than what we call a critical mass some three or four inches in diameter, most of the neutrons are trapped and the whole thing blows up. That is what we call a fission bomb, which is often referred to incorrectly as an atomic bomb.

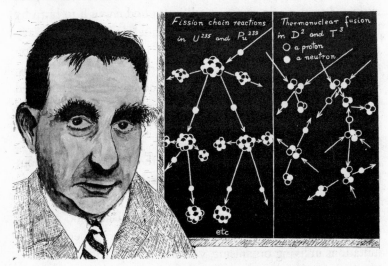

Although the names sound similar, fission and fusion are entirely different processes

'But much better results can be obtained working on the other end of the periodic system of elements where nuclear attractive forces are stronger than electric repulsion. When two light nuclei come into contact they fuse together as do two droplets of mercury on a saucer. This can happen only at a very high temperature, since the light nuclei approaching each other are kept from coming in contact by the electric repulsion. But when the temperature reaches tens of millions of degrees, electric repulsion is impotent to prevent the contact, and the fusion process starts. The most suitable nuclei for the fusion process are deuterons, i.e. the nuclei of heavy hydrogen atoms. There on the right is a simple scheme of thermonuclear reactions in deuterium. When we first thought about the hydrogen bomb, we thought that it would be a blessing to the world, since it produces no radioactive fission products which spread through the atmosphere of the earth. But we were not able to produce such a "pure" hydrogen bomb because deuterium, being the best nuclear fuel which can readily be extracted from ocean water, is still not good enough to burn by itself. Thus we had to surround the deuterium core by a heavy uranium shell. These shells produce a large amount of fission fragments and some people call them "dirty" hydrogen bombs. A similar difficulty is encountered in designing the controlled thermonuclear deuterium reaction, and, in spite of all efforts, we still do not have one. But I am sure this problem will be solved sooner or later.'

'Dr Tallerkin,' asked somebody from the audience, 'what about those fission products from the bomb tests which produce harmful mutations in the population of the entire globe?'

'Not all mutations are harmful,' smiled Dr Tallerkin, 'a few of them are leading to the improvement of progeny. If there were no mutations in living organisms, you and I would still be amoebae. Don't you know that the evolution of life is entirely due to natural mutations and the survival of the fittest?'

'You mean,' shouted a woman in the audience hysterically, 'that we all have to produce children by dozens, and, keeping a few of the best, destroy the rest of them?!'

'Well, Madame,—' started Dr Tallerkin, but at that moment the door of the auditorium opened and in came a man in a pilot suit.

'Hurry, Sir!' he cried, 'your helicopter is parked at the entrance and if we don't start immediately you will miss the connexion with your jetliner at the airport.'

'Sorry,' said Dr Tallerkin to the audience, 'but I must go now. *Isten velük*!' And out they both rushed.

13

The Woodcarver

It was a large and heavy door with an impressive sign, KEEP OUT
—HIGH TENSION, right in the middle of it. However, this first
inhospitable impression was somewhat softened by the word
'welcome' written large on the door mat, and, after a minute's
hesitation, Mr Tompkins pressed the door bell. Let in by a young

assistant, Mr Tompkins found himself in a large room a good half
of which was occupied by a very complicated and fantastic looking machine.

'This is our large cyclotron or "atom-smasher", as they call it
in the newspapers,' explained the assistant, putting a loving hand
on one of the coils of the giant electromagnet which represented
the main part of this impressive looking tool of modern physics.

'This is our large cyclotron or "atom-smasher"'

'It produces particles with energy up to ten million electron volts,' he added proudly, 'and there are not many nuclei which can withstand an impact of a projectile moving with such terrific energy!'

'Well,' said Mr Tompkins, 'these nuclei must be pretty tough! Imagine having to build a giant thing like that just to crack the tiny nucleus of a tiny atom. How does this machine work anyway?'

'Have you ever been to the circus?' asked his father-in-law emerging from behind the giant frame of the cyclotron.

'Err...yes, of course,' said Mr Tompkins, rather embarrassed by this unexpected question, 'you mean you want me to go to the circus with you tonight?'

'Not exactly,' smiled the professor, 'but that will help you to understand how a cyclotron works. If you look between the poles of this large magnet, you will notice a circular copper box which serves as a circus ring on which various charged particles, used in experiments on nuclear bombardment, are being accelerated. In the centre of this box is located the source from which these charged particles, or ions, are produced. When they come out, they possess very small velocities, and the strong field of the magnet bends their trajectories into tiny circles around the centre. Then we begin to whip them up to higher and higher velocities.'

'I see how you can whip a horse,' said Mr Tompkins, 'but how you do the same thing with these tiny particles is rather above my head.'

'Nevertheless, it is very simple. If the particle is moving in a circle, all one has to do is to apply to it a series of successive electric shocks each time it passes a given point on its trajectory, just as a trainer in the circus stands on the edge of the ring and whips the horse each time it passes by.'

'But the trainer can see the horse,' protested Mr Tompkins. 'Can *you* see a particle rotating in this copper box to give it a kick just at the proper moment?'

'Of course I can't,' agreed the professor, 'but it isn't necessary. The whole trick of this cyclotron arrangement is that, although the accelerated particle always moves faster and faster, it always executes one complete turn in the same period of time. The point is, you see, that with the increasing velocity of the particle, the radius, and consequently the total length, of its circular trajectory also increases proportionately. Thus it moves along an unwinding spiral, and always comes to the same side of the "ring" at regular intervals. All one has to do is to place there some electric device to give the shocks at regular intervals, and we do it by means of an oscillating electric circuit system, which is very similar to those you can see at any broadcasting station. Each electric shock produced here is not very strong, but their cumulative effect speeds up the particle to extremely high velocities. This is the great advantage of this apparatus; it gives an effect equivalent to that of many million volts, although nowhere in the system are such high tensions actually present.'

'Very ingenious indeed,' said Mr Tompkins thoughtfully. 'Whose invention is it?'

'It was first built by the late ERNEST ORLANDO LAWRENCE at the University of California a number of years ago,' answered the professor. 'Since then cyclotrons have been growing in size and spreading through physical laboratories with the speed of rumour. They seem to be really more convenient than the older devices which used cascade transformers, or machines based on the electrostatic principle.'

'But can't one really break the nucleus without all these complicated devices?' asked Mr Tompkins, who was a great believer in simplicity, and didn't quite trust anything more complicated than a hammer.

'Of course one can. In fact when Rutherford made his first famous experiments on the artificial transformation of elements, he just used ordinary alpha-particles emitted by naturally radioactive bodies. But that was over twenty years ago and, as you can see, the techniques of atom smashing have made considerable progress since then.'

'Can you show me an atom actually being smashed?' asked Mr Tompkins, who always preferred to see things for himself rather than to listen to lengthy explanations.

'Gladly,' said the professor. 'We were just starting an experiment. Here we are making a further study of the disintegration of boron under the impact of fast protons. When the nucleus of a boron atom is hit by a proton hard enough to permit the projectile to pierce the nuclear potential barrier and get inside, it breaks into three equal fragments which all fly in different directions. This process can be directly observed by means of the so-called "cloud chamber" which enables us to see the trajectories of all the particles involved in the collision. Such a chamber, with a piece of boron in the middle, is now attached to the opening of the acceleration chamber, and as soon as we start the cyclotron working you will see the process of nuclear cracking with your own eyes.'

'Will you please switch on the current,' he said, turning to his assistant, 'while I try to tune up the magnetic field.'

It took some time to get the cyclotron started, and left alone Mr Tompkins wandered idly around the lab. His attention was drawn to a complicated system of large amplifier tubes glowing with a faint bluish light. Being quite unaware of the fact that the generating electric tensions used in the cyclotron, though not high enough to crack a nucleus, can easily floor an ox, he leaned forward to look at them more closely.

There was a sharp crack, like that of a lion tamer's whip, and Mr Tompkins felt a terrible shock running through his entire body. The next moment everything went black and he lost consciousness.

When he opened his eyes, he found himself prostrate on the floor where the electric discharge had thrown him. The room around him seemed the same, but all the objects in it had changed considerably. Instead of the towering cyclotron magnet, shining copper connexions, and dozens of complicated electric gadgets attached to every possible spot, Mr Tompkins saw a long wooden work table covered with simple carpenter's tools. On the old-fashioned shelves attached to the wall, he noticed a large number of different wood carvings of strange and unusual shapes. An old, friendly-looking man was working at the table, and, looking more closely at his features, Mr Tompkins was struck by his strong resemblance both to the old man Gepetto in Walt Disney's Pinocchio, and the portrait of the late Lord Rutherford of Nelson hanging on the wall of the professor's lab.

'Excuse my intrusion,' said Mr Tompkins, raising himself from the floor, 'but I was visiting a nuclear laboratory, and something strange seems to have happened to me.'

'Oh, you are interested in nuclei,' said the old man, setting aside the piece of wood he was carving. 'Then you came to just the right place. I make all kinds of nuclei right here and will be glad to show you around my little workshop.'

'You say you *make* them?' said Mr Tompkins rather stupefied.

'Yes, of course. Naturally, it requires some skill, especially in the case of radioactive nuclei, which may fall apart before you even have time to paint them.'

'*Paint* them?'

'Yes, I use red for the positively charged particles and green for the negative ones. Now you probably know that red and green are what one calls "complementary colours", and cancel each other out if mixed together.* This corresponds to the mutual cancellation of positive and negative electric charges. If the nucleus is made up of an equal number of positive and negative charges moving rapidly to and fro, it will be electrically neutral

---

* The reader must keep in mind that the mixture of colours pertains only to light rays and not to the paints themselves. If we mix red and green paint we shall simply get a dirty colour. On the other hand if we paint one half of a toy top red, and the other green, and then spin it rapidly, it will look white.

and will look white to you. If there are more positive or more negative charges, the whole system will be coloured red or green. Simple, isn't it?'

'Now,' continued the old man, showing Mr Tompkins two large wooden boxes standing near the table, 'this is where I keep the materials from which various nuclei can be built. The first box

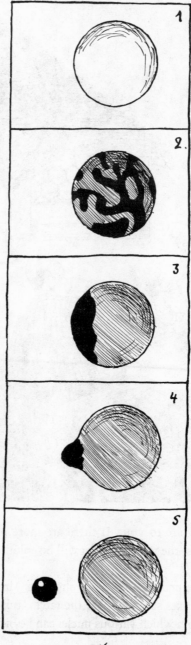

contains *protons*, these red balls here. They are quite stable and keep their colour permanently, unless you scratch it off with a knife or something. I have much more trouble with the so-called *neutrons* in the second box. They are normally white, or electrically neutral, but show a strong tendency to turn into red protons. As long as the box is closed tight, everything is all right, but as soon as you take one out, see what happens.'

Opening the box, the old woodcarver took out one of the white balls and placed it on the table. For a while nothing seemed to happen, but just when Mr Tompkins had about lost patience, the ball suddenly came alive. Irregular reddish and greenish stripes appeared on its surface, and for a short while the ball looked like one of the coloured glass marbles children like so much. Then the green colour became concentrated on one side, and finally separated itself entirely from the ball, forming a brilliant green droplet which fell on to the floor. The ball itself was now left completely red, no different from any of the red-coloured protons in the first box.

'You see what happens,' he said, picking the drop of green paint, now quite hard and round, up from the floor. 'The white colour of the neutron broke up into red and green and the whole thing split into two separate particles, a proton and a negative electron.'

'Yes,' he added, seeing the surprised look on Mr Tompkins's face, 'this jade-coloured particle is nothing but an ordinary electron, just like any other electron in any atom or anywhere else.'

'Gosh!' exclaimed Mr Tompkins. 'This certainly tops any coloured handkerchief trick I have ever seen. But can you change the colours back again?'

'Yes, I can rub the green paint back on to the surface of the red ball and make it white again, but that would require some energy, of course. Another way to do it would be to scratch the red paint off, which would take some energy too. Then the paint scratched from the surface of the proton will form a red droplet, that is, a positive electron, about which you have probably heard.'

'Yes, when I was an electron myself. . . ,' began Mr Tompkins, but checked himself quickly. 'I mean, I have heard that positive and negative electrons annihilate each other whenever they meet,' he said. 'Can you do that trick for me too?'

'Oh, it's very simple,' said the old man. 'But I won't take the trouble to scratch the paint off this proton, as I have a couple of positrons left over from my morning's work.'

Opening one of the drawers, he extracted a tiny bright red ball, and, pressing it firmly between finger and thumb, put it beside the green one on the table. There was a sharp noise, like a fire-cracker exploding, and both balls vanished at once.

'You see?' said the woodcarver, blowing on his slightly burned fingers. 'That is why one cannot use electrons for building nuclei. I tried it once, but gave it up right away. Now I use only protons and neutrons.'

'But neutrons are unstable too, aren't they?' asked Mr Tompkins, remembering the recent demonstration.

'When they are alone, yes. But when they are packed tightly in the nucleus, and surrounded by other particles, they become quite stable. However, if there are, relatively speaking, too many neutrons, or too many protons, they can transform themselves, and the extra paint is emitted from the nucleus in the form of negative or positive electrons. Such an adjustment we call a beta-transformation.'

'Do you use any glue, in making the nuclei?' asked Mr Tompkins with interest.

'Don't need any,' answered the old man. 'These particles, you see, stick to each other by themselves as soon as you bring them into contact. You can try it yourself if you want to.'

Following this advice, Mr Tompkins took one proton and one neutron in each hand, and brought them together carefully. At once he felt a strong pull, and looking at the particles he noticed an extremely strange phenomenon. The particles were exchanging colour, becoming alternately red and white. It seemed as if the red paint were 'jumping' from the ball in his right hand to the one in his left hand, and back again. This twinkling of colour was so fast that the two balls seemed to be connected by a pinkish band along which the colouring was oscillating to and fro.

'This is what my theoretical friends call the exchange phenomenon,' said the old master, chuckling at Mr Tompkins' surprise. 'Both balls want to be red, or to have the electric charge, if you want to put it that way, and as they cannot have it simultaneously, they pull it to and fro alternately. Neither wants to give up, and so they stick together until you separate them by force. Now I can show you how simple it is to make any nucleus you want to. What shall it be?'

'Gold,' said Mr Tompkins, remembering the ambition of the medieval alchemists.

'Gold? Let us see,' murmured the old master, turning to a large chart hanging on the wall, 'the nucleus of gold weighs one hundred and ninety-seven units, and carries seventy-nine positive electric charges. That means I have to take seventy-nine protons and add one hundred and eighteen neutrons to get the mass correct.'

Counting off the proper number of particles, he put them into a tall cylindrical vessel and covered it all with a heavy wooden piston. Then, with all his strength, he pushed the piston down.

'I must do this,' he explained to Mr Tompkins, 'because of the strong electric repulsion between the positively charged protons. Once this repulsion is overcome by the pressure of the piston, the protons and the neutrons will stick together because of their mutual exchange forces, and will form the desired nucleus.'

Pressing the piston in as far as it would go, he took it out again and quickly turned the cylindrical vessel upside down. A glittering pinkish ball rolled out on the table, and, watching it more closely, Mr Tompkins noticed that the pinkish colour was due to an interplay of red and white flashes among the rapidly moving particles.

'How beautiful!' he exclaimed. 'So this is an atom of gold!'

'Not an atom yet, only the atomic nucleus,' the old woodcarver corrected him. 'To complete the atom you must add the proper number of electrons to neutralize the positive charge of the nucleus, and make the customary electronic shell around it. But that is easy, and the nucleus itself will catch its electrons as soon as there are some around.'

'Funny,' said Mr Tompkins, 'that my father-in-law never mentioned that one could make gold so simply.'

'Oh your father-in-law and those other so-called nuclear physicists!' exclaimed the old man with a touch of irritation in his voice. 'They put on a fine show but they can actually do very little. They say they cannot compress separate protons into a complex nucleus because they cannot exert great enough pressure to do the job. One of them even calculated that one would need to impose the entire weight of the moon to make the protons stick together. Well, why don't they get the moon if that is their only trouble?'

'But still they produce *some* nuclear transformation,' remarked Mr Tompkins meekly.

'Yes, of course, but awkwardly and to a very limited extent. The quantity of the new elements they get is so small they can hardly see it themselves. I will show you how they do it.' And, taking a proton, he threw it with considerable force against the gold nucleus lying on the table. Nearing the outside of the nucleus, the proton slowed down a little, hesitated a moment and then plunged inside it. Having swallowed the proton, the nucleus shivered for a short time as though in a high fever and then a small part of it broke off with a crack.

'You see,' he said, picking up the fragment, 'this is what they call an alpha-particle, and if you inspect it closely you will notice that it consists of two protons and two neutrons. Such particles are usually ejected from the heavy nuclei of the so-called radioactive elements, but one can also kick them out of ordinary stable nuclei if one hits them hard enough. I must also call your atten-

tion to the fact that the larger fragment left on the table is not a
gold nucleus any longer; it has lost one positive charge and is now
a nucleus of platinum, the preceding element in the periodic table.
In some cases, however, the proton which enters the nucleus will
not cause it to split in two parts, and as the result you will get the
nucleus that follows gold in the table, i.e. the nucleus of mercury.
Combining these and similar processes one can actually transform
any given element into any other.'

'Oh, now I see why they use fast proton beams produced by the
cyclotron,' said Mr Tompkins, beginning to understand. 'But
why do you say this method is no good?'

'Because its effectiveness is extremely low. First of all they cannot aim their projectiles the way I can so that only one in several
thousand shots actually hits the nucleus. Second, even in the case
of a direct hit, the projectile is very likely to bounce off the nucleus
instead of penetrating into the interior. You may have noticed
when I threw the proton into the gold nucleus that it hesitated
somewhat before going in, and I thought for a moment that it was
going to be thrown back.'

'What is there to prevent the projectiles from going in?' asked
Mr Tompkins with interest.

'You could have guessed it yourself,' said the old man, 'if you
had remembered that both the nuclei and the bombarding protons
carry positive charges. The repulsive force between these charges
forms a kind of barrier which is not so easy to cross. If the bombarding protons manage to penetrate the nuclear fortress, it is only
because they use something like the Trojan horse technique; they
go through the nuclear walls not as particles but as waves.'

'Well, you have got me there,' said Mr Tompkins sadly, 'I don't
understand a word you are saying.'

'I was afraid you wouldn't,' said the woodcarver with a smile.
'To tell you the truth, I'm a workman myself. I can do these
things with my hands but I'm not too strong on this theoretical
abracadabra either. However the main point is that, as all these

nuclear particles are made out of quantum material, they can always go, or rather leak, through obstacles ordinarily considered impenetrable.'

'Oh, I see what you mean!' exclaimed Mr Tompkins. 'I remember that once, shortly before I met Maud, I visited a strange place where billiard-balls behaved exactly the way you describe.

'Billiard-balls? You mean real *ivory* billiard-balls?' repeated the old woodcarver eagerly.

'Yes, I understand they were made from the tusks of quantum elephants,' answered Mr Tompkins.

'Well, such is life,' said the old man sadly. 'They use such expensive materials just for games, and I have to carve protons and neutrons, the basic particles of the entire universe, out of plain quantum oak!'

'But,' he continued, trying to hide his disappointment, 'my poor wooden toys are just as good as all those expensive ivory creations and I will show you how neatly they can pass through any kind of barrier.' And, climbing on the bench, he took from the top shelf a very strange carved figure looking like the model of a volcano.

'What you see here,' he continued, gently brushing off the dust, 'is the model of the barrier of repulsive forces surrounding any atomic nucleus. The outer slopes correspond to the electric repulsion between the charges, and the crater to the cohesion forces which make the nuclear particles stick together. If I now flip a ball up the slope, but not hard enough to bring it over the crest, you would naturally suppose that it would roll back again. But see what actually happens...,' and he gave the ball a slight flip.

'Well, I don't see anything unusual,' said Mr Tompkins, when the ball, after rising about half way up the slope, rolled back again on the table.

'Wait,' said the woodcarver quietly. 'You shouldn't expect it at the first trial,' and he sent the ball up the slope once more. This

time it failed again, but at the third attempt the ball suddenly disappeared just when it was about half-way up the slope.

'Well, where do you suppose that one went?' said the old
woodcarver triumphantly with the air of a magician.

'You mean it is in the crater now?' asked Mr Tompkins.

'Yes, that is exactly where it is,' said the old man, picking out
the ball with his fingers.

'Now, let us get it in reverse,' he suggested, 'and see if the ball
can get out of the crater without rolling over the top,' and he
threw the ball back into the hole.

For a while nothing happened, and Mr Tompkins could hear
only the slight rumbling of the ball rolling to and fro in the crater.
Then, as by a miracle, the ball suddenly appeared in the middle of
the outer slope, and quietly rolled down to the table.

'What you see here is a very good representation of what happens in radioactive alpha-decay,' said the woodcarver, putting the
model back into its place, 'only there, instead of the ordinary
quantum-oak barrier, you have the barrier of repulsive electric
force. But in principle there is no difference whatever. Sometimes these electric barriers are so "transparent" that the particle
escapes in a small fraction of a second; sometimes they are so
"opaque" that it takes many billion years, as for example in the
case of the uranium nucleus.'

'But why aren't all nuclei radioactive?' asked Mr Tompkins.

'Because in most nuclei the floor of the crater is below the outer
level, and only in the heaviest known nuclei is the floor sufficiently
elevated to make such an escape possible.'

It is difficult to say how many hours Mr Tompkins spent in the workshop with the kindly old woodcarver, who was always so eager to communicate his knowledge to anyone who came along. He saw many other unusual things, and above all a carefully closed, but apparently empty casket labelled: NEUTRINOS. *Handle with care and don't let out.*

'Is there something in it?' asked Mr Tompkins, shaking the casket near his ear.

'I don't know,' said the woodcarver. 'Some people say yes, some say no. But you can't see anything anyway. That's a fancy casket given to me by one of my theoretical friends, and I don't quite know what to do with it. Better leave it alone for the time being.'

Continuing his inspection, Mr Tompkins also discovered a dusty old violin, which looked so old that it must have been made by Stradivari's grandfather.

'Do you play the violin?' He turned to the woodcarver.

'Only gamma-ray tunes,' answered the old man. 'It is a quantum-violin, and it doesn't play anything else. Once I had a quantum-cello, for optical tunes, but somebody borrowed it and never brought it back.'

'Well, play me a gamma-ray tune,' asked Mr Tompkins. 'Never heard one before.'

'I will play you "*Nucléet in Th C Sharp*",' said the woodcarver, raising the violin to his shoulder, 'but you must be prepared for it to be a very sad tune.'

The music was very strange indeed, unlike anything Mr Tompkins had ever heard before. There was a steady noise of ocean waves running on sandy shores, interrupted from time to time by a shrill tune reminding him of the whistle of a passing bullet. Mr Tompkins was not exactly musical, but this tune had a weird and powerful effect on him. He stretched himself comfortably in an old armchair and closed his eyes. . . .

14

Holes in Nothing

Ladies and Gentlemen:

Tonight I will request your special attention, since the problems which I am going to discuss are as difficult as they are fascinating. I am going to speak about new particles, known as 'positrons', possessing more than unusual properties. It is very instructive to notice that the existence of this new kind of particle was predicted on the basis of purely theoretical considerations several years before they were actually detected, and that their empirical discovery was largely helped by the theoretical preview of their main properties.

The honour of having made this prediction belongs to a British physicist, Paul Dirac, of whom you have heard and who arrived at his conclusions on the basis of theoretical considerations so strange and fantastic that most physicists refused to believe them for quite a long time. The basic idea of Dirac's theory can be formulated in these simple words: 'There should be holes in empty space.' I see you are surprised; well, so were all physicists when Dirac uttered these significant words. How can there be a hole in an empty space? Does this make any sense? Yes, if one implies that the so-called empty space is actually not so empty as we believe it to be. And, in fact, the main point of Dirac's theory consists in the assumption that *the so-called empty space, or vacuum, is actually thickly populated by an infinite number of ordinary negative electrons packed together in a very regular and uniform way*. It is needless to say that such an old hypothesis did not come to Dirac's mind as the result of sheer fantasy, but that he was more or less forced to it by a number of considerations pertaining to the theory of ordinary negative electrons. In fact, the theory leads to an inevitable conclusion that, besides the quantum states of motion in atoms, there is also an infinite number of special 'negative quantum states' belonging to a pure vacuum, and that, unless one prevents electrons from going over into these 'more comfortable' states of motion, they will all abandon their atoms and will be, so to speak, dissolved into empty space. Since, furthermore, the only way of preventing an electron from going where it pleases, is to have this particular spot 'occupied' by some other electron (remember Pauli), one must have *all* these quantum states in vacuum completely filled up by an infinity of electrons distributed uniformly through the entire space.

I am afraid that my words sound like some kind of scientific abracadabra, and that you cannot make head or tail of all this, but the subject is really very difficult, and I can only hope that if you keep on listening attentively you will be able finally to get some idea about the nature of Dirac's theory.

Well, one way or another, Dirac arrived at the conclusion that empty space is thickly filled with electrons, distributed with a uniform but infinitely high density. How does it happen that we do not notice them at all, and consider the vacuum as an absolutely empty space?

You may understand the answer if you will put yourself in the position of a deepwater fish suspended in the ocean. Does the fish, even if it is intelligent enough to put such a question, realize that it is surrounded by water?

These words brought Mr Tompkins out of a doze into which he had fallen during the beginning of the lecture. He was a bit of a fisherman, and he felt a fresh breeze off the sea and the gently rolling blue waves. But although he was a good swimmer he could not stay on the surface and began to sink deeper and deeper toward the bottom. Strangely enough, he did not feel the lack of air and was quite comfortable. Maybe, he thought, this is the effect of a special recessive mutation.

According to palaeontologists, life originated in the ocean, and the first fishy pioneer to get out on to dry land was the so-called *lungfish* who crawled out to a beach, walking on its fins. According to biologists, these first lungfish, which are called Neoceratodus in Australia, Protopterus in Africa, and Lepidosiren in South America, gradually evolved into land-dwelling animals, like mice, cats, and men. But some of them, like whales and dolphins, after learning of all the troubles of life on dry land, returned to the ocean. Getting back to the water, they retained the qualities acquired during their struggle on the land, and

P. A. M. Dirac was engaged in conversation with a dolphin

remained mammals, the females bearing their progeny inside their bodies instead of just dropping caviar and having it fertilized later by the males. Wasn't it a famous Hungarian scientist named LEO SZILARD* who said that dolphins are more intelligent than human beings?

His thoughts were interrupted by a conversation carried on somewhere deep under the ocean's surface by a dolphin and a typical *homo sapiens* whom Mr Tompkins recognized (from a photograph he had once seen) as the physicist Paul Adrien Maurice Dirac, from Cambridge University.

* Leo Szilard, *The Voice of the Dolphins and Other Stories* (Simon and Schuster, New York, 1961).

'Look here, Paul,' the dolphin was saying, 'you contend that we are not in a vacuum but in a material medium formed by particles with negative mass. As far as I am concerned, water is not different at all from empty space; it is completely uniform and I can move freely through it in all directions. I heard a legend from my pre-pre-pre-pre-predecessor that dry land is quite different, however. There are mountains and canyons which one cannot cross without effort. Here in the water I can move in any direction I choose.'

'You are right in the case of ocean water, my friend,' answered P.A.M. 'Water exerts friction on the surface of your body and if you do not move your tail and fins you will not be able to move at all. Also, because the water pressure changes with the depth, you can float upwards or sink downwards by expanding or contracting your body. But if water had no friction and no pressure gradient you would be as helpless as an astronaut who ran out of rocket fuel. My ocean, which is formed by electrons with negative masses, is completely frictionless and therefore unobservable. Only the *absence* of one of the electrons can be observed by physical instruments, since the absence of a negative electric charge is equivalent to the presence of a positive electric charge, so that even Coulomb could notice it.

'In comparing my electron's ocean with the ordinary ocean we must however make one important exception in order not to be carried too far away by this analogy. The point is that since electrons forming my ocean are subject to the Pauli principle, not a single electron can be added to that ocean when all the possible quantum levels are occupied. Such an extra electron will have to remain above my ocean's surface and can be easily identified by the experimentalists. The electrons discovered first by SIR J. J. THOMSON, the electrons circling around atomic nuclei, or those flying through vacuum tubes, are such excess electrons. And until I published my first paper in 1930 the rest of space was considered to be void, and it was believed that the physical reality belongs only to the occasional splashes rising above the surface of zero energy.'

'But,' said the dolphin, 'if your ocean is unobservable because of its continuity and absence of friction, what is the sense of talking about it?'

'Well,' said P.A.M., 'assume that some external force lifted one of the electrons with negative mass from the depth of the ocean to above its surface. In this case the number of observable electrons will increase by one, which would be considered as a violation of the conservation law. But the empty hole in the ocean from which the electron was removed will now be observable, since the absence of negative charge from a uniform distribution will be perceived as the presence of an equal amount of positive charge. This positively-charged particle will also have a positive mass and will move in the same direction as the force of gravity.'

'You mean it will float up instead of sinking down?' asked the dolphin with surprise.

'Certainly. I am sure you have seen many objects sinking to the bottom, being pulled down by gravity forces: things thrown overboard from ships, or sometimes ships themselves. But look here!' P.A.M. interrupted himself, 'See these small silvery objects rising up to the surface? Their motion is caused by the force of gravity, but they move in the opposite direction.'

'But those are just bubbles,' retorted the dolphin. 'They are probably escaping from something containing the air which turned over or broke, hitting the rocks on the bottom.'

'Right you are, but you would not see bubbles floating up in vacuum. Hence my ocean is not void.'

'Very clever theory,' said the dolphin, 'but is it true?'

'When I proposed it in 1930,' said P.A.M., 'nobody believed it. It was to a large extent my own mistake because I originally suggested that these positively charged particles are nothing else but protons, well known to the experimentalists. You know, of course, that protons are 1840 times heavier than electrons, but I hoped that by some mathematical trick I would be able to explain this increased resistance to acceleration under the action of the given force, and to obtain theoretically the number 1840. But it did not work, and the material mass of the bubbles in my ocean was coming to be exactly equal to that of an ordinary electron. My colleague, Pauli, to whom I must certainly ascribe a sense of humour, was running around professing what he called "the Second Pauli Principle". He calculated, you see, that if an ordinary electron comes close to a hole produced by removal of an electron from my ocean it will fill it up within a negligible period of time. Thus if the proton of a hydrogen atom is really a "hole", it will be instantaneously filled by the ordinary electron rotating around it, and both particles will disappear in a flash of light—or a flash of gamma-rays, should I say. The same would happen, of course, to the atoms of all other elements. Now, the Second Pauli Principle demanded that any theory proposed by a physicist would immediately apply to the matter forming his body, so that I would be annihilated before I had a chance to tell my idea to anybody else. Just like that!' And P.A.M. vanished with a brilliant flash of radiation.

'Sir,' said an irritated voice at Mr Tompkins's ear, 'it is your privilege to sleep at a lecture, but you shouldn't snore. I cannot hear a word of what the professor is saying.'

And, opening his eyes, Mr Tompkins saw again the crowded lecture room and the old professor, who continued:

Let us now see what happens when a travelling hole encounters a surplus electron which is looking for a comfortable place in Dirac's ocean. It is clear that, as the result of such an encounter, the surplus electron will inevitably fall into the hole, filling it up, and the surprised physicist observing the process will register the phenomenon as *the mutual annihilation* of a positive and a negative electron. The energy set free in the fall will be emitted in the form of short-wave radiation, and will represent the only remainder of two electrons who have eaten each other up like the two wolves in the well-known children's story.

But one can also imagine a reverse process in which a pair con-

sisting of a negative and a positive electron are 'created from nothing' by the action of a powerful external radiation. From the
point of view of Dirac's theory, such a process consists simply in
kicking out an electron from the continuous distribution, and
should be considered actually not as a 'creation' but rather as a
separation of two opposite electric charges. In the diagram which
I now show you, these two processes of electronic 'creation' and
'annihilation' are represented in a very crude schematic way, and

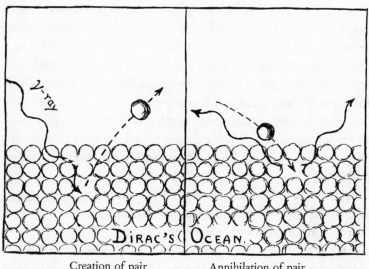

Creation of pair   Annihilation of pair

you see that there is nothing mysterious about the matter. I must
add here that, although strictly speaking the process of pair-creation may take place in an absolute vacuum, its probability would
be extremely small; you may say that the electron-distribution of a
vacuum is too smooth to break it up. On the other hand, in the
presence of heavy material particles, which serve as the point of
support for the gamma-ray digging into the electronic-distribu-
tion, the probability of pair-creation is largely increased and it can
be easily observed.

It is clear however that positrons created in the way described above will not exist very long and will soon be annihilated in an encounter with one of the negative electrons which possess large numerical superiority in our corner of the universe. This fact constitutes the reason for the comparatively late discovery of these interesting particles. In fact, the first report on positive electrons was made only in August 1932 (Dirac's theory was published in 1930) by the Californian physicist CARL ANDERSON who, in his studies of cosmic radiation, found particles which resembled in all their aspects ordinary electrons with the only important difference that instead of a negative electric charge they carried a positive one. Soon after this we learned a simple way of producing electron pairs under laboratory conditions by sending a powerful beam of high-frequency radiation (radioactive gamma-rays) through any kind of material substance.

On the next plate I am going to show you, you will see the so-called 'cloud-chamber photographs' of the cosmic-ray positrons, and of the process of pair-creation itself. But before doing so I must explain the way in which these photographs were obtained. The cloud-, or Wilson-chamber, is one of the most useful instruments of modern experimental physics, and it is based on the fact that any electrically-charged particle moving through a gas produces a large number of ions along its track. If the gas is saturated with water vapours, tiny droplets of water will condense on these ions, thus forming a thin layer of fog extending all along the track. Illuminating this foggy band by a strong beam of light on a dark background we obtain perfect pictures, showing all the details of motion.

The first of the two pictures now projected on the screen is the original photograph by Anderson of a cosmic-ray positron, and is, by the way, the first picture of this particle ever taken. The broad horizontal band going across the picture is a thick lead plate placed across the chamber, and the track of the positron is seen as a thin curved scratch going through the plate. The track is curved because during the experiment the cloud-chamber was placed in a strong magnetic field influencing the motion of the particle. The lead plate and magnetic field were employed in order to determine the sign of the electric charge carried by the particle, which can be done on the basis of the following argumentation. It is known that the deflexion of the trajectory produced by the magnetic field depends on the sign of the charge of the moving particle. In this particular case the magnet was placed in such a way that negative electrons would be deflected to the left of the original direction of their motion, whereas positive electrons would be deflected to the

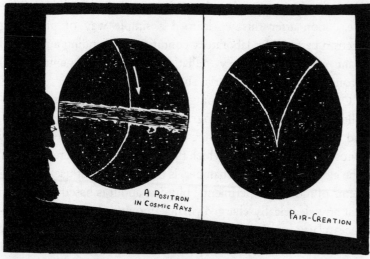

A POSITRON IN COSMIC RAYS

PAIR-CREATION

right. Thus if the particle in the photograph was moving upwards it may have had a negative charge. But how to tell which way it was moving? That is where the lead plate comes in. After crossing the plate the particle must have lost some of its original energy, and hence the bending effect of the magnetic field must be larger. In the present photograph the track is bent more strongly *under* the plate (it can hardly be seen at first glance, but comes out in the measurement of the plate). Consequently the particle was moving downwards, and its charge was positive.

The other photograph was taken by JAMES CHADWICK at the University of Cambridge and represents the process of pair creation in the air of the cloud chamber. A strong gamma-ray entering from below, and producing no visible track in the photograph, produced an electronic pair in the middle of the chamber, and the two particles are flying apart, being deflected in opposite directions by the strong magnetic field. Looking at this photograph you may wonder why the positron (which is on the left) is not annihilated on its way through the gas. The answer to this question is also given by Dirac's theory and will be easily understood by anyone who plays golf. If, in putting on the green, you hit the ball too hard, it will not fall into the hole even if your aim is true. In fact a rapidly moving ball will simply jump over the hole and roll on. In the very same way a fast moving electron will not fall into Dirac's hole until its velocity is considerably reduced. Thus a positron has a better chance of being annihilated at the end of its trajectory when it is slowed down by collision along the track. And, as a matter of fact, careful observations show that the radiation which accompanies any annihilation process is actually present at the end of the positron's trajectory. This fact represents an additional confirmation of Dirac's theory.

There remain now two general points still to be discussed. First of all I have been referring to negative electrons as the overflow of Dirac's ocean and to positrons as the holes in it. One can, however, reverse the point of view and consider ordinary electrons as the holes, giving to positrons the role of thrown-out particles. To do this we have only to assume that Dirac's ocean is not overflowing, but that, on the contrary, there is always a shortage of particles. In such a case we can visualize Dirac's distribution to be something like a piece of Swiss cheese with a lot of holes in it. Owing to the general shortage of particles the holes will exist permanently, and if one of the particles is thrown out of distribution it will soon fall back again into one of the holes. It should be stated, however, that both pictures are absolutely equivalent from physical as well as mathematical points of view, and there is actually no difference no matter which one we choose.

The second point can be put in the form of the following question: 'If in the part of the world in which we live there is a definite preponderance in the number of negative electrons, are we to suppose that in some other parts of the Universe this is reversed?' In other words, is the overflow of Dirac's ocean in our neighbourhood compensated for by the lack of these particles somewhere else?

This extremely interesting question is a very hard one to answer. In fact, since atoms built by positive electrons rotating around negative nuclei would have exactly the same optical properties as ordinary atoms, there is no way to decide this question by any spectroscopic observation. For all that we know, it is quite possible that the material forming, let us say, the Great Andromeda Nebula is of this topsy-turvy type, but the only way to prove it would be to get hold of a piece of that material and see whether or not it is annihilated by contact with terrestrial materials. There would be a terrible explosion, of course! There has recently been some talk about the possibility that certain meteorites exploding in the terrestrial atmosphere are formed of this topsy-turvy material, but I don't think that much credit should be given to it. In fact it may very well be that this question of the overflow and draught of Dirac's ocean in different parts of the Universe will remain unanswered forever.

15

Mr Tompkins Tastes a Japanese Meal

One weekend Maud went away to visit her aunt in Yorkshire, and Mr Tompkins invited the professor to have dinner with him in a famous sukiyaki restaurant. Sitting on the soft cushions at a low table, they were enjoying all the delicacies of the Japanese kitchen and sipping sake from little cups.

'Tell me,' said Mr Tompkins. 'The other day I heard Dr Tallerkin saying in his lecture that the protons and the neutrons in a nucleus were held together by some kinds of nuclear forces. Are those the same forces which hold electrons in an atom?'

'Oh, no!' answered the professor. 'Nuclear forces are something quite different. Atomic electrons are attracted to the nucleus by ordinary electrostatic forces first studied in detail by a French physicist, CHARLES AUGUSTIN DE COULOMB, toward the end of the eighteenth century. They are comparatively weak and decrease in inverse proportion to the square of the distance from the centre. Nuclear forces are quite different. When a proton and a neutron come close to each other but not yet in direct contact, there are practically no forces between them. But as soon as they come into contact, there appears an extremely strong force which holds them together. It is like two pieces of adhesive tape which do not attract each other at even a small distance but stick together like brothers as soon as they come in touch with each other. Physicists call these forces 'strong interaction'. They are independent of electric charge of the two particles, and are equally strong between a proton-neutron pair, two protons, or two neutrons.'

'Are there any theories which explain these forces?' asked Mr Tompkins.

'Oh, yes. In the early thirties HIDEKEI YUKAWA proposed

that they are due to the exchange of some as yet unknown particles between the two nucleons; a nucleon is a collective name for a proton and a neutron. When two nucleons come close to each other these mysterious particles begin to jump to and fro between them, leading to a strong binding force which holds them together. Yukawa was able to estimate theoretically their mass, which came to about 200 times larger than the mass of an electron or about 10 times smaller than the mass of a proton or a neutron. Thus they called them "mesatrons". Then the father of Werner Heisenberg, who was a professor of classical languages, objected to this violation of the Greek. The name 'electron', you see, was derived from the Greek ἤλεκτρον meaning *amber*, while "proton" comes from the Greek πρῶτον meaning *first*. But the name of Yukawa's particle is derived from the Greek μέσον meaning *middle*, which has no letter *r* in it. Thus at an international physics meeting Heisenberg proposed to change the name mesatron to "meson". Some French physicists objected because, independent of spelling, meson sounds like *maison*, the French word for home or house. But they were overruled and now the term meson is firmly established. But look at the stage! They are just going to perform a meson show.'

And, indeed, six geishas came out and began to perform a *bilboquet* act in which they were throwing a ball to and fro between two cups which they held in their hands. A man's face appeared in the background singing:

> For a meson I received the Nobel Prize,
> An achievement I prefer to minimize.
> Lambda zero, Yokohama,
> Eta keon, Fujiyama—
> For a meson I received the Nobel Prize.

They proposed to call it *Yukon* in Japan.
I demurred, for I'm a very modest man.
   Lambda zero, Yokohama,
    Eta keon, Fujiyama—
They proposed to call it *Yukon* in Japan.

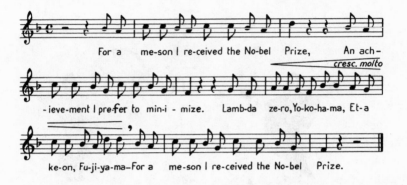

For a me-son I re-ceived the No-bel Prize, An ach-
-ieve-ment I pre-fer to min-i-mize. Lamb-da ze-ro, Yo-ko-ha-ma, Et-a
ke-on, Fu-ji-ya-ma—For a me-son I re-ceived the No-bel Prize.

'But why are there three pairs of geishas?' asked Mr Tompkins.

'They represent three possibilities of meson exchange,' said the professor. 'There may be three kinds of mesons: positively charged, negatively charged, and electrically neutral. Maybe all three of them take part in producing nuclear forces.'

'So now there are eight elementary particles,' said Mr Tompkins, counting on his fingers, 'neutrons, protons (positive and negative), negative and positive electrons, and the three kinds of mesons.'

'Ho!' said the professor, 'not eight but closer to eighty. First it was found that there are two kinds of mesons: the heavy and the light mesons designated by the Greek letters π and μ and called *pions* and *muons*. Pions are produced at the fringes of the atmosphere by the impact of the very high energy protons against the nuclei of the gases which form the air. But they are very unstable, and break up, before they reach the Earth's surface, into muons and—most mysterious particle of them all—neutrinos which have neither mass nor charge and are just energy carriers. Muons live somewhat longer, about a few microseconds, so that they manage to reach the earth's surface and decay under our eyes into ordinary electrons and two neutrinos. Then there are also particles designated by the Greek letter κ known as keons.'

Three geishas were playing some unusual *bilboquet* game

'Which kinds of particles did these geishas use in their play?' asked Mr Tompkins.

'Oh, probably pions, the neutral ones, those being the most important, but I am not sure. The majority of new particles which are now being discovered almost every month are so short-lived that, even moving with the speed of light, they decay within the distance of a few centimetres from their origin, so that even the gadgets sent into the atmosphere on balloons do not notice them.

'However, we have now powerful particle accelerators which speed up protons to the same high energy as they reach in cosmic rays: many thousand million electron volts. One of these machines, called the Lawrencetron, is located close by here right up the hill and I will be glad to show it to you.'

A short automobile drive brought them to a large building housing the particle-accelerating machine. Entering the structure, Mr Tompkins was impressed by the complexity of this giant gadget. But, as the professor assured him, it was not more complicated in principle than the slingshot used by David to kill Goliath. The charged particles were entering into the centre of that giant drum, and moving along the unwinding spiral trajectories, being speeded up by alternating electric impulses and kept in line by a strong magnetic field.

'I think I have seen something like that before,' said Mr Tompkins, 'when I visited the Cyclotron, which they used to call an "atom smasher" some years ago.'

'Oh, yes,' said the professor, 'the machine which you have seen before was originally invented by Dr Lawrence. The one you see here is based on the same principle but, instead of accelerating the particles to several million volts, it can speed them to many thousand million volts. Two of them have recently been constructed in the United States. One of them is in Berkeley, California, and is called the Bevatron because it produced particles with the energy of billions of electron volts. It is a strictly American name because in that country a 'billion' is one thousand million. In the United Kingdom a 'billion' means one million million and nobody in good old England has yet tried to achieve that mark. Another American particle accelerator in Brookhaven, Long Island, is called the Cosmotron, which is somewhat over-doing it, because natural cosmic rays often have much higher energy than the Cosmotron can provide. In Europe, at CERN (near Geneva), they have built accelerators comparable to the two American ones. In Russia, not far from Moscow, there is still another machine of that kind, familiarly known as the Khruschev-tron, which will probably now be renamed the Brezhnevtron.'

Looking around, Mr Tompkins noticed a door carrying a sign:

ALVAREZ'S LIQUID HYDROGEN
BATHING ESTABLISHMENT

'What is over there?' he asked.

'Oh!' said the professor, 'the Lawrencetron here produces more and more different elementary particles, with higher and higher energies, and one has to analyse them by observing their trajectories and calculating their masses, lifetimes, interactions and

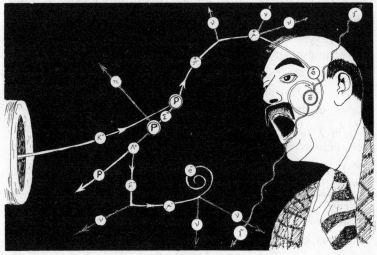

Particles were multiplying like rabbits

many other properties such as strangeness, parity, etc. In olden times one used the so-called cloud chamber invented by C. T. R. WILSON, who received a Nobel Prize for it in 1927. At that time, the fast, electrically-charged particles of a few million electron volts' energy, which were being studied by physicists, were sent through a chamber with a glass top filled with air saturated almost up to the limit by water vapour. When the bottom of the chamber was jerked down, the air in it was cooled by expansion, and the water vapour became *over*saturated. Thus, a fraction of vapour had to condense into tiny water droplets. Wilson discovered that such a condensation of vapour into water goes much faster around ions, i.e. electrically-charged particles of the gas. But gas is ionized along the trajectories of the electrically-charged projectiles passing through the chamber. Thus the foggy stripes of fog, illuminated by a light source located on the side of the chamber, became visible on the black painted bottom of the chamber. You must remember my showing these photographs at the previous lecture.

'Now, in the case of cosmic ray particles with energies a thousandfold larger than those we used to study before, the situation is different because their tracks are so long that the cloud chambers filled with air are too small to follow the tracks from their beginning to their end, and only a small part of the entire picture could be observed.

'A large step forward was made recently by a young American physicist, DONALD A. GLASER, which secured the Nobel Prize for him in 1960. According to his story, he was once sitting gloomily at a bar watching bubbles rising in the beer bottle which stood in front of him. Well, he suddenly thought, if C. T. R. Wilson could study liquid droplets in gas, why can't I do better by studying gas bubbles in liquid? I am not going to discuss technical details,' continued the professor, 'and the difficulties connected with the design of the gadget; it would all be well over your head. But it turned out that, in order to function properly, the liquid in what we now call the bubble chamber had to be liquid hydrogen, the temperature of which is about five and a half hundred degrees Fahrenheit below the freezing point of water. In the next room is a large container built by Louis Alvarez and filled with liquid hydrogen; they usually call it "Alvarez's Bath Tub".'

'Brrrr...it is a bit cold for me!' exclaimed Mr Tompkins.

'Oh, you will not need to get into it. You will just watch the trajectories of the particles through the transparent walls.'

The bathtub was operating as always, and the flash cameras located all around it were taking a continuous row of snapshots.

The bathtub was placed inside of a large electromagnet which was bending the trajectories in order to estimate the speed of their motion.

'It takes only a few minutes to produce a single photograph,' said Alvarez, 'which adds up to several hundred pictures a day, provided that the apparatus does not get out of order and has to be repaired. Each photograph has to be carefully inspected, each track analysed and its curvature carefully measured. It may take anywhere from several minutes to an hour, depending on how interesting the picture is, and how fast the girl analysing it works.'

'Why did you say "girl"?' interrupted Mr Tompkins. 'Is this a purely feminine occupation?'

'Oh no,' said Alvarez, 'many of these girls are actually boys. But in this kind of business we use the term *girl* irrespective of sex, simply as the unit of efficiency and precision. When you say "a typist" or "a secretary" you think about a woman and not a man. Well, to analyse on the spot all the photographs obtained in our laboratory we would need hundreds of girls, which would constitute a problem. Thus we send a large number of our photographs to other universities that do not have enough money to construct the Lawrencetrons and Bubble Baths, but can afford to buy gadgets for analysing our photographs.'

'Are you the only institution doing this job?' inquired Mr Tompkins.

'Oh no! Similar machines exist in Brookhaven National Laboratory on Long Island, New York; in CERN (Corporation Européenne de Recherche Nucléaire) Laboratory near Geneva in Switzerland, and in Shchelkunchik (Nutcracker) Laboratory near Moscow in Russia. They are all looking for a needle in a haystack, and, by God, they find one once in a while!'

'But why is all this work being done?' asked Mr Tompkins in surprise.

'To find new elementary particles, which is more difficult than finding a needle in a haystack, and to study the interaction among

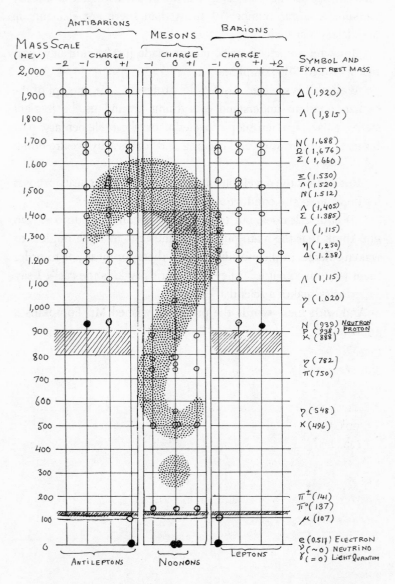

More complicated than Mendeleev's table! (After G. F. Chow, M. Gell-Mann and A. H. Rosenfeld, in *Scientific American*, February 1964.)

them. Here on the wall hangs a chart of particles, and it already contains a larger number of them than there are elements in Mendeleev's system.'

'But why are such terrific efforts made just to find new particles?' asked Mr Tompkins.

'Well, this is science,' replied the professor, 'the attempt of the human mind to understand everything around us, be it giant stellar galaxies, microscopic bacteria, or these elementary particles. It is interesting and exciting and that is why we are doing it.'

'But doesn't the development of science serve practical purposes by improving the comfort and well being of people?'

'Of course it does, but this is only a secondary purpose. Do you think that the main purpose of music is to teach buglers to waken soldiers in the morning, to call them for meals, or to order them to go into battle? They say "curiosity kills the cat"; I say "Curiosity makes a scientist".'

And with these words the professor wished Mr Tompkins a good night.